Effective Governance Under Anarchy

Policy makers and academics alike have mistakenly promoted an agenda which takes well-governed democratic and consolidated "Weberian" states as the model for the world and the goal of development programs. Whilst Western industrial democracies are the exception, areas of limited statehood where state institutions are weak and ineffective, are everywhere, and, this books argues, can still be well-governed. Three factors explain effective governance in areas of limited statehood: Fair and transparent institutions "fit for purpose," legitimate governors accepted by the people, and social trust among the citizens. Effective and legitimate governance in the absence of a functioning state is not only provided by international organizations, foreign aid agencies, and non-governmental organizations but also by multi-national companies, rebel groups and other violent non-state actors, "traditional" as well as religious leaders, and community-based organizations. Börzel and Risse base their argument on empirical findings from over a decade of research covering Latin America, the Middle East, Sub-Saharan Africa, and Asia.

Tanja A. Börzel is professor of political science and holds the chair for European Integration at the Otto Suhr Institute of Political Science, Freie Universität Berlin. She is the author of *Why Noncompliance: The Politics of Law in the European Union* (Cornell, 2020); and co-editor of *The Oxford Handbook of Governance and Limited Statehood* (2018).

Thomas Risse holds the chair of international relations at the Otto Suhr Institute of Political Science, Freie Universität Berlin. He is co-editor of *The Oxford Handbook of Governance and Limited Statehood* (2018) and of *The Oxford Handbook of Comparative Regionalism* (2016).

Effective Governance Under Anarchy

Institutions, Legitimacy, and Social Trust in Areas of Limited Statehood

Tanja A. Börzel

Freie Universität Berlin

Thomas Risse

Freie Universität Berlin

CAMBRIDGE
UNIVERSITY PRESS

CAMBRIDGE
UNIVERSITY PRESS

University Printing House, Cambridge CB2 8BS, United Kingdom

One Liberty Plaza, 20th Floor, New York, NY 10006, USA

477 Williamstown Road, Port Melbourne, VIC 3207, Australia

314–321, 3rd Floor, Plot 3, Splendor Forum, Jasola District Centre, New Delhi – 110025, India

79 Anson Road, #06–04/06, Singapore 079906

Cambridge University Press is part of the University of Cambridge.

It furthers the University's mission by disseminating knowledge in the pursuit of education, learning, and research at the highest international levels of excellence.

www.cambridge.org
Information on this title: www.cambridge.org/9781107183698
DOI: 10.1017/9781316872079

© Tanja A. Börzel and Thomas Risse 2021

This publication is in copyright. Subject to statutory exception
and to the provisions of relevant collective licensing agreements,
no reproduction of any part may take place without the written
permission of Cambridge University Press.

First published 2021

Printed in the United Kingdom by TJ Books Limited, Padstow Cornwall

A catalogue record for this publication is available from the British Library.

ISBN 978-1-107-18369-8 Hardback
ISBN 978-1-316-63504-9 Paperback

Cambridge University Press has no responsibility for the persistence or accuracy of URLs for external or third-party internet websites referred to in this publication and does not guarantee that any content on such websites is, or will remain, accurate or appropriate.

Contents

Figures

Tables

Preface

In the late 2000s, we both participated in a guided tour through the Langa township near Cape Town, South Africa. While most of the wealthy South Africans (irrespective of race) live in gated communities that are heavily guarded by armed security, we walked through areas with shacks located side by side with middle-class houses with beautifully maintained gardens. In the course of our conversations, we asked our guide how public security was being maintained in the township (since we could not see any police cars anywhere around). Answer: "The community is taking care of it. And besides, we do not have many problems, since we know our people." Okay, we asked, but what about capital crimes, such as armed robbery or even murder? Answer: "Yes, indeed, we need to call in Cape Town police in such cases. Mainly to protect the perpetrators from our community members who might take matters in their own hands ..."

Langa is what the book is about. Conventional wisdom has it that "areas of limited statehood," such as Langa, where state institutions are too weak to maintain order and enforce the law are crime- or violence-infested places where chaos prevails. In contrast, we show in this book that "governance under anarchy" is not only possible, but that it can work rather well under specific conditions. The provision of collective goods and services in areas of limited statehood is effective if it can rely on social trust relations among community members, adequate institutional rules and regulations, and social acceptance of those who govern (the "governors").

Since this book includes a lot of theoretical and empirical material from a variety of sources, here is a reader's guide: If you are mainly interested in theory, you should read the introduction, chapters 2 and 3, as well as the conclusions. Chapters 4 to 7 contain the empirical material to back up our claims.

Our book has been in the making for quite some time. In 2002, we started initial discussions with colleagues at Freie Universität Berlin and beyond about a major research initiative at the Otto Suhr Institute of

Political Science (OSI). A few years later, the theme "Governance in Areas of Limited Statehood" was born with a focus on countries featuring weak state institutions with limited abilities to implement and enforce central decisions and/or to uphold the monopoly of the use of force. In 2006, the *Deutsche Forschungsgemeinschaft* (DFG = German Research Foundation) decided to generously fund our *Sonderforschungsbereich 700* (SFB = Collaborative Research Center) "Governance in Areas of Limited Statehood,"[1] which ran until the end of 2017 and was located in *Binger Straße 40* in Berlin-Wilmersdorf. We had the privilege of being able to engage in a sustained research effort for more than ten years, together with our colleagues from political science, history, law, economics, and area studies. This book largely grew out of the engaged and heated debates in the seminar room of *Binger Str. 40*. It is impossible to mention here all the colleagues, postdocs, PhD researchers, and research assistants from whom we received invaluable input over the years. Our special thanks go to Ulla Lehmkuhl (co-coordinator of the SFB 700 with Thomas from 2006 to 2010), Stefan Rinke (Thomas' co-coordinator from 2010–2017), as well as to Marianne Beisheim, Marianne Braig, Lars Brozus, Sven Chojnacki, Michael Daxner, Anke Draude, Lottje de Vries, Thomas Eimer, Henrik Enderlein, Stefan Esders, Barbara Fritz, Harald Fuhr, Robin Geiß, Tim Glawion, Cilja Harders, Adrienne Héritier, Lasse Hölck, Jana Hönke, Daniel Jacob, Christopher Kahn, Jan Köhler, Matthias Kötter, Nicole Kranz, Heike Krieger, Bernd Ladwig, Markus Lederer, Luisa Linke-Behrens, Andrea Liese, Susanne Lütz, Andreas Mehler, Klaus Mühlhahn, Markus-Michael Müller, Nicole Kranz, Gregor Reisch, Beate Rudolf, Marco Schäferhoff, Cord Schmelzle, Ursula Schröder, Folke Schuppert, Sören Stapel, Eric Stollenwerk, Christian Thauer, Esther Thomas, Vera van Hüllen, Gregor Walter-Drop, and Christoph Zürcher. The book builds on their work and also summarizes, as well as updates, key publications, including Risse and Lehmkuhl (2007), Risse (2011a), Beisheim et al. (2011c), Krasner and Risse (2014a), Risse, Börzel, and Draude (2018).

In addition, we are extremely grateful to the various guest scholars and visitors of SFB 700 who critically commented on our work over the years, among them Michael Barnett, Arthur Benz, Jeff Checkel, Thomas Debiehl, Christopher Daase, Nicole Deitelhoff, Marty Finnemore, Philipp Genschel, Edgar Grande, Ralph Hamann, Katharina Holzinger, Stephen Krasner, the late Stephan Leibfried, Renate Mayntz, Dirk Messner, Harald Müller, Shalini Randeria, Fritz Scharpf,

---

[1] www.sfb-governance.de/, last access October 27, 2019.

Jim Scott, Moliehi Shale, Kathryn Sikkinik, Beth Simmons, Dietlind Stolle, Klaus Dieter Wolf, Bernhard Zangl, and Michael Zürn.

While research for this book was mainly conducted in Berlin (and in field research around the globe), we wrote most of the manuscript in Centennial, Wyoming, population 200, and 8,000 feet high in the middle of the Rocky Mountains. In a way, Centennial represents another area of limited statehood, even though more by choice rather than by lack of capacity. Security and order is maintained by the local Sheriff. Other than that, the state is only visible in terms of a US post office (and the US state owns most of the land, including the National Forest nearby). Everything else is run by volunteers, including the local fire department, the museum, and the public library. Centennial is reasonably well governed by the equivalent of community-based organizations held together through relationships of trust (we rarely lock our house). In a way, Centennial resembles many areas of limited statehood about which we write in this book.

While writing up the book, a number of people helped us tremendously. Anke Draude, Hyeran Jo, Aila Matanock, Melissa Lee, Cord Schmelzle, and Eric Stollenwerk were so kind to read the entire manuscript and to provide us with critical comments. They deserve our heartfelt gratitude, as do the following scholars who served on book panels at the annual conferences of the American Political Science Association (APSA) and the International Studies Association (ISA): Sameer Azizi, Ana Covarrubias, Gini Haufler, Hyeran Jo, David Lake, Aila Matanock, Amanda Murdie, Bill Reno, and Beth Simmons.

Special thanks also go to Maria-Sophia Dellasega and Lukas Müller-Wünsch, who checked the bibliography for us. Last but not least, we are very grateful to the professional team at Cambridge University Press and elsewhere who helped us with the book throughout the production process. This includes John Haslam, our editor at the press, Diana Witt, the indexer, Dhivya Elavazhagan and Vinoth Kumar, our project managers, as well as Tobias Ginsberg and Robert Judkins.

Abbreviations

ACLED	Armed Conflict Location & Event Data Project
AFISMA	African-led International Support Mission
ALS	Areas of Limited Statehood
ANSF	Afghan National Security Forces
ASEAN	Association of South-East Asian Nations
AU	African Union
BRICS	Brazil, Russia, India, China, South Africa
BTI	Bertelsmann Transformation Index
CAR	Central African Republic
CBO	Community-Based Organization
CICIG	International Commission Against Impunity in Guatemala
CSR	Corporate Social Responsibility
DAC	Development Assistance Committee (of the OECD)
DRC	Democratic Republic of Congo
ECOWAS	Economic Community of West African States
EITI	Extractive Industries Transparency Initiative
EPP	Electoral Participation Provisions
ETI	Ethical Trading Initiative
EU	European Union
EUFOR	European Union Force (in Kosovo)
FAO	Food and Agriculture Organization
FARC	Fuerzas Armadas Revolucionarias de Colombia (Revolutionary Armed Forces of Colombia)
FATA	Federally Administered Tribal Areas (Pakistan)
FLA	Fair Labor Association
FSC	Forest Stewardship Council
FWF	Fair Wear Foundation
GAIN	Global Alliance for Improved Nutrition
GAM	Free Aceh Movement
GAVI	Global Alliance for Vaccines and Immunization
GCC	Gulf Cooperation Council

GDA	Governance Delegation Agreement
GDP	Gross Domestic Product
GF	Global Fund to Fight AIDS, Tuberculosis and Malaria
GIZ	Gesellschaft für Internationale Zusammenarbeit
GRI	Global Reporting Initiative
HIV/AIDS	Human Immunodeficiency Virus/Acquired Immuno Deficiency Syndrome
ICRC	International Committee of the Red Cross
ICSECR	International Covenant on Social, Economic, and Cultural Rights
IHL	International Humanitarian Law
IL	International Law
IMF	International Monetary Fund
(I)NGO	(International) Non-Governmental Organization
INTERFET	International Force East Timor
IO	International Organization
IR	International Relations (as a field of study)
IS	Islamic State/Daesh
ISAF	International Security Assistance Force (Afghanistan)
ISO	International Standardization Organization
KFOR	Kosovo Force (NATO)
LAS	League of Arab States
MDG	Millennium Development Goals
MILF	Moro Islamic Liberation Front
MLG	Multi-Level Governance
MNC	Multi-National Corporation
MONUC	Mission de l'Organisation des Nations Unies en République Démocratique du Congo (Mission of the United Nations Organization in the DRC)
MSF	Médecins Sans Frontières (Doctors Without Borders)
MSP	Multi-Stakeholder Partnership
NAAMSA	National Association of Automobile Manufacturers of South Africa
NAFTA	North American Free Trade Agreement
NATO	North Atlantic Treaty Organization
NPFL	National Patriotic Front of Liberia
NRA	National Resistance Army (Uganda)
NSJI	Non-State Justice Institutions
OAS	Organization of American States
ODA	Official Development Assistance

OECD	Organization of Economic Cooperation and Development
OSCE	Organization for Security and Cooperation in Europe
PMC/PSC	Private Military Company/Private Security Company
PPP	Public Private Partnership
R2P	Responsibility to Protect
RAMSI	Regional Assistance Mission to the Solomon Islands
RGIL	Rebel Groups and International Law Database
RO	Regional Organization
SA 8000	Social Accountability 8000
SADC	Southern African Development Community
SDG	Sustainable Development Goals
SSR	Security Sector Reform
UN	United Nations
UND	United Nations Development Program
UNGC	United Nations Global Compact
UNICEF	United Nations Children's Fund
UNMIL	United Nations Mission in Liberia
UNRWA	United Nations Relief and Works Agency for Palestine
UNSC	United Nations Security Council
VNSA	Violent Non-State Actors
VPSHR	Voluntary Principles on Security and Human Rights
WFO	World Food Organization
WFP	World Food Programme
WHO	World Health Organization
WSUP	Water and Sanitation for the Urban Poor

1   Introduction

The World Is Not Denmark!

Somalia is considered the quintessential failed state. The Fund for Peace's Fragile States Index 2019 counts it as the second most failed state in the world (No. 1 is Yemen).[1] The Bertelsmann Transformation Index (BTI) 2018 lists Somalia at the very bottom of its 26 listed failed states (out of 129 states altogether).[2] Indeed, the country has not had a central government since the previous dictator, Siad Barre, was ousted from power in 1991. There have been various attempts at re-creating a central government since then, but whoever was in charge in Mogadishu, the capital, never had much control inside, let alone outside, the city. It is also true that central Somalia, the region where the capital is located, has been haunted by widespread violence from various rebel and terrorist groups since the early 1990s (see Chapter 5).

Yet, this is only half of the truth. There is also the province of Somaliland where 3.5 million people live, roughly one-quarter of Somalia's population. Since about the mid-1990s, Somaliland has been rather peaceful. It has been governed by councils of elders representing the various clans and sub-clans. While it has not become a Western-style democracy, the province has managed to restore at least some degree of the rule of law and has protected basic human rights. Last but not least, Somalilanders are way better off with regard to the provision of public goods and services than they were under the dictatorship of Siad Barre. The Global Fund, for instance, a transnational Multi-Stakeholder Partnership (MSP) to fight malaria, tuberculosis, and HIV/AIDS, has successfully instituted public health governance in most parts of Somaliland (Schäferhoff 2014a). A study of development indicators for the whole of Somalia concludes that "Somalis are better off under anarchy than they were under government" (Leeson 2007, 689;

---

[1] https://fragilestatesindex.org/data/, last access August 10, 2019.

[2] https://atlas.bti-project.org/share.php?1*2018*GV:SIX:0*CAT*ANA:REGION, last access August 10, 2019.

see also Kaplan 2008; Lake, D. 2016, ch. 5; Menkhaus 2006/2007; Richards 2014).

The Democratic Republic of Congo (DRC) is another one of the world's most famous failed states that has been stricken by civil wars and violence for decades. Yet, courts and (international) non-governmental organizations (INGOs) in eastern DRC have been able to effectively prosecute gender crimes and sexual violence against women and, thus, to restore important aspects of the rule of law (Lake, M. 2018). Governance under anarchy?

Somalia and the DRC are extreme cases of failed states, but they share important features with most countries on the globe: they are *areas of limited statehood* (ALS) in which central state institutions are too weak to implement and enforce central decisions and/or to uphold a monopoly of the use of force. Somaliland and the eastern DRC have in common that they disconfirm the conventional wisdom according to which areas of limited statehood are ungovernable or ungoverned. While they are not "Denmark" and will probably never be, they are reasonably well governed in some areas.

This book starts from the proposition that "limited statehood" is not a historical accident or some deplorable deficit of most Third World and transition countries that has to be overcome by the relentless forces of economic and political modernization in an era of globalization. Rather, we suggest that "limited statehood" is here to stay – even in so-called Western and modern societies (see also Chowdhury 2018). Governance research has to take limited statehood into account. We therefore ask *how effective and legitimate governance is possible under conditions of limited statehood. How can political rule as well as security and other collective goods be provided when the state is weak or even absent?*

In addressing this question, the book establishes four claims:

1. Areas of limited statehood are ubiquitous. While most states in the contemporary international system are neither fragile nor failed, they contain areas – whether territorial spaces or policy domains – in which weak state capacity prevails – up to the point where the state lacks a monopoly of the use of force. As a result, from a global as well as a historical perspective, the modern ("Western") nation-state with full control over its territory and sufficient capacity to enforce the law is the exception rather than the rule. The world is not Denmark and never will be.[3]

---

[3] And, even in Denmark, more than one-third of the population feels too insecure to walk around alone at night. According to 2014 data, see www.nationmaster.com/country-info/profiles/Denmark/Crime/Fear-of-crime, last access August 10, 2019.

2. Areas of limited statehood are neither ungoverned nor ungovernable. Somebody or some group always seeks to rule or to govern, from rebels to "traditional" authorities, companies, (I)NGOs, and foreign governments. In particular, we observe a multitude of non-state governors. Effective and legitimate *governance under anarchy* is possible under particular circumstances. This pertains to the provision of collective goods and services, such as security, human rights, and the rule of law, democracy, health, education, food security, and others. It also includes binding rules and regulations.

3. Three drivers, alone or in combination, explain effective governance under anarchy: first, the governing actors – "governors" – and institutions must enjoy legitimacy and social acceptance by the people and, thus, the "right to govern."[4] Second, governance institutions, including what remains of the state, have to be "fit for purpose," adequately resourced, as well as inclusive, fair, and transparent. Third, social trust relations among citizens and within local communities are crucial in enabling collective action capacity "under anarchy."

4. The three drivers complement and reinforce each other; they also include several feedback loops. In particular, inclusive institutions enhance the (input) legitimacy of the governors, while effective governance tends to increase their output legitimacy in a virtuous circle from effectiveness to legitimacy. Last but not least, social trust relations enhance the legitimacy of governors and also foster their effectiveness by facilitating collective action.

Limited Statehood as the Default

Afghanistan, the Islamic State in Iraq and Syria, the global financial crisis in 2008–2009, or the migration flows in Europe and the Americas have heavily colored contemporary debates about world order with state failure and limited statehood as their alleged root cause. The various crises have corroborated the agenda of policy makers and academics alike, which sees well-governed liberal democracies of the Global North as the ultimate *telos* of world history and the goal of foreign policy and development programs.

Yet, the world is not Denmark. Nor is the world Afghanistan or Syria. Rather, some areas of limited statehood are reasonably well governed,

---

[4] The literature on legitimacy usually defines the concept as the "right to rule." However, since "ruling" often implies only hierarchical authority (*Herrschaft* in the Weberian sense), we use the term in this book interchangeably with the "right to govern."

resembling Somaliland, while others are war zones where violence and chaos prevail – with many shades of partially effective governance in between. In other words, becoming Denmark is not the only way to escape the fate of Afghanistan and Syria. This book argues that better governance for most places in the contemporary world does not require turning them into Denmark.

Denmark exemplifies consolidated statehood, democratic political institutions, and a well-governed welfare regime inside the European Union (EU). It is also prototypical for what North et al. call "open access orders" (North, Wallis, and Weingast 2009). It is, therefore, no wonder that many development theories, particularly modernization theories, have adopted a teleological perspective according to which the "end of history" (Fukuyama 1992) should be the – Western – consolidated, democratic, and welfare state. This state of Western modernity is undergoing transformation (Hurrelmann et al. 2007; Leibfried et al. 2015) and is increasingly challenged by alternative models outside and beyond the "West" (Acharya 2014; Katzenstein 2012). Yet, it still exemplifies the endpoint of historical evolution in the eyes of many scholars (Fukuyama 1992; Huntington 1993).

In contrast, we maintain that areas of limited statehood, where central authorities are too weak to adopt, implement, and enforce central decisions, not only represent the default condition in the contemporary world order as well as historically (see also Chowdhury 2018). They are likely to remain that way in the future. Limited statehood refers to a lack of what Krasner called "domestic sovereignty," i.e., "the formal organization of political authority within the state and the ability of public authorities to exercise effective control within the borders of their own polity" (Krasner 1999: 4). Most countries with ALS are still internationally recognized (even the failed state of Somalia remains internationally sovereign), but they cannot enforce their laws everywhere and with regard to some policy areas or certain groups of people. Some even lack the monopoly of the use of force in some parts of their territory.

Note that our focus is on state *capacity* to uphold the monopoly of the use of force as well as to implement and enforce decisions and provide collective goods and services. Limited statehood as introduced here has little to do with a state's (un-)*willingness* to rule or to provide certain services. While it is often hard to dis-entangle lack of capacity and unwillingness empirically (see Chapter 2), the focus in this book is not on the "neoliberal state" (Plant 2010), which has decided to refrain from, privatize, or de-regulate certain public services.

By focusing on capacity rather than willingness, we do not want to imply that areas of limited statehood are confined to the postcolonial world of the Global South. Even the "Denmarks" of the world contain areas where state authorities – e.g. the police – lack the ability to enforce the law, if only temporarily (Chapter 2). Moreover, ALS in the Global North and the Global South show other similarities. Some are "no go areas" (such as many inner cities), while others are reasonably well governed (e.g. self-governance in various rural areas).[5] Thus, the binary of the "underdeveloped" Global South and the "modern" as well as "developed" Global North misses the fact that ALS have existed across history (Esders, Hölck, and Rinke 2018) and constitute a global phenomenon in our present time (Brandel and Randeria 2018; Schlichte 2018). As a result, we submit that our approach is generalizable even though this book concentrates on examples from the Global South.

The Governance Puzzle

The book's main contention is that the absence of hierarchical governance by the state (anarchy) does not equal chaos. As argued above, areas of limited statehood are neither ungoverned nor ungovernable. We understand "governance" as institutionalized modes of social coordination to produce and implement collectively binding rules, or to provide collective goods and services (see Chapter 2). Governance is about rule-making for a given (imagined) community as well as the provision of goods and services, such as security, health, education, a clean environment, and so forth. Modes of governance can be hierarchical – command and control, order and obedience; it can also be non-hierarchical – governance through negotiations as well as deliberation. Governance, hence, covers hierarchical steering by the state ("governance by government"), governance via cooperative networks of state and non-state actors ("governance with government"), as well as rule-making by non-state actors ("governance without government"). We expect that non-hierarchical modes of governance are more common in ALS than hierarchical modes (though not completely absent, see particularly Chapter 5 on security governance). Those who govern ALS – the "governors"[6] – encompass a multiplicity of actors, state as well as non-state, local/domestic as well as external/international/transnational: international and regional organizations (IOs and ROs); foreign governments; foreign aid agencies; (I)NGOs; and (multinational) companies; (weak)

---

[5] For a report about ALS in the Swedish city of Malmo see "Malmo, a segregated city – separating fact from fiction," https://euobserver.com/social/146538?utm_source=euobs&utm_medium=email, last access July 3, 2020.

[6] We borrow that term from Avant, Finnemore, and Sell 2010a.

national or local governments; rebel groups, warlords, and other violent non-state actors (VNSA); as well as tribal chiefs, clan leaders (so-called traditional authorities), and Community-Based Organizations (CBO).[7]

This brings us to our "governance puzzle": We find huge variation in the extent to which rules and regulations are being adopted, implemented, and enforced, and/or public services are being provided in areas of limited statehood. While the eastern provinces of the DRC are war zones, its western provinces have remained relatively peaceful.[8] The same holds true for central Somalia, a war zone, as compared to stable peace in Somaliland (see above and Chapter 5). While biodiversity in South Africa scores rather high, water pollution is a serious problem due to the lack of effective waste water treatment.[9]

There is not only variation within and across areas of limited statehood. There is no linear and strong relationship between degrees of statehood, on the one hand, and the provision of governance, on the other (Lee, Walter-Drop, and Wiesel 2014). The scatterplot below shows our "governance puzzle." Each mark represents the governance performance of one country in a particular issue-area using "objective" data for key indicators (see Figure 1.1). The better the performance, the higher the mark on the y-axis. The x-axis measures degrees of (limited) statehood with values higher than 0.8 representing consolidated statehood and values lower than 0.5 indicating fragile and failed statehood (for a discussion of these measurements see Chapter 2). Of course, the data here have their own limitations. They are aggregated per country rather than per ALS using only one indicator per issue-area. We provide more details on these measurements in Chapters 5–7.

Despite its shortcomings, the scatterplot shows, first, that consolidated statehood (top-right corner of Figure 1.1) and high service provision indeed go together, as expected. Denmark is a consolidated state that provides most collective goods to its citizens. Second, at the other end of the spectrum, with statehood values of 0.4 and below, we find a few fragile and failed states.[10] Even though none of these states reach the best performance levels of 0.9 and higher, the variation is still considerable.

---

[7] We put "traditional" in parentheses for two reasons. First, the term is often used in a pejorative sense – in contrast to "modern," i.e., Western, rationality. Second, what counts as "tradition," is usually a social construction (Förster and Koechlin 2018).

[8] According to www.acleddata.com/dashboard/#180, last access August 11, 2019.

[9] According to the 2018 Environmental Performance Index, https://epi.envirocenter.yale .edu/sites/default/files/2018-zaf.pdf, last access August 8, 2019.

[10] One problem for measuring governance performance in extremely fragile and failed states is the availability of valid and reliable statistics. Missing data constitute a major issue here, see Chapter 2 for details.

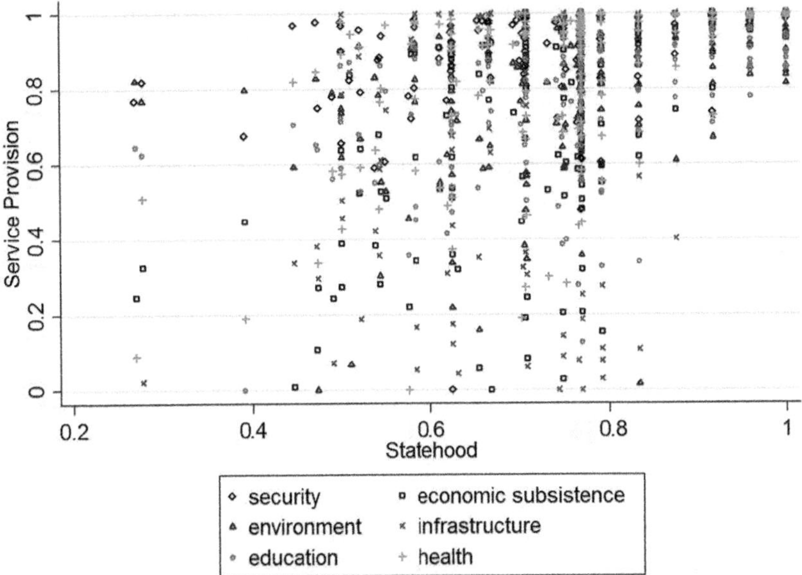

Figure 1.1 The "governance puzzle"

Source: Krasner and Risse 2014b, 553. The x-axis measures statehood by using indicators for both the state monopoly over the means of violence and the administrative capacity of states. For details see Lee, Walter-Drop, and Wiesel 2014. The y-axis measures various composite indicators for service provision based on a variety of data sources: World Bank, UN Statistics Development Indicators, United Nations Office on Drugs and Crime, WHO, CIA, SIPRI, UNESCO, UCDP etc. See Lee, Walter-Drop, and Wiesel 2014 for a detailed description of each indicator. Each dot represents a particular type of service provision by country. For instance, the + dot at 0.3/0.1 represents (extremely poor) health provision in a failed state.

This corroborates our contention above that even failed states can be reasonably well governed in some issue-areas. Third, this holds even more for countries with medium levels of statehood between 0.4 and 0.8, that is, the vast majorities of states in the contemporary international system (see Chapter 2 for details). This category includes Brazil, South Africa, Kenya, Thailand, the Philippines, but also Italy and Greece. These countries have in common that they contain both areas where the state is in full control and areas of limited statehood (such as the Amazon region in Brazil). The scatterplot demonstrates for this group of countries the enormous variation with regard to governance effectiveness. The variation ranges from the worst (0) to the best (1.0) performance. Note that governance effectiveness in one issue-area, e.g. security, does not tell us much about performance in another one, e.g. health or education. As we will discuss throughout this book, there is not only little correlation between degrees of statehood and governance effectiveness. There is also variation between issue-areas in one and the same country. For instance, the People's Republic of China – certainly not a failed state – is able to provide public security for most of its citizens, but its environmental performance is wanting since it lacks the means to enforce even its own laws. Its air quality ranks at number 177 of the180 countries for which measurements exist.[11]

Solving the "Governance Puzzle"

This book seeks to solve this "governance puzzle." We explain why some areas of limited statehood are reasonably well governed, while others are not. We not only focus on effective governance, but also on legitimate governance, that is, the provision of rules and collective goods in a manner that is acceptable to the people that are governed. Our main task is to explain effective and legitimate governance "under anarchy," i.e., in ALS where central or local governments lack the ability to steer hierarchically. In a way, our endeavor resembles the efforts by International Relations (IR) scholars to account for "cooperation under anarchy" (Oye 1986; see also Axelrod 1984; Keohane 1989a). IR scholars have long struggled to explain under which conditions effective international cooperation and problem-solving are possible in the absence of an international authority that has the capacity to enforce binding agreements and sanction non-compliance (inter alia Baldwin 1993; Katzenstein 1996; Katzenstein, Keohane, and Krasner 1998).

Our theoretical points of departures combine insights from both rationalist and sociological institutionalism, which Scharpf sought to integrate in the framework of "actor-centered institutionalism" (Scharpf 1997; cf. Hall and Taylor 1996; March and Olsen 1989, 1998). Acknowledging the importance of institutions, we take actors seriously (Sikkink 2011; see also Checkel 1998; Finnemore 1996). We conceive of actors as both rational utility maximizers driven by the logic of consequentialism and social agents, who are deeply embedded in social structures and, thus, follow a logic of appropriateness (see March and Olsen 1998 on these terms).

To explain effective and legitimate "governance under anarchy" in areas of limited statehood, we need to answer two sets of questions:

---

[11] See 2018 data in https://epi.envirocenter.yale.edu/sites/default/files/2018-chn.pdf, last access August 11, 2019.

1. Why and when are – state and non-state, international, transnational, and domestic – actors motivated to govern in ALS, and how do they govern?
2. Under what conditions is "governance under anarchy" effective and legitimate?

The two questions require separate answers, since the motivation to govern does not necessarily lead to effective and legitimate performance. Take Haiti's "Republic of NGOs" in the aftermath of the horrendous earthquake of January 2010:[12] we can safely assume that most (I)NGOs have been motivated to improve governance and – in this particular case – to provide humanitarian assistance. Yet, there was a tremendous lack of coordination, which not only resulted in ineffective governance, but also rendered what remained of the weak Haitian state even weaker. At the same time, it is hard to imagine that actors are able to govern effectively, if they lack any motivation to engage in rule-making or the provision of goods and services.

The same holds true for the "how" question, which refers to the modes of governance. Here, we distinguish primarily between hierarchical steering (command and control; rule-setting through law), on the one hand, and non-hierarchical modes of governance on the other (Risse 2018b). The latter involves negotiations and bargaining, persuasion, as well as deliberation. There is no strong relationship between modes of governance and effectiveness, but we claim that, on average, non-hierarchical modes of governance have certain advantages under conditions of ALS.

Rational choice as well as sociological institutionalism point us to three broad concepts that help us in answering the two questions:

- *Institutions* and their design, including residual statehood (e.g. Goldstein et al. 2000; Koremenos, Lipson, and Snidal 2001; North 1986);
- *Legitimacy* as a social relationship between governors and governed, by which the latter bestow the "right to rule" on the former and socially accept the results, which then enables voluntary compliance with costly rules and against one's immediate self-interest (Hurd 1999; Scharpf 1999; also Schmelzle 2015);[13]

---

[12] See www.usip.org/sites/default/files/resources/PB%2023%20Haiti%20a%20Republic%20of%20NGOs.pdf, last access August 11, 2019.

[13] Note that we refer to *empirical legitimacy* here, that is, the actual perception of the governors and of governance institutions as rightful. This is to be distinguished from *normative legitimacy*, that is, the determination according to normative criteria that the rulers and their institutions *should* have the "right to rule." Empirical legitimacy and

- *Social trust* (understood here as "upfront risk-taking" [Luhmann 1989] and the belief that others will honor cooperative commitments) as the social glue among members of relevant communities enabling them to govern (and to solve collective action problems, see Ostrom, Gardner, and Walker 1994) and to accept governance as legitimate.

As regards the first question about the motivations of actors to govern, the answer is not trivial in the absence of consolidated and democratic statehood. For some "governors" in ALS – namely IOs, foreign aid agencies, (I)NGOs – contributing to the public good is constitutive. This does not mean that these actors are not self-interested and that they can never be corrupted. But it is their institutionally defined purpose or action orientation (Scharpf 1997) to protect the environment, defend human rights, or fight HIV/AIDS.

What we need to explain, though, is under which conditions primarily self-interested actors, such as companies, warlords, or rent-seeking governments, are willing to engage in governance. Functioning state institutions that are bound by the rule of law not only ensure that such (state) actors pursue the public interest (and are sanctioned through democratic procedures and the court system if they do not). Consolidated statehood also casts an effective "shadow of hierarchy" (Börzel 2007; Scharpf 1997) to induce private actors to provide governance. For instance, governments of consolidated states can threaten to pass laws if self-interested non-state actors, such as companies, do not contribute to service provision and other collective goods. Neither direct hierarchical steering nor a more indirect "shadow of hierarchy" are available to governments under conditions of limited statehood.

We argue in this book that all three factors mentioned above play a role in motivating actors to become governors (see Chapter 3): First, there are functional *institutional* equivalents to consolidated state institutions casting a "shadow of hierarchy" as incentive structures for non-state actors, such as companies, to provide governance (Börzel and Risse 2010). Here, we distinguish between:

- "external shadows of hierarchy," e.g. the trusteeships whereby external states intrude in the "Westphalian sovereignty" of states with ALS (Kosovo, Iraq, or Afghanistan as most recent examples), but also home state laws binding Multi-National Corporations (MNCs) in their host states, such as the US Foreign Corrupt Practices Act or the 2015 UK Modern Slavery Act;

social acceptance by the citizens do not tell us much about normative legitimacy. Many dictators have enjoyed empirical legitimacy for long periods of time.

- the "shadow of anarchy," i.e., the risk of violence, chaos, and disorder in ALS preventing non-state actors from achieving their own goals, which then incentivizes them to engage in governance.

Second, the quest for *legitimacy* and social acceptance serves as a powerful inducement for self-interested (non-state) actors to provide governance. For instance, consumer preferences in the Global North push MNC toward complying with human rights, social, and environmental standards, and punish them through boycotts if they violate these rules (Börzel and Thauer 2013). Rebel groups and other violent non-state actors (VNSA) who control territory and require at least some collaboration from the citizens are likely to engage in governance, once they need domestic as well as international legitimacy.

Third, *social trust* relations serve as enabling conditions for communities to solve collective action problems and to engage in self-governance in the absence of a functioning state (see below). At the same time, the action capacity of communities enabled through social trust casts a "shadow of the community," incentivizing self-interested actors such as companies, but also VNSA, to provide governance services. Examples include mining companies, but also rebel groups.

Our second question asks under what conditions governance in ALS will be effective and legitimate. We answer it with reference to the above three factors:

1. The *institutional design* of the governance arrangement matters. Governance institutions can only perform effectively if they are "fit for purpose," that is adequate for the task at hand (Koremenos, Lipson, and Snidal 2001), which includes having sufficient material and ideational resources (such as – local – knowledge) as well as process management capable of flexibly adapting to local conditions (Beisheim and Liese 2014b). For instance, distributing anti-malaria bednets constitutes a rather simple task, whereas combating and preventing HIV/AIDS requires complex governance institutions, repeated interventions, and coordination among many different actors. Moreover, governance institutions have to be inclusive and fair, not only to be effective, but also to generate input as well as throughput legitimacy. The experience of inclusive and fair institutions has also been found to build generalized trust among citizens (Rothstein and Stolle 2008a).

2. (Empirical) *legitimacy*, that is, the acceptance of the governance actors or of the governance institutions as "rightful," constitutes a crucial condition for effective rule-making and provision of services in ALS (see Krasner and Risse 2014b). This is the main reason why most comprehensive external state-building interventions have been

unsuccessful, since they could not satisfy the rather demanding legitimacy requirements for intruding deeply into a country's "Westphalian sovereignty." Once people bestow the "right to rule" on governors, their effectiveness increases drastically. This extends not only to foreign interveners, but also to companies and rebel groups, as well as other VNSA. Moreover, a virtuous circle is likely to emerge between legitimacy fostering effectiveness and governance effectiveness generating (output) legitimacy (Risse and Stollenwerk 2018a; Schmelzle and Stollenwerk 2018).

3. Last but not least, *social trust* matters, too, for effectiveness. This is obvious with regard to the collective action capacity of local communities enabling them to govern themselves "under anarchy" (Ostrom 1990, 2002; see also Börzel and Risse 2016). But social trust is also important for various governors. For instance, the ability of "traditional" authorities, such as tribal leaders, chiefs, and elders, to govern hierarchically and to enforce decisions (absent a monopoly of the use of force) largely derives from their embeddedness in trust relations of local communities. Moreover, the sustainability of post-conflict peace settlements largely depends on whether the former opponents develop relationships of trust (Kreutz and Nussio 2019; Matanock 2017).

Given the significance of (empirical) legitimacy for effective governance, we also identify the following sources of legitimacy: first, the more those being governed have a say or input in the policy-making process and the more this process is regarded as efficient, fair and transparent, the more governors and governance institutions are accepted as legitimate (input and throughput legitimacy; see Scharpf 1999). The development literature discusses input legitimacy as the "ownership" principle (Brett 1996; Lopes and Theisohn 2003). To come back to our example of Somalia above: the Global Fund to Fight AIDS, Tuberculosis and Malaria, a global multi-stakeholder partnership (MSP), was rather successful in its anti-HIV/AIDS campaign in Somaliland, precisely because it included local, particularly tribal, leaders. The campaign failed in other provinces, since the Global Fund did not bother to engage local stakeholders (Schäferhoff 2014a). The example further points to the importance of establishing inclusive institutions to foster legitimacy as a driver of effective governance. Procedural fairness, in turn, does not only generate social acceptance (Tyler 1997b). If people perceive the provision of rules and collective goods and services as fair, this throughput legitimacy is also conducive to the building of social trust (see below).

Second, the more governance outcomes (rules, collective goods, and services) are perceived or anticipated as effective by the governed, the more the "governors" are seen as legitimate. Here we find the above-mentioned virtuous (or vicious) cycle between effectiveness and legitimacy in governance. (In-) effective governance breads (il-) legitimate governance – and vice versa. To point to the case of Afghanistan: household surveys conducted in northeast Afghanistan since 2007 demonstrated that popular support for external military interveners (such as the International Security Assistance Force, or ISAF, led by the North Atlantic Treaty Organization – NATO) increased, the more the latter were perceived to be effective. This in turn enabled ISAF to combat the Taliban more effectively, since the latter had lost their support among the locals. Years later, though, the reverse relationship has been observed, since external military forces failed to provide public security in the eyes of the local population (Koehler 2014; Koehler and Zürcher 2007; Stollenwerk 2018b).

Third, social trust not only motivates communities to self-govern, it also enhances the legitimacy of governance. Generalized trust increases the diffuse support for governance institutions beyond local scales. Here, we find another virtuous (or vicious) circle at play, namely between the perception of political institutions (whether state or non-state) as fair and transparent, on the one hand, and generalized trust, on the other (Rothstein and Stolle 2008a, b). In other words, throughput legitimacy leads to generalized trust and the two reinforce each other. A study of non-state justice institutions (NSJI) in rural Bangladesh demonstrated that the more underprivileged groups (e.g. poor women) gained access to these non-state courts and were treated fairly, the more they started trusting these institutions and the more they felt accepted in their communities (Berger 2017; see also Berger and Lake 2018).

In sum, the conditions for effective and legitimate governance in ALS should be regarded as configurations. They complement each other, but they can also substitute for each other, at least partially. And they influence each other. This book discusses these scope conditions in detail using empirical findings from Latin America, the Middle East, Sub-Saharan Africa, and Asia (see Chapters 4–7). While we do not provide a strict empirical test of if-then hypotheses, we use the existing literature to compare cases of successful with failed governance in ALS so as to demonstrate the validity of our theoretical framework.

Contribution to Theory-Building

This book takes issue with prevailing approaches in the relevant literatures and provides an alternative account to them that neither relies on Western modernity as the "end of history" (Fukuyama 1992) nor on consolidated and well-functioning statehood as a prerequisite for effective and legitimate governance (see also Krasner 2018). First, we challenge the (implicit) teleology of modernization theories in its various versions (e.g. Boix 2011; Przeworski 1991; Przeworski and Limongi 1997; Rustow 1968). The ultimate driver of 'good governance' is economic growth. Once states are on the "growth escalator,"[14] democratic and effective governance is likely to follow. Unfortunately, the empirical record of these theories, which have informed many development policies up to date, is rather mixed. There are many emerging economies, including Singapore, Hong Kong, Turkey, and China, with high growth rates and large urban middle classes (the two drivers of modernization), which have remained authoritarian and illiberal for a long time. Moreover, reaching the level of high-income countries is extremely hard and probably only an option for a handful of countries. Last but not least, modernization theories are inherently biased toward Western-type modernization, ignoring alternative forms of modernity (Eisenstadt 2002, 2007).

Second, this in-built Western bias is even more visible in the literature on fragile and failed states (e.g. Carment 2003; Dorff 2005; Rotberg 2003, 2004b). While this literature is rather a-theoretical in the sense that it does not elaborate main drivers for state success, it builds on what could be called a "deficit theory" of limited statehood (Schuppert 2009 on this point). Failed states lack all ingredients of modern consolidated statehood and are therefore badly governed. Since statehood and governance performance are lumped together, this literature cannot conceptualize the puzzle of well-governed areas of limited statehood, the starting point of this book (see Chapter 2).

Third, we criticize the main challengers of modernization theories, namely various approaches focusing on strong state institutions. Huntington's classic critique of modernization theory (Huntington 1968) emphasized strong, effective, and legitimate political institutions and, thus, "consolidated statehood" in our terminology, as the main precondition of modernization. Huntington's work has been the predecessor of theories of the "developmental state" (Kwon 2005; Woo-Cumings 1999). Once the developmental state has provided the conditions for economic growth (the "Asian tiger" model, e.g.), countries are on the escalator toward liberal democracy and good governance. Huntington's work has also inspired Fukuyama's study on "Political Order and Political Decay" where he establishes the primacy of the functioning state

---

[14] We owe this metaphor to Stephen Krasner.

over economic growth as the main pillar of social order (Fukuyama 2014). Yet, as argued above, limited statehood is the default condition, both historically and in the contemporary international system, and, thus, Huntington's and Fukuyama's main drivers are not available to them. Nevertheless, many areas of limited statehood are reasonably well governed and provide public goods and services without relying on a functioning state.

Fourth, recent works by North, Wallis, and Weingast, as well as by Acemoglu and Robinson, emphasize growth, strong state institutions, and liberal democracy ("open access orders") as pre-conditions for good governance (Acemoglu and Robinson 2012; Cortright, Seyle, and Wall 2017; Norris 2012; North, Wallis, and Weingast 2009). Our approach is closer to their arguments insofar as we also identify the inclusiveness of governance institutions as a scope condition for effective governance. We contend, though, that in ALS, legitimacy more often than not is not state-based and that non-state governance arrangements can draw on their own sources of legitimacy (Bernstein and Cashore 2007). Moreover, Western-type democracy is not the only source of legitimacy. However, similar to Huntington and Fukuyama, North et al. are still Western-centric insofar as Denmark and other Western democracies remain the linchpin of their analysis. They assume that consolidated statehood is the necessary condition for good governance. We agree that Western modernity as embodied by consolidated, democratic, and welfare states is a most successful model of effective and legitimate governance in world history. But we challenge the implicit assumption of this work that central control of violence in the sense of strong statehood and domestic sovereignty is a necessary condition. Effective and legitimate governance is possible also in ALS, and we show why and how.

The failure of modernization theories, Huntington-type institutional-ism, and the North et al. open access order approach to account for governance in ALS is at least partly related to a major weakness this scholarship shares: it is overly structural. There is only limited agency in these literatures, actors drop out or are not properly theorized. As a result, neither North et al. nor Acemoglu and Robinson nor Fukuyama offer satisfactory explanations for why some countries make the transi-tion from "limited" to "open access" orders, while others do not. In a way, "limited access orders" are doomed. In contrast, our main explana-tory variables – institutional design, legitimacy, and social trust – do not come out of thin air, but can be shaped by actors and their behavior. Whether external state actors or Northern consumers set the right incen-tives for companies to engage in governance depends on the formers' behavior. The extent to which governance institutions are "fit for purpose" is a matter of designing them in the appropriate way. Whether "governors" gain legitimacy through the acceptance of the people is significantly influenced by their own behavior. The social mobilization of communities has a strong role in social trust helping to solve collective action problems.

The actor-centered and institutionalist framework to governance we develop in this book overcomes the Western bias exemplified by state-centrism in the dominant literatures. It integrates our explanatory variables and specifies the causal mechanisms through which they affect effective and legitimate governance in ALS. Our interest in governance under anarchy notwithstanding, we do not dismiss the role existing state structures may play for governance in ALS. Yet, we acknowledge the ambivalent effect they can have and explore when statehood fosters rather than impairs the effective and legitimate provision of rules and of collective goods and services (see Chapter 8). More importantly, we do not treat statehood or hierarchy as the *sine qua non* for good governance, but identify conditions under which alternative forms of governance emerge and are effective and legitimate, respectively.

Normative, Political, and World Order Implications

The arguments advanced in this book have significant normative, political, and world order implications (see Chapter 8 for a discussion). From a *normative* point of view, we join the growing literature challenging mainstream social science as inherently Euro- or Western-centric with regard to their central concepts and theories. We share this criticism with the postcolonial literature (Said 1979; Williams and Chrisman 1994; Young 2001). Removing the Western model of the liberal capitalist welfare state as the teleological center in the social sciences opens up space for both considering multiple modernities (Eisenstadt 2007; Schmidt 2006) and different institutionalized forms of effective and legitimate governance that do not rely on consolidated "Western" statehood. While we do not go as far as Scott's "cheers for anarchism" (Scott 1998, 2009, 2012), we maintain that consolidated statehood only constitutes one way of improving the human condition, both historically and in the contemporary global order. As Scott reminds us, however, the state is often part of the problem and not part of the solution. Building or strengthening the Leviathan without taming it tends to result in "bad governance" by repressive and corrupt states (Börzel and Pamuk 2012).

The *political implications* of our argument are rather straightforward. For the past 20 years, Western powers engaged in – mostly futile –

attempts at state-building – from Iraq to Afghanistan (for critiques see Lake, D. 2016; Lake and Farris 2014). Our findings imply that a paradigm shift in international development strategies is necessary – from state-building to governance-promotion (Brozus 2011). Rather than focusing on the whole-sale transfer of Western-type state institutions to areas of limited statehood, we advocate concentrating on specific governance tasks and the provision of particular rules, goods, and services. External governance promotion has proven to be rather effective and sustainable – under the scope conditions specified in this volume.

Last but not least, we consider the *world order implications* of our findings. First, the traditional dichotomy of juxtaposing the international system as an anarchic order (classical versions: Bull 1977; Waltz 1979) and domestic political orders as hierarchical does not work. Areas of limited statehood are similar to the international system in the sense that there is no central authority with the capacity to enforce rules and the monopoly of the use of force. Yet, governance and order are possible both internationally and in ALS, as our book documents. Chapter 8 explores the consequences of this finding for the international-domestic divide that has structured the social sciences, setting the field of International Relations apart from other disciplines.

Second, public international law and the various international regimes and institutions are based on the ideal type of consolidated statehood. In other words, states, which commit to international law and the various treaties, are thought of being capable of implementing and enforcing these rules domestically (Krieger 2018). Non-compliance with international law then becomes a question of (un-) willingness rather than lack of capacity (Börzel and Risse 2013). Systematically considering limited statehood changes the perspective: capacity issues and the "management perspective" in compliance research (Chayes and Chayes 1991, 1995) become front and center with regard to the domestic implementation of international law. At the same time, international law can also deploy its empowering potential in ALS even when it is no longer the state that is able to enforce it (Simmons 2009). It may serve as a legitimating device for governance under conditions of limited statehood.

Organization of the Book

This book relies on a multitude of theoretical and empirical sources, both quantitative and qualitative. We would not have been able to write this book without more than 12 years of research in the *Collaborative Research*

Center (*Sonderforschungsbereich*) "Governance in Areas of Limited Statehood," which was generously funded by the German Research Foundation (*Deutsche Forschungsgemeinschaft*) and included dozens of individual research projects, about 100 PhD researchers, and more than 20 postdocs.[15] However, the book does not only rely on the empirical research conducted in Berlin. We also include other scholarship in order to demonstrate the validity of our theoretical arguments.

Concepts and Theory

The book is organized in the following way. The first two chapters set the stage. *Chapter 2* introduces the main concepts, namely "areas of limited statehood" and "governance." We discuss functional and institutional conceptualizations of the state and explain why we settle for an institutional understanding in the tradition of Max Weber (Weber 1978 [1922]). Accordingly, we avoid defining statehood through the various governance functions a (modern and Western-type) state is expected to perform. We then conceptualize areas of limited statehood as referring to those (territorial, policy, or social) spaces where state institutions are too weak to implement and enforce central decisions and/or to uphold a monopoly of the use of force. We continue by discussing measurement issues and providing empirical examples for measuring limited statehood, including subnational levels.

We then turn to introducing our understanding of "governance," which we define as institutionalized modes of social coordination to adopt and implement collectively binding rules, or to provide collective goods and services. We discuss governance as structure and process with the latter including the various modes of hierarchical as well as non-hierarchical governance. The chapter concludes with a discussion of several issues emerging when one applies the governance concept to areas of limited statehood. This concerns, on the one hand, the distinction between the "public" and the "private" spheres common to Western modernity that has to be adjusted to conditions of limited statehood. On the other hand, the inherent intentionality and normativity of the governance concepts needs to be taken into account.

Chapter 3 elaborates our theory of governance in areas of limited statehood. We start with a brief discussion of the shortcomings of existing theories, such as modernization theory, statist institutionalism in the tradition of Huntington leading to the state-building paradigm, as

---

[15] See www.sfb-governance.de/en/index.html, last access August 12, 2019.

well as inclusive institutionalism with its distinction between "open" and "closed access orders," and the good governance paradigm. This overview leads to the conclusion that, while these approaches address certain pieces of our "governance puzzle," none of them offers a satisfying answer.

We continue to develop our own approach centring on the three concepts of institutions, (empirical) legitimacy, and social trust. After defining these concepts, we turn to developing the theoretical framework for answering our first research question, namely how to explain when (particularly self-interested) actors are motivated to engage in governance. As to the role of (state) institutions, we argue that the shadow of hierarchy and the shadow of anarchy go a long way to incentivize external state actors as well as companies and violent non-state actors to become governors. The same holds true for the quest for (international as well as domestic) legitimacy and social acceptance motivating companies and rebel groups in particular to provide governance services. Last but not least, personalized trust relations within and among local communities not only helps overcoming collective action problems, but also leads to the demand for governance contributions by "traditional" authorities, such as tribal or religious leaders.

Next, we introduce our theory of effective and legitimate governance in areas of limited statehood, answering our second research question. We start by conceptualizing "effective" governance as consisting of both "objective" (measurable) and "subjective" (relating to perceptions) dimensions. We then turn to our three explanatory factors. First, institutional conditions fostering effective governance consist of institutional design ("fit for purpose"), inclusiveness, and fairness (leading to input and throughput legitimacy), and – last but not least – residual statehood that, however, can be both a blessing and a curse. Second, empirical legitimacy and social acceptance of the governors and the governance institutions matters hugely for effectiveness. It is virtually impossible to govern effectively in ALS without legitimacy (Krasner and Risse 2014b). Finally, personalized, group-based or particularistic, and generalized trust constitutes a further enabling condition for effective governance. The more people trust each other – both governors and governed – the more they are able to effectively solve collective action problems and to provide goods and services under conditions of limited statehood.

The chapter ends by discussing the various sources of legitimacy, such as inclusive and fair institutions, effective governance, and – once again – relationships of trust. In other words, the three explanatory factors reinforce each other, but they also complement each other. And there are various feedback loops and virtuous (as well as vicious) circles between them.

Actors and Modes of Governance

The empirical part of the book puts our theoretical framework to work. We summarize numerous empirical studies and interpret the findings by applying our theoretical framework. The empirical part starts with *Chapter 4* focusing on the various governors in areas of limited statehood. For each of these actors, we discuss their motivation to govern as well as the – hierarchical or non-hierarchical – modes of governance they use. We start with external state governance, including IOs and ROs, development agencies, and foreign governments. We find the entire spectrum of potential reasons to engage – from the "shadow of anarchy" and other self-interested reasons to humanitarian motives. The same holds true for the modes of governance whereby IOs and ROs mostly employ negotiation and deliberation, while foreign governments might also use military interventions, not always out of humanitarian motives.

We then turn to the non-state sector, starting with (I)NGOs and MSPs. While humanitarian motives are constitutive for them and their engagement in governance, this does not exclude self-interested reasons, such as fund-raising. As to their modes of engagement, they focus on negotiations and deliberations and often try to foster local ownership, including community-based organizations. A very different type of actor are (multinational) companies who are usually not inclined to become governors to begin with. In general, they need to be confronted with rather strong shadows of hierarchy, of anarchy, and of (local) communities to become governors. In contrast, "traditional" authorities, such as tribal chiefs and community leaders, as well as non-state justice institutions (NSJI), tend to be among the most important indigenous governors in many ALS. Their motivation to govern derives mostly from their embeddedness in relationships of social trust. Moreover, they have the entire repertoire of modes of governance at their disposal, including hierarchical command and control with strong social sanctioning capacities. Interestingly enough, many NSJI fulfill the criteria of deliberative governance in an almost Habermasian sense, which have been formulated for a totally different – mostly Western – context. A rather unlikely group of governors are violent non-state actors, such as rebel groups or even warlords. For them to engage in governance, they need to become "stationary bandits" (Olson 1993) controlling territory. Under these conditions, their governance motivations mostly stem from the shadows of anarchy and of local communities and from their need to gain international as well as domestic legitimacy so that they can achieve their political goals. Once they become governors, however, they have the entire range of governance modes at their disposal, from the use of force and command-and-control all the way to inclusive and participatory governance.

In sum, we find a whole variety of different actors motivated to engage in governance in ALS under certain conditions – state and non-state, local, national, transnational, as well as international. Moreover, we find the entire range of modes of governance, from hierarchical steering including the use of force to inclusive, participatory, and deliberative governance.

Effective and Legitimate Governance

Chapters 5–7 of the book look at the effectiveness and legitimacy of governance in ALS in various policy areas. While our choice of issue areas may sound Western-centric at first glance, we submit that security (Chapter 5), human rights, the rule of law, and democracy (Chapter 6), as well as economic subsistence, health, and a clean environment (Chapter 7), are universally accepted values and collective goods (to judge from the ratification rates of international treaties covering these issue areas). We do not have a pre-conceived notion of how these issue areas should be governed or by whom. Nor do we think that there is a "hierarchy of goods" as suggested by Rotberg (2004a, 3–5). Rather, the whole point of the book is to demonstrate the enormous variety of (good) governance, even under rather adverse conditions of limited statehood (Draude 2012). Each chapter of this part of the book begins with an assessment of the particular governance puzzle in the issue-area under investigation.

SECURITY GOVERNANCE

We start with the provision of public security in *Chapter 5*. We begin by contesting the notion that ALS are mostly violent places where civil war prevails. The opposite is the case, particularly when one moves to the sub-national level and even in countries having experienced civil war for decades (such as Somalia and the DRC). We then move on to analyze peace-keeping missions, military interventions from the outside, as well as externally promoted security sector reform. We point to a paradox in this case (see also Lake, D. 2016, 2018): the more intrusive the interventions and the more they resemble comprehensive state-building efforts from the outside, the less successful they are on average. In contrast, more limited external governance fostering post-conflict peace-building and security sector reform is more effective, particularly the more inclusive it is. The main reason for the difference in effectiveness concerns the extraordinarily high requirements for domestic legitimacy in the case of intrusive (military) interventions that can rarely be met, as theorized by our framework.

We then look at the conditions under which VNSA can provide public security in the territory that they control. Warlord governance tends to be rather ineffective, particularly since warlords are likely to turn security into a private or club good that is only available for their clientele. Rebel groups and more politically motivated VNSA tend to score better, particularly if and when they face high legitimacy needs and local communities with strong trust-based action capacity to hold them accountable. Under these conditions, strong and efficient internal organizational capacities can actually be used to maintain public security rather than to terrorize civilians.

Finally, Chapter 5 looks at tribal groups and leaders as rather effective peace-keepers. While they normally lack military enforcement capacity, they can rely on strong social norms to maintain security in communities. Here, legitimacy and social trust relations are key, as the example of Somaliland demonstrates (see above).

We conclude Chapter 5 with an ambivalent assessment: on the one hand, "security under anarchy" is possible in ALS, even under rather adverse conditions. On the other hand, our findings cast serious doubts on whether public security governance can be sustainable in the long run, if a (state) monopoly of the use of force is not restored at some point, e.g. as a result of an inclusive peace process that includes former combatants (Matanock 2017).

HUMAN RIGHTS, THE RULE OF LAW, AND DEMOCRACY

Chapter 6 investigates an equally demanding governance task, namely to protect human rights, institute the rule of law as well as participatory institutions ("democracy") under anarchy. Here we conclude with a slightly more positive assessment than in Chapter 5, namely that democratic governance is possible, even if state capacities to enforce rules and decisions are weak or absent. After having established our particular governance puzzle for the issue-area, we discuss the peculiar human rights problematique in areas of limited statehood. The take home message in this section is that simply strengthening state capacity might do human rights and the rule of law more harm than good, resulting in autocratic and repressive statehood (see also Börzel and Risse 2013).

As in Chapter 5, we continue to discuss the effectiveness of various actors. Here, we start by focusing on the role of regional organizations

(ROs) as promoters and protectors of human rights and democracy. ROs tend to be more effective in these tasks, the more they are equipped with sufficient resources and their institutional rules and procedures enable collective action. Moreover, the more ROs can rely on the domestic acceptance and legitimacy of the (democratic) norms they promote, the more successful they are.

We then move on to the effectiveness of (I)NGOs and NSJI to provide fair and transparent access to justice as a crucial component of the rule of law. We show that – based on various micro studies – NSJI can indeed accomplish these goals, the more their institutional design enables deliberative negotiations through fair and transparent procedures. Moreover, their legitimacy among local communities is crucial for their success.

The remainder of the chapter discusses the effectiveness of companies and rebel groups to engage in human rights and democratic governance. We find that it is one thing to expect companies to comply with human rights norms. It is quite different to ask them to actively promote human rights and the rule of law beyond their premises (and beyond supply chains), as we argue with regard to the limited success of the Voluntary Principles on Security and Human Rights. Interestingly enough, VNSA are more likely to provide effective human rights and inclusive governance, particularly if they require international and domestic legitimacy in order to control territory, on the one hand, and if they are faced with trust-based communities with their own collective action capacity, on the other (see also Huang 2016).

We conclude Chapter 6 with a discussion of empirical legitimacy in this context, particularly the various feedback loops between legitimacy, effectiveness, and institutional design. The greater the legitimacy of the democratic and human rights norms promoted by governors in a given context, the lesser the need for an institutional capacity necessary to enforce the rule of law and democratic rules.

WELFARE GOVERNANCE

Chapter 7 of the book deals with welfare governance concerning health, education, food security, and environmental protection in ALS. We document that the provision of collective goods and services with regard to welfare is possible "under anarchy" and – with regard to less complex tasks – even under the rather adverse conditions of civil war. Available data show that there has been a general improvement on average across a wide range of governance services and including many countries with ALS over the past decades. Moreover, governors other than the state contribute regularly to effective welfare governance in ALS. The chapter covers a wide variety of such actors – from IOs and foreign donors to (multinational) companies, MSPs, (I)NGOs, VNSA, and "traditional" authorities. We find that most governors covered in this chapter are able to provide effective governance services. With regard to IOs, foreign donors, MSPs, (I)NGOs and "traditional" authorities, we are rather optimistic. More recent studies focusing on the sub-national level demonstrate that foreign aid actually improves local conditions – without weakening the state even further, but – on the contrary – contributing to increased state legitimacy. For these governors and governance services, the two conditions specified in the theoretical framework are particularly relevant, namely institutional designs that are inclusive and "fit for purpose," on the one hand, and domestic legitimacy and social acceptance, on the other hand.

As to business and VNSA, their contribution to effective welfare governance is more circumscribed. Business as governors will step in as subsidiary service providers as long as nobody else is providing governance and its primary goals are not threatened. But the institutional conditions and legitimacy requirements for effective governance contributions of business are quite demanding. As discussed above with regard to human rights, it is easier for companies to avoid negative externalities from their activities (e.g. environmental pollution) than to make positive contributions to governance, e.g. with regard to public health. As to VNSA, legitimacy needs lead them to provide effective welfare governance. However, this circle from effective governance to output legitimacy is likely to be disrupted by their opponents, e.g. by state actors fighting them. It follows that rebel groups are most likely to sustain effective governance if they are close to victory, i.e., if they turn from governors to governments (see Jo 2015).

Thus, effective welfare governance is possible in ALS. But there are two crucial scope conditions that appear to require some residual statehood, the more complex the governance tasks at hand are: the absence of large-scale violence and at least some degree of public security, on the one hand, and a minimum infrastructure (such as roads and electricity), on the other.

Conclusions and Implications

Chapter 8 of the book begins by summarizing our key findings. In general, the conceptual and theoretical framework developed in Chapters 2 and 3 holds up well in light of the empirical evidence: governance under anarchy can be effective and legitimate under specific conditions. In this context, we also explore the various feedback loops between legitimacy, institutional design, social trust, and effective governance.

We then move on to discuss various implications of our findings. First, we turn to the ambivalent role of the – residual – state in areas of limited statehood. On the one hand, effective governance in most issue-areas is not possible without some degree of security, pointing to the need for a monopoly of the use of force, and without some basic infrastructure. On the other hand, the residual state in ALS often behaves as a governance spoiler rather than an active supporter. We conclude that residual statehood may be important but needs to be tamed by the rule of law and participatory institutions. We also discuss similarities between the (residual) state in ALS and the transformation of statehood in Western democracies toward "governance management" and meta-governance in terms of rule-setting about rules.

Second, we discuss the implications for international affairs. On the one hand, the international system shares important features with areas of limited statehood. The "anarchy problematique" – the absence of an ultimate authority with the capacity to enforce decisions and to uphold a monopoly of the use of force – is common to both. At the same time, neither the international system nor ALS are ungoverned or ungovernable. It follows that many IR theories are highly relevant for explaining effective governance in ALS – and vice versa. On the other hand, the global governance system and ALS are firmly intertwined in a multi-level governance system. This has numerous advantages insofar as the international community cannot simply ignore governance challenges in ALS – without creating severe repercussions for the international system, for global stability, and for peace, security, and the wealth of consolidated states. However, governance in ALS as multi-level governance creates its own problems since international law presupposes consolidated states and because of diverging legitimacy and accountability issues.

Third, we turn to the political implications of our findings. If areas of limited statehood are here to stay, what does this mean for Western democracies and IOs when dealing with ALS? Most analysts and policy-makers alike agree that comprehensive state-building efforts in ALS have largely failed. But does this mean that we have to lower our normative standards when we deal with, say, Kenya rather than Denmark, as the "good enough governance" proposal implies (Grindle 2004)? We submit that this is the wrong way to pose the normative questions. We suggest a paradigm shift from state-building to governance promotion and spell out what this means (see Brozus, Jetzlsperger, and Walter-Drop 2018). In particular, external (state) actors and IOs should not only deal with state actors in ALS, but support the governance contributions of non-state actors as well as focus on specific governance tasks.

Part I

Setting the Stage: Concepts and Theories

Areas of Limited Statehood and Governance
Concepts and Measurements

Governance has become a central topic of research within the social sciences.[1] This research is motivated by a widespread hope that governance will help to achieve certain normative standards, such as human rights, democracy, and the rule of law, as well as to provide common goods, such as security, welfare, and a clean environment (Ladwig and Rudolf 2011; Rothstein 2011; Ruggie 2004b). Yet, the governance discourse has remained centered on an ideal type of modern statehood – with full internal and external sovereignty, a legitimate monopoly of the use of force, and checks and balances that constrain political rule and authority (Bevir 2008; Börzel 2010c; Pierre and Peters 2000). Similarly, the "global governance" debate in international relations, while focusing on "governance without government" (Czempiel and Rosenau 1992) and the rise of private authority in world politics (e.g. Avant, Finnemore, and Sell 2010b; Cutler, Haufler, and Porter 1999; Hall and Biersteker 2002; O'Brien et al. 2000), has assumed that functioning states are capable of implementing and enforcing global norms and rules. "Denmark," the modern consolidated democratic and welfare state of the late twentieth century, has been the (implicit) benchmark of the governance discourse.

As outlined in the introduction, this book challenges the idea that modern consolidated statehood constitutes what is "normal" in the contemporary international system or from a historical perspective. In contrast, we argue that limited statehood is the default and has also been with us for most of known human history (see e.g. Chowdhury 2018; Clunan and Trinkunas 2010; Conrad and Stange 2011; Rinke, Contreraz Saiz, and Hölck 2011; Scott 1998). We also submit that "governance by government" has been the exception rather than the standard, not only in history, but also in the contemporary world. Even in OECD countries with their consolidated statehood, the classical or

---

[1] This chapter contains material from Börzel, Risse, and Draude 2018 and Risse 2011b.

"heroic" state has transformed itself over the past decades from a regulator and enforcer into a governance manager (Deitelhoff and Geis 2010; Genschel and Zangl 2008a; Kooiman 1993). Rather than monopolizing the provision of collective goods and services, the negotiating, cooperating, or enabling state seeks to involve non-state actors to achieve more effective and legitimate governance (cf. Jessop 1998; Kooiman 1993; Mayntz 1993; Schuppert 2009).

This chapter introduces the book's key concepts, namely *areas of limited statehood* (ALS) and *governance*. We then discuss some conceptual and methodological issues that arise when the concept of *governance* is applied to *areas of limited statehood*.

Areas of Limited Statehood

This book argues that limited statehood is central for capturing governance challenges in the twenty-first century. We will state our case by, first, distinguishing statehood and "the state" from other forms of political order. Second, we will clarify how our understanding of "limited statehood" differs from other concepts, such as "weak," "fragile," or "failed" states.

Statehood: Functional vs. Institutional Understandings

Theories of the state abound (see e.g. Benz 2001; Hay, Lister, and Marsh 2006; Hobson 2000; Schuppert 2009; vom Hau 2015). However, this book is not concerned with theories of state formation (e.g. Fukuyama 2012; Tilly 1975; and others). Neither do we seek to explain states as institutionalized class relations (Marxist theories, for an overview see Barrow 1993), as social contracts (liberal approaches, see North, Wallis, and Weingast 2009), or as cultural representations in the Foucauldian sense (see vom Hau 2015 for an overview over these various traditions). Rather, we look for a definition of the state that helps us clarify our concept of statehood.

Most scholars would probably agree that the state constitutes a particular type of political order, a political system, or a polity. A tribe forms a political order, but it is not a state. Global governance, with its many international institutions, also constitutes a political order, but there is no world state. So, how do we know a state when we see it? We find two different conceptualizations of the state in the literature that help us clarify our concept of statehood (for the following see also Eriksen 2011).

FUNCTIONAL CONCEPTUALIZATIONS OF THE STATE

Functional conceptualizations of state focus on the functions it is supposed to perform. States exist to provide rule structures and deliver public goods and services within their territory. The following quote is typical for such a performance-based approach:

We define weak states as countries that lack the essential capacity and/or will to fulfil four sets of critical government responsibilities: fostering an environment conducive to sustainable and equitable economic growth; establishing and maintaining legitimate, transparent, and accountable political institutions; securing their populations from violent conflict and controlling their territory; and meeting the basic human needs of their population. (Rice and Patrick 2008, 3; see also Rotberg 2014)

In other words, functioning states are effective service providers – from security to education and a clean environment. A functional understanding of the state has informed most of the scholarly literature on "fragile" and "failed" states, the various datasets measuring degrees of statehood, as well as the state-building programs of development agencies and international organizations (e.g. Carment 2003; Carment et al. 2015; Ghani and Lockhart 2009; Helman and Ratner 1992; Messner et al. 2015; Messner et al. 2016; Rotberg 2003, 2004b, 2014; Schneckener 2004). Using state performance to define functioning states is prone to tautological reasoning (cf. Cingolani 2013; Lindvall and Teorell 2016; Soifer 2008). For instance, the OECD 2015 Report on State Fragility claims that fragile states lag behind other states in reaching the Millennium Development Goals (MDG; see The Development Assistance Committee 2015). At the same time, it uses economic growth, educational years, and health capacities among others as indicators for state fragility. No wonder that fragile states form the "bottom billion" (Collier 2007) and are among the poorest states in the world.

Functional understandings of the state are not only analytically problematic (for a similar critique see Wolff 2011); tautological reasoning also leads to bad policy advice, since we have no clue what is the cause of what if we use poverty as an indicator for state fragility and then argue that state fragility causes poverty (for a thorough critique of the "failed state" concept see also Woodward 2017). Fighting poverty is not the same as state-building. Nor does the strengthening of state institutions necessarily reduce poverty. Finally, such functional understandings obscure the politically highly relevant distinction between states that are unwilling to provide governance services, and those that are unable to do so (see below).

A related issue is the confusion of definitional issues and research questions. If we define a state through the functions it performs, a non-performing state is no longer a state at all, strictly speaking. Moreover, defining rule of law or transparent, accountable, and inclusive institutions as state functions tends to conflate regime type (democracy, autocracy, etc.) and statehood. We might find autocratic systems, such as Russia or Saudi Arabia, morally questionable, but they certainly constitute states. Functional, performance-oriented conceptualizations of the state prevent us from posing the questions we are most interested in: under which conditions do states or other types of polities perform well by providing rule structures and delivering goods and services? What capacities does a state need to perform certain tasks? How much statehood is necessary to lead to governance that is effective and legitimate? To what extent can non-state actors provide collective goods and services, compensating for the governance failure of states?

Last but not least, most functional typologies in the literature and datasets on fragile states, failing states, or "states at risk," reveal a normative orientation toward highly developed and democratic states, such as Denmark. The benchmark is usually the democratic and capitalist state governed by the rule of law (Leibfried and Zürn 2005). This is normatively questionable, because it reflects Eurocentrism and a bias toward Western concepts as if statehood equals the combination of Western liberal statehood and market economy.

INSTITUTIONAL CONCEPTUALIZATIONS OF THE STATE

The second understanding of state, which we follow here, is institutional and conceptualizes a state as a particular type of organizational structure. Weber has provided the quintessential definition:

A compulsory political organization with continuous operation (*politischer Anstaltsbetrieb*) will be called a "state" insofar as its administrative staff successfully upholds the claim to the *monopoly* of the *legitimate* use of physical force in the enforcement of its order. (Weber 1978 (1922), 54)

A state constitutes an authoritative rule structure, a *Herrschaftsverband*, which has the capacity and the right to rule hierarchically, based on the control over the (legitimate) use of violence within its territory, and can expect obedience to its commands. This is an institutional understanding of the state as a hierarchical rule structure. It does not imply that states rule hierarchically via command and control all the time, only that statehood implies the ability and (the claim to) the legitimate right to do so.

Among contemporary authors, Fukuyama, Holsti, Jackson, and Krasner share this institutionalist understanding of statehood (see Fukuyama 2004, 2012; Holsti 2004; Jackson 1990; Krasner 1999; for a similar emphasis on state enforcement capacity see also D'Arcy and Nistotskaya 2016; Lambach, Johais, and Bayer 2015). Equally important, this institutional understanding conforms to international law, in particular the Montevideo Convention of 1933 (see Grant 1998–1999; also Jellinek 1900 [1922]). Accordingly, a state possesses a permanent population, occupies a clearly defined territory, operates an effective government over its territory, and displays capacity to fulfill international treaty obligations. Weber's conceptualization of the state conforms to the third and fourth criteria mentioned here, if we understand "effective government" as entailing some degree of hierarchical enforcement capacity, what we call statehood. States command what Stephen Krasner called "domestic sovereignty," i.e., "the formal organization of political authority within the state and the ability of public authorities to exercise effective control within the borders of their own polity" (Krasner 1999, 4). This is what the US and China have in common, for all their other differences. They are both states in a Weberian or institutionalist sense.

The control of the monopoly of the use of force captures the coercive or military dimension of state capacity (Fortin 2010; Gurr 1988). And the setting and enforcement of rules requires some tax and spending capacity (Levi 1988; Tilly 1995) as well as some sort of administration or professional bureaucracy (Rauch and Evans 2000; Skocpol 1985). Our institutionalist understanding of statehood leaves out what the literature discusses as the developmental capacity of the state to shape, innovate, or permeate the economy and the society (Migdal 1988, 2001; Rueschemeyer and Evans 1983; see also Mann 1984).

Our Weberian understanding of statehood allows us to strictly distinguish between the state as an institutional structure of authority that can set and enforce rules and controls the monopoly of the use of force, on the one hand, and the kind of governance it provides, on the other. The latter is an empirical not a definitional question. Statehood understood as the capacity to govern hierarchically is part of the definition. Whether statehood is used to provide collective goods and services is part of our research question. North Korea certainly commands statehood in terms of coercive and enforcement powers, but it does not use it to provide many goods and services for the population. Moreover, as the North Korean example shows, statehood has nothing to do with regime type (democracy, autocracy, etc.) or what North et al. call "open" versus "closed access orders" (North, Wallis, and Weingast 2009).

Separating statehood from governance avoids the fallacies of functional conceptualizations. Most importantly, it allows for the possibility that other actors than the state engage in governance. This is particularly relevant in areas of limited statehood (see below). As this book discusses particularly in Chapter 4, what if non-state actors, such as warlords or rebel groups, gain the ability to maintain a monopoly of the use of force in a territory controlled by them and are also capable of enforcing their decisions? As Tilly has argued, European states came about precisely because such violent non-state actors (VNSA) acquired at least some degree of statehood (Tilly 1975, 1985). In the contemporary international system, however, the difference between a state and a territory controlled by warlords or rebel groups is recognition by other states ("international sovereignty" in Krasner's terminology, Krasner 1999). As a result, and for mostly pragmatic reasons, we confine the term statehood in this book to those political entities that are internationally recognized and legitimated as such, even though warlords or rebel groups might claim statehood, too (Huang 2016).

Conceptualizing Limited Statehood

The institutional understanding of the state enables us to define more precisely what limited statehood means. While areas of limited statehood are located inside internationally recognized states, it is the domestic sovereignty of these states that is severely circumscribed. ALS constitute those aspects of a country *where state authorities (such as national, regional, or local governments) lack the ability to implement and enforce rules and decisions and/or in which they do not control the use of force.*

The opposite of limited statehood is not "unlimited" but "consolidated" statehood, i.e., those areas of a country in which the state enjoys the monopoly of the use of force and/or the ability to make and enforce central decisions most of the time.

"Limited statehood" refers to lack of capacity, not lack of willingness. While this distinction is conceptually clear-cut, applying it empirically is much more difficult, since capacity might be endogenous to willingness and vice versa. First, the "neoliberal state" that has withdrawn from regulating particular policy areas (e.g. capital flows) or from providing particular public services (e.g. telecommunications) by way of political decisions does not qualify as an "area of limited statehood." These are mostly consolidated and democratic states that are not of concern here, since they can still cast a "shadow of hierarchy" and, thus, see to it that private actors provide the various public services (Börzel 2010c; see Chapter 4 for details).

Second, however, (lack of) willingness and capacity often go together empirically, which makes it very hard to disentangle them empirically: the Mexican central state might not have the overall capacity to ensure public security in Mexico City and in the various federal states given the threats posed by drug cartels and other VNSA. However, the decision to police certain – mostly wealthy – areas and city quarters and not others is a question of political choice, not capacity (Braig and Stanley 2007; Müller 2012). The example also shows that ALS emerge, sometimes, because certain threats and challenges overwhelm state capacities. For instance, climate change is likely to turn coastal areas in many parts of the world into ALS, since the Netherlands might be able to cope with it, but Bangladesh certainly cannot (Hamann, Hönke, and O'Riordan 2018). Last but not least, states might decide to focus their limited capacity on enforcing rules and providing public services in one policy area, while neglecting another one. A state's choice to invest in public health might turn public education into an ALS, because the government lacks the capacity to take care of both. A more common example concerns investing in military defense and security, thereby turning other policy issues into ALS.

Third, there are the so-called cunning states (Randeria 2003; see also Brandel and Randeria 2018) whereby political and social elites deliberately keep state institutions weak in order to reap economic and political benefits or to increase their rents. Randeria has argued that India represents such a state that avoids accountability to its citizens domestically while seeking to retain as much foreign aid as possible internationally. Reno makes a similar argument about the state in Sub-Saharan Africa whereby state institutions are captured by rent-seeking warlords to feed their clientelistic networks (see Reno 1998b; also Bates 2008).

Whether limited statehood results from a lack of capacity or of willingness by ruling elites (or a combination of both) is ultimately an empirical question. Moreover, it needs to be clarified what is endogenous to what. In the case of the "neoliberal" state, keeping the state out of certain parts of the economy has been a political decision that has little to do with weak state institutions in general. The "neoliberal" US or UK states are perfectly capable of enforcing the law with regard to national security issues and command enormous resources in this regard. Moreover, they can revoke the political choice of rolling back the state and re-regulate markets. With regard to "cunning states," in contrast, elite choices to keep the state weak are endogenous to limited statehood and not the other way around. African or Indian clientelistic networks are only capable of capturing state institutions and preventing the development of institutional capacities because these states have been weak to begin with.

The above examples also show that limited statehood is not confined to territorial space. The ability to set and enforce rules or to control the use of force can be limited along various dimensions: 1) territorial,

Table 2.1 *Configurations of limited statehood (examples)*

Dimensions of limited statehood	Examples
Territory	Amazon region (Brazil)
	Most Sub-Saharan African countries
Policy area	Environment (China)
	Health (South Africa)
Social	Mafia (Italy)
	Al Qaeda and Daesh (Middle East)

i.e., parts of a country's territorial spaces; 2) sectoral, that is, with regard to specific policy areas; and 3) social, i.e., with regard to specific parts of the population. Each of the three dimensions can also be temporarily limited with regard to statehood. Table 2.1 contains empirical examples for each dimension. As to temporarily limited statehood, New Orleans in the immediate aftermath of Hurricane Katrina would constitute an example, when the US state authorities lost the monopoly of the use of force for a short period of time.

Measuring Areas of Limited Statehood – Problems and Pitfalls

Figure 2.1 provides a very rough first glance at how widespread areas of limited statehood are in the contemporary international system. The world map uses various indicators to measure state administrative capacity and the state monopoly of the use of force. It shows that consolidated states (light grey colors) are the exception to the rule in the contemporary international system covering mostly the "Global North" of highly industrialized and democratic states. This is not to argue that ALS are confined to the "Global South" of the developing world. France, Spain, and Italy are marked as countries with areas of limited statehood in the world map below. The example of New Orleans during Hurricane Katrina in 2005 has already been mentioned. The "no go" areas in many American and European inner cities constitute another example of areas of limited statehood. Nevertheless, and for better or worse, most ALS are located in countries of the Global South, as Figure 2.1 reveals.

At the same time, Figure 2.1 shows that ALS do not equal "failed states" per se where the state has completely lost the monopoly of the use of force and the ability to enforce rules and decisions. Among the failed and fragile states mentioned in the various indices (e.g. Fund for Peace 2019), only Somalia shows up in Figure 2.1 (black color), while

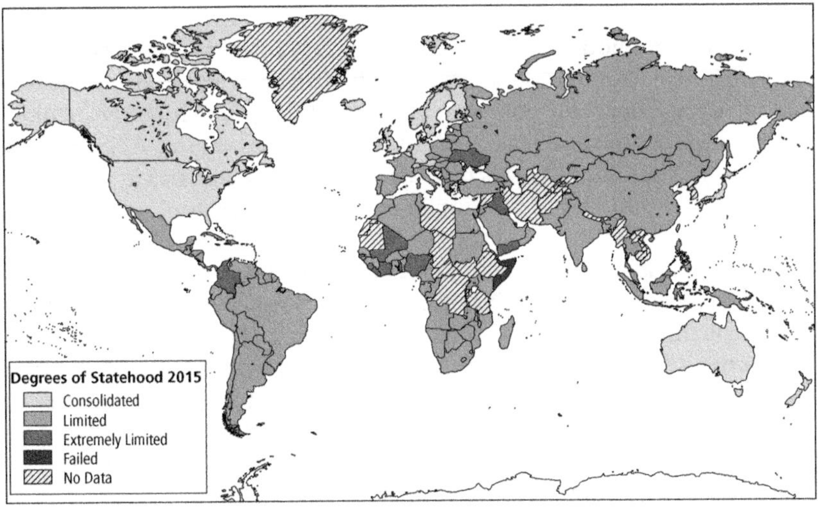

Figure 2.1 World map of countries with areas of limited statehood (2015)

Legend: Statehood is measured here by combining two components and their empirical measurements: 1) the state's monopoly of the use of force and 2) the state's administrative capacity. Concerning the monopoly of the use of force, an index is generated through combining two variables from the Political Instability Task Force (PITF) datasets. The variable MAGAREA measures the proportion of a country affected by fighting. The variable MAGFAIL measures the failure of state authority. For details see Lee, Walter-Drop, and Wiesel 2014; on PITF see http://www.systemicpeace.org/index.html, last access January 28, 2017. Administrative capacity is measured with the International Country Risk Guide (ICRG)-Dataset using their Bureaucracy Quality indicator. For ICRG Dataset see: http://epub.prsgroup.com/products/ international-country-risk-guide-icrg, last access January 28, 2017. The index and the world map have been generated by Eric Stollenwerk (see Stollenwerk and Opper 2017).

Afghanistan, South Sudan, or the DRC are not included because of missing data. Somalia is an interesting case insofar as it contains at least one province – Somaliland – that has developed into a quasi-state. While not recognized internationally, Somaliland nevertheless exhibits a provincial government with almost complete domestic sovereignty (Bryden 2004; Debiel et al. 2009; Menkhaus 2006/2007; Renders and Terlinden 2010). In fact, Somaliland constitutes a prima example of a rather well-governed ALS within a failed state.

The main message of Figure 2.1 is two fold: first, areas of limited statehood are ubiquitous in the contemporary international system. The vast majority of contemporary states exhibit ALS with regard to parts of the territory, particular policy areas, parts of the population, or combinations thereof. Second, most countries, while exhibiting ALS, are not failed or fragile states. This is true for most of the countries in the Global South. Take the People's Republic of China, for example: the Chinese authorities probably control the use of force in most provinces. Yet, state capacity to implement and enforce environmental laws is rather limited, as any visitor to its mega-cities can testify. In other words, the environment constitutes a policy ALS in China (Man 2013).

But the world map in Figure 2.1 also points to various methodological and empirical problems with regard to measuring ALS: first, the map is misleading because of methodological nationalism as a result of which data are aggregated on the national level rather than with regard to sub-state or even local entities, policy areas, or social groups (Amelina et al. 2012; Zürn 2002). Brazil, for example, is a prominent member of the group of emerging economies called BRICS (Brazil, Russia, India, China, South Africa). The Brazilian state cannot be regarded as failed or fragile, but state authorities do not command the capacity to enforce the law in many *favelas* of Rio de Janeiro or in vast areas of the Amazon. China as a state exhibiting various policy ALS has already been mentioned. The government of South Africa has been unable and unwilling for years to deal with the HIV/AIDS pandemic in the country (Börzel and Thauer 2013). With regard to social ALS, whereby the government is unable to enforce the law concerning parts of the population, Southern Italy and the Mafia have to be mentioned (Piattoni 2001), as well as drug cartels and street gangs in the Americas (Sullivan and Bunker 2002), or the transnational terrorist networks in the Middle East (Sageman 2011). In sum, we need much more nuanced data to map reliably ALS beyond methodological nationalism.

A second problem of the world map in Figure 2.1 is that it cannot completely avoid the problem of measuring statehood functionally, i.e., via the functions a state can or cannot perform. For instance, one of the indicators for the monopoly of the use of force measures the proportion of a country affected by fighting (Stollenwerk and Opper 2017, 12). It is assumed rather than demonstrated empirically that in areas without fighting the state retains its monopoly of the use of force. What if people kept the peace anyway, irrespective of the presence of state police forces and the military? While the institutional conceptualization of statehood developed above can be clearly distinguished from the functional one, it is much more difficult to operationalize statehood empirically without at least partially also using functional indicators for state performance.

Third, the indicators used to produce Figure 2.1 cannot fully distinguish between a lack of state capacity to implement and enforce decisions, on the one hand, and a state's willingness to do so, on the other hand (see the discussion above).

In sum, measuring ALS empirically and coming up with valid indicators present a daunting task in and of itself (see also Stollenwerk 2018a). However, there have been various efforts at tackling the measurement issues, if not at solving them. First, there have been several attempts at generating sub-national data for ALS and, thus, at overcoming methodological nationalism (for a similar approach with regard to "failed states" see Lambach and Dertwinkel 2007). Figures 2.2 and 2.3 provide two examples for mapping degrees of statehood with regard to the federal states of Nigeria. Figure 2.2 uses data measuring, on the one hand, instances of violence threatening the state monopoly of the use of force (Armed Conflict Location & Event Data Project [ACLED], see Raleigh et al. 2010). On the other hand, data measuring administrative capacity are taken from the Nigerian National Bureau of Statistics and pertaining to the ratio of vehicles stolen vs. vehicles recovered by state agencies (for details see Stollenwerk 2017).

Figure 2.3 maps the Nigerian federal states using the accuracy of state-generated statistical data (e.g. census data) on age distribution as a proxy for limited state capacity (for details see Lee and Zhang 2017). Lee and Zhang argue that the less a state knows about its citizens and the less valid and reliable the data, the more limited state capacity to provide public goods is.

The two maps of Nigerian federal states demonstrate the enormous variation within a state that – as a whole – qualifies as an area of severely limited statehood (see Figure 2.1). Both maps show that areas of severely limited statehood are located mostly in Northern Nigeria. At the same time, the two figures exhibit quite some differences depending on the chosen indicators for limited statehood. This suggests further caution with regard to measuring limited statehood, but also that state capacity is composed of a variety of different factors depending on the issue area in question. While Figure 2.2 includes data on the monopoly of the use of force, Figure 2.3 solely focuses on statistical data as a proxy for administrative capacity.

Second, scholars have used a variety of indicators to measure limited statehood both at the national and subnational level. Indicators for (a lack of) the monopoly of the use of force internally include areas of a country affected by fighting (Lee, Walter-Drop, and Wiesel 2014) and

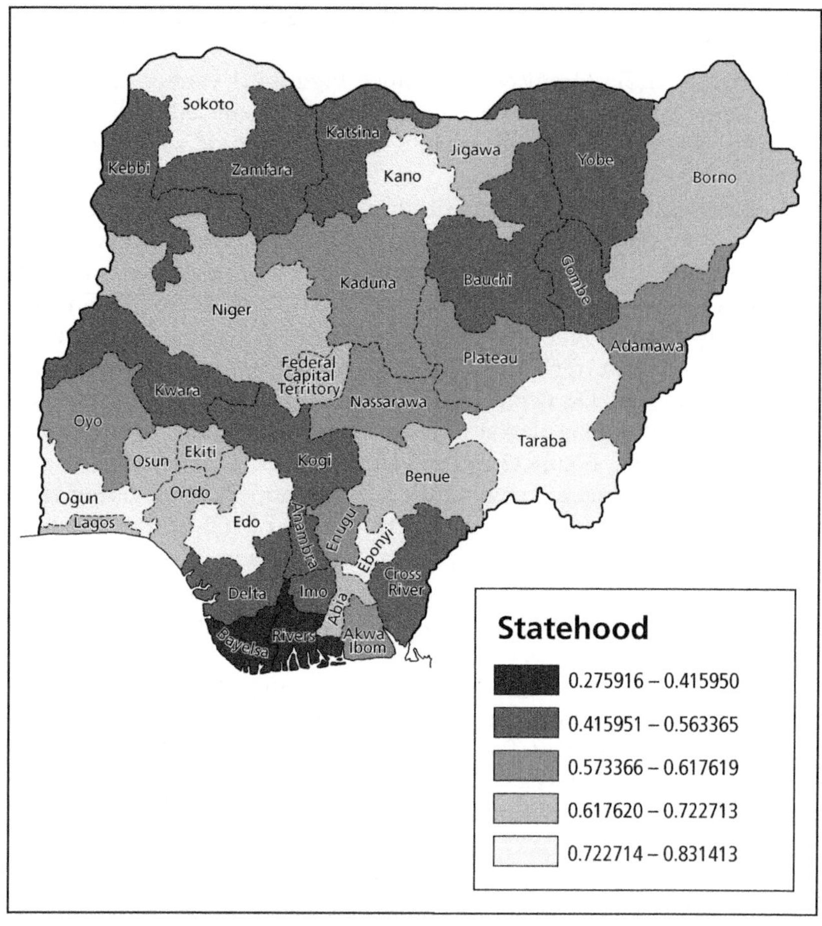

Figure 2.2 Statehood mapping by federal state in Nigeria 2009
Legend: The darker the color, the more limited statehood in the
respective federal state.
Source: Stollenwerk 2017, courtesy of Eric Stollenwerk.

violent acts threatening the monopoly of the use of force (Stollenwerk
2017). Externally, the monopoly of the use of force is operationalized by
a state's control over its borders, preventing intruders from entering its
territory (Simmons 2019, particularly p. 265). In this context, Lee has
focused on the ability of "hostile neighbors" to interfere with the domestic sovereignty of states and, thus, to further weaken areas of limited
statehood (Lee 2018). The (lack of) state capacity to implement and
enforce decisions has been measured by – among others – the ability of

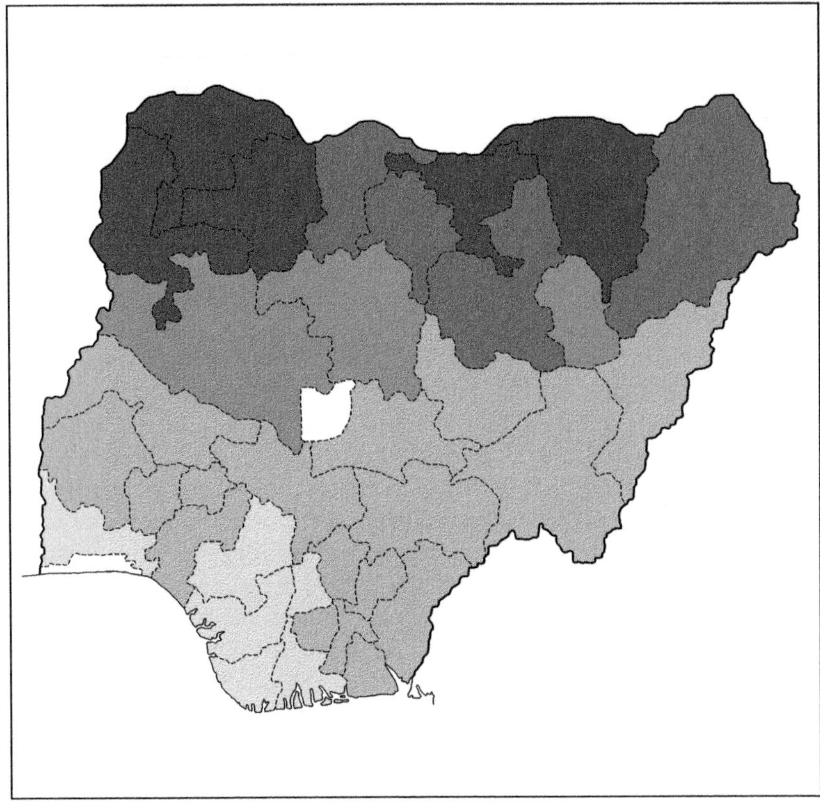

Figure 2.3 Age heaping data, state capacity, and the federal states of
Nigeria
Legend: The map uses degrees of "age heaping," that is, the tendency of
humans to round up or down their age for lack of exact knowledge, as a
measurement for the state (in-) capacity to generate correct statistical
data about the age distribution of the population. Thus, the darker the
color of the respective federal state, the more age heaping and the less
state administrative capacity.
Source: Courtesy of Melissa Lee, see Lee and Zhang 2017 for details of
measurement.

the central state to collect the taxes it is owed (Lee, Walter-Drop, and
Wiesel 2014; see also Lambach and Dertwinkel 2007), or the extent to
which states possess cadastral records on land ownership (D'Arcy and
Nistotskaya 2016), which appears to measure similar features as the
accuracy of state-generated statistical data used by Lee and Zhang (Lee
and Zhang 2017). Last but not least, Koren and Sarbahi have measured

state capacity on the local level by using night-time light emissions as a proxy (Koren and Sarbahi 2018).[2]

This overview shows that measuring ALS in a valid and reliable way represents a daunting task. The literature has not agreed on a set of common indicators. The various measurements discussed here all have their advantages and shortcomings. Future research needs to tackle the double challenge of overcoming methodological nationalism and the functional understanding of statehood.

Limited Statehood and Sovereignty

As argued above, ALS are located within states, which enjoy international sovereignty but lack domestic sovereignty over parts of their territory or population in some or all policy areas for an extended time. We cannot emphasize enough that ALS have been the rule rather than the exception, both historically and with regard to the contemporary international system (Chowdhury 2018). States only acquired the monopoly of the use of force in the nineteenth century (see e.g. Osiander 2001; Reinhard 2007; Thomson 1994, 1995). For centuries, they had fought mercenaries and pirates in order to reap the means of violence from the various contenders. As Tilly argued, state-making was war-making and war made the state (Tilly 1985, 1995). According to Krasner, sovereignty amounted to not much more historically than "organized hypocrisy" (Krasner 1999). Many states have not enjoyed full "Westphalian" sovereignty,[3] i.e., freedom from outside intervention; they have been invaded and conquered and invaded again by external powers. In comparison, international military interventions today are heavily regulated by strong international norms (Finnemore 2003).

Rather than the fully sovereign Weberian state, we are witnessing different combinations of sovereignty (see also Beisheim et al. 2011b; Genschel and Zangl 2008b):

- States may or may not enjoy domestic sovereignty, but most of them are internationally recognized. South Sudan is a prime example of a state that has failed from the very beginning and was recognized as

---

[2] However, this latter measurement uses state provision of critical infrastructure, electricity in this case, and, thus, again conflates service provision and state capacity as it assumes that electricity is provided solely by the state.

[3] We put "Westphalian" in quotes, because the principle of non-interference in domestic affairs was not established by the 1648 Peace of Westphalia, as many International Relations scholars still believe (see Osiander 2001). Rather, this principle emerged over a much longer time.

"sovereign," even though its government has never had domestic sovereignty and failed to fulfill any of the Montevideo criteria discussed above.

- Conversely, state-like entities abound in the current world order that have full domestic sovereignty but are denied or do not seek international sovereignty. Taiwan and Somaliland are cases in point (Bryden 2004; Jackson 1990; Kingston and Spears 2004).
- There are also internationally sovereign states, which not only lack domestic sovereignty. They have given away their "Westphalian" sovereignty or parts thereof by accepting – some voluntarily, others not – external intervention in their rule and authority structures to (re-)gain domestic sovereignty (Lake, D. 2016). Iraq and Afghanistan used to be prominent examples, Kosovo, the Solomon Islands,[4] and countries which have accepted UN peace-keeping missions under Chapter 6 of the UN Charter are cases in point.
- Recently, a group of self-declared "fragile states"founded their own international organization, with a secretariat and regular meetings among members, the "G7+."[5] Founding members are Afghanistan, the DRC, Haiti, Liberia, South Sudan, Sierra Leone, and East Timor. They employ their international sovereignty to compensate for the lack of domestic sovereignty, possibly to avert a violation of their "Westphalian" sovereignty.

The ubiquity of areas of limited statehood and the different combinations of (lacking) domestic, "Westphalian," or international sovereignty stand in sharp contrast to the fiction upheld by international law and the sovereignty discourse prevailing in the international community that the world is populated by sovereign Weberian states enjoying consolidated statehood. Moreover, international law and the legalization of world politics have embedded states in a net of legal and other binding obligations in almost every policy area (Goldstein et al. 2000). Yet, legalization assumes that states are fully capable of implementing and enforcing international law (for a discussion see Krieger 2018). Most international donor agencies and most international state-building and democratization programs – from the World Bank to the EU and the US – also presuppose that the modern Western nation-state is the model for "good governance" (Magen, Risse, and McFaul 2009). This "governance package," consisting of an effective government, the rule of law,

---

[4] In the case of the Solomon Islands, the Regional Assistance Mission to the Solomon Islands (RAMSI) has taken over large parts of the police, military, and judiciary system as part of a Governance Delegation Arrangement. See Matanock 2014.

[5] See www.g7plus.org/en, last access November 29, 2016.

human rights, democracy, market economy, and some degree of social welfare, constitutes a world cultural script (Meyer 1987). The good governance script is promoted by international organizations, states, and NGOs, particularly in developing and transition countries as well as in failing and failed states (Börzel and van Hüllen 2015a).

If full sovereignty and consolidated statehood are close to fiction, this has serious implications for the way we approach governance in ALS. First, the familiar distinction in IR theories (Waltz 1979; but see Lake, D. 2009) between domestic orders where hierarchy prevails, and the international realm of "anarchy" falls by the wayside. (Domestic) ALS share by definition characteristics of the international system, namely the absence of a central enforcement authority. There is no world state that can regularly rule authoritatively and hierarchically over the countries in the world, even though some international organizations, such as the UN Security Council, have the capacity to exercise hierarchical authority. The same holds true for ALS where central state authorities – while not absent – lack the capacity to enforce central decisions and/or to maintain the monopoly of the use of force.

Second, the binary distinction between state and non-state actors becomes blurred and problematic (Mitchell 1991). Not only do states support, authorize, or even organize non-state actors. The distinction between state and non-state actors usually rests on the assumption that state actors enjoy international, domestic, as well as "Westphalian" sovereignty, while non-state actors do not. As argued above, most states only enjoy sovereignty to some degree and in various combinations. Moreover, the ability to rule hierarchically is not confined to states, but non-state actors do so, too – from warlords to the Catholic Church (see Chapter 4, this volume; see also Risse 2018b). As we will show in this book, both state and non-state actors govern in ALS and it is often less than clear who the "governors" are in particular places (on this term see Avant, Finnemore, and Sell 2010b).

This brings us to our third point: most ALS are not anarchic in the Hobbesian sense where life is "solitary, poor, nasty, brutish, and short" (Hobbes 1987 (1651), ch. 13). ALS are neither ungovernable nor ungoverned. Again, this is what they have in common with other "anarchic" environments, such as the international system. There is no supreme authority governing these spaces. Yet, the international system and ALS are equally full of norms, rules, and procedures, both formal and informal. As we will show in this book, some ALS are reasonably well governed, while others are not and the provision of basic collective goods and services is lacking. Just because the Brazilian police cannot enforce the law in many *favelas* of Rio de Janeiro (or the South African police in many townships, for that matter), this does not mean that all Brazilian *favelas* or all South African townships are crime-infested places per se where governance is completely absent.

Governance

Governance has made quite a career in the social sciences during the 1990s and the 2000s. There is a growing number of handbooks, edited volumes, special issues, and research centers that are dedicated to global, transnational, multi-level, new, or experimental governance (Bevir 2011; Enderlein, Wälti, and Zürn 2010; Hale and Held 2011; Levi-Faur 2012; Mayntz 2009; Pierre and Peters 2000; Sabel and Zeitlin 2010; Schuppert 2005; Schuppert and Zürn 2008; Zürn 2013). So, has governance become an "empty signifier" (Offe 2009)? We do not think so, but the confusion surrounding the concept requires clarification (see Börzel 2010a and Risse 2011b for the following).

In its most general version, governance refers to all modes of coordinating social action in human society. However, such a broad understanding that identifies governance with any kind of social ordering does not appear useful for our purposes. For instance, markets do not qualify as governance structures since they constitute a "spontaneous order" (Hayek 1948) that leaves "no place for 'conscious, deliberate and purposeful' effort to craft formal structures" (Williamson 1996, 31). After all, we are not interested in how markets allocate values and resources (but see below). Nor are we concerned with how families deal with conflicts. Rather, we want to know how collective goods and services can be provided in the absence of a well-functioning state. In other words, we are interested in politics as the regulation of public affairs for a society.[6] This involves finding out "who gets what, when, how?" (Laswell 1936) in what David Easton defined as the "(authoritative) allocation of values for a society" (Easton 1953, 131).[7]

As a result, this book employs a somewhat narrower concept, which situates governance in the context of politics. By *governance*, we mean *institutionalized modes of social coordination to produce and implement collectively binding rules, or to provide collective goods and services.*

This conceptualization follows closely the understanding of governance that is widespread within political science, law, and IR (see e.g. Benz 2004a; Kohler-Koch 1998; Mayntz 2004, 2009; Schuppert 2005;

---

[6] As we show below, even the notion of "public" is problematic in ALS.

[7] We put "authoritative" in parenthesis here, since it should not be conflated with hierarchical. For a discussion see Czempiel 1981.

Schuppert and Zürn 2008). Accordingly, governance is inherently linked to the provision of collectively binding rules as well as collective goods and services. Simply curbing negative externalities of private goods' production does not qualify as governance in our understanding (while setting up rules to avoid negative externalities does). We can then distinguish three types of governance contributions:

- The direct delivery of collective goods and services (first-order governance),[8] such as security, public health, education, or clean environment;
- The formulation and implementation of collectively binding rules for regulating social life (e.g. human rights) as well as for the delivery of collective goods and services (second-order governance);
- The establishment of institutions regulating the rule-making itself and coordinating the governance contributions of others (meta-governance).

As to first-order governance, we follow the definition of collective goods as characterized by non-exclusive access and/or non-rivalry in consumption (see Héritier 2002). At least one of these conditions has to be present for a good to qualify as collective. Thus, our understanding includes pure public goods (non-exclusive access *and* non-rivalry in consumption, e.g. lighthouses), common goods or common pool resources (non-exclusive access and rivalry in consumption, e.g. fish stocks), and club goods (exclusive access and non-rivalry in consumption, e.g. security in gated communities), but not private goods (exclusive access and rivalry in consumption, e.g. cars). Note, however, that the degree of collectiveness with regard "collective goods" is usually a question of political or social choices. There are very few natural collective goods. For instance, security in a given territory can be provided as a public good for everybody, as a club good (when access to the territory is restricted, see the example above), or as a private good (e.g. bodyguards).

As to governance in areas of limited statehood, we concentrate on a continuum that ranges from club goods to public goods. This is particularly important with regard to our understanding of what constitutes effective governance, the main dependent variable of our endeavor. Effectiveness ultimately relates to the successful and non-arbitrary provision of a collective good – security, public health, or clean water – and the compliance with binding rules for an ever-more inclusive population in a given context (space and time). We come back to this point below.

---

[8] See also Holm's distinction between first- and second-order institutions (Holm 1995).

Governance as Process

Governance defined as institutionalized modes of social coordination consists of a structural and a process dimension (Scharpf 1997, 97; Mayntz and Scharpf 1995b, 19). Governance as institutionalized rule structures relate to the institutions and actor constellations, while governance processes are modes of social coordination by which actors adjust their behavior (for further discussion see Börzel 2010c).

Research on governance usually distinguishes three different types of institutionalized rule structures: hierarchy (states), market (competition systems), and networks (negotiation systems, such as associations or public-private partnerships; see overviews in Levi-Faur 2012). Hierarchy, market, and networks are ideal types, which differ with regard to the type of actors involved and the degree of coupling between them. Within these three governance structures, actors can coordinate their actions in hierarchical or non-hierarchical ways, which relates to the process dimension.

Hierarchical coordination usually takes the form of authoritative decisions (e.g. law, administrative ordinances, court decisions). Authoritative directives define normative expectations that actors *must* obey. Hierarchical coordination, hence, creates obligations that can force actors to act against their self-interest. In order to ensure compliance with these obligations, actors may be either physically coerced by the use of force or legally obliged by legitimate institutions (law).

Non-hierarchical coordination, by contrast, is based on voluntary compliance. Conflicts of interests are solved by negotiations. Voluntary agreement is either achieved by negotiating a compromise and granting mutual concessions (side-payments and issue-linkage) on the basis of fixed preferences (bargaining), or actors engage in processes of non-manipulative persuasion (arguing), through which they develop common interests and change their preferences accordingly (see below). Coordination in competition systems is also non-hierarchical. Actors compete over meeting certain performance criteria, to which they adjust their behavior accordingly. They are largely motivated by egoistic self-interests but pursue a common goal or some scarce resources of which they wish to obtain as much as possible by performing better than their competitors. Markets do not qualify as governance structures; however, market mechanisms can be institutionalized to coordinate actors' behavior in the provision of collective goods through competition.

The most common forms of governance include hierarchical coordination by the state ("governance by government"), non-hierarchical coordination via networks of state and non-state actors ("governance with government"), and rule-making or self-regulation by non-state actors ("governance without government;" cf. Benz 2004a; Czempiel and Rosenau 1992; Grande and Pauly 2005; Zürn 1998). We come back to this point in Chapter 4.

While being analytically distinct, governance structures and processes are inherently linked since institutionalized rule structures constitute arenas for social coordination, regulate access, and may constrain actors in their choices for social coordination mechanisms (Scharpf 1997). It is important to keep in mind that governance structures do not determine, but rather promote, specific modes of coordination. Hierarchy allows for hierarchical and non-hierarchical modes of coordination. Institutions bestow upon the government the power to impose decisions unilaterally, but they can refrain from invoking their hierarchical authority when they bargain or argue with others. Negotiation and competition systems, by contrast, can only rely on bargaining and arguing. Which mode of coordination actors choose within their institutional limits, is, again, influenced by institutions, which render certain modes more appropriate or socially acceptable than others.

Hierarchy and hierarchical coordination constitute the essence of the (Western) nation-state. It provides a structure of rule and authority that enables and legitimates state actors to hierarchically set and enforce central decisions. Today, democracy and the rule of law belong to the generally accepted norms of these institutions for authoritative rule-making. They "tame the Leviathan" by restraining the use of force and by binding it to the provision of collective goods. The Western nation-state has the task to protect the internal and external security of its citizens, as well as to create economic stability, guarantee minimal social security and public health, education, and maintain a clean environment. In short, the Western nation-state provides governance with regard to rule-making and enforcement, on the one hand, and with regard to collective goods such as security, welfare, and a clean environment, on the other (Rotberg 2004a, 3–5). The classical state has transformed itself into the modern state by compromising its authority to hierarchically set and enforce rules (Hurrelmann et al. 2007; Leibfried and Zürn 2005). Yet, its ability to ultimately make, implement, and enforce decisions is beyond doubt, even when the "neoliberal" state privatizes or de-regulates previously public services and pools and delegates its sovereignty at the international level. In other words, modern statehood is restrained by domestic and international institutions. Yet, it is still consolidated, even in the age of (neoliberal) privatization and de-regulation (Börzel 2008). Governments can still step in if markets and networks fail to deliver collective goods and services as they did during the financial crises that hit the world in 2008.

Conditions in areas of limited statehood are profoundly different. While states still exist as hierarchical rule structures, governance cannot rely on their capacity to set and enforce central rules or to provide collective goods and services directly. We have to look for functional equivalents to modern statehood (see Draude 2007 on this point) – unless we want to give up the normative proposition that human beings have a right to a decent authority structure, to security, to other collective goods etc. (Ladwig 2007; Ladwig and Rudolf 2011). For more details see Chapters 3 and 4.

Alternatives to Governance by the State

Governance with/out the state in ALS differs according to the actors involved, on the one hand, and the modes of social coordination, on the other. As to the actors, we find various combinations of state and non-state actors governing ALS (see Chapter 4). *State actors* include national governments (the "central state"), foreign governments and their agencies (e.g. development agencies), as well as international (inter-state) organizations (IOs), such as the UN, its agencies, the World Bank, or the International Monetary Fund (IMF; see Lederer 2018 for details). *Non-state actors* are not recognized as states, nor made up of states (such as international organizations). They comprise a whole variety of actors, including companies and other for-profit organizations (Börzel and Deitelhoff 2018), (international) non-governmental organizations (I-NGOs), multi-stakeholder partnerships (MSPs, see Beisheim, Ellersiek, and Lorch 2018),[9] local "traditional" authorities,[10] such as tribal and religious leaders (Förster and Koechlin 2018), and even violent or criminal non-state actors, such as warlords and rebel groups (Berti 2018).

Regarding modes of governance, the modern (Western) nation-state has the ability of hierarchical steering, that is, to enforce the law authoritatively, ultimately through policing and "top down" command and control based on its monopoly of the use of force. It is precisely this ability of the state, which is limited or lacking in ALS. To the extent that hierarchical steering and authoritative rule do take place in ALS, we have to look for actors other than the respective national governments.

---

[9] Note that most multi-stakeholder partnerships bring together state and non-state actors, including IOs, INGOs, and often business. As a result, they are often called public-private partnerships (PPP, see Schäferhoff, Campe, and Kaan 2009).

[10] We put "traditional" in parenthesis, because such "traditions" are invented social constructions more often than not, see Förster and Koechlin 2018.

Warlords and local "big men" sometimes exert hierarchical control in war-torn ALS (Berti 2013; Chojnacki and Branovic 2011). The same holds true for "traditional" authorities (Baldwin 2016). Moreover, IOs as well as – mostly Western – states often interfere authoritatively, particularly in the modern protectorates such as Kosovo or previously Afghanistan, which have all but lost their "Westphalian sovereignty" (Lake, D. 2018; Lake and Farris 2014). As we argue in Chapter 3, hierarchical governance does takes place in ALS, even though central state authorities do not have the ability for it.

We also posit that forms of governance emerge under conditions of limited statehood, which the contemporary social science literature discusses as "new" modes of governance or the privatization of authority. These new modes involve governance with or without, rather than governance by, the state. They are by no means specific to the contemporary international system (Cutler, Haufler, and Porter 1999; Grande and Pauly 2005; Hall and Biersteker 2002) or the modern national state (Kohler-Koch 1996; Kooiman 2003). The colonial state, for example, constituted an area of limited statehood as we understand it, as a result of which governance took place through colonial rulers ("states"), transnational "public-private" companies (cf. the Hudson Bay Company in North America or the East India Companies in Asia), and local non-state actors, such as settlers (Conrad and Stange 2011; Esders, Hölck, and Rinke 2018).

What these modes of governance have in common is their reliance on non-hierarchical modes of governance in the sense that they have to depend on voluntary acceptance and compliance (see also Göhler, Höppner, and De La Rosa 2009). We find evidence for both ideal types of non-hierarchical coordination, which, however, often occur together in empirical reality (overview in Risse 2018b):

- In bargaining processes, actors strive to come to agreements on the basis of fixed interests and preferences. This type of non-hierarchical governance also involves creating and manipulating incentives and "benchmarking." Positive incentives, but also negative sanctions, are meant to affect the cost-benefit calculations of the relevant actors and to induce the desired behavior. This variety of non-hierarchical governance is based on a social logic of rational choice or consequentialism. Actors know what they want to achieve and try to achieve their goals through coordination with others by way of give and take.
- We also find negotiations in ALS that resemble more deliberative processes. Actors mutually challenge and justify their interests and preferences based on moral reasoning or with regard to some empirical

"facts." Such arguing processes aim at achieving a reasoned consensus, the introduction of shared rules and norms, and at mutual learning processes. The underlying social logic is one of communicative rationality and/or of appropriateness (see March and Olsen 1998; Müller 2004; Risse 2000). As we argue in Chapter 6, such "Habermasian" processes are not absent in ALS, particularly with regard to NSJI (Kötter et al. 2015). However, much more common are "deliberative negotiations" (Warren, Mansbridge, and André Bächtiger et al. 2013). Here, actors enter negotiations with their interests and preferences in mind, but the talks are fair, transparent, and non-exclusive, and the participants are open to persuasion.

The Distinction between the "Public" and the "Private" Spheres

The governance concept as outlined above provides a lens that allows for uncovering rule-making and service provision by actors other than the state in areas of limited statehood and, thus, seeks to avoid a state-centric view of politics. The approach also sheds light on modes of social coordination beyond simplistic top-down and command-and-control. Thus, the governance concept is particularly suitable to look at the politics and policies in ALS (for further elaboration see Draude 2012).

At the same time, the understanding of governance employed in this book largely follows conceptualizations of governance and politics in American and European social sciences. The way in which the governance concept has been developed in the social sciences (and has become part of political practice) is strongly influenced by the experiences of Western modernity and of modern statehood as discussed above. As a result, there is the risk of some implicit biases toward Western modernity when studying governance in areas of limited statehood. This appears to be particularly problematic with regard to the distinction between the "public" and "private" realms that is often built into the governance concept. The distinction stems from modern statehood in its Western and Eurocentric understandings (Kumar 1997) raising questions whether we can simply apply the governance concept to other historical contexts and/or to other cultural experiences in the contemporary international system.

Historically speaking, the modern Western notion of the "private sphere" is connected to processes of individualization and personalization that only emerged in the second half of eighteenth-century Europe, leading to the separation of the public and the private (Böckenförde 1976; Keane 1988). Thinking of the "public" and the "private" spheres as binary categories is inherently problematic with regard to colonial rule

(Conrad and Stange 2011). The differences between state-funded administrative personnel and "private" actors among the colonizers were marginal at best. For instance, the "private" East India Companies exercised "public" authority on behalf of the British Empire and the Dutch state. The same holds true for the definition of indigenous elites as "private" actors, since local "chiefs"were often given the authority to rule hierarchically by the colonizers.

Applying the public-private distinction to contemporary areas of limited statehood involves similar difficulties. Of course, we can still distinguish formally between the state and the non-state sector including for-profit companies, on the one hand, and the not-for profit NGO and civil society sector, on the other. But what does this mean in countries in which state institutions are so weak that government actors can easily exploit state resources for private purposes, while so-called private actors, such as companies, provide much-needed collective goods with regard to education, public health, or infrastructure (Börzel and Thauer 2013; Thauer 2014b)? In other words, the implicit assumption of the public-private distinction, according to which governments govern and private actors mind their own business, is often turned on its head in ALS.

In many cases, rent-seeking governments distribute state revenues, including development aid, to maintain their rule via clientelistic networks (the so-called neo-patrimonial state in sub-Saharan Africa, the Southern Caucasus, and elsewhere, see Erdmann 2013; Erdmann and Engel 2007). In other words, they transform public goods into club or even private goods through corruption, which is both an indicator and a consequence of limited statehood (Börzel and van Hüllen 2014; Mungiu-Pippidi 2015). With regard to failing and failed states, formal state institutions have largely ceased to provide governance services and have become semi-private organizations. In such cases, "shadow states" often emerge, i.e., informal governance institutions providing social and political order as well as collective goods, thereby preventing the country or the region from completely collapsing into anarchy. In the Southern Caucasus and Central Asia, such shadow states have survived over extended periods of time (Koehler and Zürcher 2004; Zürcher 2007).

These examples challenge distinctions that come with Western modernity, according to which "state = public" and "non-state = private." They also reveal the implicit normative connotations of the distinction (see Jacob, Ladwig, and Schmelzle 2018; Ladwig and Rudolf 2011). We usually expect that state actors contribute to governance, i.e., to act in the public rather than their private interest. While policy-makers might be power-seeking, state institutions in a consolidated state are supposed to orient their actions toward governance in the public interest. If they abuse their power, public actors are held accountable through democratic procedures or the rule of law. Likewise, business is legally accountable for corrupt practices or misleading customers and stakeholders. However, in ALS, legal and political institutions, which hold actors engaging in governance accountable, are weak. There are alternatives to democracy and the rule of law, such as community membership (cf. Hönke and Börzel 2014). However, such mechanisms of social accountability tend to blur the boundaries between private (family, tribal) relations and the public interest. Likewise, companies are pushed into public roles when corporate social responsibility norms not only ask them to respect but to enforce human rights in ALS (Börzel and Hönke 2012).

To conclude, certain assumptions with regard to the "public-private" distinction at best partially apply in ALS. At least, they should not be taken for granted. The conceptual problem cannot be solved easily. For instance, we could speak of hybrid regimes or hybrid forms of governance in order to avoid the distinction between the public and the private realms or between state and non-state actors (see e.g. Bendel, Croissant, and Rüb 2002). Yet, such a solution only sidesteps the problem to discern who provides governance services and who does not, and under which conditions. A possible way out would be to investigate empirically who serves as a governance actor – irrespective of its institutional role in the political system or in society. In other words, one would search for functional equivalents of "public" actors (Draude 2008). This would still leave us with the normative problem, though, when "private" actors assume public functions. "Public" actors are expected to be accountable to the citizens whom they serve (Jacob, Ladwig, and Schmelzle 2018). Accordingly, companies that provide health and education to citizens should no longer be just accountable to their stakeholders, but also to the recipients of their governance contributions. How to institutionalize such accountability? We come back to these and other normative questions throughout this book.

Intentionality and Normativity of Governance

Considerations about the "public" and the "private" raise a second problem with regard to the applicability of the governance concept to ALS. Governance is geared toward producing and implementing collectively binding rules and/or providing collective goods and services. This implies intentional action (Mayntz 2004, 67). This does not mean that governance actors have to be motivated necessarily by the public interest, even though such motivations do not hurt. Politicians, for example, can still be egoistic power-maximizers. Yet, in a consolidated state, such public actors are embedded in governance structures that institutionalize the intentionality of governance toward providing services for the community.[11] If they fail to do so, they are politically and legally accountable.

The inherent intentionality of governance becomes problematic when applied to ALS. First, as noted above, we cannot simply assume that governance institutions, such as the state, orient actors toward providing collective goods. Second, we need to distinguish between the provision of collective goods or services as the unintended consequence of "private" activities, on the one hand, and the explicit regulation of social issues and intentional provision of collective goods, on the other hand. Only the second understanding would qualify as governance according to our conceptualization.

For example, transnational mining companies routinely use private security companies to protect their production facilities in ALS (Jakobi and Wolf 2013; Krahmann 2010). Since the latter make their profit by selling a collective good (security) to clients, this transforms security into a private good or a club good in some cases. Protecting industrial sites might have positive externalities for the surrounding neighborhoods insofar as the security firms might unintentionally deter armed gangs or militias from attacking nearby villages, too. In this sense, the firms, while primarily providing a private good for mining companies, would also contribute to public security, albeit indirectly. Yet, we would not call this "security governance" because of the lack of intentionality. Only if mining companies explicitly instruct their security firms to protect, not only the production facilities, but also the surrounding villages, could this activity be called governance (for a critical discussion see Hönke 2013b).

In other cases, we are faced with a continuum ranging from governance in the above-defined sense to "racketeering": the warlord who uses his militias to provide public security for the area of his rule can be regarded as a governance actor or "governor."[12] However, the more he uses the same militias to threaten the safety of the community and then re-sells security for a protection fee, the more the warlord transforms public security into a club or private good. The latter would be "racketeering" (Chojnacki and Branovic 2011; Schuppert 2007, 479).

---

[11] Note that the effectiveness and problem-solving capacity of governance is not part of the definition. Institutionalized intentionality toward regulating social issues and providing collective goods is all that is needed.

[12] We use this term in a generic way, see Avant, Finnemore, and Sell 2010a. "Governors" are those who govern or who provide governance.

Applying governance to ALS highlights the unavoidable intentionality and implicit normativity of the concept. If we mean by governance – as is common in the social sciences – that collectively binding rules are made and implemented and that collective goods are provided, we cannot refrain from acknowledging that governance is linked normatively toward what is supposed to be in the public interest. But who are those in ALS in whose name the "public interest" is being pronounced? What is the relevant public, community, or collectivity for whom governance is being provided? Once again, these issues are clearly decided in the ideal typical modern Western state (Schmelzle 2015, ch. 4): In most cases, governance is provided for the people or the citizens living in a given territory defined by the borders of the state. While some services are only accessible to the citizens rather than the residents, even non-citizen residents enjoy some basic rights as well as access to at least some public services, e.g. emergency health care.

All this becomes problematic in areas of limited statehood. In many cases, it remains unclear who are the addressees of governance, who is subject to which rules and entitled to which governance services, and who actually receives them in practice (cf. Hönke and Thomas 2012). At least, we cannot assume that the group for which governance is provided is clearly defined. Take border regions in sub-Saharan Africa, for example, that are beyond the control of central governments. Are the people living on a given territory entitled to receiving governance? What about members of particular tribal and/or ethnic communities? Who decides who is entitled to receive what, particularly in cases of extremely scarce resources? Is it still governance if collective goods become club goods in the sense that only particular ethnic, religious, or gendered communities are entitled to receive them? The latter constitutes a common practice in many ALS, both historically and in the contemporary international system.

Researching governance in ALS requires us to take a step back and refrain from "all or nothing" conceptual solutions. If governance is overburdened with too strong a normative orientation toward the common good or the public interest, we will hardly find much governance in ALS by definition (see Schuppert 2007 on this point). In this case, governance does not travel very far outside the developed world of liberal democracies and consolidated statehood. At the same time, if we strip the concept of governance of all normative underpinnings, everything is governance and the privatization of collective goods has equal normative weight as the provision of pure public goods.

We suggest an intermediary position as a way out: we should consider governance as both a process and a continuum. The more inclusive the social group for which goods and services are provided or rules are formulated and enforced, the more we should consider this as governance. To put it in theoretical terms of defining collective goods, non- or at least limited exclusivity with regard to access should be the defining characteristics of governance. In contrast, the more particular goods and services are only provided for exclusive groups (clientelistic networks, the rich and wealthy, an ethnic or religious group) and the more collective goods are transformed into club or private goods accessible only to those who pay for them or who belong to specific (and small) communities, the less we should conceptualize this as governance. In sum, the cut-off point with regard to what can or cannot be regarded as governance from both an analytical and a normative point of view is located within the realm of club goods. An exclusive club to which only few people compared to the larger population in a given polity are entitled to have access should not be regarded as a governance structure. The gated communities, to which only the rich and wealthy have access, do not provide governance. In contrast, let us assume a situation in which security is provided for the ethnic majority in a given territory. In this case, it is still a club good (and might even be questionable on normative grounds), but we do enter the realm of governance here. This is also the case if the territorial scope of service provision is limited. Companies build and, at times, even run health clinics in the communities in which they have their operations. If they limit access to workers and their families, health provision resembles a club good. If other community members receive treatment, too, corporate health provision becomes more inclusive. If anyone in need of medical assistance, irrespective of his or her employment or residence, is being treated, the company governance contribution becomes a public good.

In short, applying the notion of collective goods to ALS requires a differentiated conceptualization of the collectivity for which governance is provided. In many cases, those entitled to receiving collective goods, such as security, are distinct from the addressees of governance services, which also differ from those who factually receive governance (Chojnacki and Branovic 2011; De la Rosa, Höppner, and Kötter 2008). The weaker and the more fragile the state, the less it makes sense to judge governance services according to benchmarks derived from modern developed states, since the degree of governance is also a question of the resources that are available. Thus, we should strive for minimum normative standards in these cases (Keohane 2007; Ladwig and Rudolf 2011).

Conclusions

The social science debate on governance implicitly or explicitly remains wedded to an ideal type of Western statehood that historically originated in Europe – with full domestic sovereignty that is restrained by democracy and the rule of law. From a global as well as a historical perspective, however, the Western modern nation state constitutes the exception rather than the rule. Outside the developed OECD world, we find mostly areas of limited statehood that lack domestic sovereignty. Even fully developed Western states often encompass ALS, too, if only temporarily.

This chapter has introduced the two main concepts employed in this book. First, areas of limited statehood are those territorial, policy, or social spaces in which state authorities lack the capacity to implement and enforce central decisions ("the law") and/or lack the monopoly of the use of force, at least temporarily. Second, however, as argued in Chapter 1 of this book, ALS are neither ungoverned nor ungovernable. Governance is understood here as institutionalized modes of social coordination to produce and implement collectively binding rules, or to provide collective goods and services. The "governors" can be state or non-state actors, domestic or inter- and transnational. Modes of governance can be hierarchical, but, more often than not, they are non-hierarchical in ALS involving various types of negotiation systems.

This chapter has also argued that there are some implicit biases in the governance concept as it has been developed in the context of Western-based social sciences and of modern statehood. However, we should not throw out the baby with the bathwater. The governance concept provides a useful tool to analyzing policies and politics in ALS, precisely because it directs our attention to the role of non-state actors, on the one hand, and non-hierarchical modes of coordination, on the other. As a result, governance overcomes the state-centric bias implicit in the literature on failed and failing states as well as the modernization bias of most development studies.

The following chapter uses the concepts developed here to provide a theoretical model for governance in areas of limited statehood.

3 Theorizing Governance in Areas of Limited Statehood

This chapter develops the theoretical argument of the book. How can we explain that some areas of limited statehood have succeeded in providing effective and legitimate governance in many issue-areas, while others have not (see Chapter 1)? Accordingly, a theory of governance in areas of limited statehood must answer two questions:

1. Why and when do actors – whether state or non-state, domestic, transnational, or international – engage in governance?
2. What makes their governance effective and legitimate under conditions of limited statehood?

We argue that existing theories of development, with their focus on economic growth, the state, or democracy, as well as good governance, fall short of being able to account for the variation. We use standard institutionalist theories from International Relations (IR) and comparative politics – informed by rational choice, historical, and sociological institutionalism – to develop a unified theoretical framework answering both questions. Our theoretical framework consists of three principal components:

- (state) institutions;
- legitimacy and social acceptance;
- social trust.

These three components are necessary for *any* theory of governance or political order for that matter (Fukuyama 2012, 2014). Political orders – state or not – require, first, a set of institutions designed to maintain the order and to provide governance as defined in Chapter 2. Second, political orders – except for pure tyranny – require some minimum degree of social acceptance by the inhabitants in order to be sustainable so that the governors acquire a "right to govern." Legitimacy (or the lack thereof) concerns the way in which a population of a given polity relates to their rulers and authorities. Last but not least, political orders rely on some degree of social fabric, order, and community rather than anomy.

Social trust provides the glue that binds individuals together in a community.

In the following, we concentrate on areas of limited statehood where state institutions are weak or non-existing by definition. As a result, (non-state) governance institutions, legitimacy, and relations of social trust have to do more of the "heavy lifting" in order to compensate for limited statehood (see Draude 2007 for a discussion of functional equivalents to consolidated statehood).

In response to the first question with regard to actor motivations to become "governors," we need to explain under what conditions and when particularly self-interested and utility-maximizing (non-state) actors – such as foreign governments, companies, or violent non-state actors (VNSA) – start engaging in governance. We point to three factors:

- (lack of) institutions: the risk of anarchy and a "shadow of hierarchy" cast by external (consolidated) statehood;
- the need for (international and domestic) legitimacy;
- collective action facilitated by the demand for governance resulting from personalized trust relations among relevant community members.

As to the second question, our main task in this book is to explain the variation in governance in areas of limited statehood, that is, the provision of collective goods and services as well as the adoption of and compliance with binding rules. We claim that governance in ALS is effective, the more three factors or a combination thereof are present:

- the better designed ("fit for purpose") and inclusive the governance institutions (including residual state institutions) are;
- the more the "governors" and the governance institutions enjoy empirical legitimacy or social acceptance bestowed by the governed in the respective ALS;
- the more social, in particular generalized, trust relations prevail among the governed citizens and relevant communities.

Our main *explanandum* or dependent variable in this book is governance effectiveness under conditions of limited statehood. Here, we argue that empirical legitimacy or social acceptance of the governors and the governance institutions is key. Without legitimacy, no effective governance can be sustained in ALS (Krasner and Risse 2014b)! Thus, we consider legitimacy crucial for compensating state weakness (see also Schmelzle 2015). Given the significance of legitimacy for effective governance, we cannot take it for granted in ALS, but have to endogenize it. To do this, we point to various feedback loops among the explanatory factors discussed above. First, perceived effective governance tends to generate output legitimacy that induces voluntary compliance, increasing the effectiveness of rule and service provision, particularly in ALS. Second, inclusive governance institutions are likely to generate input and throughput legitimacy. Finally, social trust relations within and among communities will also lead to more legitimate governance.

This chapter proceeds in the following steps. First, we delve into various theories of development and discuss their shortcomings with regard to governance in ALS. Second, we identify the scope conditions under which – mostly self-interested – actors become governors. Third, we develop our theoretical framework to account for effective and legitimate governance in ALS.

Theories of Development and Their Shortcomings

The obvious starting point for looking for answers to our governance puzzle of the observable variation in effective governance in areas of limited statehood are the various theories of development. Most of them assume that limited statehood and development are inversely related (Krasner 2018). While we do not wish to equate development with governance, the provision of collective goods and services, such as security, education, or health, serves as important indicators for development. Likewise, consolidated statehood is a major quality of developed countries. They control the use of force and have the capacity to set and enforce central decisions. At the same time, their consolidated statehood is restrained by democracy and the rule of law.

The various approaches differ in what they consider the main drivers of development. Where modernization theories emphasize economic growth, statist approaches focus on strong political institutions. The literature on "failed states" is derivative of these latter theories (see Chapter 2). Last but not least, some authors stress the participatory quality of political orders or the type of political regime (autocracy vs. democracy) as a pre-condition for development.

Modernization Theories and the "Escalator to Denmark"

Starting with the original formulations by Lipset and Lerner in the 1950s, modernization theories conceive of economic growth as the ultimate driver of development and good governance (Lerner 1958; Lipset 1959; Rustow 1968). Once countries are on a path to economic growth, state institutions and democracy will inevitably follow. Economic growth leads to social transformations, particularly the rise of urban middle classes, which become increasingly better educated. These middle classes then demand strong state institutions and the rule of law to protect their property rights. They also favor democracy over dictatorship, since they want to have a say over their own fate. Since the ruling elites depend on the middle classes for economic growth, democratic institutions will be established eventually – hence the "escalator to Denmark"![1]

While the original modernization theory was developed during the 1950s and 1960s, scholars have gathered quite some evidence in its support. More recently, Inglehart and Welzel have argued that economic development is the ultimate driver of vast cultural changes leading to secular societies, gender equality, and "post-materialist" values. These cultural changes then foster democratization processes and mitigate class conflicts (Inglehart and Welzel 2005). Indeed, empirical data indicate that rich countries are most likely democratic and that democratic consolidation correlates with a certain income level (Boix 2011; Przeworski and Limongi 1997; see also Krasner 2018). Of course, this raises the question of causality: Are countries democratic, because they are rich, or are they rich, because they are democratic? As Acemoglu and Robinson put it:

Modernization theory is both incorrect and unhelpful for thinking about how to confront the major problems of extractive institutions in failing nations. The strongest piece of evidence in favor of modernization theory is that rich nations are the ones that have democratic regimes, respect civil and human rights, and enjoy functioning markets and generally inclusive economic institutions. Yet interpreting this association as supporting modernization theory ignores the major effect of inclusive economic political institutions on economic growth... (I)t is the societies with inclusive institutions that have grown over the past hundred years and have become relatively rich today. (Acemoglu and Robinson 2012, 454)

Moreover, this version of modernization theory is clearly and unapologetically teleological. The "end of history" (Fukuyama 1992) is the fully developed and democratic welfare state of the Western OECD world. Once countries are on the escalator of economic growth, they will inevitably end up where Europe or North America currently are. Slowly but surely, areas of limited statehood will disappear. While fully consolidated states might still have "pockets of limited statehood," modernization will contain the problem. The only question then becomes how to put countries on the path to economic growth – an issue that cannot be easily solved theoretically, since neither strong state institutions nor democracy

---

[1] We owe this metaphor to Stephen D. Krasner.

nor the rule of law are thought to foster economic growth. According to the causal logic of the theory, these factors are derivative of economic development.

Moreover, equating modernization with Western-type modernization leaves no room for multiple modernities (Eisenstadt 2002, 2007) or entangled modernities (Conrad and Randeria 2013). In modernization theory, the yardstick remains Denmark. Areas of limited statehood are either doomed or have to be put on the escalator to Western modernity.

Yet, what about the empirical record of modernization theory? If we look at the governance puzzle in Figure 1.1 of Chapter 1, the upper top-right corner more or less conforms to modernization theory. It is mostly populated by rich, territorial, rule of law governed, democratic, and interventionist consolidated states (Leibfried and Zürn 2005). So far, so good – but what about the vast majority of countries with ALS? Economic growth only loosely coincides with development. The analysis by Lee et al., for instance, shows that mean income is only correlated with service provision in some cases (Lee, Walter-Drop, and Wiesel 2014).

Moreover, what about the relationship between development and democracy? According to modernization theory, developing countries should turn democratic eventually. Yet, China and Singapore have consistently experienced high growth rates and a rise of urban middle classes over the past decades, but have remained authoritarian. In contrast, Turkey under Erdogan, Russia under Putin, or Venezuela under Chavism have seen similar economic growth and urbanization patterns, used democratization to get rich, but then slid back into authoritarianism. If modernization theory were correct, China and Singapore would not be able to sustain their autocratic systems in the end, but will inevitably democratize. In contrast, Turkey's, Russia's, or Venezuela's relapses into authoritarianism should be temporary at best. Some might argue that the verdict is still out where China, Singapore, Turkey, or Russia will be turning – for the past ten years, however, they appear to be stuck on the escalator or sliding down.

Recently, Boix has developed a more sophisticated and less teleological version of modernization theory (Boix 2015). Using a whole range of ethnographic data, he, first, argues that "cooperation under anarchy" (to quote Oye 1986) is possible in stateless societies, as long as two conditions are met: human beings perceive and treat each other as equals and there is very limited technological change. Second, once technological change takes place, inequality will be on the rise and lead to the formation of political orders. These take the form of states that are either republics or monarchies, depending on the equilibrium between the producers of wealth, on the one hand, and those controlling the means of violence, on the other. Third, Boix argues against earlier versions of modernization theory that the path to European industrialization resulted from a unique combination of economic growth in urban centers and military developments that was contingent upon time and place.

While Boix's approach gets rid of the teleological version of modernization theory, the consequences of his argument for the governance problematique in areas of limited statehood remain unclear. On the one hand, he concedes that cooperation in stateless societies – "governance" in our understanding – is possible, but under very constrained conditions. On the other hand, his central causal variable – technological change – appears to emerge from nowhere and outside social relations – and certainly outside institutional pre-conditions, since he explicitly criticizes them (Boix 2015, ch. 2). Statist institutionalism focuses on these latter conditions.

Statist Institutionalism and the State-Building Paradigm

The main challenger of modernization theories are various approaches focusing on strong political institutions. Samuel Huntington's classic critique of modernization theory emphasized strong, effective, and legitimate political institutions: "The most important political distinction among countries concerns not their form of government, but their degree of government" (Huntington 1968, 1; for a discussion see Krasner 2018). Statists in the tradition of Huntington, thus, emphasize "consolidated statehood" in our terminology, as the main drivers of modernization. As Fukuyama put it: "Having a state is a basic precondition for intensive economic growth" (Fukuyama 2012, 469). Huntington's work has been the predecessor of theories of the "developmental state" (Kwon 2005; Woo-Cumings 1999). Once the developmental state has provided the conditions for economic growth (the "Asian tiger" model, e.g. Taiwan, Singapore, South Korea), countries should be on the escalator toward liberal democracy and good governance. Huntington's thinking has also inspired Fukuyama's recent work where he establishes the primacy of a functioning state over economic growth as the main pillar of social order (see the above quote; Fukuyama 2004, 2012, 2014). Bates and Collier have made similar arguments with regard to explaining civil war and poverty, particularly in Sub-Saharan Africa (Bates 2008; Collier 2007). Statists in the tradition of Thomas Hobbes' *Leviathan* (Hobbes 1987 [1651]) typically reverse the causal order of modernization theory: strong state institutions that control the use of force and have the capacity to enforce decisions are a pre-condition for economic growth. States provide basic infrastructure and basic public services, i.e., governance, as enabling factors for economic development. Conversely, limited statehood is a major impediment to development. At later stages of this process, however, the dynamics of modernization theory take over, resulting in the rule of law, human rights, and democracy. The result is still "Denmark," but through a different causal pathway.

Modernization theory essentially argues that economic growth will eventually overcome the problems of limited statehood. In contrast, Huntingtonians of the various kinds suggest that state-building does the trick. Accordingly, well-governed areas of limited statehood are an oxymoron. At least, they are not sustainable. Fukuyama has been careful not to advocate simplistic institutional transfer models that ignore local conditions (Fukuyama 2004, 82–91). The literature on fragile and failed states, in contrast, has had no problems with taking cues from Western models of consolidated statehood (e.g. Carment 2003; Dorff 2005; Rotberg 2003, 2004b; for various critiques see Clunan and Trinkunas 2010; Lake 2016, 2018; Thomas 2015; Woodward 2017). While the failed states literature is rather a-theoretical in the sense that it does not elaborate on main drivers for state success, it builds on what could be called a "deficit theory" of limited statehood (see Schuppert 2009 on this point). Failed states lack all ingredients of modern consolidated statehood and are badly governed. Since statehood and governance performance are lumped together, this literature cannot conceptualize the puzzle of well-governed areas of limited statehood, the starting point of this book. The reason is that it conflates an institutionalist and a functionalist understanding of statehood, as we have discussed in Chapter 2.

Moreover, there is a logical flaw in a functional and Hobbesian story of state formation, as Boix argues (Boix 2015, 10–11, 254–255; for an extensive treatment see Hampton 1986). If humans were unable to cooperate in stateless societies in the first place, why would they voluntarily give up their freedoms and individual rights to a strong state – the Leviathan – rather than continue fighting each other? He also shows that cooperation in stateless societies is possible – albeit up to a certain point (see above). Scott goes a step further and argues that the formation of strong states has been part of the problem, not of the solution (see particularly Scott 1998, 2009). Huntingtonians describe the emergence of states from agricultural societies as a history of civilization and of overcoming violent (dis-)orders. Scott analyzes the same history as one of plundering, exploitation, and violent expansionism. In that, his analysis resembles Tilly's description of European state-building as "organized crime" (Tilly 1985). Scott's history of the "hill people" in upland

Southeast Asia describes deliberate attempts to escape the violent orders of the state (Scott 2009). Scott also reminds us that, through most of recorded history, state-like orders were insignificant:

The very earliest states in China and Egypt – and later, Chandra-Gupta India, classical Greece, and republican Rome – were, in demographic terms, insignificant. They occupied a minuscule portion of the world's landscape, and their subjects were no more than a rounding error in the world's population figures. (Scott 2009, 5)

Of course, this situation has changed. In the contemporary international system, there are very few territorial spaces that do not belong to an internationally recognized state (see Chapter 2). Nevertheless, areas of limited statehood remain ubiquitous and all-pervasive. While Scott's book title is questionable (stateless societies are still being governed), his fundamental insight remains correct: consolidated statehood is no guarantee for (good) governance. If statehood is not constrained by the rule of law, if not democracy, it can be as predatory, violent, and oppressive as the "stateless" society it seeks to replace. Hitler's German Reich, Stalin's Soviet Union, and Mao's "People's Republic" of China were all consolidated states with few ALS. Likewise, colonial states heavily relied on violence to control their territory. Violent suppression of rebellion and insurgency is not only a cause of colonial state collapse resulting in ALS. It was a major part of colonial state-building (Anderson and Killingray 1991; Anderson and Rolandsen 2014).

Yet, as we have shown in Chapter 1, some ALS are reasonably well governed – if they are not, it is often due to an autocratic and predatory "rump" state that uses what is left of its control over the use of force and capacity to set binding rules for rent-seeking. Using key development indicators, Leeson has shown that parts of Somalia are considerably better off today as compared to the time its last dictator, Siad Barré, governed the country and was able to enforce his decisions (Leeson 2007; see also Chapter 1 and Kaplan 2008; Renders and Terlinden 2010; Richards 2014).

At the same time, one should not throw out the baby with the bathwater. The fundamental insight of statist institutionalism is probably correct – political institutions matter for social and economic development and it is highly unlikely that sustained economic growth is possible without an institutional framework that is effective and legitimate. What is problematic, however, is the conflation of political institutions with the modern (Western) state and the emphasis on strong statehood in terms of unconstrained domestic sovereignty. For Huntington, for instance, political order comes first, while democracy, the rule of law, and human rights follow: "Men may, of course, have order without liberty. But they cannot have liberty without order" (Huntington 1968, 7–8).[2]

As to Huntington's first point, statist institutionalism cannot imagine that there might be sustainable and non-violent political orders that rely on non-hierarchical modes of governance without the enforcement capacities of a strong state. We demonstrate in this book that this is empirically false and offer a theoretical explanation for why. Huntington's other point, namely the primacy of order over liberty and constraints on the exercise of authority, is heavily criticized by the third approach discussed here, focusing on the openness of political orders.

Inclusive Institutionalism and "Good Governance"

The third approach to be discussed here focuses on effective and inclusive institutions as pre-conditions of development. Acemoglu and Robinson in particular have turned the causal logic of modernization theory on its head:

Countries such as Great Britain and the United States became rich because their citizens overthrew the elites who controlled power and created a society where political rights were much more broadly distributed, where the government was accountable and responsive to citizens, and where the great mass of people could take advantage of economic opportunities. (Acemoglu and Robinson 2012, 3–4)

Rather than democratization following economic growth, it is economic growth that resulted from democratization. Interestingly enough, statehood as defined above by a monopoly over the use of force and the ability to enforce central decisions forms part of what Acemoglu and Robinson refer to as "inclusive political institutions":

We will refer to political institutions that are sufficiently centralized and pluralistic as inclusive political institutions. When either of these conditions fails, we will refer to the institutions as extractive political institutions. (Acemoglu and Robinson 2012, 81)

To phrase it in our conceptualization, extractive political institutions are those that encompass areas of limited statehood as defined above and/or are not democratic and governed by the rule of law. In contrast, the modern Western state, of course, exemplifies inclusive political institutions.

---

[2] Note that Huntington's analysis served as an ideological justification for U.S. support for authoritarian regimes in Latin America during the late 1960s and 1970s. For a balanced discussion see Dominguez 2001.

In a similar way, North, Wallis, and Weingast define what they call "open access orders" as encompassing beliefs about the equality of all citizens; open access to economic, political, and other activities and organizational forms; impartial enforcement of the rule of law; and impersonal exchange (North, Wallis, and Weingast 2009, 114). In contrast, "limited access orders" or "natural states" are characterized by polities without the consent of the governed, a relatively small number of organizations, smaller and centralized governments, and a predominance of social relationships along personal lines including privileges, social hierarchies, and the like (ibid., 12). North et al. then formulate so-called doorstep conditions to enable transitions from limited to open access orders (ibid., ch. 5): rule of law for elites, perpetual organizations that are not tied to particular rules, and central control of the military. In other words, statehood in the Weberian sense, as defined in Chapter 2, constitutes one of the necessary doorstep conditions toward open access orders (ibid., 121–122).

In contrast to modernization theory and to some variants of statist institutionalism, neither Acemoglu and Robinson nor North et al. adopt a teleological perspective. In fact, they argue that natural states or limited access orders are the norm, both historically and in the contemporary system. North et al. reckon that only approximately 15 percent of the world's population today lives in open access orders, i.e., the developed and democratic OECD world of Western consolidated states. In contrast to modernization theory, there is no chance for limited access orders to open up, unless they meet the doorstep conditions that are themselves rather demanding. According to this line of thinking, areas of limited statehood are by definition limited access orders that have to be overcome in order to ensure economic growth and development.

We take from this strand of theorizing about economic, political, and social development that inclusive institutions and the rule of law are important for effective governance in terms of rule-making and the provision of collective goods and services. Our own approach incorporates the arguments by North et al. as well as Acemoglu and Robinson through an emphasis on legitimacy as the "right to rule" bestowed upon the governors by those being governed. One important source of (input) legitimacy is, of course, the inclusiveness of political institutions (see below).

Where we depart from both North et al. and Acemoglu and Robinson is the statism that is still an intrinsic part of their arguments (see also, e.g. Cortright, Seyle, and Wall 2017; Norris 2012). They share with modernization theorists as well as statist institutionalists the assumption that consolidated statehood is an integral part of development. The three approaches differ with regard to their causal arguments. Modernization theorists emphasize economic growth as the key to social and political development, while statist institutionalists argue that consolidated statehood leads to economic growth. Inclusive institutionalism, finally, adds to the picture pluralism and openness incorporating the rule of law.

Yet, all three approaches offer little hope for areas of limited statehood. Modernization theorists claim that they will disappear, once sustainable economic growth has been achieved. Statists in the tradition of Huntington argue that limited statehood has to be replaced by a functioning state in order to achieve human development, including economic growth. Inclusive institutionalists agree with Huntingtonians, but make the process even more demanding by adding freedom, participatory institutions, and the rule of law to the equation.

As a result, none of these approaches can explain the "governance puzzle" outlined in the introductory chapter of this book. How do we account for the variation in governance in areas of limited statehood where economic growth is at best moderate, state institutions are too weak to enforce central decisions or even lack a monopoly of the use of force, and democracy and the rule of law are weak or absent? We can only explain the variation if we depart from the assumption that fully consolidated and democratic statehood is necessary for effective governance, as defined in Chapter 2 of this book. At the same time, we agree that (political) institutions including the state matter, even in ALS. Therefore, institutions form part of our explanatory framework developed below. Yet, governance institutions do not have to be synonymous with the state.

We also differ from all three approaches discussed above in terms of ontology, that is, the assumption derived from rational choice that human beings are nothing but short-term utility maximizers.[3] Instead, we submit that human beings not only follow a logic of consequentialism, but also a logic of appropriateness (see March and Olsen 1989, 1998, on these concepts). Actors care about socially expected and accepted behavior. They seek to "do the right thing" rather than merely pursue short-term egoistic interests (March and Olsen 1989, 1998). Moreover, they also have a logic of communicative action at their disposal (Habermas 1981), that is, human beings are able to reason and to deliberate about what is in their best interest and how they ought to behave in the world. If we consider the other two social logics, we can better understand how legitimacy and social trust enable governance, even under adverse conditions of limited statehood. With this, we now turn to our own theoretical framework.

---

[3] North et al. are explicit about this. See North, Wallis, and Weingast 2009, 27–29.

Explaining Governance in Areas of Limited Statehood: A Theoretical Framework

In the following, we develop our conceptual framework, which will then be used to solve our governance puzzle in the empirical chapters of this book. As argued above, explaining governance in areas of limited statehood requires answering two questions:

1. Why and when do actors become governors?
2. What makes their governance effective and legitimate?

Our theoretical framework is embedded in the various institutionalisms as used in International Relations and comparative politics. As a unifying framework, we adopt actor-centered institutionalism as developed by Scharpf and Mayntz (Mayntz and Scharpf 1995a; Scharpf 1997). Actor-centered institutionalism tries to integrate the various institutionalist approaches – from rational choice (or neoliberal) institutionalism that informs most of the work discussed above (North 1990; for international relations Keohane 1989a) to historical (Fioretos, Falleti, and Sheingate 2016; Hall and Taylor 1996) and sociological institutionalism with its emphasis on the logic of appropriateness (March and Olsen 1989, 1998). Actor-centered institutionalism also allows us to incorporate insights from IR theories, whose conceptualization of IR as "cooperation under anarchy" (Oye 1986) in an international system without a central state authority to enforce the rules resembles our problematique of governance under conditions of limited statehood. We come back to this point in the conclusions (Chapter 8).

Our theoretical framework consists of three factors (or "bundles of factors") that we consider crucial for successful governance "under anarchy," namely institutions, legitimacy, and social trust. We do not conceive of this set of factors as "independent variables," which are then conducive to "if-then" hypotheses. Rather, these factors form configurations leading to effective and legitimate governance in ALS. They complement each other, influence each other, but they can also partially substitute for each other. In other words, we employ a configurative understanding of causality in the following (Byrne 2009; Rihoux and Ragin 2008).

(State) Institutions, Legitimacy, Social Trust: Defining Key Explanatory Factors

In the following, we briefly define the three explanatory sets of factors of our theoretical framework and then go on to develop it further to answer the two questions above.

(STATE) INSTITUTIONS

According to a standard definition, institutions are "persistent and connected sets of rules (formal and informal) that prescribe behavioral roles, constrain [as well as enable] activity, and shape expectations" (Keohane 1989c, 161 [authors added]). This book concentrates on political or governance institutions, that is, institutions designed for rule-making and/or the provision of collective goods and services (see our understanding of governance as developed in Chapter 2). In accordance with our understanding of state and statehood, state institutions are a subset of governance institutions with a claim to international and domestic sovereignty, i.e., they are recognized by other states and have the capacity to implement and enforce central decisions and/or to uphold the monopoly of the use of force.

In the following, and unless specified otherwise, we use the term "institutions" as a shortcut for political or governance institutions including, but not limited to, state institutions.

LEGITIMACY

The second factor explaining both the motivations of actors to become governors and the effectiveness of their governance contributions is *legitimacy*. In most general terms, legitimacy refers to the "right to rule" or the "license to govern"[4] (cf. Gehman, Lefsrud, and Fast 2017; the classic treatment is Weber 1978 (1922); for a detailed discussion see Schmelzle 2015). (Political) institutions as well as rulers are considered legitimate if and when they have the right to govern. The literature then distinguishes between normative, legal, and empirical legitimacy. While a normative perspective assesses whether an actor or institution should have the right to govern according to various normative principles, a legal perspective considers whether the actor or institution is legitimate from a formal legal point of view (see Hollis 2002; Tyler 1997a).

In contrast, we focus on *empirical legitimacy* as social acceptance. We define the empirical legitimacy of governance actors and institutions as a given social group's or population's sense of obligation or willingness to accept their authority. This conceptualization does not only allow for considering the legitimacy of the state as well as of external and non-state actors. It also avoids conflating possible sources of legitimacy with the concept itself. Thus, we understand empirical legitimacy as diffuse

---

[4] In the following, we use the terms "right to rule" interchangeably with the "right to govern" or "license to govern." Ruling often connotes only hierarchical governance (in the Weberian sense of *Herrschaft*) which we extent here to all modes of governance (see Chapter 2).

support for governance actors and/or institutions in an Eastonian sense (Baranyi 2012; Easton 1975). However, while Easton focused on political systems, such as the state, we broaden the perspective to include international organizations, foreign governments, as well as non-state actors, such as companies or (I)NGOs as recipients of diffuse support. Other than that, we follow Easton's analysis according to which legitimacy or diffuse support allows governance actors to carry out policies effectively even if they lack specific support. To put it differently, (empirical) legitimacy induces actors' voluntary compliance with costly rules even if they disagree with their substance (Hurd 1999). Legitimacy is, thus, tied to the logic of appropriateness according to which actors aspire to "do the right thing" rather than pursuing short-term egoistic interests (see above).

Social acceptance or empirical legitimacy tells us very little about the normative or legal status of governors or institutions. The so-called Islamic State (IS) is certainly not a legitimate actor according to international law and its normative legitimacy is surely extremely questionable. Nevertheless, it has enjoyed at least some empirical legitimacy among its members and supporters (Fromson and Simon 2015).

Note that we are first and foremost interested in empirical legitimacy as a main cause of effective governance, particularly if state institutions lack the capacity to set and enforce rules and provide collective goods and services (for a treatment of the normative questions involved see Jacob, Ladwig, and Schmelzle 2018; Ladwig and Rudolf 2011). Since we consider social acceptance (empirical legitimacy) a crucial explanation for effective governance under conditions of limited statehood, we need to endogenize it in our analysis. As a result, we are particularly concerned about the various sources of legitimacy in ALS (Risse and Stollenwerk 2018a). In this sense, legitimacy becomes a second dependent variable in our analysis.

The literature distinguishes three different sources of legitimacy (see Scharpf 1999 and Schmidt 2013 on these concepts; also Risse and Stollenwerk 2018a):[5]

1. *Input legitimacy* refers to legitimacy through participation. Social acceptance hinges on the possibility for those who are affected by collectively binding decisions to participate in the decision-making process, e.g. via elections, community meetings, or tribal councils.
2. *Output legitimacy* concerns legitimacy through performance. Effective governance generates social acceptance since it helps solve collective

---

[5] Strictly speaking, we should call these types of legitimacy, input-based, output-based, and throughput-based, since legitimacy is only generated through these various mechanisms, which create social acceptance in the eyes of the governed. However, we use the short terms here following the way these concepts are used in the literature.

problems. Effectiveness, hence, does not only depend on legitimacy; it is also an important source of legitimacy resulting in a virtuous circle (see below).

3. *Throughput legitimacy* is legitimacy through due process. Social acceptance arises from the perception of the decision-making process as fair, impartial, and transparent.

All three sources of legitimacy are shaped by the institutional design of the governance arrangements. As we will discuss below in more detail, they can complement, substitute, and reinforce each other.

SOCIAL TRUST

"Trust is largely understood as a cooperative attitude towards other people based on the optimistic expectation that others are likely to respect one's own interests" (Draude, Hölck, and Stolle 2018, 354; see also Börzel and Risse 2016). Luhmann has conceptualized trust as "upfront risk-taking" (*riskante Vorleistung*, Luhmann 1989), that is, deliberately abstaining from checking whether my interaction partner tells the truth about not defecting or keeping her commitments. Kydd defines trust as "a belief that the other side prefers mutual cooperation to exploiting one's own cooperation, while mistrust is a belief that the other side prefers exploiting one's cooperation to returning it" (Hardin 2002, 12; Kydd 2005, 6). Relationships of trust induce a sense of appropriate behavior among actors that is no longer based on cost-benefit calculations.

Three types of social trust can be distinguished (Börzel and Risse 2016; Draude, Hölck, and Stolle 2018):

1. *Personalized trust* among people living in the same neighborhood or community who trust each other because they know each other; personalized trust develops out of face-to-face interactions.
2. *Particularistic* or *group-based trust* among people who do not know each other personally, but trust each other, because they belong to the same social group; particularistic or group-based trust evolves out of particular social identities (e.g. ethnic, religious, gender, race).
3. *Generalized trust* beyond face-to-face interactions and group membership; generalized trust constitutes an abstract form of trust that does not have any group boundaries and includes the widest scope of people.

In the following, we argue that (state) institutions, legitimacy, and social trust, and their combination, explain to a large degree why and when actors are prepared to engage in governance in ALS (first question). The three factors also provide the scope conditions for governance effectiveness (second question). We start with the first question.

Why and When Do Actors Become Governors in Areas of Limited Statehood?

As noted above, we need to separate the question of whether actors are motivated to govern from the issue of whether their attempts at governance are effective and or not. Here, we concentrate on the first question.

The literature often focuses on those actors for whom it is constitutive to provide governance. Special agencies of the UN and other IOs, for example, have it in their mandate to contribute to governance. The same holds true for foreign aid agencies of various states as well as for (I)NGOs (e.g. Oxfam), religious organizations (e.g. the Catholic Church), or private foundations (e.g. the Bill and Melinda Gates Foundation), as well as MSPs (e.g. UN Global Compact or the Extractive Industry Transparency Initiative).

For these type of actors, the motivation to become governors in ALS lies in their mandate. Of course, they might be ineffective or they might even fail completely (see Chapters 5–7). In some cases, they have done more harm than good, e.g. when UN peace-keepers and other IOs commit violations of human rights (Heupel, Zürn, and Hirschmann 2017). As to (I)NGOs, it would be equally wrong to treat them solely as altruistic actors (Prakash and Gugerty 2010). However, we do submit that it is constitutive for them and for other actors to engage in governance, particularly under conditions of limited statehood. As a result, we do not need a lengthy discussion of their motivations here. What matters is what is expected of actors and this is defined by the institutions in which they are embedded rather than whether they are driven by intrinsic values as opposed to material concerns.

Yet, there are various other actors in ALS whose main social purpose or institutional mandate is not to govern. The most prominent group are private companies, whether MNCs or local firms. We can safely assume that their primary motivation is to make profit or to gain and to expand market shares. Another group are violent non-state actors (VNSA), such as warlords, rebel groups, or transnational terrorists. Their main interest is to control territory and to keep the state out (which might, however, motivate them to govern their territory, see below).[6] Foreign governments are also unlikely to prefer governing ALS. In some cases, hostile neighboring states might actually choose to keep the state out of

---

[6] We owe this and the following point to Melissa Lee.

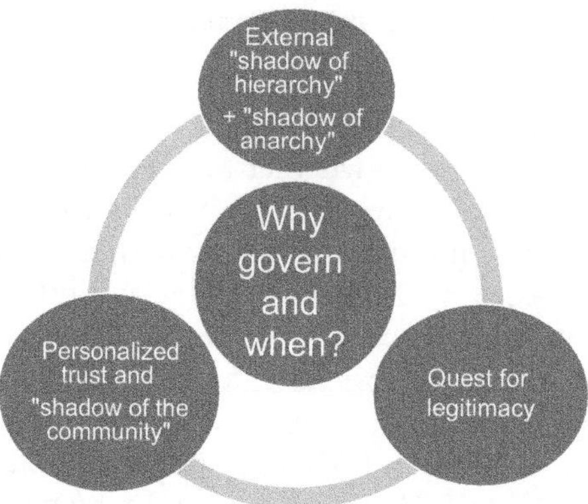

Figure 3.1 Why govern and when?

ALS and leave them ungoverned (Lee 2018). Last but not least, (autocratic) governments of weak states often have no intention to govern, but to exploit the resources available in ALS. They become predatory states (Ostrom 1999; Reno 2015b; Scott 1998).

The literature has mostly treated these actors as governance spoilers, and rightly so (see e.g. Chan and Ross 2003; Stedman 1997). Without denying the "public bads" companies, rebel groups, predatory governments, and others have laid on ALS, we argue that they might engage in governance under particular conditions. We do not need to assume a logic of appropriateness here, but can treat these actors as egoistic utility-maximizers. For instance, foreign governments might become governors in ALS for strategic reasons, be it security (negative externalities of civil war) or economic considerations (access to resources such as energy sources). Under certain conditions, even autocratic national or local state actors engage in governance in ALS rather than merely using their access to rents, taxes, and the like for private purposes.

Figure 3.1 summarizes our argument answering the first question of this book, namely, why and when particularly self-interested and utility-maximizing actors – whether state or non-state, whether local/domestic or inter-/transnational – engage in governance. We elaborate these scope conditions below.

STATE INSTITUTIONS AND THE LACK THEREOF

Statehood and the External "Shadow of Hierarchy" A prominent condition under which self-interested actors engage in governance has to do with the so-called shadow of hierarchy (Mayntz and Scharpf 1995b; Scharpf 1997).[7] This argument has originally been developed to explain governance provisions by private actors, particularly companies, in consolidated states. Research on modes of governance in the OECD world has demonstrated that public-private cooperation and private self-regulation are usually most effective under the "shadow of hierarchy." The threat of governments to impose rules hierarchically provides a major incentive for non-state actors to engage in the provision of collective goods, such as a clean environment. The shadow cast by the threat of hierarchical coordination also prevents non-state actors from reneging on their voluntary commitments, e.g. to reduce packaging waste or increase the number of female members in the boards of directors. This implies, however, that state agencies are able to supervise private regulatory efforts and/or issue and enforce state regulation if business does not get its act together and does not provide collective goods in the necessary quality (see e.g. Börzel 2008, 2012; Héritier 2003). Hierarchical coordination or the threat to do so is a major pre-condition for the successful emergence and effectiveness of non-state governance. In other words, non-hierarchical modes of governance involving non-state actors complement rather than substitute for regulatory activities by national governments or supranational institutions, such as the EU. Paradoxically, strong states or strong supranational organizations are required for non-hierarchical modes of steering to be effective and to enhance the problem-solving capacity of governance (Börzel 2010a, d; Héritier and Rhodes 2010). In other words, consolidated statehood is necessary to cast a "shadow of hierarchy."

Areas of limited statehood are by definition characterized by weak state capacities to implement and enforce decisions and therefore cannot cast a credible "shadow of hierarchy" either. If this were all there is to it, state authorities in ALS would be doomed twice: they cannot provide governance themselves for lack of capacity *and* they cannot induce others to govern. Being unable to enforce their own laws, a threat to issue laws is empty. Moreover, the contribution of non-state actors to the provision of collective goods has to substitute for governance by governments rather than to complement it, as is the case in countries with consolidated statehood.

Fortunately, national or local state authorities are not the only actors able to cast a "shadow of hierarchy" inducing other actors to provide governance in ALS. External actors, such as IOs and foreign governments, can commit non-state actors to engage in governance. First,

---

[7] For an expanded version of the following see Börzel and Risse 2010.

external actors may directly exercise domestic sovereignty, including the monopoly of the use of force, as well as enforcing decisions authoritatively (Linke-Behrens and van Hoof-Maurer 2016). IOs and foreign governments that might themselves be motivated for a variety of reasons (see above) can interfere in the "Westphalian sovereignty" of countries with ALS (for a comprehensive treatment see Lake, D. 2016). Prominent examples have been the modern protectorates from Bosnia-Herzegovina to Afghanistan. Moreover, the UN Security Council might invoke the "responsibility to protect" (R2P) if a lack of governance results in gross violations of human rights in ALS. If external actors control the means of violence and can effectively enforce decisions in protectorates or trusteeships, they are also able to cast a credible "shadow of hierarchy," at least in principle. Note that we do not discuss here the effectiveness of external state-building efforts (for a skeptical view see Lake, D. 2016; see also Chapters 5 and 6). Our point is simply that external actors can cast a credible shadow of hierarchy in ALS through (the credible threat of) (military) interventions.

Second, a less intrusive "shadow of hierarchy," which can induce other – mostly state – actors to provide governance in ALS is political conditionality. The EU, for example, has often tied foreign aid and other instruments to human rights and rule of law provisions in ALS (Börzel and Hackenesch 2013; Holland 2003). In contrast to military interventions, political conditionality still leaves local actors some choice, even though this choice might be rather limited under severe conditions of poverty and limited statehood.

Third, national governments of (consolidated and democratic) states, where MNCs and (I)NGOs have their headquarters, may also legally coerce non-state actors to contribute to governance in ALS. Home country laws can be in place, which require non-state actors, such as companies, their sub-contractors, and suppliers, to comply with standards of good governance or other regulations (e.g. environmental laws) irrespective of where they invest or operate. While their scope is still limited, home-country regulations can help commit companies in particular to contribute to governance in ALS (Börzel and Thauer 2013; Thauer 2014b; Deitelhoff and Wolf 2010a, 212–214; Flohr et al. 2010, 52–66). Two causal mechanisms link home-country regulations to governance contributions of companies in ALS. First, companies can be legally bound to comply with regulatory standards of their home country when they invest abroad. While the scope and enforcement is still limited, US extraterritorial jurisdiction on human rights, bribery, and national security issues shows the potential for national governments to regulate their companies abroad (Flohr et al. 2010; skeptical Ruggie

2018). The 2015 UK Modern Slavery Act and the 2017 French Duty of Vigilance (*Devoir de Vigilance*) Act have essentially transposed the 2011 UN Guidelines on Business and Human Rights into national law, making its provisions obligatory for UK and French companies as well as their subsidiaries.[8]

The second mechanism is more indirect and works through markets in a globalized economy. Firms producing for markets with a high degree of state regulation (e.g. in the realm of human rights or environmental standards) and targeting high-end consumer markets have little incentive to use different production standards in ALS thereby, say, polluting the environment or violating human rights. They tend to transport their regulatory standards abroad as these are interpreted as "quality signals" (Potoski and Prakash 2006) by business partners and customers (Börzel et al. 2011; Kolk, van Tulder, and Welters 2005; Murphy 2000). Rather than "racing to the bottom," production networks in a globalized economy result in firms providing governance in ALS, adopting and even lobbying for environmental and social regulation going beyond legal requirements (Greenhill, Mosley, and Prakash 2009; Haufler 2001b; Prakash 2000; Vogel and Kagan 2004). There are limits to the extent to which home-country regulations can be used to induce firms to provide governance in ALS, though (Flohr et al. 2010). These rules are often confined to product regulation (Vogel and Kagan 2004) and rarely extend to supply chains beyond the first or second supplier (Héritier, Müller-Debus, and Thauer 2009).

Last but not least, international law itself can cast a "shadow of hierarchy," even though its enforcement capacity is limited. International law does oblige (I)NGOs, companies, and local actors to comply with standards of good governance in ALS (Ladwig and Rudolf 2011; Rudolf 2007). If a state government is no longer capable of living up to international standards under conditions of limited statehood, actors who then step in as governors are obligated by the same international rules as the state government. In other words, standards of international law hold non-state actors directly accountable to provide governance under conditions of limited statehood. Whether this results in effective and sustainable governance is an altogether different question. The problem is, of course, who enforces international law in ALS.

In sum, the external "shadow of hierarchy" discussed here still requires some consolidated statehood to produce at least a credible

---

[8] www.ethicaltrade.org/blog/france-adopts-new-corporate-duty-care-law, last access July 28, 2019.

threat to set and to enforce the law. It is located outside the ALS, except for direct military interventions in the "Westphalian" sovereignty of states. While often weak and selective, this external shadow of hierarchy can induce other actors – state or non-state alike – to engage in governance.

The "Shadow of Anarchy" An external "shadow of hierarchy" provides incentives for self-interested state and non-state actors to engage in governance in areas of limited statehood. The same holds true for the exact opposite, what we call the "shadow of anarchy" (Mayntz and Scharpf 1995b, 23, Fn. 5) in terms of the absence of any political order. If the state is not capable of adopting and enforcing collectively binding decisions (as in ALS), actors face the possibility that there is no governance at all, including the risk of widespread violence and chaos. This anarchy problematique in ALS closely resembles the international system in the absence of an enforcer or hegemon. Transnational or global governance has to cope with the problem that there is no world state to enforce compliance with costly rules or to provide governance. Rather, in the case of international regimes, individual states have to voluntarily comply with and enforce norms and rules on others (Krasner 1983; Rittberger 1993). At the same time, the various international institutionalisms (overviews in Hasenclever, Mayer, and Rittberger 1997; Keohane 1989b; Simmons and Martin 2002) have convincingly demonstrated that "cooperation under anarchy" (Oye 1986) is indeed possible if and when egoistic actors cannot reach their goals unilaterally or if and when their unilateral action produces negative externalities for everybody involved.

A similar point can be made with regard to areas of limited statehood: the "shadow of anarchy" in terms of the risk of chaos and any lack of governance provides actors with a major incentive to step in and to fill the governance gap (Börzel 2010c; Börzel and Thauer 2013; Ruggie 2004a), under at least one of two conditions:

1. They are "stationary" rather than "roving" bandits, i.e., they cannot simply leave the area of limited statehood in question (on the distinction see Olson 1993). As Olson argued, autocratic regimes as "stationary bandits" in ALS are likely to deliver collective goods and services in order to stay in power and to be able to continue extracting rents for their patronage networks. The same argument can be made with regard to other potential governors.

2. They depend on the provision of certain common goods (security, basic infrastructure) and collectively binding rules (e.g. property rights) in the pursuit of their self-interests in the respective ALS.

This argument applies to almost all self-interested state and non-state actors – domestic as well as inter- or transnational – mentioned above. It also holds true for rebel groups, warlords, and other VNSA – as long as they need to hold on to a certain territory for various reasons (see Berti 2013, 2018; Chojnacki and Branovic 2011; Weinstein 2007). For instance, Weinstein has shown that rebels sometimes even commit to rather inclusive and participatory institutions, as long as their rule depends on the consent of the governed, at least to some extent (see also Arjona, Kasfir, and Mampilly 2015b). The argument resembles Tilly's historical account of modern state formation in Europe as one of the transformation of military actors to governors and then national governments in emerging states (Tilly 1995).

The "shadow of anarchy" may also induce companies to engage in governance, if they cannot easily disinvest and move away from areas of limited statehood. Extractive industries as well as MNCs that have heavily invested in infrastructure and human capital are cases in point. If the pursuit of their individual profits depends on the provision of certain common goods and collectively binding rules to produce them, respectively, and the state is not capable or unwilling to provide them, companies are motivated to compensate. Take the case of HIV/AIDS in South Africa (Börzel and Thauer 2013; Thauer 2014b): multinational automobile companies, such as BMW, Mercedes Benz, or General Motors, require skilled labor that, however, suffer from the HIV/AIDS pandemic. In the absence of a functioning public health system, including public education on the risks of the pandemic, companies have been stepping in to provide health and education services not only for their workers, but also for their families and the larger communities. In other words, these companies have become public health governors.

Last but not least, the "shadow of anarchy" has been a major incentive for Western states, their foreign aid agencies, but also international organizations to engage in governance in ALS, whether through state-building interventions or "softer" modes of interference. Following 9/11, the discourse on "fragile and failed states" and the negative security and economic externalities that they might entail for the developed world (from harboring transnational terrorism to refugee flows; for a critical analysis of this discourse see Woodward 2017) has motivated OECD countries and IOs to become governors in ALS. Once again, whether these efforts have been effective or not is irrelevant here, since we only want to explain why self-interested actors start engaging in governance in the first place.

In sum, whether real or not, the perceived risk of anarchy, violence, and chaos provides a major incentive for self-interested actors with some stake in ALS (as "stationary bandits" or with regard to negative externalities) to become governors.

THE QUEST FOR LEGITIMACY

The desire for recognition and legitimacy can be a major reason why self-interested and utility-maximizing actors are prepared to engage in governance. Let us start with Olson's argument about "stationary bandits" mentioned above. Similar to multinational companies, warlords or rebel groups are often considered as part of the problem of, not the solution to, limited statehood (see above). However, once these actors become stationary, they might require legitimacy, both domestic and international, to pursue their interests. With regard to local populations, constant plundering, oppression, and violence are extremely costly to ensure community compliance with their rule. In contrast, providing collective goods and services is likely to induce output legitimacy, which in turn leads to compliance and obedience by local populations. Thus, the quest for domestic legitimacy can transform VNSA into governors. The literature on warlords and rebel groups appears to support this argument (see e.g. Arjona 2016; Arjona, Kasfir, and Mampilly 2015b; Berti 2018; Jo 2015; Weinstein 2007).

Hyeron Jo, for instance, has argued, that VNSA are likely to seek international recognition and legitimacy, the closer they are to victory (Jo 2015; Jo and Bryant 2013). As a result, they have incentives to engage in governance, including a monopoly over the use of force, thereby assuring security as a public good in the territory, which they control. International recognition and legitimacy (for either secession or control of the national government) often constitute pre-conditions for access to humanitarian as well as foreign aid, including loans by the World Bank. In other words, access to international resources provides a strong incentive structure for VNSA to become governors on "their" territory in order to gain recognition and legitimacy bestowed by the international community.

Similar considerations might also induce national governments in areas of limited statehood to engage in governance rather than exploitation, rent-seeking, and corruption. Particularly autocratic regimes need to generate output legitimacy and social acceptance, unless they have to rule by pure force and oppression, which is rather costly. What is true for Belarus, Russia, or China, should even more apply to autocratic governments in ALS with their weakened enforcement capacities. Dependency on foreign aid and other international economic and monetary resources might further induce them to become governors.

The quest for social acceptance as an incentive to engage in governance is increasingly relevant for private companies, too, albeit in different ways.[9] First, companies are likely to contribute to the provision of collective goods and services for local communities in order to increase their social acceptance other than simply providing jobs. This is all the more the case, since local communities often expect (foreign) companies to invest in the common good in return for extracting resources (Börzel and Hönke 2011).

Second and more important, particularly producing for global markets in ALS, MNCs often need social acceptance in their home markets in order to be able to sell their products (see Börzel and Risse 2010 for the following). (I)NGOs and transnational social movements launch international campaigns naming and shaming companies who fail to contribute to the provision of common goods in ALS. As a result, environmental and human rights norms have started to creep into the core business of many companies, particularly multinational corporations with a "brand name" to defend and whose products target markets in (consolidated and democratic) states where consumers care about the provision of common goods (see e.g. Flohr et al. 2010; Potoski and Prakash 2006; Prakash and Potoski 2007; Thauer 2014b). Moreover, more and more pension funds have started investing in companies that conform to certain social standards or are listed in various social indices such as the Dow Jones Sustainability Index.

This is an interesting case in which the logic of appropriateness intersects with the logic of consequences. The more consumers of companies' products, particularly in high-end markets, care about governance in ALS, including human rights and environmental standards (the logic of appropriateness), the more they use market mechanisms inducing firms to comply with these norms (the logic of consequentialism). This then translates into reputational concerns for companies, particularly those with a brand name to defend (Börzel and Thauer 2013).

---

[9] Strictly speaking, legitimacy as the "right to rule" is not at stake here, but reputation and social acceptance in general. We thank Eric Stollenwerk for alerting us to this point, which we will revisit in the concluding chapter.

In sum, the quest for legitimacy and social acceptance, as well as reputational concerns, serve as another powerful motivation for a variety of self-interested and utility-maximizing actors to engage in governance in areas of limited statehood.

(PERSONALIZED) TRUST AND THE "SHADOW OF THE COMMUNITY"
A third factor motivating various actors to engage in governance relates to the social relations among the governed. As argued above, trust relations among community members constitute a fundamental glue for societies and for social integration. In our context, we particularly focus on personalized trust emerging from face-to-face interactions among community members (see Börzel and Risse 2010; Börzel and Risse 2016 for the following). First, as numerous studies have shown, personalized trust enables actors to solve collective action problems in the absence of hierarchy (Gambetta 1988b; Ostrom 1990, 2002; Ostrom, Gardner, and Walker 1994). In other words, personalized trust facilitates self-governance without hierarchy in local communities in ALS. In some cases, such trust relations can even be scaled up to larger territories, as the example of Somaliland demonstrates (Glawion 2017, 2020; Kaplan 2008; Richards 2014).

Second and closely related to the first point, personalized trust enhances the action capacity of local communities. For instance, a study on conflicts between multinational mining companies and neighboring communities in Tanzania and Guinea demonstrates that local communities with high levels of trust have a higher capacity to engage with companies to manage conflicts. In many cases, local communities have, thus, induced companies, but also other non-state actors, such as rebel groups, to provide governance in terms of e.g. local security and infrastructure (Thomas 2014; see also Arjona, Kasfir, and Mampilly 2015b; Beisheim, Janetschek, and Sarre 2014).

Third, trust among community members with their own standards of appropriate behavior holds governors – whether state or non-state – accountable to the community. Areas of limited statehood are often inhabited by indigenous communities with their own normative standards of what would be considered in the public interest. Using comparative case studies of public service provision in rural China, Lily Tsai has shown that state representatives that are embedded in inclusive societal institutions at the local level are more likely to strive for collective goods provision than those who are not embedded or in areas with no inclusive societal institutions (Tsai 2007). Likewise, Hönke and Börzel find that local communities in Sub-Saharan Africa exhibiting high levels of trust restrain local state representatives and customary authorities in the use of their powers (Hönke and Börzel 2014). This "shadow of the community" holds state representatives accountable in the absence of formal institutions through which citizens could voice their claims. Community institutions, thus, affect the willingness of state or non-state actors that are external to the community to engage in governance.

The South African mining industry has been exposed to this mechanism in a particular way. Mining companies used to have a terrible record with regard to environmental pollution and workers' rights during Apartheid. In post-Apartheid South Africa, local communities in mining towns and NGOs used naming and shaming practices to induce companies to provide governance with regard to social rights and cleaning up the environment. At the same time, companies turned to corporate social responsibility for rebuilding relationships with the African National Congress (ANC) government for regaining legitimacy in the wider public and for avoiding state regulation against them (Hamann 2004; Hönke 2010a, 257–285).

In sum, personalized trust in local communities enhances their action capacity and, thus, enables them to self-govern as well as to use the "shadow of the community" to induce other actors – from local authorities to companies – to engage in governance according to community norms.

We now turn to the second question concerning the effectiveness and legitimacy of governance in areas of limited statehood.

What Makes Governance Effective and Legitimate?

DEFINING AND MEASURING "EFFECTIVE GOVERNANCE"

The main dependent variable or *explanandum* of this book is governance effectiveness. Before we engage in developing our explanatory framework, we need to clarify what we mean by "effective governance." On a most general level, effective governance means that *binding rules are actually implemented and complied with and that collective goods and services are indeed delivered for as many people as possible in areas of limited statehood* (Schmelzle 2011). As to the former and under conditions of limited statehood, rule compliance implies that rules are being followed voluntarily, particularly if they are costly and/or against the interests of the people concerned. For instance, companies have to refrain from environmental pollution even if there is a lack of enforcement capacity by state authorities. Police officers have to comply with human rights norms, even if the state is too weak to punish wrong-doing. As to the latter, governance is the more effective, the more various collective goods are actually delivered and are accessible for everybody concerned, improving living conditions. Take public health: the ultimate measure of effective health governance is not only that there is universal healthcare available for a given population, but also that, say, infant mortality is actually declining. In the case of education, effective governance not only means that every child has access to a school, but that children also learn how to read and write.

While it is, thus, possible to define governance effectiveness conceptually and in the abstract, the term nevertheless raises some thorny issues, as the never-ending debate about compliance demonstrates (overview in Börzel 2020). To begin with, what is effective is often in the eye of the beholder. As a first cut, one might argue that governance effectiveness means that the actors in charge manage to reach their own goals. In the public health example above, the World Health Organization (WHO) might consider it a governance success if 90 percent of the population have access to healthcare in a town or region. A more demanding understanding would imply that infant mortality actually declines and that common diseases are cured and prevented in a sustainable way through comprehensive immunization campaigns, and the like. As to rule compliance, who is to decide authoritatively (particularly in areas of limited statehood) that actors' behavior is rule-consistent or whether a violation actually occurred? In consolidated states, court systems serve as the ultimate arbiter of compliance issues. That is, their interpretation of the law in question *becomes* the law. In areas of limited statehood, however, things are more complicated, particularly since many state court systems are corrupt (see Chapter 6 for a discussion).

Even if we have managed to solve issues of interpretation, measuring governance effectiveness in an intersubjectively transparent way is at least as daunting (see Stollenwerk 2018a for a detailed discussion). Governance effectiveness has both objectively measurable as well as subjective features. With regard to collective services, for instance, we can measure to what extent governance achieves public security in terms of largely absent instances of violence, public health in terms of widely reduced infant mortality rates, or environmental protection in terms of improving air and water quality. We can also measure rule consistent behavior, for instance, by looking at human rights violations or child labor. However, one problem is the availability of valid and reliable data, particularly in ALS where statistical offices are often lacking, as we discussed in Chapter 2.

More important, it is unclear what the appropriate standard of measurement with regard to governance is. If governance is supposed to be "for the people," a major benchmark ought to be the subjective perceptions of governance effectiveness by the governed rather than "objective" measurements. But, what if perceptions of effectiveness and quasi-

Figure 3.2 What makes governance effective?

objective data differ, as many studies have shown (Stollenwerk 2018a, 116). For instance, Stollenwerk has collected data on antenatal care for the federal states of Nigeria provided by the National Bureau of Statistics (see also Figure 2.2 in Chapter 2). He has then compared these "objective" data with the subjective perception of public health provision derived from Afrobarometer data (Stollenwerk 2018a, 117–119). For many federal states in Nigeria, "objective" data and subjective perceptions do not match. In some cases, citizens perceive healthcare as more inadequate than the data indicate; in other federal states, they evaluate it as much better. Koehler reported a similar divergence between the "objective" measurement of violence and subjective perceptions of security for northeastern Afghanistan (see e.g. Koehler 2008, 2014).

It is impossible to solve these problems in this book. Instead, we seek to be as explicit about the data and their reliability as we possibly can. We will both use "objective" data and subjective perceptions of governance effectiveness. The latter are particularly relevant for the various feedback loops between effectiveness and legitimacy, as we discuss below.

We now turn to our explanatory framework with regard to governance effectiveness and legitimacy. The three factors that induce actors to become governors also influence their effectiveness in areas of limited statehood in the absence of a central state that can set and enforce rules, decisions, or engage in large-scale collective service provision.

As we will see, institutions, legitimacy, and social trust do not only affect governance effectiveness in different ways. They also influence each other. Last but not least, there are various feedback loops to be considered, particularly between legitimacy and effectiveness. Figure 3.2 depicts the three factors that we discuss below in more detail.

INSTITUTIONAL SETTINGS

As expected from an institutionalist perspective, the design and settings of the governance arrangements themselves account largely for the effectiveness of governance in ALS. We submit that three institutional features are particularly relevant for effective governance under conditions of limited statehood: 1) the design of the governance arrangement in terms of its resources, task adequacy, and coordination mechanisms; 2) the inclusiveness of the institutions; and 3) the remaining role of – albeit limited – statehood.

Institutional Design First, governance institutions – from (non-state) judicial systems to educational institutions, public health governance, etc. – must be "fit for purpose" in order to be effective. This is a straightforward functional argument that – in International Relations – has been made by rational institutionalists (see e.g. the situation structure approach by Zürn 1992 and Martin 1992a, as well as the argument about "rational design," Koremenos, Lipson, and Snidal 2001). A pure coordination problem requires a different institutional design as compared to coordination games with distributive consequences and a collaboration problem of the prisoners' dilemma variety (see Stein 1990 on these distinctions). IR approaches are particularly helpful in our context of limited statehood, since they also assume "governance under anarchy."

For areas of limited statehood, enforcement is a major problem by definition. In the absence of a central authority, non-state actors, such as companies, should have a common interest in cooperating to provide collective goods and services under the "shadow of anarchy" (see above). Yet, even though it may be in their best interest, they are likely to forgo cooperation because of the risks of being cheated upon and of free rider problems. To give three examples: first, food and beverage companies rely on clean water for their production. At the same time, their production processes are a main source of pollution. If public authorities fail to set or enforce water quality standards, companies sharing the same water source may be motivated to engage in collective self-regulation. Since curbing pollution is costly, however, they also have an incentive to defect, assuming that others will comply and they can reap the benefits, free-riding on the costs. Thus, the risk of being cheated by others is a major impediment to voluntary self-regulation (see Kranz 2013 for the case of South Africa).

Second, multi-stakeholder partnerships (MSPs) often have to deal with similar problems involving distributional conflict, cheating, or free-riding. Distributional conflicts may arise when information for decision-makers, e.g. on the success of MSP projects, lends itself to policy conclusions that benefit some members more than others. Moreover, when MSPs provide services, such as access to water and sanitation in low-income communities, their members undertake substantial investments in designing and implementing projects. Others can benefit without sharing the costs (Beisheim and Campe 2012).

Third, peace-keeping missions face a similar collective action dilemma: a prominent example concerns the Trilateral Contact Group on Ukraine, which consisted of representatives from Ukraine, Russia, and the Organization for Security and Cooperation in Europe (OSCE), and brokered a peace plan in 2014. The conflict parties pledged to stop the use of violence. In January 2015, however, the ceasefire collapsed because Ukraine and Russia considered themselves better off without agreement than if one of them had unilaterally defected to extend its control over territory.

Institutions can help avoid these collective action dilemmas by providing effective monitoring and sanctioning mechanisms. Companies can delegate the setting of standards and their supervision to a public-private partnership that provides a verification or certification scheme (Kaan 2014). MSPs can have their project evaluated on a regular basis and sanction failure by suspending or ending membership (Beisheim and Campe 2012). For instance, the effectiveness of the Global Compact significantly increased after it had institutionalized monitoring and reporting mechanisms to prevent companies from reaping the reputational rewards of membership without adhering to its standards (Kahn 2014). In the case of Ukraine, the collective action problem could have been mitigated by a robust UN peace-keeping mandate.

However, not all governance problems in ALS resemble a prisoners' dilemma requiring institutions with enforcement capacity. Institutionalized monitoring and sanctioning is less relevant for coordination games where actors' interests converge and where they have no incentive to cheat. Nor do they help tackling distribution problems. Pure coordination games are self-enforcing once actors have reached an agreement that helps them avoid their least preferred outcome. The proliferation of governance actors often results in organizational overlap and competition over resources and influence. To avoid problems of ineffectiveness caused by complexity and fragmentation, the governance actors have an incentive to coordinate their activities by establishing joint institutions and agreeing on some division of labor among themselves (Faude 2014; Gehring and Faude 2014). In the food sector, for instance, a multitude of international organizations, including the United Nations Children's Emergency Fund (UNICEF), the Food and Agriculture

Organization (FAO), the World Food Organization (WFO), the World Health Organization (WHO), and the World Bank, seek to address malnutrition (Clapp 2015; Holzscheiter 2018). The World Food Council or the Committee of World Food Security are to provide for the coordination and cooperation among these agencies to ensure the effective allocation of food aid (Holzscheiter, Bahr, and Pantzerhielm 2016).

Coordination becomes more challenging, however, when the costs are not equally distributed. With regard to MSPs, for example, IOs may not be prepared to have private donors interfere with their public mandate and claim the coordination authority (Beisheim and Liese 2014a: 205–208). Or some stakeholders benefit more from a certain policy option than others (Beisheim and Campe 2012). Once a solution is found, however, no actor has an incentive to defect. The problem is to come to an agreement in the first place. Institutions can facilitate side-payments and issue-linkages, which compensate agencies for the concessions they make. They can also turn coordination into an iterated game in which responsibilities rotate among the agencies involved.

Task complexity matters for coordination, too (Krasner and Risse 2014b): distributing anti-malaria bednets or child immunization are relatively simple tasks that require little coordination among actors and few repeated interventions. In contrast, combating and preventing HIV/ AIDS is a complex task that necessitates the coordination of at least the health and education sectors and requires repeated interventions over many years (Schäferhoff 2014a). Institutions governing these tasks must be able to ensure sufficient material and ideational (e.g. knowledge) resources for their partners and the recipients of their services to be able to perform their functions. Companies fighting HIV/AIDS depend on a substantial number of highly qualified personnel trained in prevention and treatment (Thauer 2013a).

Finally, institutional designs must be flexible to adapt to local circumstances. Effective governance institutions require flexible process management and in-built capacities enabling organizational learning and change management. An independent secretariat that is well-equipped and employs full-time staff appears to be crucial for good process management (Beisheim and Campe 2012; Beisheim and Liese 2014b; Beisheim et al. 2014).

Inclusiveness Irrespective of the type of problem and the degree of complexity they face, governance institutions must be open, inclusive, fair, and transparent in order to be effective. We agree with Acemoglu and Robinson about the necessity of inclusive institutions to foster governance and development (Acemoglu and Robinson 2012; see above). Where we part ways is that these institutions do not have to be linked to the state. In fact, inclusiveness is probably even more important if the governance arrangements lack enforcement capacities, as is common in areas of limited statehood, because it fosters voluntary compliance through input legitimacy and social trust. Institutional rules and procedures according to which IOs, states, (I)NGOs, and companies take unbiased decisions, inform about their governance activities in a transparent way, and take responsibility for their outcomes ensure inclusiveness as well as effectiveness (Brinkerhoff and Brinkerhoff 2002; Klingebiel 2012). The effectiveness of MSPs, for instance, crucially depends on the ownership they build of their legally non-binding standards among those who shall adhere to them (Beisheim and Dingwerth 2010; cf. Beisheim and Liese 2014b; for a more critical view see Booth 2012; Sjöstedt 2013).

Inclusive institutions foster effective governance mostly in an indirect way, since they influence the other two factors discussed here, namely legitimacy and social trust (see also below). If those being governed have a say in the institutional decision-making processes, this is likely to generate input legitimacy as a major source of social acceptance. The same holds true for rule-based, fair, and transparent governance processes that ensure accountability. Fair and transparent institutions have also been found to contribute creating generalized social trust (Freitag & Bühlmann 2009; Knight 2001; Rothstein and Stolle 2008b). Last but not least, inclusive governance institutions are likely to allow for deliberative processes as a non-hierarchical mode of governance (see Chapter 2), which will also enhance effectiveness, as we discuss in Chapter 4.

In sum, inclusive institutions are likely to generate both legitimacy and social trust and, thus, to lead to effective governance in a more indirect way.

Residual Statehood While the state is weak by definition in areas of limited statehood, it is not completely absent. To some extent, the design of governance institutions outside the state can compensate for its weak capacity. Yet, any remaining state capacity comes in handy in ALS, particularly when state actors are embedded in the governance institutions. First, the control of violence is often a basic pre-condition for non-state actors, such as MSPs or companies, to engage in governance in the first place (Beisheim et al. 2014; Börzel and Thauer 2013; Liese, Janetschek, and Sarre 2014, 139–142). Second, even where other governors seek to fill the void left by the state, successful implementation often relies on some regulatory capacity of the state. Governance without government can be, and sometimes needs to be, strengthened by governance by government in the same area in order to be comprehensive and effective (see also Amengual 2010). Third, basic infrastructure and administrative organization are necessary for governance actors to deliver services and broaden access. They require roads, ports, and airports for their operations (Beisheim et al. 2011c, 2014). Moreover, particularly complex governance contributions, such as HIV/AIDS workplace programs, have to rely on some basic administrative structure of the state to be broadly accessible and sustainable (Beisheim et al. 2011c; Börzel, Hönke, and Thauer 2012; Schäferhoff 2014a). Fourth, external and non-state actors are more likely to engage in governance in ALS if they can "partner" with state actors instead of entirely taking over (Beisheim et al. 2011b; Börzel, Hönke, and Thauer 2012; Deitelhoff and Wolf 2010a). Finally, state capacity is important to coordinate governance interventions by other actors. Rather than regulating, it is about orchestrating the multiplicity of governance contributions as to make sure that they complement each other (Beisheim et al. 2011b). We have called this meta-governance in Chapter 2.

However, residual statehood in ALS can also be a curse rather than a blessing. On the one hand, particularly very weak states have been found to stay out of the way of external governors, e.g. in the cases of Governance Delegation Agreements (Matanock 2014; see Chapter 4). On the other hand, autocratic weak states might use their residual capacity to interfere with the governance of non-state actors and to act as spoilers if not predators. They may use their residual statehood for private rent-seeking rather than the provision of collective goods and services (Börzel, Hönke, and Thauer 2012; Lake 2014). In the sensitive area of security, e.g. government authorities often seek to demonstrate and reinforce their claim to sovereignty, which is closely linked to controlling the use of force, e.g. by preventing companies from providing human rights training to the police (Hönke 2010b). Likewise, the South African government has resisted non-state engagement in combating HIV/AIDS as an interference with its sovereignty to (not) provide for the welfare of its citizens (Sehovic 2014; see also Beisheim, Janetschek, and Sarre 2014). We come back to this ambivalent role of residual statehood in the concluding Chapter 8.

Last but not least, the necessity of residual statehood to make non-state governance effective is likely to vary depending on the issue-area and on task complexity. For instance, if no actor holds a monopoly of the use of force and violent orders emerge, it is unlikely that any but the most simple governance tasks can be accomplished (see Schäferhoff 2014a for public health in Somalia).

In sum, the more the institutional design is functional for the governance task at hand, the more inclusive and transparent the governance institutions, and the more the residual state capacity can be brought to bear to enhance governance, the more effective governance is likely to be in areas of limited statehood.

LEGITIMACY

There is a huge literature on the legitimacy of transnational governance (see e.g. Benz and Papadopoulos 2006; Clark 2005; Dingwerth 2007; Hurd 1999; March and Olsen 1998; Risse 2006; Schmelzle 2011; Zürn 2000).[10] However, this literature often does not distinguish adequately between *empirical* and *normative* legitimacy (see above on these concepts). We concentrate on empirical legitimacy and argue that the social acceptance of the governors and of the governance institutions by those being governed constitutes a crucial condition for the effectiveness of governance itself. It is rather unlikely that effective governance can be achieved if the governors do not enjoy a "license to govern" and if the governance institutions are not considered legitimate by the population or the local elites. As argued above, diffuse support for the governors and the governance institutions leads to voluntary compliance with costly rules and to cooperative attitudes with regard to service delivery. Both are crucial in ALS. Thus, empirical legitimacy of the governors and the governance institutions can compensate for the lack of enforcement capacity in ALS, an argument that has been made by Hurd for the international system (Hurd 1999). As to rule compliance, legitimacy instills a logic of appropriateness according to which rule-following is the "right thing to do," irrespective of whether the rules are enforced or not. As to service delivery, it is hard to see how even rather simple tasks, such as child immunization, or the distribution of anti-malaria bednets, let alone more complex endeavors, such as education, can be accomplished if the governed refuse to cooperate, because they consider the governors and their institutions illegitimate.

Who bestows legitimacy on whom? Who are the relevant "legitimacy audiences" (Zaum 2013) for different actors? The relative importance of legitimating actors in the respective area of limited statehood – national or local, elites or ordinary citizens – depends on the activity involved and on domestic political structures. For instance, service provision by

---

[10] For the following see also Krasner and Risse 2014a.

external actors – whether state or non-state – will be impossible unless local actors regard these activities as legitimate. For activities that target national governance structures, legitimation by local actors will be less important than validation from national political elites. Particularly external actors face daunting legitimacy requirements. If they are being considered alien or if they do not align with domestic or local actors including elites, they are very unlikely to gain enough social acceptance to be able to accomplish anything (Schmelzle and Stollenwerk 2018). This explains why governance by imposition from the outside – e.g. military interventions or trusteeships – is very unlikely to be effective because of the legitimacy requirements it faces (Lake, D. 2018; Lake and Farris 2014). External interveners have to rely almost exclusively on output legitimacy or on expectations about it (see below). They might be effective governors, if the recipients anticipate them as being likely to be effective. Otherwise, they run into resistance, as the international community has learned the hard way in Afghanistan and other places.

To illustrate our point: we expect peace-keeping missions that require the consent of the national governments (e.g. UN Chapter 6 missions)[11] to be more effective than missions that occur irrespective of the agreement of the national authorities (e.g. UN Chapter 7 missions, see Doyle and Sambanis 2006; Matanock 2014). The same holds true for so-called Governance Delegation Agreements (GDAs) whereby national or local state authorities contract out governance tasks to external actors, thereby providing them with some initial input legitimacy (Matanock 2014). The difference between "Chapter 6" and "Chapter 7" missions also points to the difference between international and domestic legitimation. International legitimation is irrelevant for governance effectiveness unless it is taken up and used in local or domestic discourses. To put it bluntly: whether the UN Security Council approves an intervention in the "Westphalian" sovereignty of an ALS is only relevant for its effectiveness as long as domestic actors care about a UN mandate.

Companies as governors also face their own legitimacy problems (see above). As for-profit organizations, they have to convince their target audiences that their contributions to governance are motivated toward the common good rather than constituting a more subtle way to maximize their profit. One way to do this is to rely on certification schemes by third parties, including (I)NGOs (e.g. the Forest Stewardship Council as a certification scheme for the wood-working industry, see Esguerra 2014).

---

[11] The reference is here to the respective chapter of the UN Charter.

In sum, empirical legitimacy appears to be a powerful explanation for governance effectiveness in ALS, precisely because it will lead to rule-following and cooperation with the governors based on the logic appropriateness rather than some cost-benefit calculations. Diffuse support and bestowing the "right to rule" to governance actors and institutions are probably the single most important driver of effective governance in ALS. As a result, the more the governors as well as the governance arrangements are considered legitimate by domestic as well as local elites and populations, the less statehood by (state) institutions is required to enforce governance and make it effective. Moreover, as we will elaborate below, there are likely to be interactions effects between legitimacy and effectiveness (via output legitimacy), institutions (via input and through-put legitimacy), and social trust (as a source of legitimacy).

SOCIAL TRUST

Social trust does not only affect the preparedness of actors to govern, it is also likely to result in greater effectiveness. Yet, the three types of social trust – personalized, group-based/particularistic, and generalized trust – discussed above will have different effects on the problem-solving capacity of governance (see Börzel and Risse 2016; Draude, Hölck, and Stolle 2018, for the following).

Personalized Trust Personalized trust has been found to be a functional equivalent for weak or dysfunctional state institutions in ALS and, thus, helps to explain the governance puzzle. Neighborhoods and local communities where people know each other often exhibit personalized trust. It contributes to the effective provision of governance in the absence of functioning state institutions in at least two ways. To begin with and as mentioned above, personalized trust enables actors to solve local collective action problems (Gambetta 1988b). Elinor Ostrom demonstrated through experimental designs that local communities where members trust each other are likely to govern themselves and to produce common pool resources without having to refer to strong institutions with their monitoring and sanctioning mechanisms (Ostrom 1990, 2002; Ostrom, Gardner, and Walker 1994). Personalized trust, thus, enhances the action capacity of local communities. Besides providing collective goods and services themselves, community-based organizations often also faciliate governance by external actors. MNCs and transnational MSPs equally rely on neighborhood or traditional communities to tap into local resources and build local ownership (Börzel and Hönke 2012; Liese, Janetschek, and Sarre 2014, 153–155).

Finally, the "shadow of the community" based on mutual respect and shared norms tends to exhibit strong social monitoring and sanctioning capacities, which serve to ensure cooperation and compliance with costly rules. The quest for social approval and the threat of social exclusion from the community serve as a powerful incentive to comply with the rules and to provide collective goods. One should not underestimate the sanctioning potential of these informal institutions – ranging from social ostracism to physical punishment (Hönke and Börzel 2014; Paller 2014; see also Boix 2015, ch. 1, on the sanctioning capacities of stateless societies).

Thus, the presence or absence of local trust accounts for parts of the variation in effective governance in areas of limited statehood. At the same time, its governance potential or "collective efficacy" (Sampson, Raudenbush, and Earls 1997) can be captured by internal power struggles and can also be turned against external governors (Börzel and Hönke 2012; Hönke 2013b; Liese, Janetschek, and Sarre 2014). Moreover, personalized trust remains limited to neighborhoods and local communities (Sampson 2012; Sutherland, Ian, and Jackso 2013). Collective goods and service provison more often than not requires governance beyond the neighborhood. Not only are local resources too limited to provide complex collective goods and services, such as health, education, and infrastructure. Many collective goods problems, such as environmental pollution or pandemics, have to be addressed on a larger scale to be effectively solved.

Group-Based or Particularistic Trust Scaling-up governance in the absence of functional and effective state institutions requires the extension of trust to people not personally known. A first step is trusting strangers because they are members of the same social group based on kinship, a shared ethnic background, faith, values, common history or language, geographical proximity, or behavioral similarities (Brewer 1981; Tanis and Postmes 2005). This group-based or particularistic trust may generate what Putnam calls "bonding social capital" (Putnam 2000, 22). It enables groups to cooperate more effectively and to provide collective goods and services, at least for group members and way beyond personalized networks.

However, group-based or particularistic trust can also hinder the upscaling of governance. First, social groups do not have to use their trust to engage in governance. Criminal or terrorist networks, such as the mafia, Hamas or Hisbollah, are built on relationships of trust, too (Portes 1998, 15–18; Stolle and Rochon 1998). Second, if a group only encompasses parts of a society, group-based trust produces at best club goods whose consumption is confined to the members of the group. At worst, it undermines rather than advances governance altogher (Putnam 1995, 665). "Groups segregated by class, occupation or ethnicity may build cooperation and trust only among group members, perhaps even encouraging distrust between members and non-members" (Knack 2003, 343; Stolle and Rochon 1998). Group-based trust might foster in-group favoritism (Hammond and Axelrod 2006) and reinforce in-group/outgroup divisions. This is particularly relevant for areas of limited statehood, which are often socially heterogeneous post-conflict societies with deep cultural- or identity-based cleavages. In addition, ethnically partitioned groups that are split across borders (as is the case resulting from many of the former colonial borders in Sub-Saharan Africa) are likely to be associated with transnational civil wars (Michalopoulos and Papaioannou 2016).

Generalized Trust Upscaling governance in areas of limited statehood beyond "islands of excellence" (Krasner 2018) in local communities ultimately requires some degree of *generalized trust* in "imagined communities" (Anderson 1991). Generalized trust is necessary for governance to function in ALS beyond local communities. People who trust each other irrespective of personal relationships, shared kinship, or common religious beliefs are prepared to pay a price for their loyalty (e.g. taxes), to cooperate with the governance institutions, and to comply with costly rules (Draude, Hölck, and Stolle 2018; Putnam 1993, 2000; Rothstein and Stolle 2003).

How is generalized trust possible in ALS characterized by social and cultural heterogeneity and strong cleavages? We suggest two causal mechanisms, one for the generalization of group-based trust through the inclusiveness of social identities and the other for the building of generalized trust through the impartiality of institutions.

First, whether or not group-based trust leads to generalized trust, furthering better governance and the provision of public goods and services, in ALS and beyond depends crucially on the social construction of the group identity itself. According to Social Identity Theory, people who share a strong sense of group identity cooperate more within their group than with outsiders (Tajfel 1974). Group identities can be more or less inclusive and accommodating to strangers. The more inclusive a group identity is, the more easily it can be extended to encompass other groups. Moreover, the number of groups is crucial with which individuals identify in heterogeneous societies. Self-categorization theory tells us that individuals naturally identify with several social groups holding multiple identities (Abrams and Hogg 1990; Turner 1987).

These identity categories can be nested or blended into each other (I can identify with my village, my district, and my nation); they can also be cross-cutting or overlapping (e.g. gender identities and ethnic identifications; see Brewer 2001; Herrmann and Brewer 2004). Once in-group trust is built, it makes the generalization of trust more likely when combined with inclusive identities, which allow for the emergence of multiple, overlapping communities: "The more identity-categories overlap in the positive cooperation experience, the easier the transfer of trust to society at large" (Stolle 2002, 405). Cross-cutting cleavages can, thus, moderate the harmful effect of social fragmentation and diversity (Buzasi 2014; Dunning and Harrison 2010; cf. Coser 1956).

Second, where lasting cultural patterns of social interaction, or voluntary associations and networks of civic engagement, are absent, social capital formation has to rely on formal political, administrative, and legal institutions (Braithwaite and Levi 1998; Hartmann 2011; Herreros 2012; Levi and Stoker 2000; Rothstein and Stolle 2008b). Institutionalist approaches to social capital center on "government institutions and policies" (Rothstein and Stolle 2008a, 279) rather than the civil society as a source of social capital generation. State institutions foster trust in others by being perceived as efficient, fair, and impartial (Knight 2001; Freitag and Bühlmann 2009; Rothstein and Stolle 2008b). Rothstein and Stolle argue that political, legal, and administrative institutions that are in charge of implementing government policies are most "important for the creation, nurturing and maintenance of generalized trust" (Rothstein and Stolle 2008a, 283). More precisely, the local practices of administrative or executive agents matter. The practices of local police, judges, teachers, or doctors signal to people the moral standards of society. If they perform their governance functions effectively and impartially, people will infer from their experience to the behavior of others thereby developing generalized trust.

At this point, the inclusiveness of governance institutions emphasized by Acemoglu and Robinson becomes crucial (Acemoglu and Robinson 2012; see above). The more governance services are provided in an impartial, transparent, and procedurally fair way, the more they help generating and maintaining generalized trust as an enabling condition for the up-scaling of governance – even in the absence of functioning state institutions. In other words, there seems to be a causal pathway from the perception of inclusive and impartial institutions to the emergence of generalized trust as a major factor for enhancing effective governance.

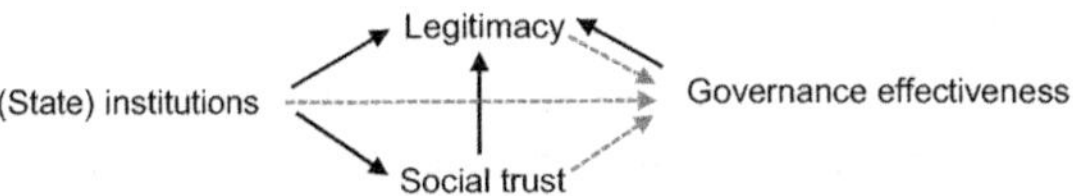

Figure 3.3 Institutions, legitimacy, trust, and effectiveness

ENDOGENIZING LEGITIMACY: INDIRECT EFFECTS, FEEDBACK
LOOPS, AND OTHER SOURCES

So far, we have argued that the institutional setting of the governance
arrangements, the legitimacy of the governors and the governance institutions, as well as the social trust between governors and the governed,
each have an independent effect on governance effectiveness.
Accordingly, the three factors can not only reinforce and support each
other but also substitute for each other. The more legitimate the governors and the stronger the social trust relations within (local) communities,
the less demanding are the necessary institutional monitoring and sanctioning capacities to ensure governance effectiveness. The opposite, of
course, also holds but is less relevant in areas of limited statehood, which
are defined by the weakness or absence of central enforcement authorities. Traditional leaders and companies therefore often rely on relationships of social trust and their social acceptance in their relevant
communities, to overcome collective action problems in the provision
of collective goods and services.

Institutions as a Source of Legitimacy Since legitimacy plays a key
role for governance effectiveness, we seek to endogenize it in our
framework. Our discussion so far has identified an indirect effect of
institutions on governance effectiveness as a source of legitimacy as
well as a feedback loop from governance effectiveness to legitimacy
marked by the straight black arrows in Figure 3.3 (the grey dotted
arrows indicate the independent effects of institutions, legitimacy, trust
on governance effectiveness).

Input as well as *throughput legitimacy* can be generated by designing
inclusive and impartial governance institutions. The development community uses the terms "ownership" or "stakeholder" principles (Fransen
and Kolk 2007; Fukuda-Parr and Lopes 2013; Theisohn and Lopes
2013). In many cases, however, "ownership" is implemented as a top-
down socialization process by which domestic or local elites are supposed
to accept externally derived governance arrangements (Booth 2012;
Sjöstedt 2013; von Billerbeck 2015). Local "ownership" then gives rise

to various adaptation and resistance processes in the translation from the "global" to the "local" level. As argued above, external actors are more likely to enjoy input legitimacy and, hence, to be effective if they are operating through inclusive institutional arrangements that were created through contracting rather than imposition. Contracts are voluntary and will only be signed if all parties perceive themselves to be better off. The negotiated delegation of "Westphalian sovereignty" to external actors is rare in areas of limited statehood. However, such Governance Delegation Agreements are likely to be more legitimate and, thus, more effective than trusteeships or protectorates, which are externally imposed (Matanock 2014; on the latter see Lake, D. 2016, 2018).

Inclusive institutions in ALS often face the problem of reaching out to all (that consider themselves to be) the owners of a governance arrangement. Even if they do, this may impair their performance. MSPs often compromise on inclusiveness because of the pressure they face from donor organizations to produce timely and effective results (Beisheim and Liese 2014b). Throughput legitimacy may compensate at least to some extent for weak input legitimacy as efficient and impartial procedures do not require the possibility for all relevant actors to participate in the decision-making. Moreover, procedural fairness is conducive to generalized trust, which, in turn, strengthens the legitimacy of governors and governance institutions. This points to social trust as a source of legitimacy. The more governors – such as tribal or religious leaders – are embedded and firmly integrated in their communities, the more the ensuing relationships of trust are likely to generate social acceptance and the "right to rule" to these governors.

Effectiveness as a Source of Legitimacy Since output legitimacy is based on performance, there is a feedback loop from governance effectiveness to legitimacy. This feedback mechanism works through the perception of effectiveness by those being governed, i.e., the people. The more they perceive governors or governance institutions to deliver the desired collective goods and services, the more this perceived effectiveness is likely to generate (output) legitimacy as well as social trust (Hutchison and Johnson 2011, 2017; for a more skeptical view see McLoughlin 2015). To avoid circular reasoning, we consider output legitimacy with regard to two processes: On the one hand, local or domestic actors and communities might consider governors as legitimate in anticipation of their performance. On the other hand, a virtuous circle might evolve over time in which the initial performance meets the expectations of local communities, which then increases the governance legitimacy and, hence, its effectiveness (see Schmelzle and Stollenwerk

2018 for a detailed analysis; see also Stollenwerk 2018c). Here, governance effectiveness feeds back into legitimacy, as we discuss further in Chapters 5–7. Of course, output legitimacy relies heavily on perceptions of governance performance. If the governors do not deliver what is expected from them, their social acceptance will suffer and a vicious circle is likely to develop, as the external interveners learned the hard way in Afghanistan (Koehler and Gosztonyi 2014; Stollenwerk 2018b; see also Chapter 5).

Other Sources of Legitimacy There are sources of legitimacy, which are outside our framework as they relate to ascribed properties of the governors themselves. Some of these sources are rather peculiar for areas of limited statehood, while others are more widespread. *Moral* or *knowledge-based* (epistemic) authority induces legitimacy, insofar as the governed accept governors as holders of particular moral values or normative beliefs and/or as sources of particular knowledge and causal beliefs. For instance, (I)NGOs as governors in ALS usually claim moral as well as knowledge-based (epistemic) authority and, if they are perceived as such, they are likely to be effective in providing goods and services (Murdie 2014; Murdie and Hicks 2013; Lake, M. 2018). The same holds true for religious leaders with claims to moral authority, particularly in areas with strong religious communities. Last but not least, what Weber called "*traditional*" authority (Weber 1978 [1922]) is widespread in many ALS. Local chiefs and tribal leaders can be very effective governors, precisely because their legitimacy derives from group-based, often ethnic identities (Baldwin 2016; Förster and Koechlin 2018). Once again, Somaliland is a case in point (Kaplan 2008; Renders and Terlinden 2010; Richards 2014).

Conclusions

This chapter has developed a theoretical framework to explain the "governance puzzle" outlined in Chapter 1 of this book. Such a framework must account for, first, the motivation of actors to contribute to governance under conditions of limited statehood, and, second, for the differences in effective governance in terms of rule-making and service provision.

We have argued that the three main approaches to explain development – modernization theory, statist institutionalism, and inclusive institutionalism – are of only limited value to explain our puzzle, for two reasons. First, they tend to be rather Western- or Euro-centric, assuming that it is the modern European or Western state that constitutes the model of development. While modernization theory is explicitly teleological, the other two approaches at least concede that "Denmark" as the exemplary consolidated and inclusionary state is still the exception. Second, all three approaches are state-centric in the sense that they take consolidated statehood in the (Weberian) sense discussed in Chapter 2 as a pre-condition for effective development and governance. As a result, areas of limited statehood appear to be doomed almost by definition.

In contrast, we argue that governance under anarchy can work under certain conditions. Three factors and their combination account for both the motivation of (self-interested and utility-maximizing) actors to become governors and for the effectiveness of their governance contributions:

- the design and make-up of formal governance institutions, including their functionality, inclusiveness, and transparency as well as the presence or absence of remaining statehood;
- the empirical legitimacy of both the governors and the governance institutions in terms of diffuse support conveying the "right to govern" by the governed;
- social trust among the people in ALS, such as personalized trust in local communities, group-based or particularistic trust grounded in collectively shared social identities, and generalized trust among strangers.

The following chapters adopt this framework to illustrate our arguments empirically. We start with a discussion of how and why various actors – state and non-state, domestic/local as well as inter-/transnational – become governors and of the modes of governance in ALS, hierarchical as well as non-hierarchical.

Part II

Governance in Areas of Limited Statehood: Empirical Evidence

4 Who, Why, and How? Actors and Modes of Governance

This and the following chapters provide the empirical evidence for the concepts and theories discussed in the previous chapters. Chapter 4 examines the various actors who become "governors" in areas of limited statehood, at least temporarily. We look at external state actors, such as international and regional organizations (IOs and ROs) as well as foreign governments, at multi-stakeholder partnerships (MSPs) and the not-for-profit sector, at the role of business, and at "traditional" authorities, including tribal leaders and non-state justice institutions, as well as the conditions under which violent non-state actors (VNSA) assume governance roles. In doing so, we investigate the reasons and motivations of these actors to become "governors," drawing on the arguments developed in Chapter 3. We also explore the modes of governance employed by these actors in ALS (see Chapter 2). Our analysis demonstrates that hierarchical modes of steering are not necessarily absent just because central state institutions are weak. However, the various non-hierarchical modes of governance feature prominently, of which we pay particular attention to deliberation.

External State Actors: International and Regional Organizations, Development Agencies, and Foreign Governments

Governance in ALS regularly involves international state actors providing basic services, but also rules and decision-making procedures. This includes foreign governments and development agencies, as well as IOs, such as the UN and its sub-organizations, but also regional organizations (ROs; overview in Lederer 2018). The German Society for International Cooperation (GIZ; *Gesellschaft für Internationale Zusammenarbeit*), for instance, describes its "products and services" as "management services, rural development, sustainable infrastructure, security, reconstruction and peace, social development, governance and democracy, environment and climate change, as well as economic development and employment."[1] This self-understanding as governance provider is rather typical for the various development agencies. Rather than merely providing governance services, they increasingly engage in supporting the (re-) building of governance institutions, developing governance programs, and adjusting their budget allocation accordingly (Lederer 2018).

Development cooperation as governance provision is by no means restricted to the Global North, but includes also many Southern states and emerging economies, including China, India, Brazil, or South Africa (Gray and Gills 2016). There exists even an organization of self-described fragile and post-conflict states engaged in fostering governance, the G7+.[2] Moreover, the majority of UN peace-keeping troops come from the Global South. For some, South-South cooperation, however, is less about governance promotion than about resource extraction (Burges 2014; Hackenesch 2018; McEwan and Mawdsley 2012).

As to IOs and ROs as governors, some constitute so called "general purpose organizations" that offer a multitude of governance services to their members and other countries. Others concentrate on specific governance tasks, such as health, environment, or security (Lenz et al. 2015). The UN or the EU are general purpose organizations engaging in governance in areas of limited statehood. So are many ROs in the Global South, which have considerably broadened the scope of their governance mandate since the end of the Cold War (Börzel 2013; Börzel and van Hüllen 2015a). The World Health Organization (WHO), the Artic Council, or the Food and Agricultural Organization (FAO) concentrate on specific tasks or issue-areas. Last but not least, some IOs and ROs provide meta-governance with regard to ALS, such as the Development Assistance Committee (DAC) of the Organization for Economic Cooperation and Development (OECD), and the EU in the area of democracy and the rule of law (Berger and Lake 2018).

Foreign governments have been prominent governors in ALS, too. A lot of scholarly attention in this context is devoted to (military) interventions for humanitarian or state-building purposes (overviews in Fearon and Laitin 2004; Finnemore 2003; Krasner 2004; Lake, D. 2016, 2018). In these cases, foreign governments directly interfere in the "Westphalian sovereignty" of states with ALS – with or without a UN mandate. However, the attention devoted to military interventions for humanitarian purposes and/or to combat terrorism overlooks that the vast majority of these missions occur with the explicit consent of host

---

[1] See www.giz.de/en/ourservices/range_of_services.html, last access August 25, 2017.
[2] www.g7plus.org/en, last access August 25, 2017.

governments. Moreover, most military interventions are not only complemented by diplomatic missions but by comprehensive development cooperation (Mosse 2011). As a result, defense and foreign ministries, as well as development agencies, do not monopolize governance provision in ALS. Finance ministries and central banks, as well as sector-specific government departments, such as environment, energy, and even home affairs, have increasingly become involved (Lederer 2018).

In other words, "shared sovereignty" is an empirical reality in many states that lack the ability to enforce central decisions (Krasner 2004). The division and distribution of political authority across transnational, national, and local levels does not only characterize modern statehood in the OECD world (Leibfried and Zürn 2005; Slaughter 2004). "Multi-level governance" prevails in areas of limited statehood in the sense that external actors directly participate in governance. The enormous literature on multi-level governance that predominantly deals with the EU has not yet realized that similar phenomena are all too common in the Global South (but see Beisheim et al. 2011b; on multi-level governance in the Western context see e.g. Benz 2004b; Hooghe and Marks 2001, 2003; Kohler-Koch and Eising 1999).

Why do these external state actors engage in governance in areas of limited statehood in the first place?

Why Govern? Humanitarianism, the Responsibility to Protect, and the Threat of "Failed Statehood"

"We live in a world in which the international community vigorously protects and promotes the quality of human life" (Barnett 2017b, 1). For many governments, service delivery IOs and ROs, as well as development agencies (see the quote from GIZ above), governance provision is constitutive and part of the external state actors' mandate. In this context, humanitarian assistance as well as development aid appear to be part of a global script embodying a particular logic of appropriateness, as Lumsdaine already pointed out many years ago (Lumsdaine 1993). It is simply the right and legitimate thing to do to prevent human suffering and this moral principle extends beyond one's own national borders. IOs and ROs increasingly follow the global script by setting and increasingly also enforcing standards for effective and legitimate governance in their member states (Börzel and van Hüllen 2015b). The same holds true for the norm of "humanitarian intervention" legitimizing the use of force even against the will of the host government (Finnemore 2003). This norm has recently been enshrined in the – albeit heavily contested – principle of the "Responsibility to Protect" (R2P). Accordingly, the international community has the responsibility (not the duty) to protect civilian populations in cases of massive human rights violations, humanitarian crises, and civil wars, if and when the national government is unwilling or incapable of ensuring the survival its own people (for a critical discussion see Bellamy 2011; Krieger 2018). Most recently and particularly after the intervention in Libya in 2011, the R2P has become ever more contested internationally, since its proponents – particularly in the West – have been accused of using double standards and of using R2P as a pretext for more mundane purposes, including economic interests (Bazirake and Bukuluki 2015; Pingeot and Obenland 2014).

Foreign governments, development agencies, IOs, and ROs do not only have humanitarian reasons why they become governors in ALS. There are also many short- and long-term economic and geopolitical interests at work here (Dreher, Lang, and Ziaja 2018; Hoeffler and Outram 2011; Pugh 2005). For centuries, states have intervened in each other's internal affairs for a variety of reasons (Krasner 1999) – from securing access to economic and other resources to preventing hostile take-overs of allied governments. Foreign aid has been given to protect security alliances and friendly regimes as well as to gain access to markets. Moreover, IOs often become vehicles of member states using them to pursue their own interests (Lall 2017).

More recently and particularly in the post-9/11 environment, ALS have been increasingly perceived as presenting direct security threats to consolidated states in the Global North, but also beyond (Paris 2011; Rotberg 2004a). Governance breakdowns pose the "risk of anarchy" (see Chapter 3) in the sense of producing negative externalities for even far-away countries – including harboring transnational terrorist groups, preventing access to crucial economic resources, or initiating refugee and migration flows. As the 2017 German Government Guidelines for Preventing Crises, Managing Conflicts, and Building Peace put it:

There is rarely a crisis, which we do not feel at some point in Europe and Germany. Civil wars, ethnic and religious conflicts, repression and violation of human rights, but also poverty, lack of perspectives, as well as lack of access to natural resources prepare a breeding ground for ideological radicalization and terrorism. (our translation, Die Bundesregierung 2017, 5)

The interconnectedness of the governance problematique in areas of limited statehood with perceived security threats in the Global North has given rise to the so-called failed/fragile state discourse (see Chapter 2), which then served as a justification for external actors providing governance in ALS, including military interventions. As we have pointed out above (see Chapter 3), this discourse – including its reverberations in the scholarly literature (e.g. Fukuyama 2004; Messner et al. 2015; Rotberg 2003, 2004b; Schneckener 2004) – uses Western consolidated statehood as the standard model of political and economic development (for a thorough critique see Woodward 2017). State-building interventions and institutional transfers in war-torn ALS then became standard answers to the governance problem (for a critical analysis see Lake, D. 2018; Lake and Farris 2014) thereby legitimizing all sorts of interventions, including military solutions.

In Chapter 5, we discuss in more detail why state-building has mostly failed. Suffice it to mention here that the risks emanating from "failed/ fragile states" have provided a powerful incentive for consolidated states of the Global North as well as a variety of international and regional organizations to engage in state-building governance in ALS. The EU, for instance, has developed the European Neighbourhood Policy as a comprehensive policy framework to promote peace, stability, and prosperity in its eastern and southern neighborhood by seeking to export its governance institutions (Börzel 2016). The rise and spread of Islamist terrorism and the European migration crisis in 2015 have fueled the securitization of the development discourse by transforming development and governance export into a national security issue for the Western world (on securitization in general see Buzan, Waever, and Wilde 1998). Limited statehood does not only challenge development in the Global South. Governance breakdowns and civil wars in ALS threaten the security of the Global North, too.

At the same time, as Lee points out (Lee 2018), states neighboring ALS do not only have benign motivations to contribute to governance in order to prevent governance breakdown and violent conflict. They often exploit state weakness for their own purposes. Lee shows that rivaling neighbors, rather than contributing to governance, often have a significant effect on weakening the state even further and intervening in its "Westphalian sovereignty." Russian intrusions in the Ukraine, Moldovia, Georgia, and elsewhere serve as a prominent example. We come back to the ambivalent role of states in Chapter 8. In the following, we primarily focus on external state governors with the intention of improving governance in ALS.

How Govern? Interventions, Delegation Agreements, Conditionality, and Socialization

External state actors have the entire range of modes of governance at their disposal when attempting to provide governance in areas of limited statehood – from the use of force and hierarchical steering to non-hierarchical modes, including persuasion and deliberation.

As argued above, the state-building paradigm and various perceived security threats emanating from war-torn ALS have given rise to various (military) interventions in ALS – from the 1991 US-backed UN intervention in Somalia to the interventions in the Western Balkans following the post–Yugoslav wars of the early-to-mid 1990s, the 2001 intervention in Afghanistan and in Iraq in 2003, up to 2011 when R2P was invoked by the UN Security Council to legitimize a regime-changing intervention in Libya (for a critical discussion see Lake, D. 2016). With a few exceptions (e.g. Kosovo 1999 and Iraq 2003), these interventions were legitimized by Chapter 7 ("threat to international peace and security") resolutions of the UN Security Council (e.g. Somalia, most post-Yugoslav interventions, Afghanistan, Haiti, and Libya). Most cases involved varying "coalitions of the willing" (Somalia, Afghanistan, Iraq, Libya, and others), while others were carried out by international or regional organizations, such as NATO (Bosnia-Herzegovina and Kosovo) or the Economic Community of West African States (ECOWAS) under the leadership of Nigeria (Hartmann and Striebinger 2015). What these cases have in common is that the interveners intruded in the "Westphalian sovereignty" of states without the consent of their national governments, at least temporarily, and then tried to establish a monopoly of the use of force. In addition, major state-building interventions – e.g. Bosnia-Herzegovina, Kosovo, Afghanistan, and Iraq – established some sort of trusteeships by the UN, NATO, and other IOs and ROs (e.g. the EU in the post-Yugoslav cases).

While a lot has been written about these hierarchical interventions (overview in Lake, D. 2016, 2018), they are the exception rather than the rule. Most interferences with "Westphalian" sovereignty occur with the explicit consent of the host states. This concerns, for example, the vast majority of the 14 UN peace-keeping missions operational in 2017 under Chapter 6 of the UN Charter.[3] The same holds true for the 18 peace operations led by the EU in 2018, as well as the various missions conducted by regional organizations, particularly in Africa.[4] Such hierarchical external interferences in the domestic authority structures of weak states often take the form of so-called Governance Delegation Agreements (GDA) whereby weak states in ALS delegate hierarchical rule to external actors (Matanock 2014). In 2003, Australia

---

[3] https://peacekeeping.un.org/en/where-we-operate, last access July 31, 2019.

[4] www.zif-berlin.org/fileadmin/uploads/analyse/dokumente/veroeffentlichungen/ZIF_World_Map_Peace_Operations_2018.pdf, last access July 31, 2019.

led the Regional Assistance Mission to the Solomon Islands (RAMSI) in order to restore peace and the rule of law on these islands in the Southern Pacific. More than 2,000 foreign troops, police officers, and other personnel took over essential governance functions upon request by the state authorities of the Solomon Islands. While RAMSI represents a rather comprehensive delegation agreement, the International Commission Against Impunity in Guatemala (CICIG) has been a more limited example of consent-based external interference in the judicial system of Guatemala. In 2006, the UN and Guatemala signed an agreement that set up and empowered the CICIG as an independent body to investigate and prosecute sensitive and difficult cases (Maihold 2016; Nyberg 2015). GDAs are peculiar insofar as host governments voluntarily delegate to external actors the authority to govern hierarchically, even though – or precisely because – they lack the ability to enforce the agreements. In order to (re-)gain their domestic sovereignty, governments in ALS use their international sovereignty to compromise their "Westphalian sovereignty."

Last but not least, as explained above (Chapter 3), foreign governments in consolidated states often contribute indirectly to governance in ALS insofar as they are able to cast an "external shadow of hierarchy" thereby inducing non-state actors, such as companies, to become governors in their own right.

While external (state) actors sometimes intervene forcefully and hierarchically in ALS, most governance contributions by external state actors occur in non-hierarchical fashion – from the EU's attempts to foster good governance and anti-corruption policies in its eastern neighborhood (Börzel and Schimmelfennig 2017; Börzel and Van Hüllen 2014) to international organizations and development agencies in the Global South (Lederer 2018). Some African regional organizations have the authority to deploy military force in case of a coup d'état against a democratically elected government (Hartmann and Striebinger 2015). But they mostly rely on financial and technical assistance, as well as learning and persuasion, to make their member states adhere to mutually agreed governance standards. Even diplomatic and financial sanctions are hardly used (Börzel and van Hüllen 2015a).

First, IOs, foreign aid agencies, and external state actors usually enter contractual relationships with host governments to perform specific governance tasks. These are often cases of delegated authority, particularly with regard to service provision in security sector reform (Schröder 2018), public health (Holzscheiter 2018), education (Ellersiek 2018), food security (Liese 2018), the environment (Hamann, Hönke, and O'Riordan 2018), and elsewhere. Given the reliance of host governments on external governance assistance, the terms of delegation are negotiated rather than imposed.

Second, external governors use conditionality to induce state and non-state actors in ALS to engage in governance. The World Bank and the International Monetary Fund make loans and grants conditional on structural adjustments to improve governance (Santiso 2001). So do most donors of development aid (Stokke 2013), China being a prominent exception (Hackenesch 2018). The EU, the Council of Europe, and NATO use closer cooperation and membership to reward improvements in effective and democratic governance (Börzel and van Hüllen 2015a).

Third, many external actors simultaneously make use of socialization efforts through means of persuasion and communication in order to increase local ownership and "buy in" into governance efforts (see e.g. Schröder, Chappuis, and Kocak 2013 on security sector reform, Börzel and van Hüllen 2014, 2015a on governance export by regional organizations, and Finnemore 1993 on IOs as teachers of norms). Even the EU, which heavily relies on conditionality to induce governance reforms in post-conflict areas, such as the Western Balkan states, supports its efforts through persuasion and by emphasizing that human rights, democracy, and the rule of law are constitutive for the EU and its member states (Börzel and Grimm 2018; Elbasani 2013).

In sum, external state-actors – from foreign governments to development agencies, IOs and ROs – are motivated by the "shadow of anarchy" (Chapter 3) and other instrumental reasons (e.g. economic or geopolitical interests) as well as by the logic of appropriateness and by humanitarian reasons to provide governance in areas of limited statehood. At the same time, they employ the entire spectrum of modes of governance – from hierarchical and intrusive interventions, to non-hierarchical coordination including conditionality and persuasion as well as socialization. We assess their effectiveness in Chapters 5–7. Suffice it to state here that there seems to be a negative correlation between the degree of coercion and intrusiveness into the "Westphalian sovereignty" of states, on the one hand, and the governance effectiveness (let alone legitimacy on the ground), on the other. In contrast, less intrusive and non-hierarchical modes of governance appear to be less costly as well as more effective and legitimate. We now turn to the vast not-for-profit sector.

Not-for-Profit Non-State Actors: (I)NGOs and Multi-Stakeholder Partnerships (MSPs)

The not-for-profit sector is heavily involved in governance in areas of limited statehood. It is made up by non-state actors – both transnational and national/domestic – whose sole purpose is to engage in both rule-making and service delivery. It is hard to estimate the size of the sector with regard to governance. Beisheim et al. report that ca. US$19 billion, i.e., more than 17 percent of official bilateral development aid of the OECD members of the Development Assistance Committee (DAC), was channeled through so-called civil society organizations, mostly (I) NGOs (see Beisheim, Ellersiek, and Lorch 2018, 211). The world's largest (and Christian) development INGO, World Vision International, had an annual budget of US$2.8 billion in 2011, which is bigger than the foreign aid budget of 12 of the 23 DAC member states (according to Morton 2013, 333). Next to (I)NGOs, private foundations and charities engage in various governance activities. The largest of them, the Bill and Melinda Gates Foundation, spent US$3.4 billion in 2016 on global development and global health; this is only a little less than the annual budget of the World Health Organization (WHO), the largest IO in the public health sector.[5] The Aga Khan Development Network, another huge (Islamic) private development foundation, spends ca. US$950 million annually on development projects.[6]

Last but not least, MSPs have developed into important governors in ALS. Unlike (I)NGOs, foundations, and charities, MSPs consist of both state and non-state actors (Beisheim and Liese 2014b; Schäferhoff, Campe, and Kaan 2009). Prominent examples include the Global Fund to Fight AIDS, Tuberculosis, and Malaria (GF, see Schäferhoff 2014b), the Global Alliance for Improved Nutrition (GAIN, see Nishtar 2004), or the UN Global Compact (Mwangi, Rieth, and Schmitz 2013). Official Development Aid (ODA) projects involving MSPs totalled US $377 million in 2012. However, the Global Fund alone spends ca. US$4 billion a year on various public health projects, while the Global Alliance for Vaccines and Immunization (GAVI), another giant among the MSPs, spent ca. US$1.2 billion in 2018.[7] Since they combine the resources of private and public actors, MSPs have been hailed as a more effective means to reach international targets, such as the UN Sustainable Development Goals (Benner, Streck, and Witte 2003; Reinicke and Deng 2000; Witte and Reinicke 2005).

---

[5] www.gatesfoundation.org/Who-We-Are/Resources-and-Media/Annual-Reports/Annual-Report-2016, last access August 27, 2017. The WHO's approved program budget for 2016-2017 was ca. US$ 4.2 bln, according to www.who.int/about/finances-accountability/budget/PB2018-2019_en_web.pdf?ua=1, p. 5, last access August 22, 2019.

[6] According to www.akdn.org/frequently-asked-questions, last access July 31, 2019.

[7] According to www.theglobalfund.org/en/financials/, last access July 31, 2019. On GAVI, see www.gavi.org/results/disbursements/, last access August 22, 2019.

In sum, the not-for-profit sector of transnational and domestic/national non-state actors yields a considerable influence with regard to the provision of governance services in ALS. Its financial resources are compatible to those of state actors. Likewise, (I)NGOs and MSPs cover the entire spectrum of governance activities – from poverty reduction and service provision in health, education, environment, or energy to peace-building and security provision, to human rights and the rule of law (cf. Beisheim, Ellersiek, and Lorch 2018). But why do these actors engage in governance?

Why Govern? Mandate, Legitimacy, and Fundraising

The short answer to the "why"-question pertains to the very mandate of the not-for-profit sector, namely, that governance provision is their organizational purpose and institutional mandate (as in the case of many IOs and development agencies). However, while altruism, "other help," and an orientation toward the common good are constitutive for these actors and provide a crucial source of their legitimacy, this only consti-tutes part of the picture. First, altruism and paternalism are often two sides of the same coin, the latter defined as "the substitution of one actor's judgment for another's in order to improve the object's welfare, interests, and happiness" (Barnett 2017a, 316). In other words, the motivation to "do good" might result in the neglect of the right of the governed to self-determination (for a critical analysis see Barnett 2017c; see also Ladwig 2007). The Gates Foundation, for example, has been repeatedly accused of promoting a particular neoliberal ideology thereby neglecting the needs of the poor (see e.g. Curtis 2016). (I)NGOs have also faced criticism for promoting new forms of colonialism, being donor driven, focusing on low-hanging fruit, and neutralizing local dissent and resistance (Feldman 2003; Khan, Munir, and Willmott 2007; Merz 2012). The same holds true for MSPs, which are often described as fostering the interests of private business and Western donors (see e.g. Banerjee 2018; Brühl 2007; Bull and McNeill 2007; Khan, Munir, and Willmott 2007; Merz 2012; Utting and Zammit 2009).

Second, the logic of appropriateness driving the governance activities of the not-for-profit sector does not exclude self-interested behavior (Prakash and Gugerty 2010). To begin with, both the private and the public markets for financial resources to provide governance in ALS are limited. Many (I)NGOs, for example, are dependent on humanitarian aid as well as ODA from OECD countries and, thus, have to position themselves to acquire these resources (Ly 2012; Merz 2012). The same holds true for the market of private donations. (I)NGOs have to conduct extensive fund-raising campaigns in the Global North in order to be able to provide governance in the Global South. Their primary mandate to further the common good in ALS might be compromised by their need to acquire the necessary financial resources in the Global North.

Third, actors joining MSPs might equally be motivated by self-interest, such as the need to acquire resources, to increase their power in a policy field, or simply reputational concerns (Brown and Moore 2001; Selsky and Parker 2005). The Bill and Melinda Gates Foundation, for instance, used its considerable power to substantially influence the institutional design of GAVI, thereby overcoming the resistance of the WHO and of UNICEF, the two UN organizations working in this policy field (Beisheim, Liese, and Vosseler 2014, 114–118).

Fourth, the legitimacy of not-for-profit groups largely depends on their moral authority combined with claims to expert knowledge. At the same time, as mentioned above, some private foundations, (I)NGOs, and MSPs command substantial financial resources and are likely to wield quite some power, particularly in ALS with weak state authorities and, thus, limited capacities to regulate these non-state actors. Abuse of power is a distinct possibility, particularly when the mechanisms to hold non-profit actors accountable are also weak and marginalized interests are not represented (Raynolds 2014; Riisgaard 2009; Utting 2015a). A closely related problem concerns the question of inclusiveness and conditionality. NGOs and other non-state actors usually decide unilaterally which groups of people and which types of governance problems they want to address. This raises the question of the legitimate criteria non-state actors may apply for choosing between potential beneficiaries (Jacob, Ladwig, and Schmelzle 2018; Schmelzle 2015). Is it legitimate, for example, if religious NGOs primarily provide services to fellow members of their religion or make them conditional on participation in religious activities? It is certainly possible that the not-for-profit sector commits rights abuses or provides its governance services only selectively. However, we need to put these potentially negative externalities in perspective. For instance, (I)NGOs and MSPs should be compared with state actors, such as external governments and IOs, in order to provide fair assessments (on the latter see Heupel, Zürn, and Hirschmann 2017).

Fifth, while the "risk of anarchy," including the lack of effective state institutions, constitutes a major motivation for external state actors (see above) and for companies (see below) to engage in governance in ALS, the opposite appears to be the case for the "not for profit sector." A study of MSPs, for example, has shown that they are unlikely to be active in areas where the state has completely lost the monopoly of the use of force (Liese, Janetschek, and Sarre 2014, 139–142; see also Beisheim,

Ellersiek, and Lorch 2018). Even *Médecins Sans Frontières* (MSF) withdraw from war zones if the lives of their doctors and nurses are threatened. However, there is also a less benign motif for not engaging in areas where the state is completely absent: (I)NGOs and MSPs have to prove their effectiveness to their donors. As a result, they often aim for the lower hanging fruits engaging in ALS where service delivery is easier than in others (Beisheim, Liese, Janetschek, and Sarre 2014).

In sum and despite all these caveats, the primary motivation of not-for-profit actors, such as (I)NGOs and MSPs, is to contribute to governance and to provide crucial services in ALS that would otherwise not be delivered. As Büthe et al. have shown with regard to US (I)NGOs, the need of aid recipients is the single most important driver for aid allocation by private donors (Büthe, Major, and Souza 2012). Since limited statehood is seen as a major obstacle to development and seriously mitigates aid effectiveness, (I)NGOs' and MSPs' governance contributions go beyond mere service delivery. They also engage in the (re-) building of state institutions. At the same time, however, one cannot overlook self-interested motives such as the quest for (financial) resources and influence in a crowded policy field. Yet, there is a catch: once (I)NGOs and MSPs are caught in violating their constitutive norms and, e.g. become greedy with regard to resources, such resources can dry up rather quickly, with regard to both public and private donors. In other words, the – rather competitive – market for donations provides a powerful sanction mechanism against egoistic and too self-interested behavior by (I)NGOs and MSPs (for a discussion see Risse 2010b).

How Govern? Negotiation and Advocacy

Unlike other governors in ALS, (I)NGOs and MSPs have to rely almost exclusively on non-hierarchical modes of governance. They sometimes interfere with the "Westphalian sovereignty" of states by circumventing the (weak) central state authorities and dealing directly with local communities, as was the case in Somalia (Schäferhoff 2011, 2014). In most cases, however, and particularly with regard to MSPs involving external state-actors, they cannot act as governors without the at least implicit permission of central state authorities, as weak as these might be. Yet, this does not imply that, therefore, MSPs become hierarchical governors, even though they sometimes use the remaining central authority structure of the state to implement governance services.

Unfortunately, the existing empirical evidence is not sufficient to conclude firmly on the respective mix of incentive-based versus deliberative modes of governance. We can only infer rather than show that the widespread inclusion of local community leaders, brokers, and community-based organizations (CBOs) in the governance arrangements on the ground leads to more deliberation-based modes of communication.

(I)NGOs and MSPs are voluntary organizations with regard to membership and contributions (Anheier, Kaldor, and Glasius 2012; Hamann and Acutt 2003). Many of them embrace the "ownership" principle and, thus, the inclusion of primarily local communities in governance institutions for rule-making and service delivery (Beisheim and Dingwerth 2010; Beisheim and Liese 2014b). This implies non-hierarchical modes of governance almost by definition and, the more external actors – state and non-state – take the principle seriously, the more inclusion is likely to lead to deliberative modes of governance (Brown and Moore 2001; Lowndes and Skelcher 1998).

A prominent example concerns the project setup of the MSP Water and Sanitation for the Urban Poor (WSUP) in Kibera, the largest informal settlement in Kenya (Beisheim, Janetschek, and Sarre 2014b, 172–173), which closely involved CBOs and local leaders. As to rule-making partnerships, the final negotiations leading up to the foundation of the Forest Stewardship Council (FSC) closely resemble deliberative processes in terms of equal access for all stakeholders, an emphasis on fair and transparent process, and the receding into the background of power asymmetries, particularly between industry and indigenous communities (Esguerra 2017). Monitoring and verification of compliance, however, relies on market-based incentives in form of consumer campaigns or inter-firm purchasing decisions. The Fair Labor Association (FLA), The Fair Wear Foundation (FWF), and the Ethical Trading Initiative (ETI) create supply chain policing systems, which involve the various stakeholders. Buyers have access to information (O'Rourke 2006, 903–906). At the same time, some of the MSPs encourage learning from best practice among their members. The ETI was explicitly designed to diffuse information about how to effectively implement labor codes along the supply chain, e.g. by conducting projects on how to best monitor standards and conduct audits across different country settings (O'Rourke 2006, 904). Moreover, MSPs do not only monitor and verify but also help local companies build the capacity to comply with international standards. Finally, some have started to facilitate participation by local stakeholders, including workers and community representatives. This also involves negotiations over how to address compliance problems (O'Rourke 2006, 908–909).

Last but not least, a rather prominent contribution of advocacy networks and advocacy (I)NGOs to governance in ALS concerns capacity-building and empowerment of particularly poor populations. As Berger shows with regard to rural communities in Bangladesh, the presence or absence of advocacy NGOs was crucial in securing decisions by non-state justice institutions (NSJI) that favored poor women and furthered gender rights (Berger 2017). In a similar fashion, Lake demonstrates that NGO presence helped victims of sexual and gender violence to gain justice in informal courts in remote areas of the Democratic Republic of Congo (DRC; see Lake, M. 2018). As we argue below, deliberative modes of governance are particularly prominent in such NSJI in ALS. Yet, in the absence of strong formal institutions, it is often advocacy networks that have to ensure that power relations are absent or remote in the deliberations (on advocacy networks in general see Keck and Sikkink 1998).

In sum, (I)NGOs and MSPs are among the most widespread governors in ALS. While providing governance and public services is constitutive for them, this does not exclude self-interested behavior. As to the modes of governance, the not-for-profit sector mostly employs non-hierarchical means, tries to implement "local ownership," and to include CBOs. We discuss its effectiveness in Chapters 5–7.

For-Profit Governors: Business

For the most part of the twentieth century, the role of business in governance was perceived to be one of maximizing profit within publicly defined (i.e., state-controlled) margins to support and increase the well-being of society.[8] The state defined and enforced the rules for the market, in which companies worked and competed. Thus, business was mainly a target of governance, not a partner or its provider. In the 1990s, this started to change. Nowadays, business is generally expected to contribute to governance beyond generating welfare by making profit. It engages in governance by accepting, establishing, and complying with codes of conduct to regulate its way of doing business, by providing resources or direct governance services to societies, and by setting and implementing regulations for the provision of collective goods in the first place, e.g. with regard to social and environmental standards. In other words, companies have turned into partners in governance, not only in modern states but also at the global level. Global codes of conduct and MSPs (see also above), such as the UN Global Compact, the Extractive Industry Transparency Initiative (EITI), or the Voluntary Principles on Security

---

[8] The following draws on Börzel and Deitelhoff 2018.

and Human Rights (VPSHR), testify to the preparedness of business to take up its governance responsibility, usually referred to as corporate social responsibility (Dashwood 2012; Tsutsui and Lim 2015).

The rise of corporate social responsibility notwithstanding, areas of limited statehood still seem to be least likely cases for business contributions to governance, particularly when it comes to multinational companies (MNCs). They often shift their operation sites to states with limited capacity to set and enforce rules in order to reap the profit from lower labor standards and wages, but also to exploit natural resources (Avant 2005; Banerjee 2008b). For the same reason, companies that call ALS their home have few incentives to push for stricter regulation (Ballentine and Nitzschke 2004, 50; Flohr et al. 2010, 81–94). The literature has criticized this behavior of firms for their complicity in conflicts (Le Billon 2006; Tripathi 2005) and for driving states into a "race to the bottom" (Chan and Ross 2003; Singh and Zammit 2004). The competitive downsizing of regulation or "regulatory freeze" (Madsen 2009, 1298) led to the degradation of natural resources and the compromising of social standards for the sake of potential economic growth or the attraction of short-term foreign investment.[9] Likewise, companies finance and corrupt authoritarian regimes and armed groups, and participate in human rights violations, to maintain their business operations (Le Billon 2006; Wettstein 2012). Coca-Cola appeared to collude with paramilitary groups in Columbia, while British Petroleum was accused of funding death squads (Richani 2005). If the business of business is business (Friedman 1970),[10] why should companies engage in governance?

Why Govern? "Shadows of Hierarchy and Anarchy" as well as Social Norms

State regulation is not only an incentive for escaping governance (Brühl et al. 2001; Chan and Ross 2003; Kaufmann and Segura-Ubiergo 2001; Lofdahl 2002; Rudra 2002). States in ALS, by definition, lack the capacity to threaten credibly the setting and enforcing of strict(er) regulation that would make business commit to governance and ensure compliance with their commitments. However, such a "shadow of hierarchy" can

---

[9] Inter alia Andonova, Mansfield, and Milner 2007; Brühl et al. 2001; Chan and Ross 2003; Eden and Lenway 2001; Kaufmann and Segura-Ubiergo 2001; Lofdahl 2002; Rudra 2002; Xing and Kolstad 2002.

[10] In fact, the title of Friedman's article in the *New York Times* of September 13, 1970 was "A Friedman Doctrine: The social responsibility of business is to increase its profits." See also Banerjee 2008a.

also be cast externally, as we discussed in Chapter 3. National governments of (consolidated and democratic) states, where many MNCs have their headquarters, may force companies to contribute to governance in ALS. In some cases, home country laws are in place and enforceable, which require companies to comply with standards of good governance or other regulations (e.g. environmental or labor laws) irrespective of where they invest or operate. High-regulating countries are reluctant to regulate their companies outside their territory, the Alien Tort Claim Act of the US and recent UK as well as French legislation being exceptions (Deitelhoff et al. 2010, 213). Courts appear more responsive to business violations of good governance, including environmental damage, violent submission of protesters, rape, and forced evictions. French courts charged the French cement group Lafarge with complicity in crimes against humanity and financing terrorist groups in Syria. The Syrian subsidy allegedly paid armed groups, including IS/Daesh, nearly €13 million to keep its Jalabiya plant running in Northern Syria during the civil war.[11] Likewise, the Canadian HudBay Mining Inc. faced a negligence case filed by 11 women that were gang-raped and evicted by (security) officials of a subsidiary in Guatemala.[12] If courts recognize the responsibility of parent companies to monitor their subsidiaries, multinational companies face liability at home for incidents that occur abroad.[13] They are as accountable as states or state agents which gives individuals and communities adversely affected by business activities access to remedies (Muchlinski 2001).

Besides being legally coerced, international firms often transport their regulatory standards abroad as these are interpreted as "quality signals" (Potoski and Prakash 2006) by business partners and customers (Kolk, van Tulder, and Welters 2005; Miura and Kurusu 2015; Murphy 2000; Vogel 2007). Moreover, compliance with diverse standards in heterogeneous regulatory environments creates transaction costs and carries the risk of competitive disadvantages (Flohr et al. 2010; Greenhill, Mosley, and Prakash 2009; Perkins and Neumayer 2012; Prakash and Potoski 2007). German automobile firms, for instance, apply German environmental regulations in South Africa to level the playing field (Thauer 2014a). Finally, Vogel's "California effect" (Vogel 1995), which he used

---

[11] www.theguardian.com/world/2018/jun/28/lafarge-charged-with-complicity-in-syria-crimes-against-humanity, last access October 6, 2018.

[12] www.businesspress24.com/pressrelease1247895/ontario-court-rules-that-lawsuits-against-hudbay-minerals-regarding-shootings-murder-and-gang-rape-at-its-former-mine-in-guatemala-can-proceed-to-trial-in-canada.html, last access March 13, 2018.

[13] More than 50 percent of the world's publicly listed exploration and mining companies have their headquarters in Canada.

to explain why political jurisdictions would tighten their environment or other regulatory standards because others have done so, also works for companies operating in ALS. Involvement in global value chains induces "trading up" or "investing-up" behavior, such as the upgrading of labor standards, among companies that seek to signal quality to their supply chain partners and hope to attract foreign investors (Distelhorst, Hainmueller, and Locke 2016; Malesky and Mosley 2018). Likewise, multinational companies seek to impose their social and environmental standards on their suppliers, particularly if they have a brand name to protect (Héritier, Müller-Debus, and Thauer 2009, Thauer 2014b).

At the same time, it may be precisely the absence of the threat of strict (er) state regulation that creates an incentive for companies to engage in governance. Companies are affected by conflict and domestic turmoil and have a vital interest in securing their investments, demanding law enforcement and security measures (Oetzel and Getz 2012; Rittberger 2004). If the pursuit of their individual profit depends on the provision of certain collective goods and collectively binding rules to produce them, respectively, and states do not provide them, the "shadow of anarchy" induces companies to step in and fill the governance gap (Börzel 2010c; Börzel and Thauer 2013; Ruggie 2004a; see Chapter 3). This is particularly the case if companies cannot relocate easily because they need specific natural resources (Rittberger 2004), their initial investments have been very high, and/or the presence of the production site has already lasted for a long time (Sherman 2001, 8–11; Thauer 2014b). Likewise, local businesses may have no choice to relocate and are particularly inclined to contribute to governance to protect their long-term investments (Börzel and Thauer 2013).

Business engages in governance for economic self-interest, "doing well while doing good" (Conzelmann and Wolf 2007; cf. Boddewyn and Brewer 1994). However, maximizing profit does not only depend on material factors, such as market structures, state regulations, or the absence thereof. We do not argue that corporate social responsibility (CSR) norms have become constitutive for business. Rather, expectations of society towards business have changed. The "social license to operate" increasingly depends on corporate engagement in governance (see also Prakash and Griffin 2012, 2). Public shaming can result in consumer boycotts, loss of reputation and market shares, falling stock market prices, and criticism by shareholders (Hendry 2006; Waygood 2006; Wheeler 2001). Companies that rely on a brand product and/or whose products are highly visible to end-consumers are particularly vulnerable to reputational loss. At the same time, they can gain a competitive advantage vis-à-vis competitors if they take the lead position in their industry, e.g. with respect to strict self-regulatory standards (Auld, Bernstein, and Cashore 2008; Epstein 2008; Smith 2008). Similar concerns drive companies selling their products to the so-called LOHAS (Lifestyles of Health and Sustainability) market segment, i.e., consumers that value and demand sustainable products and the respect of social and environmental standards and are willing to pay a premium for this (Haufler 2001b; Mol 2001, 97–100). High-end consumer markets are often absent or only emerging in ALS. Authoritarian statehood also renders naming and shaming campaigns of (trans)national NGOs difficult. However, companies that are used to civil society campaigning in their home state and that have customers and stakeholders caring about governance usually display a higher inclination to engage in governance (Coni-Zimmer 2014; Flohr et al. 2010; Griffin and Prakash 2014, 475; Spar and LaMure 2003; Wenger and Möckli 2003, 116). The sweatshop campaigns against Nike and others in the early 1990s are a case in point.

Following these lines of reasoning, companies that have their headquarters outside the OECD world are less likely to contribute to governance since they have a comparatively low risk of becoming the target of naming and shaming campaigns (Ballentine and Nitzschke 2004, 42). If their home states are non-democratic, they do not have to fear public punishment for their lack of engagement abroad either (Coni-Zimmer 2014, 320; Whelan and Muthuri 2017). Chinese MNCs, for instance, have taken up CSR-programs much later than their OECD counterparts and also have a more limited CSR understanding (Coni-Zimmer 2014; Thauer 2014b; Zadek et al. 2009). Chinese companies tend to engage in environmental protection, rather than political governance, pertaining to human rights or security (Coni-Zimmer 2014).

Finally, social norms on governance contributions by business are not only institutionalized at the global level or in OECD countries inducing companies to join global CSR frameworks in their quest for being accepted as good citizens (Meyer, Pope, and Isaacson 2015; Pope 2015). ALS are often populated by traditional communities with their own social standards, even if they do not fully correspond to global standards of human rights, democracy, and good governance. While African governments may not be concerned with whether Chinese companies comply with environmental and social standards, local communities often are (Hackenesch 2015; Wegenast et al. 2017). Likewise, companies may be embedded in local communities defined by clan structures that share certain standards of appropriate behavior with regard to the provision of governance (see below). Studies on mining operations in Africa and Latin America show how demands for benefits from resource extraction in terms of collective goods and services are increasingly raised by communities at the local level, laying blame and grievances at the doorstep of companies (Hönke 2013b; Steinberg 2019; Szablowski 2007). Precisely because the state is weak or absent, mining companies are expected to fill the governance gap (Garvin et al. 2009). Such expectations may be fueled by cultural norms regarding the responsibility of social and economic institutions (An-Naim and Deng 2010). Socializing companies into providing governance contributions at the local level and holding them accountable, however, requires that local communities do not only share certain norms; they also need the collective action capacity to engage with business (Thomas 2014). Social trust relations then create the "shadow of the community," as discussed in Chapter 3.

How Govern? Consultation and Coordination

As discussed above, business contributions to governance have greatly increased in depth and breadth since the 1990s. While companies initially accepted codes of conduct to regulate their activities, they soon started to formulate new codes on their own, created local, national, and at times even transnational programs, as well as contributed directly by providing collective goods in their relevant operation sites (Flohr et al. 2010; Haufler 2001a, 2015).

Business contributions to governance typically rely on negotiation or persuasion working with best practices as well as positive and negative incentives (Börzel and Thauer 2013; Flohr et al. 2010; Jakobi and Wolf 2013; Kell and Levin 2003). There are also some, albeit, rare forms of hierarchical modes of governance. This occurs when companies hire private security or military companies to ensure the safety of their production sites and their work force in local communities (Hönke 2013b) or to protect their ships against maritime piracy (Liss 2013). Private Military Companies (PMCs) use physical coercion to provide security. Yet, they make their profit by selling a collective good (security) to clients and take an interest in privatizing security (Jakobi and Wolf 2013; Krahmann 2010). Moreover, security provision often comes at the price of other collective goods, such as human rights and social welfare, e.g. when companies use PMCs to "protect" mining sites against artisanal miners (Hönke 2013b). Therefore, the question is to what extent PMCs really engage in governance (see also Chapter 6). A more straightforward case of hierarchical coordination is when companies exercise legal coercion within their supply chains. Contractual obligations enforce regulatory standards on subsidiaries and suppliers in ALS where the state is too weak to set and enforce regulation (Héritier, Müller-Debus, and Thauer 2009; Thauer 2014b).

The vast majority of business contributions to governance take the form of private self-regulation or public-private co-regulation and is, as such, non-hierarchical (cf. Börzel and Thauer 2013; Flohr et al. 2010; Jakobi and Wolf 2013). For a start, the involvement of industry in public regulation takes place through regular and formalized stakeholder consultations at the national, regional, and local levels. In such a framework, companies may even lobby for strict(er) state regulation to keep foreign competitors out (Thauer 2013b) or raise the costs of their local competitors (Garcia-Johnson 2000). They can also take a more neutral stance when providing their expertise, e.g. as regards technical procedures. At the stage of policy implementation, companies may foster public regulation by capacity-building, i.e., by providing public actors with additional information, expertise, and money to apply and enforce state regulation. Public-private co-regulation refers to situations in which business is involved in the public policy making and implementation process as an equal partner. Business is not only consulted by public actors but also engages in negotiating policies in a formalized framework or participates in public-private partnerships. Companies share regulatory tasks with public actors by specific contracts as in PPPs (Börzel and Risse 2005; Witte, Reinicke, and Benner 2000). They often include the resources of different types of actors in the formulation and implementation of regulation, e.g. in MSPs (Bäckstrand 2008; Beisheim and Liese 2014b; Deitelhoff and Wolf 2010a; Flohr et al. 2010; Kell and Levin 2003; Khagram 2004; Taylor 2005). Forms of collective regulation without public involvement are referred to as private self-regulation. Companies may cooperate with NGOs or CBOs, engage in horizontal self-regulation via business associations or business fora, such as the International Accounting Standards Board (Büthe and Mattli 2011). Not surprisingly, in-house self-regulation without the involvement of state and other non-state actors is the most preferred form of many companies to contribute to governance. Self-regulation leaves them maximum autonomy and flexibility, which are main incentives for business to engage in governance in the first place (Börzel and Thauer 2013, Flohr et al. 2010, Hönke 2013b, Thauer 2014b).

The most comprehensive case of governance by business in ALS combining different modes are Charter Cities. Economist Paul Romer developed the concept as a way to help failing states attract foreign direct investment by granting business maximum autonomy from the host state (Romer 2010). This involves the delegation of administrative, political, judicial, and even military authority to companies. Charter Cities thereby go beyond special economic zones, by which host states offer business favorable policies with regard to investment, taxation, trading, quotas, customs, and labor regulations. Honduras was the first country to experiment with what it has dubbed "Zones for Employment and Economic Development" (*zonas de empleo y desarrollo economico*) to develop areas that have been ungoverned so far (Miller 2015; Spann 2014). The government invited business to create its own "model cities," which are ruled by a technical secretary put in charge by the Honduran parliament upon the suggestion of a committee of external experts. This committee (*Comité para la Adopcion de Mejores Prácticas*), appointed by the Honduran president, would set and enforce laws that conform to best practice. The "micro states" would also have their own courts and police force. In the end, Honduras did not follow through with its experiment due to legal concerns and public opposition.

In sum, MNCs and other companies have become major governors in ALS since at least the 1990s (but see the roles of the Hudson Bay Company or the East India Company during colonial times, Conrad and Stange 2011). As self-interested actors par excellence, they only engage in governance under the various "shadows of hierarchy, anarchy, or community" (see Chapter 3 for details). While they sometimes use hierarchical steering – particularly with regard to security governance or concerning their own supply chains – they mostly engage in non-hierarchical modes of governance based on negotiations with state actors, various stakeholders, or CBOs. Their effectiveness as governors is rather disputed in the literature, as we document in Chapters 5–7.

Self-Governance: "Traditional Authorities," Local Communities, and Non-State Justice Institutions (NSJI)

A particular group of governors that is active in ALS is often erroneously called "traditional authorities." The term usually refers to kings, village chiefs, tribal leaders, heads of clans, elders (Baldwin and Holzinger 2019b; Mamdani 2018), and, more recently, NSJI. Yet, the term "traditional" is a social construction. More often than not, "traditions" are invented, precisely because they bestow a certain legitimacy to particular actors in ALS. One could even argue that "traditional" is what communities and constituents make of it (to paraphrase Wendt 1992; see also the definition in Holzinger, Kern, and Kromrey 2016, 470; for a critique of the usage of the term see Förster and Koechlin 2018). In any event, "traditional authorities" are ubiquitous as governors in ALS. While colonial powers had incorporated them into their system of indirect rule (Mamdani 2018, ch. 3), post-colonial leaders considered traditional authorities as incompatible with modern state governance (Ubhenin 2017). With the wave of democratization toward the end of the twentieth century, however, Africa has seen a resurgence of kings, chiefs, and elders as "tax collectors," "peace-builders," "land administrators," and "development project managers" (Baldwin 2016; Buur and Kyed 2007; Englebert 2002; Rouveroy van Nieuwaal and van Dijk 1999; Ubhenin 2017, 34; Ubink 2016). To date, more than half of the UN member states politically recognize particular ethnic groups in their constitutions, and more than 60 countries explicitly acknowledge forms of "traditional" governance and customary law (data according to Holzinger, Kern, and Kromrey 2016, 469). Public opinion polls in Africa indicate that 95 percent of the citizens consider chiefs or elders to yield at least some influence on governance in their country (Baldwin 2016, 32–33).

Elders, chiefs, and tribal leaders are mostly embedded in local communities with the capacity to self-govern (Baldwin and Holzinger 2019b). Local communities and CBOs have recently gained more attention in ALS (see e.g. Kaplan 2017; Krause 2018; Steinberg 2019). Earlier work by Ostrom and others has demonstrated that local communities are able to solve collective action problems (particularly with regard to common pool resources) and to provide goods and services in the absence of a state with enforcement capacity (Ostrom 1990, 2000; Ostrom, Gardner, and Walker 1994). Ostrom's work remains highly relevant for ALS.

NSJI, such as the *jirgas* and *shuras* in Afghanistan and Pakistan, the *shalish* and "village courts" in rural Bangladesh, or the *barza inter-communitaire* in the DRC, are equally common in ALS. Apart from customary, tribal, or religious courts where the adjudicators are not lawyers, traditional or religious leaders, community mediators, and local administrators settle disputes involving marriage, inheritance, property rights, or local order issues. NSJI are pervasive in ASL, where state institutions do not exist or lack legitimacy.[14] In many parts of Sub-Saharan Africa, about 90 percent of the population are covered by such customary law systems (Tamanaha 2015, 4). 14 million South Africans have access to NSJI where "traditional" leaders solve disputes (Rautenbach 2015, 123). The same holds true for Afghanistan (Barfield, Nojumi, and Thier 2006), Pakistan (particularly the Federally Administered Tribal Areas – FATA, see Röder and Shinwari 2015), India (Eckert 2009), but also many Latin American countries (on Bolivia see Bustillos 2015). Some of

---

[14] NSJI exist in consolidated states, too. See Kötter 2015, 162, on the right of religious communities in Germany to regulate themselves, or the tribal jurisdictions in the US, Canada, or Australia.

the various NSJI are completely informal, others are incorporated into state constitutions with varying degrees of autonomy (e.g. South Africa, Afghanistan, Pakistan, Bolivia; for a discussion see Kötter 2015, 167–184).

Why Govern? Performance, Moral Standing, and the "Shadow of Anarchy"

Work on – mostly – Sub-Saharan Africa has identified chiefdoms and the like as varieties of patronage systems and neo-patrimonial, clientelistic networks (overviews in Erdmann 2013; Erdmann and Engel 2007). According to the conventional wisdom, chiefs who are not democratically elected for the most part, but rule for life, are leaders of ethnic communities and part of patronage networks operating, e.g. as "vote brokers" for African elections (e.g. Bratton and van de Walle 1994, 1997; Jackson and Rosberg 1982) or even "local despots" (Mamdani 2018).

Still, if we conceive of "traditional authorities" as mostly self-interested egoistic actors, they resemble Olson's "stationary bandits" (Olson 1993). As Baldwin put it:

Traditional chiefs are similar to Olson's stationary bandits insofar as they expect to rule for life and their material well-being is influenced by the local economy in their chiefdom. As a result, they have an interest in providing good governance, including the provision of some local public goods. Their own long-term well-being is closely tied to that of 'their subjects,' so they should take actions to improve the well-being of other community members. (Baldwin 2016, 52)

In other words, it is their quest for legitimacy – output legitimacy in this case – that motivates them to become governors in ALS. As rulers for life, they have rather long time-horizons. At the same time, the economic performance of their constituents determines their own wealth to quite some extent. "Bad chiefs" would not only lose moral standing (see below) but could not collect customary tributes from their impoverished subjects (Baldwin 2016, 26). Thus, Baldwin argues that the governance role of chiefs and other "traditional leaders" is primarily to become "development brokers" rather than "vote brokers" (Baldwin 2016, ch. 4; on brokerage in general see Hönke and Müller 2018). This is particularly the case in ALS, where the lacking capacity of the state to cater to its citizens has resulted in a resurgence of "traditional" author-ities as intermediaries between state and society (Koelble and Li Puma 2011).

By facilitating the responsiveness of elected politicians to their con-stituencies typically demanding basic infrastructure and social service, chiefs and tribal leaders do not only contribute to the provision of collective goods and services; the governance arrangements they are part of increase throughput legitimacy when the recipient perceives decision-making processes as efficient, just, and transparent. They facilitate accountability in areas where state institutions are weak and politicians have difficulties in responding to their voters.

Note that this argument resonates with claims why monarchies and other autocratic systems retain power for quite a long time based on their ability to generate output legitimacy through the provision of collective goods and services. The eight Arab monarchies survived the popular uprisings of the so-called Arab Spring that brought down authoritarian rulers in Tunisia, Libya, and Egypt, and threw Syria and Yemen into civil war. Their wealth in oil allowed them to appease public protest by stepping up on welfare and development programs (Menaldo 2012; Yom and Gause III 2012).

While engaging in governance may be rational, we should not underestimate the logic of appropriateness and social trust, which increases the more chiefs are embedded in their communities and are bound by strong relationships of social trust (Börzel and Risse 2016; Draude, Hölck, and Stolle 2018) and the more their legitimacy is based on moral or religious convictions. If chiefs and elders are commanding moral or religious authority, their ability to govern is based on more than just output legitimacy, which should enable them to generate greater diffuse support for costly rules (see discussion in Chapter 3). For instance, Tsai shows how Chinese village temples and lineage groups entailing personalized trust relations based on a shared belief in the village's guardian deities and common ancestry, respectively, play an important role in the provision of collective goods and services at the local level (Tsai 2007). Local leaders that are socially embedded in such traditional communities are more likely to deliver local development projects (cf. Baldwin 2016; Díaz-Cayeros, Magaloni, and Ruiz-Euler 2014).

Moreover, some local communities and CBOs develop their own collective action capacity to self-organize and to engage in governance. As Kaplan and Krause show with regard to Colombia, Nigeria, Indonesia, and other cases, local communities start protecting themselves against violent non-state actors (VNSA) under certain conditions (Kaplan 2017; Krause 2016, 2018; see Chapter 5): "Social cooperation and organization is therefore the key to help civilians overcome fear, manage their own communities, and deal with armed group pressure in an enduring manner" (Kaplan 2017, 4). Social trust and personal relationships are the main reason why these communities engage in security governance, while others fail to do so. Krause adds institutional capacity to these conditions (Krause 2018, 4–5).

Last but not least, the central state in ALS is likely to play an ambivalent role with regard to governance by "traditional authorities": corruption is the flip side of the coin of weak state institutions unable to enforce the law (Shen and Wiliamson 2005; Spinellis 1996). Corruption and state failure more broadly serves as another legitimation device for chiefs, elders, and other local leaders to take the law in their own hands, to establish NSJI, or to engage in the provision of other collective goods and services. In Bangladesh, for example, the corruption of the state judiciary system has been common knowledge for a long time, which served to strengthen the legitimacy of NSJI, such as the *shalish* courts (Berger 2017). As to Sub-Saharan Africa and according to Afrobarometer polls, 42 percent of the population on average ascribe the resolution of local disputes as a primary responsibility of chiefs (Baldwin 2016, 33).

The "risk of anarchy" also accounts for the engagement of traditional authorities as security providers through "community-based policing" and other "grass-root" forms of local self-protection security governance (Baker 2007; Cross 2016; Menkhaus 2006/2007, 2008; Pratten and Sen 2008; Renders and Terlinden 2010). When the Taliban regime collapsed, community-based customary structures, such as the *arbakai* (community-based policing) and *lashkar* (tribal army), filled the governance void in south-eastern Afghanistan, next to other VNSA, such as warlords, Al Qaeda, and private security providers (Schmeidl and Karokhail 2009). While the *lashkar* is to protect the tribal community against external threats, the mission of the *arbakai* is to keep the peace and stop fighting within tribal communities. The executive arm of traditional governance structures of the *jirgas* (tribal gatherings) and *shuras* (tribal councils) enforces their decisions.

Central state recognition of customary law can be regarded as a similar kind of delegation of governance authority to non-state actors as the GDA discussed above (see Kötter 2015 for details). In this case, a weak state grants "traditional" authorities the right to self-govern, including the right to solve disputes, thus adding further legitimacy to chiefs, elders, and other community leaders. In Kenya, for instance, chiefs are civil servants integrated into the provincial administration (Holzinger, Kern, and Kromrey 2017). As such, they have not only "traditional" but also bureaucratic authority. Delegating the provision of law and order to "traditional" authorities allows weak states to control areas they would otherwise not be able to govern (Anderson and Rolandsen 2014; Bagayoko, Hutchful, and Luckham 2016; on the colonial antecedents of this "negotiated" [Hagmann and Péclard 2010; Renders and Terlinden 2010] or "mediated" [Menkhaus 2008] statehood, see Branch 2009; Davis and Pereira 2003; Johson 1991).

How Govern? Social Sanctioning, Consultation, and Deliberative Negotiations

Some chiefs and headmen resemble warlords in that they command their own militias with the enforcement capacity to govern hierarchically. They may even be able to establish a monopoly of the use of force (for Afghanistan see Mukhopadhyay 2014). In general, however, and in contrast to VNSA (see below), the enforcement capacity of local chiefs is rather limited, since they do not control means of violence. However, hierarchical rule can rely on followership and voluntary obedience, because "traditional" leaders enjoy social acceptance and legitimacy, based on what Weber called charismatic and "traditional" authority (Weber 1978 [1922]); see also Chapter 3 on sources of legitimacy). In other words, chiefs may be able to rule hierarchically or to cast a "shadow of hierarchy" based on their legitimacy, which ensures compliance. In that, they resemble religious authorities who also govern hierarchically when commanding followership with regard to norms and rules. Social sanctions, such as disowning and ostracizing, also help ensure compliance with costly rules in small communities bound together through trust relations (see Boix 2015, ch. 1). The same holds true for religious sanctioning capacities. Yet, sanctions are based on incentives rather than coercion. So are material resources, e.g. the allocation of land, "traditional" leaders as governors can distribute (see Baldwin 2016, 41–44, for a critical analysis).

Unfortunately, most empirical work on ALS does not pay attention to the particular modes of governance so that we can only infer from studies if and whether non-hierarchical coordination prevails. Interestingly, the pre-colonial organization of traditional governance structures at the local level was often non-hierarchical rather than hierarchical.[15] Baldwin finds that more than 70 percent of pre-colonial leaders governed in a consultative mode (Baldwin 2016, 25). In Africa, it was the British colonial administration that introduced hierarchical rule (Baldwin 2016, 26–39). The attempts of the Spanish Empire to establish a colonial state in Latin America, in contrast, met with the resistance of indigenous tribes, such as the Mapuche in Southern Chile, who refused to establish any hierarchical structure among them. Since their total military submission was impossible, the Spaniards had to "appropriate indigenous forms of negotiation," arguing and bargaining with the hundreds of Mapuche

---

[15] Traditional kingdoms in centralized societies, e.g. in Uganda or in Northern Namibia, have been hierarchically structured (Holzinger, Kern, and Kromrey 2017) and could rely on some form of bureaucracy and military force to enforce their decisions (Baldwin 2016, ch. 2).

leaders in meetings called "parlamentos" (Esders, Hölck, and Rinke 2018, 141–142; Hölck and Rinke 2016; Hölck and Saiz 2010).

The *Usos y costumbres* (indigenous customary law) constitutes another indigenous form of participatory governance, which is practiced in Mexico. It "entails electing individuals to leadership positions through customary law in non-partisan elections, making decisions through participatory democracy, and monitoring compliance through a parallel (and often informal) system of law enforcement and community justice" (Díaz-Cayeros, Magaloni, and Ruiz-Euler 2014, 80). In China, local leaders can rely on the moral obligation toward local "solidarity groups," based on shared patrilineal descent or worship of village guardian deities, to make citizens contribute to the construction of public roads and drainage channels (Tsai 2007). Likewise, traditional leaders in Africa use local institutions to overcome collective action problems when state actors are too weak to make citizens contribute to the funding and implementing of state-sponsored development projects, such as school buildings, health clinics, and roads (Baldwin 2016). They inform, mobilize, monitor, and sanction citizens, e.g. by holding fund-raising events, organizing community labor, or enforcing contribution levels (Fanthorpe 2005; Swidler 2013). Community-based policing, like the *vigilante* village groups in Africa (Cross 2016; Pratten and Sen 2008), or the tribal police in Afghanistan, work in similar ways (Schmeidl and Karokhail 2009).

The more indigenous and local modes of governance involving "traditional" authorities are participatory and inclusive, the more we can infer their non-hierarchical nature. Local "traditional" authorities are often leaders rather than rulers (Bourdillon 1987; Olivier 1969). Many chiefs consult a council of elders, whose advice they could ignore but would usually follow. The Massai leaders in Tanzania are supported by elders, and leadership rotates among the greater families (Holzinger, Kern, and Kromrey 2017, 25). The Kikuyu councils of elders in Kenya take their decisions based on consensus. The number of elders is not limited. Anyone can become an elder depending on age, reputation, and financial means (Holzinger, Kern, and Kromrey 2017, 19).

Participation and inclusiveness suggest that traditional governance often involves deliberation as a particular mode of non-hierarchical governance (Díaz-Cayeros, Magaloni, and Ruiz-Euler 2014; Williams 2010). Once again, there is little systematic evidence available to reach firm conclusions (for a critical view see LiPuma and Koelble 2009). Yet, deliberative modes of governance can solve the compliance problem with costly rules, particularly in ALS (see Lake, D. 2018 on this point). NSJI play a prominent role for dispute resolution, which has been a core function of traditional authorities (Baldwin 2016, 27) and whose institutional design may offer important insights on the relevance of deliberation.

NSJI AS DELIBERATIVE INSTITUTIONS

Towhat extent do these NSJI allow for deliberation or deliberative nego-tiations as discussed above?[16] A deliberative body (see Risse 2018a; Warren, Mansbridge, and Bächtiger et al. 2013) should fulfill the following criteria in an ideal typical way. Note that these criteria that resemble an "ideal speech situation" in the Habermasian sense (Habermas 1981) are very rarely met completely in real life:

- equal access for affected parties;
- power asymmetries receding in the background (equal power, only better argument counts);
- reciprocal justice and procedural fairness as guiding principles;
- transparency/publicity of proceedings;
- judges or mediators as honest brokers;
- consensus- rather than compromise-oriented proceedings.

Equal Access: Many NSJI allow access for the parties affected by a conflict or a dispute within a local community. In most cases, the parties to the conflict are represented by elders, senior members of a community with a well-respected social status, or by elected members from the ethnic communities (e.g. *barza inter-communitaire* in the DRC [Clark 2008]; the *acholi* in Northern Uganda [Latigo 2008], *jirgas* in the FATA region of Pakistan [Röder and Shinwari 2015], and the *bulu-bulu* on the Fiji Islands [Merry 2006]). However, equal access is usually severely con-strained for women. In the Pakistani *jirgas* in the FATA region, for example, women are represented by men, even if they are the victims (Röder and Shinwari 2015; for the Ethiopian *amhara* see Prigge 2011). In a similar way, the *shuras* in Afghanistan are consultative bodies com-posed of senior male landowners (Koehler 2013, 276–278). In some cases, though, the lack of direct access for women is compensated by NGOs pushing for women's access to justice, as Berger has shown for the "village courts" in rural Bangladesh and Lake concerning sexual violence in the Eastern DRC (Berger 2017; Lake, M. 2018)

Equal Power: With regard to (informal) institutional rules limiting asymmetrical power resources and capabilities, existing studies on NSJI paint a mixed picture. Opinion surveys with regard to *jirgas* and *shuras* in Afghanistan and Pakistan show, for example, that more than half of the

---

[16] The following is a revised version of Risse 2018b.

respondents believed that the more powerful party to the dispute got the results it wanted, even though almost 50 percent considered members of the *jirgas* impartial (Röder and Shinwari 2015; Shinwari 2011, 89; for similar results with regard to the *amhara* in Ethiopia see Prigge 2011). More than three-quarters of the respondents to a household survey in Afghanistan considered their local *shura* to be independent from the influence of powerful people, but only 21 percent trusted it to decide in favor of the weaker party (Koehler 2013, 279). Yet, the rules of the game in Afghan *jirgas* are based on the equality of (male) participants, once disputants agree to have their conflict solved by the community (Barfield, Nojumi, and Thier 2006). As Koehler argues, compliance with the *jirga* judgments decreases, the more participants believe that the power balance is tilted in their favor (Koehler 2013, 280). As to the *barza inter-communitaire* in the DRC, Clark argues that the perception of power equality among the parties to a dispute initially contributed to its effectiveness, which broke down later when *barza* members aligned with various fighting political factions (Clark 2008). Afrobarometer data suggest that citizens perceive chiefs to be particularly powerful with regard to dispute resolution (Baldwin 2016, 43). In the case of the village courts in Bangladesh and NSJI in the Eastern DRC, the presence of (local) NGOs leveled the playing field and contributed to the equality of the parties (Berger 2017; Lake, M. 2018).

Reciprocal Justice and Procedural Fairness: Most NSJI examined here receive comparatively high marks with regard to their reciprocal and procedural fairness. This has to do with the fact that the goal of these procedures is almost always conflict resolution and the restoration of peace in a community (see for the *jirgas* in the FATA region and in Afghanistan Barfield, Nojumi, and Thier 2006, Röder and Shinwari 2015; for the Amhara people in Ethiopia see Prigge 2011). This should not be understood as a neglect of retribution for wrong-doing, though. The *Mato Oput* procedure among the Acholi people in Northern Uganda (Latigo 2008), for example, is aimed at reconciliation, but based on the full recognition and acceptance of wrong-doing by the perpetrators. It includes both retributive and restorative elements in the sense that tolerance and forgiveness is coupled to repentance for wrongdoing. Impunity is not accepted. The *gacaca* courts in Rwanda as well as other African NSJI are based on equally balanced approaches of reconciliation coupled with full accountability, including truth-telling and reparation for the victims of crimes and wrong-doing (see Huyse 2008; Ingelaere 2008).

Transparency and Publicity: All NSJI discussed here deliberate in public, and a strong presence of civil society organizations is reported in many studies. In the case of the *gacaca* courts in Rwanda, the sessions are compulsory for the public (Ingelaere 2008; for African NSJI in general see Huyse 2008). Moreover, publicity ensures that civil society organizations and NGOs can monitor the activities of NSJI in order to keep them honest, which is crucially linked to their effectiveness in dispute settlements (Huyse and Salter 2008 for Sub-Saharan Africa; Berger 2017 for Bangladesh; Lake, M. 2018 for the Eastern DRC).

Honest Brokers as Arbiters or Judges: Once again, the similarities among NSJI across continents are striking. Most African institutions appoint "traditional" arbitrators on the basis of social status or lineage (Huyse 2008, Prigge 2011). In South Sudan, chiefs act as both advocates and arbiters, lawyers are not allowed to the proceedings (Diehl, Arol, and Malz 2015). Honest brokerage also appears to be constitutive features of *Pakhtunwali* NSJI in Afghanistan and Pakistan. For the formal, i.e., government-sponsored *jirgas* in the FATA region, members must be trusted by the society, whereas members of informal *jirgas* are usually comprised of the elders of distinguished families with strong social standing and experience (Röder and Shinwari 2015; see also Shinwari 2011).

Consensus-Orientation: Since most NSJI – particularly in post-conflict environments of ALS – aim at reconciliation and mutual benefit (while not excluding retribution), they have a strong built-in consensus orientation. Whether or not the outcomes of such negotiated justice resembles a true deliberative consensus is beyond this chapter. However, it is striking that almost all NSJI considered here strive to reach a negotiated consensus.[17] This consensus orientation appears to be based on the idea that disputes are viewed as problems of the entire local community so that decisions have to be made as a voluntary process based on mutual agreements. Enforcement then works through social pressure in the group (see Draude, Hölck, and Stolle 2018; Huyse 2008). Barfield, Nojumi, and Thier describe an almost perfect deliberative setting with regard to local *jirgas* in Afghanistan (Barfield, Nojumi, and Thier 2006, 9): "Everyone sits in a circle so that no one takes priority. All members have a right to speak and binding decisions are made by common consensus rather than voting. This may take considerable time (days, weeks, or even months) or fail to come to a conclusion entirely." Unfortunately, women are excluded in this setting (see above).

To conclude: most NSJI from Sub-Saharan Africa and Asia score rather high on deliberative quality and appear to fulfill the criteria for

---

[17] For African NSJI in general see Huyse 2008; for the *barza inter-communitaire* in the DRC see Clark 2008; for the Acholi region in Northern Uganda see Latigo 2008; for the Amhara people in Ethiopia see Prigge 2011; for South Africa see Rautenbach 2015; Rautenbach, Bekker, and Goolam 2010; for the various *jirgas* in Afghanistan and Pakistan see Barfield, Nojumi, and Thier 2006; Röder and Shinwari 2015, Wardak 2004.

"deliberative negotiations" (Naurin and Reh 2018; Warren, Mansbridge, and Bächtiger et al. 2013). This is rather surprising and counter-intuitive given the often adverse conditions in ALS. Three caveats remain, though: first, as in many so-called traditional societies of ALS, women are mostly excluded from the deliberations. Second, decisions of NSJI often violate various human rights (see e.g. contributions in Kötter et al. 2015). But as Tamanaha notes, such human rights violations are often endemic to the local communities in which the NSJI are embedded and not peculiar to the NSJI (Tamanaha 2015, 19–20; see also Berger and Lake 2018). Moreover, as the cases of Afghanistan, Pakistan, Bangladesh, and others show, we need to compare NSJI to the formal state-driven courts in ALS, which are often beyond the pale with regard to the rule of law. Third, NSJI do include deliberative modes of governance, at least concerning the norms, rules, and decision-making procedures of these institutions, whether formal or informal. As to the actual practice of NSJI, the empirical evidence is still rather limited. Most studies do not engage in observing the dispute settlement procedures in action (see Berger 2017 and Lake, M. 2018 for exceptions with regard to Bangladesh and the Eastern DRC; see also Koehler 2013 and Shinwari 2011 for opinion surveys among local populations with regard to the legitimacy of NSJI in Afghanistan).

In sum, "traditional authorities" including NSJI are among the most important indigenous governors in many areas of limited statehood. While their rule and authority have been denounced as "pre-modern" and outmoded by modernization theories and other Western-centric scholarship, the governance perspective allows for a more balanced assessment of their role. As argued above, tribal leaders, chiefs, and NSJI employ the entire spectrum with regard to modes of governance, from hierarchical steering all the way to deliberation. Surprisingly enough, particularly NSJI in ALS appear to fulfill many of the criteria of deliberative negotiations, which have been formulated for very different contexts.

Violent Non-State Actors (VNSA)

A rather unlikely group of governors in ALS are often described as part of the problem rather than the solution: violent or armed non-state actors. The conventional wisdom holds that guerrilla and rebel groups, warlords, and Islamist militants[18] are not only primarily responsible for

---

[18] By treating Islamist militants, such as Hamas, the Taliban, IS/Daesh, or Hezbollah, as governors, we do not deny that they engage in brutal violence and terrorism. However,

creating ALS in the first place by denying central governments the monopoly of the use of force. They are also mostly regarded as spoilers in peace-building processes (see e.g. Krause and Milliken 2009; Marten 2012, 2013; Stedman 1997; overview and typology in Jakobi and Wolf 2013; Schneckener 2009; for a differentiated picture Reno 1998b, 2009).

However, under certain circumstances, even VNSA might turn into governors in areas of limited statehood. Mukhopadhyay tells the story of warlords Atta Mohammed Noor and Gul Agha Sherzai, who governed two provinces of post-2001 Afghanistan after the Taliban (Mukhopadhyay 2014). Blair and Kalmanovitz report the governance contributions of Ismail Khan, another powerful warlord in Afghanistan's Herat province (Blair and Kalmanovitz 2016, 435–437). Jo describes how the M23 rebel group in the North Kivu province of the DRC and the Moro Islamic Liberation Front (MILF) in the Southern Philippines started complying with international humanitarian law thereby engaging in security and humanitarian governance (Jo 2015, 134–140, 166–176). Wickham-Crowley investigates how various Latin American rebel groups provided both security and other collective goods and services in the territory they controlled (Wickham-Crowley 2015; see also Weinstein 2007 on rebel groups in Uganda, Mozambique, and Peru). Magaloni et al. focus on the governance by organized criminal groups in the *favelas* of Rio de Janeiro (Magaloni, Franco-Vivanco, and Melo 2020). Berti demonstrates that Hamas in the Gaza strip and Hezbollah in Lebanon not only engaged in security governance, but also provided public goods in the areas of education, public health, and elsewhere (Berti 2013; Berti and Gutiérrez 2016; Roy 2011). In some cases, VNSA engage in full-scale governance in a given territory ("rebelocracy"), while in other cases they provide and maintain security, but leave broader rule-making and service provision to others ("aliocracy," see Arjona 2015, 2016, on these terms; Huang 2016).

Why Govern? Resource Extraction, Territorial Control, and Recognition

We start from the assumption that VNSA, such as rebel groups or warlords, are egoistic and self-interested and, thus, not primarily inclined to engage in governance for the common good. The first distinction to be made here is Olsen's argument about "roving" versus "stationary"

they also deliver a variety of goods and services to the local population. While this may help strengthen their armed struggle, one should not ignore their contribution to governance in areas of limited statehood.

bandits mentioned above (Olson 1993). VNSA as roving bandits that move from territory to territory, plundering resources and exploiting the population, have little incentive to govern. Their calculation changes if they control territory and become stationary, e.g. because they need to exploit natural resources to generate income for their military campaign (on the "greed vs. grievance" argument with regard to the "resource curse" see Collier and Hoeffler 2004).

The first factor motivating VNSA as "stationary bandits" to become governors is derivative of the "risk of anarchy" in areas of limited statehood. As Wickham-Crowley argues for Latin America, the absence or weakness of central state institutions in remote or marginalized rural areas constitute a pre-condition for insurgents and rebel groups to become governors (Felbab-Brown, Trinkunas, and Hamid 2017; Wickham-Crowley 2015). In this context, Chojnacki and Branovic use the analogy of the market to argue that the emergence of different modes of security results from strategies of collective actors in areas where different public and private actors compete over territorial control, natural resources, and the recruitment of members (Chojnacki and Branovic 2011). The emergence of security governance depends on economic and geographic opportunity structures and on the expected utility to invest in productive means instead of unproductive fighting and (over-)looting. Weinstein has argued in this context that rebel groups tend to engage in governance the more they require civilian support, labor and material resources to sustain their military campaigns (Weinstein 2007, ch. 5; see also Reno 2010; Staniland 2012; Stewart and Liou 2017; discussion in Kasfir 2015).

Moreover, various authors point to the institutional make-up of rebel groups and other VNSA as an explanation for why they engage in governance. As to rebel groups, they need to be organized rather hierarchically with strict command-and-control structures so as to ensure that they can use violence strategically, foster local support, and make credible commitments and/or comply with international law (Jo 2015, ch. 3; Staniland 2012; Weinstein 2007, 196). This may result in the emergence of a "state within a state" (Felbab-Brown, Trinkunas, and Hamid 2017, 18), as we find it in southern Lebanon (Cammett 2014; Flanigan and Abdel-Samad 2009).

Moreover, as Mukhopadhyay has argued with regard to Afghanistan, warlords will engage in governance if two conditions are met: first, they have the institutional and administrative capacity to control a province; and, second, they face competition in their territory (Mukhopadhyay 2014). Both conditions make it likely that the (weak) central government delegates the authority to rule a province to them. In other words, the arrangement here is similar to a governance delegation agreement, as discussed above with regard to external actors.[19] In this context, the warlords are not necessarily trying to overthrow the central government, but to maintain a cooperative arrangement with it. They act as power brokers.

The study of Feblab-Brown et al. on governance by rebels, Islamist organizations, warlords, and criminals in the Middle East and Latin America corroborates that VNSA may choose to collaborate with, rather than fight against, the state. At the same time, it shows that competition among VNSA substantially decreases their propensity to engage in governance because they lose control over their territory and become more concerned about their survival (Felbab-Brown, Trinkunas, and Hamid 2017; also Arjona 2016; Cammett 2014; Metelits 2009; Reno 2010; Weinstein 2007).

Idler and Forest, finally, demonstrate that VNSA do not necessarily compete among each other either when they provide collective goods and services. Insurgents, traffickers, and tribal warlords in the Andean borderlands have set up arrangements of "complementary governance," which include tacit rules of non-interference (Idler and Forest 2015).

Even more important than the "risk of anarchy" or the institutional arrangement with a weak central state is the quest for legitimacy, be it domestic or international. As Berti and Gutiérrez explain, Hamas:

used the provision of security as a key tool to boost both its power and its political legitimacy. At the most basic level, investing in security allowed the group to increase its effective control of Gaza and its citizens as well as to rein in competing armed factions and political opponents alike. (Berti and Gutiérrez 2016, 1069)

In a similar vein, Szekely has argued that Hamas uses service provision as a tool of "political advertising" for the kind of state that it seeks to build when it gains power (Szekely 2015).

Broadening the base of support beyond their own members has also driven governance contributions by Hezbollah in Lebanon (Cammett 2014) and IS/Daesh in the territories it controlled (Barbato, Hantscher, and Lederer 2016; Felbab-Brown, Trinkunas, and Hamid 2017, ch. 4). The Taliban in Afghanistan and the Revolutionary Armed Forces of Colombia (FARC) revised their initial opposition against drug cultivation as a sin and counter-revolutionary, respectively, to win over the local population. Engaging in illicit drug trade themselves, they used part of

---

[19] We will discuss the implications of such "informal state sponsorship" (Felbab-Brown, Trinkunas, and Hamid 2017, 20) or "informal discharge" (Hönke 2010b) in Chapter 8.

the income on local policing, dispute settlement, and providing social services (Felbab-Brown, Trinkunas, and Hamid 2017, ch. 3, 8).

Providing effective basic governance services, such as law and order, health, and education, is meant to create output legitimacy for these VNSA. This in turn increases their power and control, reducing enforcement costs (Mampilly 2012) and helping them to overcome their political opponents. At the same time, the acquired social acceptance and legitimacy increases their social capital in order to carry out their armed struggles. Hezbollah, for instance, engages in extensive welfare governance in Lebanon alongside its warfare against Israel (Cammett 2014; Grynkewich 2008).

Islamist militants are equally driven by territorial control and the quest for popular support when they engage in governance. Rather than using its social facilities and programs as recruitment centers for its military wing, Roy finds that Hamas seeks to boost its domestic legitimacy and maintain popular support (Roy 2011; cf. Flanigan 2006). Domestically, welfare services not only support surviving family members of ("martyr") fighters and men killed for collaborating with Israeli military authorities. They compensate for the lack of support of Hamas' ideological agenda and ensure political survival in times of repression and excessive violence. After the signing of the Oslo Accord between Israel and the Palestinian Liberation Organization in 1993, Palestinians became increasingly disenchanted with political Islam and the military fights against Israel. As a result, Hamas started to heavily invest in the delivery of services, which the Fatah-led Palestinian National Authority was unable to provide effectively, particularly in the refugee camps and the poorest areas of the Gaza Strip (Roy 2011, 33–39). Hamas' electoral victories in 2004 through 2006 were largely based on the popular support generated by the extensive infrastructure its social service wing (*Dawah*) had established rather than its ideological agenda and the activities of its military wing (Roy 2011, 85–91, 167–168, 202–203).

Yet, trading political support for social services often produces club rather than public goods (Banerjee 2004; Wood 1997). Identity-based groups provide access to marginalized segments of the population, which may be excluded because they belong to a particular social group (see Chapter 2 on socially limited statehood). Eligibility and access constitute membership in the social group. In the end, political patronage is likely to result in fragmented welfare regimes that deepen social divisions and social inequalities and fuel contestations of the political order. Religious or ethnic parties have no interest in upscaling welfare governance to other groups (Chandra 2004; Fearon and Laitin 1996; Kasara 2007). Nor do they have the mandate (Cammett 2014, 13; cf. Brown 1998). Still, in her study on sectarian politics and welfare governance in Lebanon, Cammett (2014) finds that not all sectarian parties are restricting access to members of their own group; they may even target members of other groups. Hezbollah is far less likely to serve heterogeneous communities than the Lebanese Future Movement predominantly supported by Sunni Muslims. Both are equally well endowed with resources to engage in more inclusive welfare governance. Cammett therefore focuses on their political motivations to explain the variation. She argues that the willingness to engage in cross-sectarian welfare governance increases with a political strategy that relies on formal state institutions to pursue national power, on the one hand, and low intra-sect competition, on the other (Cammett 2014). The latter contradicts the argument by Mukhopadhyay that competition among VNSA increases their propensity to engage in governance (see above). The Future Movement is the dominant party representing Sunni Muslims in Lebanon, which allows it to claim the position of prime minister under the power-sharing agreement. Hezbollah has managed to become the dominant Shia party, runs in national elections, and has participated in government. However, it has kept its militia to pursue its armed struggle against Israel.

The quest for international legitimacy also increases the propensity of VNSA to become governors that are more inclusive. Particularly rebel groups who are close to victory (or at least maintain a balance of power with central state governments), seek domestic and international recognition as legitimate actors and not terrorists or criminals (Herr 2013; Jo 2015; Jo and Bryant 2013). They commit to international humanitarian law and become governors. In this context, the NGO "Geneva Call" has been quite successful in signing up VNSA' commitment to various international law as a signaling device to international audiences (Herr 2013; Krieger and Weingärtner 2012; Stanton 2016). International "legitimacy audiences" may include states sponsoring rebel groups and insurgents, transnational advocacy groups, such as Geneva Call, international donors, but also the international community as a whole.

Moreover, as Coggins argues, the quest for international recognition has motivated many VNSA to engage in what he calls "rebel diplomacy," not just with central state authorities, but also with international and external actors (Coggins 2015, 98): "The practice of rebel diplomacy is essential for violent non-state actors on the verge of new statehood or seeking legitimacy for a new regime."

A case in point is the efforts by the MILF in the Southern Philippines to accept the mediation efforts of the international community (Jo 2015, 173–174). Other examples for VNSA in need of gaining legitimacy in "the shadow of future statehood" (Börzel and Risse 2013), which then engaged in governance, include Museveni's National Resistance Army (NRA) in Uganda (Weinstein 2007, 175–180), the Shining Path in Peru, at least initially (Weinstein 2007, 186–192), FARC in Colombia and other Latin American cases (Wickham-Crowley 2015), some warlord factions in Afghanistan, and VNSA in Somaliland (Chojnacki and Branovic 2011, 92–95; on Afghanistan see also Koehler and Wilke 2011).

A final reason why VNSA engage in governance concerns their values and attitudes as well as their embeddedness in local communities. While most of the literature on VNSA treats them as strategic rational actors with the sole goal of achieving power over people and territories, several studies have found that their values actually matter with regard to the provision of governance (Arjona, Kasfir, and Mampilly 2015a; Felbab-Brown, Trinkunas, and Hamid 2017; Cammett 2014; Suykens 2015). Religious or political belief systems also provide an important source of legitimacy. Rebel groups, who pursue political goals of political self-determination or regime change, seek to delegitimize state actors claiming to protect the population against them (Bassiouni 2008; Felbab-Brown, Trinkunas, and Hamid 2017). This also applies to Islamist militants, particularly when they oppose a secular regime with limited statehood (Cammett 2014; Roy 2011). Even criminal groups invoke Christian imagery and religious practices to bolster their legitimacy. La Familia Michoacana, a Mexican drug cartel, subscribes to an evangelically influenced Christian ideology and distributes its own Bible authored by the leadership (Felbab-Brown, Trinkunas, and Hamid 2017, 112–113). And Afghan warlords appeal to customary forms of governance, appropriating traditional policing and military structures (*abakai* and *lashkar*; see Chapter 5), to justify their rule (Felbab-Brown 2012).

Mao Zedong's famous dictum of the guerrilla who "must move amongst the people as the fish swims in the sea"[20] already points to the need of embeddedness in local communities. This is where social trust – be it personalized, be it particularistic or group-based trust – comes in. As discussed in Chapter 3, social trust allows communities to overcome collective action problems and to increase their action capacity. Arjona shows with regard to Colombia and the FARC that pre-existing formal and informal institutions enabled trust-based communities to place specific demands on FARC rebels, including resistance to their governance efforts in a similar way as the "shadow of the (local) community"

[20] Quoted from www.brainyquote.com/quotes/quotes/m/maozedong138236.html, last access September 4, 2017.

pressures companies to provide governance (see above; Arjona 2015, 2016; for similar findings with regard to eastern Indonesia and central Nigeria see Krause 2018).

How Govern? Controlling Means of Violence and Constructing Communities

VNSA can and do employ the entire range of modes of governance discussed in Chapter 2. To the extent that warlords, rebel groups, or Islamist militants use force or even exercise a monopoly of the use of force in a given territory, they have the ability to govern hierarchically (see Marten 2012, 2013). After it won the elections in Gaza in 2007, Hamas acquired the monopoly of the use of force. The same holds true for Hezbollah in Southern Lebanon and parts of Beirut (see Berti 2013, 2016; Berti and Gutiérrez 2016, Dingel 2016). Both Hamas and Hezbollah used their capacity to set and enforce rules to provide collective goods and services (Roy 2011). At the same time, neither Hamas nor Hezbollah have become "normal" political players in the sense of refraining from violence against their opponents, both inside their territories and outside. While having become governors, they have remained VNSA that consist of both state-like bureaucracies and administrations, as well as rather sophisticated armed groups, which remain a threat to their opponents. Likewise, warlords may be contracted by external states and international organizations as security providers or be co-opted by state actors as provincial governors or members of parliament in return for their security services. Yet, their clients are unable to control the use of force, which warlords and their militias more often than not continue to also employ for private rent-seeking, e.g. by extorting informal security fees from local business (Marten 2013).

Territorial control is the pre-condition for VNSA to become governors, e.g. providing public security rather than private security in exchange for rents and taxes or delivering security as a club good for their clientele (see Chojnacki and Branovic 2011, 93, for a typology of forms of security). Hierarchical modes of governance by warlords, rebel groups, and other VNSA aimed at the effective provision of security as a public good, are often linked to the building up of state-like structures. The examples of two "strongman governors" in the Afghan provinces of Balkh and Nangahar are cases in point (Mukhopadhyay 2014). As Charles Tilly has argued, this is exactly how the modern Western state came about in Europe (Tilly 1985, 1995; cf. Davis 2009). However, the effectiveness of such security governance by warlords is an altogether different matter (see Chapter 6). So is the question whether there are any constraints on their coercive powers. The cases of Afghanistan or the FATA in Pakistan (see Koehler and Wilke 2011; Marten 2013) demonstrate how precarious and unsustainable the governance arrangements are under adverse conditions (cf. Felbab-Brown, Trinkunas, and Hamid 2017, ch. 3).

Once VNSA have established a monopoly of the use of force in areas controlled by them, they often engage in providing other collective goods and services. Hamas in Gaza and Hezbollah in Lebanon have engaged in health and education governance as well as in rule-making activities (Cammett 2014; Roy 2011). So did IS/Daesh in the territories as long as it controlled them (Barbato, Hantscher, and Lederer 2016; Felbab-Brown, Trinkunas, and Hamid 2017, 4). The FARC in Colombia represents another example for what Arjona called a "rebelocracy" (Arjona 2015, 2016), while the Free Aceh Movement (GAM) in Aceh, Indonesia, allowed other non-state actors to deliver public services, at least initially (Barter 2015).

VNSA not only use violence and threats, they also have non-hierarchical means of coordination at their disposal. Museveni's NRA in Uganda established some sort of grassroots democracy in the areas it controlled and placed authority in the hands of elected local officials. So did the Shining Path in Peru, which shared power with popular committees (Weinstein 2007, 175–180, 186–192). Weinstein argues that the governance structures established by rebel groups tend to be the more inclusive and participatory with regard to the local population, the more VNSA need civilian support and material resources, and the more they require local civilian labor because they do not have access to natural resources or external funding (Felbab-Brown, Trinkunas, and Hamid 2017; Salehyan, Siroky, and Wood 2014; Weinstein 2007). Rebel groups in Sierra Leone or the DRC could rely on diamond mining, while the Tamil Tigers in Sri Lanka drew a major part of their income from diaspora remittances. As a result, they have been less inclusive and more repressive than insurgent groups, like the Communist Party of Nepal-Maoist, which depends on contributions from local businesses and communities (Podder 2013). Increasing participation and, thus, engaging in non-hierarchical governance provides a means to gain the trust of and the domestic legitimacy among non-combatants (Felbab-Brown, Trinkunas, and Hamid 2017; Jo 2015). Participatory and non-hierarchical governance represents an attempt to build up input legitimacy rather than relying solely on output legitimacy through the delivery of collective goods.

Rebel ideology also matters. Leftist guerrillas tend to be more participatory than right-wing or Islamist groups (Arjona, Kasfir, and Mampilly 2015a; Gutiérrez-Sanín and Wood 2014; Kalyvas 2015). The embeddedness of political insurgency and criminal activities in local communities is not only a key driver for VNSA to engage in governance (Kalyvas 2006; Metelits 2009). Guerrilla forces and rebel groups in Angola, the DRC, Colombia, or Peru construct themselves as "alternative imagined communities of allegiance and reciprocity," which "provide new forms of welfare, employment and meaning" (Davis 2009, 227). Likewise, drug cartels in urban Brazil and Mexico, trafficking rings in Central and Southeast Asia, or mafia networks in Eastern Europe have developed shared loyalties based on common economic objectives. Thus, they generate loyalty and a sense of belonging that reduce the need for hierarchical governance and the use of force.

In sum, VNSA engage in governance under certain conditions. As "stationary bandits," their governance motivations stem mostly from the "shadows of anarchy and of communities," but also from the quest for (international and domestic) legitimacy. Once they become governors, they have the entire range of governance modes at their disposal, from the use of force and command-and-control all the way to inclusive and participatory governance.

Conclusions

This chapter addressed the first part of the governance puzzle: why do actors engage in rule-making and service delivery in areas where the state fails to do so, and which modes of governance do they employ? The analysis confirms that the three explanatory factors identified by our theoretical framework (see Chapter 3) induce governance contributions by external as well as internal state and non-state actors.

First, institutional conditions, that is, statehood as well as the lack of it, matter. An "external shadow of hierarchy" can substitute for the lack thereof in areas of limited statehood. Home country laws in consolidated states force multinational companies and their suppliers to not only refrain from human rights violations or environmental pollution in ALS, but also to engage in governance. Moreover, areas of limited statehood are often not ungoverned precisely because statehood is limited. The "shadow of anarchy," i.e., the absence of any governance, is a major motivation not only for foreign states, IOs, and (I)NGOs, whose public mandate and adherence to humanitarian and development norms makes them already prone to engage in governance. Companies, warlords, and rebel groups require some basic "law and order" to realize their economic and political goals. Since they have both a self-interest as well as the capacity to govern, weak states seek to enlist their help, delegating or at least tolerating the provision of security or the rule of law. Obtaining such a "license to govern" is particularly important for external actors (states, IOs, MNCs) who as foreigners often struggle for social acceptance.

The quest for (international as well as domestic) legitimacy is a second powerful driver for all actors involved in governance in ALS. States, IOs, (I)NGOs, and MSPs have to legitimate their public mandate and their humanitarian commitment by serving the common good where it is most needed. This also applies to "traditional" authorities with regard to serving their communities when the central state fails to do so. The "shadow of the community" as the embeddedness in local communities generates social expectations to engage in governance even for self-interested business and VNSA. While global norms of CSR commit multinational companies to social, environmental, and human rights standards to please their shareholders and customers, they are also confronted with local demands for providing public services at their production sites. Likewise, rebel groups not only vie for international recognition by adhering to human rights when they see a chance of taking over the state. The more they become stationary, the more they depend on the support and the social acceptance of those whom they intend to rule and/or whose resources they need to obtain victory.

Social trust, finally, reinforces social expectations to engage in governance. "Traditional" leaders seek moral standing by not betraying the trust that they provide for their community. Moreover, personalized trust eliminates a major disincentive for contributing to the provisions of collective goods and services. Members of "traditional" communities or rebel groups integrated through particularistic trust relations (see Chapter 3) do not fear that they will be cheated by others who refuse to contribute, but reap the benefit.

As to the modes of governance, we find the entire spectrum from hierarchical rule and the use of force to non-hierarchical means of negotiation and even deliberation. External state actors (through military interventions and trusteeships), VNSA (through the control of the use of force in a territory), as well as "traditional authorities" (because of their moral or religious stance or kinship relations of trust) can govern hierarchically, even if – as in the case of chiefs and tribal leaders – they do not control the use of force. Traditional authorities have the advantage of social ligatures that provide them with social sanctioning capacities. Others, such as companies, (I)NGOs or MSPs have to rely on more cooperative and non-hierarchical modes of governance that include bargaining, but also persuasion and deliberation. We even find deliberative processes in unlikely places, such as NSJI. Last but not least, there appears to be a significant link between actor motivations and modes of governance: non-hierarchical and participatory modes of governance become the more likely, the more governors require domestic (but also international) legitimacy. While many non-state actors govern to generate output legitimacy, even VNSA sometimes allow for participatory governance as a means to induce input legitimacy, the more they need the support of local communities for achieving their political goals.

This chapter presented ample evidence on a multitude of actors – domestic and international, state and non-state - engaging in governance in areas of limited statehood, both hierarchically and non-hierarchically. However, how effective and sustainable is governance by these actors, some of whom only become governors to achieve other – economic or political - goals? The motivation to govern does not equal effectiveness. Moreover, if these motivations primarily stem from self-interested reasons, such actors will cease to govern, as soon as the circumstances change and their governance contributions are no longer needed. This is different for – state and non-state – actors for whom the contribution to governance is constitutive. But, even in these cases, well-meaning does not necessarily lead to effective governance as defined above (see Chapter 3). How do we explain the variation in effectiveness (and legitimacy) of governance in areas of limited statehood? We turn to this question in the following three chapters.

5 Security

This and the following two chapters analyze the effectiveness of governance in areas of limited statehood in various issue-areas. We start with the provision of public security. While security is an essentially contested concept (see e.g. Baldwin 1997; Buzan, Waever, and Wilde 1998; Schröder 2018), we use a narrow definition, namely the absence of violence, and threats thereof, against individuals (similarly Chojnacki and Branovic 2011, 91). It follows then that security governance as the intentional provision of physical protection is the more effective, the more it resembles a public good for a given population. The following graph shows the governance puzzle with regard to "unnatural deaths" (homicides and casualties from violent conflict) and statehood in 2012 (see Figure 5.1). Each dot represents the relative (lack of) violence per country.[1] First and overall, violent deaths are rare occurrences; most countries are situated between 0.8 and 1.0, and this includes the vast majority of countries with ALS including "failed states" (with statehood levels of 0.4 and below). Second, there is virtually no correlation between degrees of statehood and violence, but quite some variation, with the spread being particularly wide in countries with medium-degrees of statehood (0.6–0.8; see also Lee, Walter-Drop, and Wiesel 2014 for similar results).

Figure 5.1 also demonstrates that a state monopoly of the use of force (countries with degrees of statehood above 0.8) does not prevent violent deaths. So, what explains the variation in the effectiveness of security governance? To explore this variation, this chapter focuses on two particular attempts at security governance in ALS: 1) efforts by external state actors in the framework of peace-keeping missions, military interventions, and Security Sector Reform (SSR); 2) security governance by violent non-state actors (VNSA), such as warlords or rebel groups. The

---

[1] Note that these data suffer from methodological nationalism and, thus, only partially reflect the security situation in the countries with regard to ALS, as we discuss in Chapter 2.

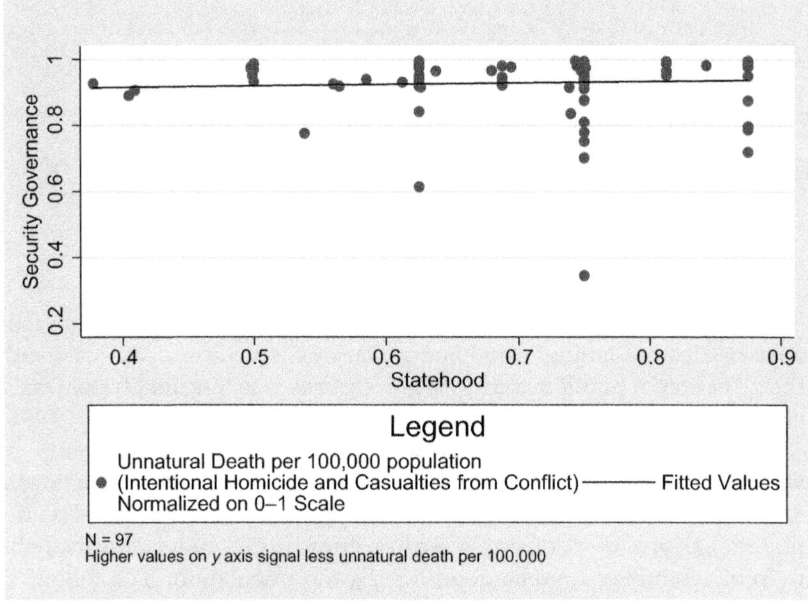

Figure 5.1 Violence and statehood (2012)
Each dot represents the value for one country.
Source: Courtesy of Eric Stollenwerk, see Stollenwerk and Opper 2017; for a description of statehood measurements see chapter 2.

first is the most extreme external interference into the sovereignty of states, raising issues of both legitimacy and effectiveness. The second presents a least likely case as violence is constitutive for warlords and rebel groups. Before we investigate the effectiveness of external state actors and VNSA as security providers, we briefly discuss the relationship between civil war and ALS.

Limited Statehood Does Not Equal Civil War

Limited statehood is frequently depicted as a major cause for civil war and violent conflict and vice versa (see e.g. the classic piece by Fearon and Laitin 2003; also Besley and Persson 2010; DeRouen et al. 2010; Fjelde and De Soysa 2009; Hendrix 2010; Sobek 2010).[2] A state that lacks the monopoly of the use of force is almost by definition incapable of preventing or quelling armed conflict between groups within its territory. Once broken out or

---

[2] This section builds on Risse and Stollenwerk 2018b.

frozen, i.e., no longer active (e.g. in South Ossetia, Georgia), violent conflicts compromise the state's monopoly of the use of force and its capacity to set and enforce collectively binding rules in parts of its territory.

The dominant discourse on fragile and failed states portrays areas of limited statehood as infested with chaos, anarchy, and violent conflict, in short, a Hobbesian state of nature where life is "solitary, poor, nasty, brutish and short" (for a thorough criticism of this discourse see Woodward 2017; see also Chapters 2 and 3). Consequently, state-building efforts are considered to be an effective tool for the prevention or ending of civil war and violent conflict (see e.g. Lockart 2018). The assumption is that more statehood will equal more governance and less civil war (DeRouen and Sobek 2004; Sobek 2010). Indeed, the lack of a state monopoly of the use of force serves as an enabling condition for violence and civil war. Yet, the reverse conclusion is wrong: limited statehood as such does not lead necessarily to civil war and violence.

While ALS are more likely to witness civil wars in their territory when compared with areas of consolidated statehood, only a small fraction of ALS are affected by civil war. In 2007, about 85 percent of countries worldwide displayed some ALS (for measurements see Chapter 2). However, the Correlates of War Project counts only 18 intra-state wars between 2001 and 2007, spread out across 12 countries. These wars occurred or are still occurring in states displaying significant degrees of limited statehood. Nevertheless, countries suffering from these conflicts comprise only 10 percent of all ALS.[3] Limited statehood as such does not correlate highly with the presence of civil wars.

Moreover, the state itself is often a source of insecurity rather than security in ALS (Müller 2012; Reno 2017). If the state acquires stronger capacities but uses them in a predatory way – not protecting but harming its citizens – state-building initiatives are counterproductive. Cases, such as Mexico, South Africa, Iraq under Nouri al-Maliki, or the Philippines under Rodrigo Duterte, illustrate that the state and, in particular, the security forces in ALS have regularly used their capacities to violently oppress and discriminate against parts of the population, thereby increasing insecurity (Ochoa and Jiménez 2012). Koren and Sarbahi use night-time light emissions as an indicator for state capacity at the sub-national level and correlate them with incidences of violence.[4] They argue that more state capacity actually leads to more violence by non-state actors

---

[3] Calculation based on Correlates of War Project intra-state conflict data. See DeRouen and Sobek 2004; Sarkees and Wayman 2010.

[4] While equating state capacity with governance (see Chapter 2), electricity constitutes a crucial infrastructure that is often provided by the state even in ALS.

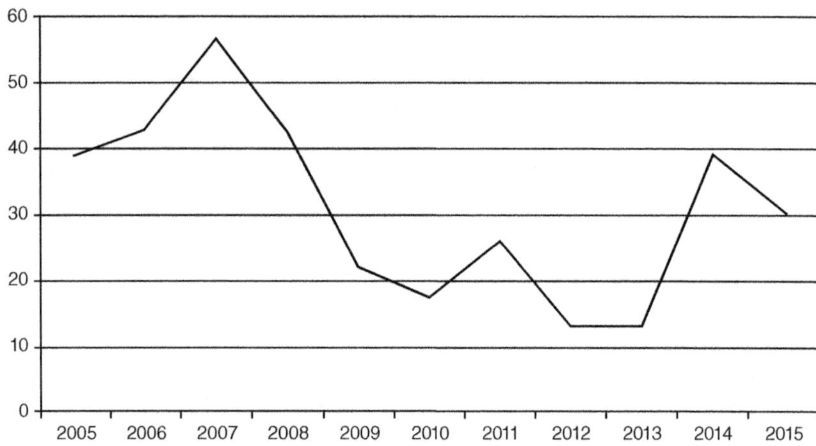

Figure 5.2 Percentage of Chadian regions affected by fighting, 2005–2015

Source: Taken from Risse and Stollenwerk 2018b, 109. Based on Armed Conflict Location & Event Data Project, "ACLED Version 6 (1997–2015)," http://www .acleddata.com/data, last access February 28, 2018.

(Koren and Sarbahi 2018). Lee demonstrates that consolidated neighboring states often interfere violently in ALS, thus hampering security rather than safeguarding it (Lee 2018). We come back to the question of how statehood affects governance in ALS in Chapter 8.

Even if we focus on countries that are affected by civil war, violence is rarely ubiquitous in time or space. Studies show that only some parts of countries are normally affected by violent conflict, while others are not (Aas Rustad et al. 2011; Buhaug and Lujala 2005). To give two prominent examples: Chad is often ranked among those countries with the lowest level of statehood on a global scale. However, during the civil war from 2005 to 2010, only some of the 23 regions of Chad were affected by conflict. In 2005, for instance, armed conflict prevailed in only nine out of the 23 Chadian regions, i.e., just 39 percent. Figure 5.2 illustrates that the proportion of the country affected by fighting from 2005 to 2015 varied over time, but never covered the entire Chadian territory. A peak was reached in 2007 with almost 60 percent of Chadian regions suffering from civil war, while 2012 and 2013 marked the lowest episodes with less than 15 percent of all regions involved in violent conflict.

The second example concerns Somalia, the quintessential failed state since the early 1990s and – according to the Armed Conflict Location & Event Data Project (ACLED) – "Africa's most violent state."[5] Figure 5.3, which maps the geo-located number of violent events

---

[5] www.acleddata.com/dashboard/#706, last access August 5, 2019.

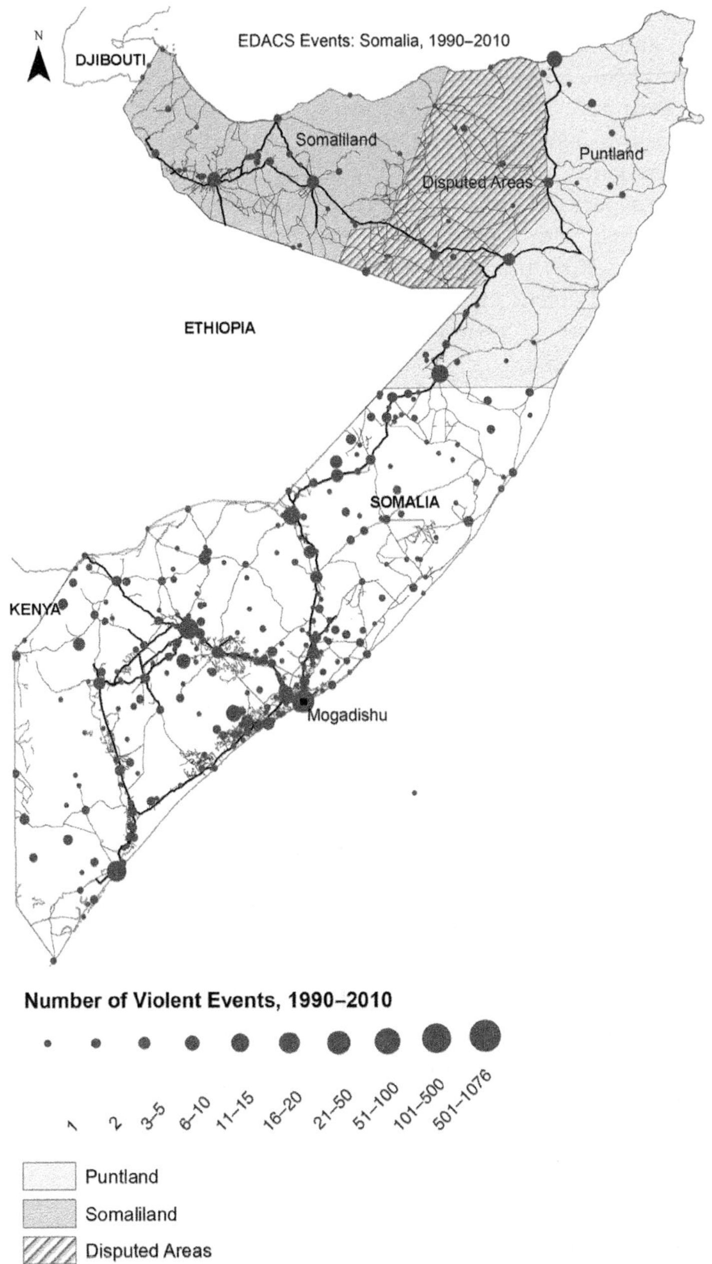

Figure 5.3 Number of violent events in Somalia, 1990–2010
Source: Courtesy of Sven Chojnacki and Johannes Ickler, based on Event Data on Armed Conflict and Security (EDACS) database, see https://www.conflict-data .org/edacs/downloads/index.html, last access February 28, 2020. See also Chojnacki et al. 2012.

from 1990 to 2010, shows a more differentiated picture. Armed conflict and other violent events are mostly located in the province of Central Somalia, around the capital of Mogadishu and along the main infrastructure roads. This is indeed the area that gave Somalia its bad name as a failed state over the years. At the same time, the provinces of Puntland (to the north of the map) and Somaliland (the northwestern part of the map in Figure 5.3) are almost completely devoid of violence, with some events occurring around Somaliland's capital of Hargeisa. Note that even the geo-referenced data cannot tell whether the lack of violence results from whoever holds a monopoly of the use of force over a territory or whether certain locations have simply remained peaceful.

In sum, civil war and other forms of violence do occur more often in areas of limited statehood than in areas of consolidated statehood. At the same time, many ALS remain peaceful, even if the central state lacks a monopoly of the use of force, as the example of Somalia shows. Once again, the question remains how the variation in the degree of violence in ALS can be explained? In the following, we discuss the effectiveness of various attempts at security governance. We start with external (state) actors.

Peace-Keeping Missions, Military Interventions, and Security Sector Reform (SSR)

Since 1948, there have been more than 70 UN peace-keeping missions with peace-keepers from more than 120 countries.[6] Since the end of the Cold War, there have been 14 so-called Chapter 7 interventions authorized by the UN Security Council (UNSC) without the consent of the country affected. In addition, the EU, the Organization for Security and Cooperation in Europe (OSCE), the African Union, and other regional organizations carried out more than 50 missions in 2018, mostly based on a UN mandate.[7] The International Military Intervention (IMI) dataset counts 1,114 interventions from 1946 to 2005, but the vast majority of them have not been conducted for humanitarian reasons (or at least a humanitarian purpose could not be ascertained).[8] A dataset compiled by

---

[6] https://peacekeeping.un.org/en/our-history, last access August 5, 2019.
[7] www.zif-berlin.org/fileadmin/uploads/analyse/dokumente/veroeffentlichungen/ZIF_World_Map_Peace_Operations_2018.pdf, last access August 5, 2019.
[8] www.k-state.edu/polsci/intervention/index.html, last access September 11, 2017.

Dembinski and Gromes identifies 41 humanitarian interventions between 1945 and 2015, including six borderline cases (Dembinski and Gromes 2017).

What these peace-keeping missions and military interventions have in common is that they constitute deep intrusions in the "Westphalian sovereignty" of states. External actors – mostly states, but also IOs and ROs such as NATO, the Economic Community of West African States (ECOWAS), or the Gulf Cooperation Council (GCC) – seek to take over the monopoly of the use of force, at least in parts of the territory. Apart from that, however, there are substantial differences in the various missions and interventions:

- Some peace-keeping missions and military interventions are rather comprehensive and part of larger attempts at state-building or liberal peace-building (e.g. Afghanistan, Iraq, and Kosovo), while others are confined to very specific tasks (e.g. UN Stabilization Mission in Haiti, EU Border Assistance Mission to Moldova and Ukraine).
- Some missions and interventions are based on the consent of the affected state (e.g. UN and EU missions in Mali, UN Mission in South Sudan or the Central African Republic), while others are not (e.g. Afghanistan 2001, UN and EU missions in Bosnia Herzegovina and Kosovo; Libya 2011). A few military interventions occurred without UN mandate (Iraq 2003, Kosovo 1999).

What can we say about the effectiveness of these external interventions in the "Westphalian sovereignty" of areas of limited statehood? First and in general, there is an emerging consensus in the literature that peace-keeping after civil wars works on average with regard to its immediate goal to end violence and mass atrocities (Doyle and Sambanis 2000, 2006; Fortna 2004, 2008; Hegre, Hultman, and Nygård 2019; Howard 2007; Hultman, Kathman, and Shannon 2016; Ruggeri, Dorussen, and Gizelis 2017). Analyzes focusing on the sub-national level showed that peace-keepers do protect civilians against rebel forces and contain local violence, but that they are more challenged in protecting people from government forces, particularly if they rely on the consent of the respective state (Fjelde, Hultman, and Nilsson 2019; Ruggeri, Dorussen, and Gizelis 2017). Studies also show that there is no endogeneity bias in the sense that international peace-keepers only pick the easy cases. On the contrary, particularly UN peace-keeping missions target the difficult conflicts. The number of casualties is a strong predictor for such external interventions, thus confirming the argument about their humanitarian mission (Finnemore 2003; Gilligan and Stedman 2003).

Second, however, there is still variation, particularly when we look at prominent cases. Even when using only minimum standards of effectiveness – keeping the peace and providing security as a public good – the Western interventions in Somalia in 1992, in Afghanistan in 2001, in Iraq in 2003, or in Libya in 2011 have substantially failed. In contrast, the UN Protection Force Missions in Croatia and Bosnia Herzegovina as well as the Kosovo intervention of 1999 can be regarded as success cases insofar as they were able to keep the peace. The same holds true for Timor-Leste in 1999, Sierra Leone in 1999, and Liberia in 2003. The above mentioned new data set on 41 humanitarian interventions from 1945 to 2015 concludes that more than a fourth ended violence within one year while almost half of them led to reduced violence. Only a quarter of interventions resulted in increased death rates or no change (Dembinski and Gromes 2017).

Comprehensive state-building and liberal peace-building interventions by external actors, in contrast – with or without UN mandate – have almost universally failed. Rather than building sustainable peace and security, they have often exacerbated domestic conflict. In the cases of Bosnia Herzegovina and Kosovo, peace has been kept successfully; however, both still require international trusteeship structures (see below). Moreover, particularly UN peace-keeping missions have been accused of human rights violations and – in some cases – gross atrocities against civilians (Hirschmann 2015, 2017).

Last but not least, and related to the various peace-keeping missions and military interventions to (re-)build a monopoly of the use of force, are efforts at SSR. The 2007 OECD Development Assistance Committee's (DAC) *Handbook on Security System Reform*, an authoritative source for external efforts at security governance, defines SSR as

the transformation of the security system – which includes all the actors, their roles, responsibilities and actions – working together to manage and operate the system in a manner that is more consistent with democratic norms and sound principles of good governance and this contributes to a well-functioning security framework. (quoted from Jackson 2011, 1810)

Most external efforts at SSR take place in post-conflict environments and are geared to restore security institutions – e.g. police forces and the military – that respect the rule of law and human rights and to re-establish a rule-based (state) monopoly of the use of force. SSR efforts have changed over time from narrow attempts at capacity-building with regard to police and the military toward a focus on human security, the rule of law, and human rights. At the same time, SSR initiatives by external actors have tried to be more inclusive with regard to the involvement of local actors as well as more context-sensitive (overviews in Jackson 2011; Schröder, Chappuis, and Kocak 2013).

The effects of SSR, however, are rather mixed. On the more positive side, most SSR initiatives seem to have increased public security, as evidence from Palestine, Liberia, Timor-Leste, Sierra Leone, and Bosnia Herzegovina suggests (Bangura 2017; Dewhurst and Greising 2017; Jackson and Albrecht 2010; Marijan 2017; Schröder, Chappuis, and Kocak 2013). At the same time, these initiatives have rarely achieved their more far-reaching goals of rule- and human rights-based security provision. They still focus on training and equipping state security agents (police, military) rather than making them democratically accountable. More often than not, SSR resulted in mixed governance models combining parts of the Western "template" and local institutional arrangements (Schröder, Chappuis, and Kocak 2014), or bolstered rather than transformed authoritarian regimes (Brockmeier and Rotmann 2018; Fisher and Anderson 2015). At the same time, more recent attempts of "second-generation SSR" (Marijan 2017, 4–5) have apparently been more successful, particularly in Timor-Leste and Sierra Leone (Bangura 2017; Dewhurst and Greising 2017).

So, how can we explain the variation?

Legitimacy: International Mandate and Local Ownership

Social acceptance or empirical legitimacy of the interveners (see Chapter 3 on these concepts) or lack thereof goes a long way to explain the variation. Interference with the "Westphalian sovereignty" of states by providing statehood – the monopoly of the use of force as well as rule enforcement (see Chapter 2) – from the outside constitutes the most extreme intrusion into a country's sovereignty. It crucially depends on the consent of those being governed – particularly in war-torn societies with strong political and cultural cleavages in areas of limited statehood (see Lake, D. 2016 for a similar argument).

Military interventions in the "Westphalian sovereignty" of states without the consent of the fighting parties are unlikely to achieve their goals. This finding holds even more for military interventions that go beyond security-building purposes and are part of larger state-building efforts in the sense of international trusteeships (Lake, D. 2016; Lake and Farris 2014). A study by Lake and Farris found no effects of peace-keeping efforts – with or without consent – on broader governance provision such as public health (Lake and Farris 2014). In fact, multidimensional peace missions appear to empower authoritarian and corrupt regimes by accommodating potential spoilers and providing incumbent elites with rent-seeking opportunities through the massive influx of resources (Brosig and Sempijja 2017; Le Billon 2008; Mac Ginty and Richmond 2016; Schröder, Chappuis, and Kocak 2014). It seems as if Germany and Japan after World War II are the two big exceptions to these findings.

The situation changes in the cases of "external interventions by invitation." Doyle and Sambanis show that if the parties to the conflict sign a peace treaty and then invite UN or other peace-keeping missions to enforce it, the likelihood of lasting absence of violence increases (Doyle and Sambanis 2000, 786, 788). Fortna finds that consent-based peace-keeping missions (such as Chapter 6 UN missions) are much more effective than enforcement missions (such as Chapter 7 UN missions or interventions without consent; see Fortna 2004, 285, 287). Matanock confirms these findings for consent-based missions between 1990 and 2003 (Matanock 2014). Finally, impartial interventions appear to be more effective in stopping violence and mass killings than biased or partisan interventions (Dembinski and Gromes 2017; Wood, Kathman, and Gent 2012).

Chapter 6 UN peace-keeping missions as well as most of the missions by the EU and other ROs resemble Governance Delegation Agreements (GDA) whereby national governments (or, in the case of peace treaties ending civil wars, the fighting parties) delegate security governance to external actors. The most prominent example of a GDA is probably the Regional Assistance Mission to the Solomon Islands (RAMSI) led by Australia and the Pacific Islands Forum, an RO (details in Matanock 2014; see also Chapter 4). RAMSI constituted a comprehensive GDA taking over almost the entire state apparatus, including the police, the judiciary, and the treasury. It is considered rather successful: incidents of violence have dropped drastically since 2003 and the rule of law has been restored.

RAMSI and other missions by invitation or delegation enjoy some degree of input legitimacy and social acceptance from the very beginning. They can still fail when they do not manage to win over the local population or when the inviting central governments are not perceived as legitimate by local actors. The UN Peacebuilding Commissions, for instance, have strongly endorsed the principle of ownership (Paris and Sisk 2009). They formally involve (I)NGOs, local communities, and other actors operating on the ground in their work on post-conflict peace-building at various stages and levels.

At the same time, successful peace-keeping is likely to reinforce the legitimacy of the external governors resulting in a virtuous cycle where perceived governance effectiveness fosters output legitimacy, which in turn increases governance effectiveness, and so forth (Sabrow 2017; Schmelzle and Stollenwerk 2018). This may explain why peace treaties correlate rather highly with peace-keeping success, even though they often fail to connect to the local population (Doyle and Sambanis 2000, 789). The EU's very first autonomous military mission, operation Artemis, supporting the UN Organization Mission in the DRC (MONUC), could claim little local ownership (Rayroux and Wilén 2014). Nevertheless, the deployment of EU troops in 2003 significantly helped decrease conflict intensity, restoring security in the town of Burnia.[9] A case study on external peace operations in the Mali conflict that broke out in 2012 corroborates that output- or performance-based legitimacy can to some extent substitute for lacking input legitimacy. Sabrow's data on the perceived legitimacy of the subsequent interventions by France, ECOWAS, and the UN show that France is appreciated but only for its effective performance, while ECOWAS as a regional organization can claim a license to intervene but no real success. The UN scores relatively low on output- and even lower on input legitimacy (Sabrow 2017).

Autesserre argues that most external peace-building interventions lack input legitimacy with regard to "peaceland," the virtual environment that most international peace-builders and interveners inhabit (Autesserre 2014b). Her ethnographic studies relating to the daily experiences of peace-builders demonstrates that most interventions, if at all, only include local elites and populations in the final stages of a project rather than in the project design. While paying lip-service to the principle of "local ownership," this is rarely practiced on the ground (Donais 2009b; Grøner Krogstad 2014; Lee and Özerdem 2015; Oosterveld and Galand 2012). Campbell's in-depth study of local peace-building in Burundi also demonstrates that the informal accountability of peace-keepers to local actors and communities was key for successful peace-building (Campbell 2018). Her work points to the connection between local legitimacy generated through accountability mechanisms, on the one hand, and institutional design with an in-built learning capacity, on the other.

External interveners often fail because they lack the necessary acceptance and support among local actors (Autesserre 2014a; Fortna 2008; Hellmüller 2013; Sabrow 2017; Talentino 2007). Moreover, they do not have the local knowledge about the particular needs and conditions on the ground either, which then translates into ill-suited institutional designs of peace-building efforts (Avant, Finnemore, and Sell 2010a; Westerwinter 2013) that are unlikely to generate output legitimacy.

---

[9] http://ucdp.uu.se/#nonstate/5248, last access March 23, 2018.

This may be the reason why the study by Call finds that ROs are perceived to make a more positive contribution to peace than IOs or Western states – the former are stronger on both input legitimacy and output legitimacy (Call 2012).

(Input) legitimacy, or the lack thereof, also appears to explain the variation with regard to various attempts at SSR led by external actors. In this case, some sort of "natural experiment" has been conducted, insofar as external SSR actors changed their modes of governance from coercive and incentive approaches to efforts at socialization and persuasion (Schröder, Chappuis, and Kocak 2013). The overall model for SSR initiatives now endorses more inclusive approaches emphasizing local ownership and the early participation of domestic and local actors (Ball 2010; Donais 2009a; Mobekk 2010; Oosterveld and Galand 2012). A series of reports from the Canadian Centre for Security Governance demonstrates particularly for Sierra Leone and Timor-Leste that the change in SSR programming toward increased input legitimacy led indeed to greater effectiveness (cf. Bangura 2016 with Bangura 2017; Dewhurst, Saraiva, and Winch 2016 with Dewhurst and Greising 2017; on Timor-Leste also Schröder, Chappuis, and Kocak 2013; on Sierra Leone Jackson and Albrecht 2010). An evaluation of the Friedrich Ebert Foundation's (FES) support for SSR in Southeast Asia, Southern Africa, and Latin America also finds that the inclusive regional-level dialogues the FES organized stimulated changes in the security sector, e.g. by broadening security toward social, economic, and human rights issues. They did so by bringing together a broad range of stakeholders from the security sector, politics, and civil society, and building trust among them (Brockmeier and Rotmann 2018).

In contrast, where local ownership failed, as it did in the DRC, SSR got paralyzed (Boege 2014; Rayroux and Wilén 2014). Local actors resisted structural changes related to the EU's civilian SSR missions (EU Police Mission – EUPOL – and EU Mission to Provide Advice and Assistance for SSR – EUSEC), not only because they were perceived as externally imposed – EUSEC was requested by the Congolese government, whereas EUPOL was part of the UN mandate. The central government sidelined other local actors, seeking to rebuild the security sector according to its own interests in strengthening the national armed forces, "prioritizing state and elite protection over the population's security in an insecure environment" (Rayroux and Wilén 2014, 38).

In contrast, Matanock shows that external actors monitoring or supporting so-called Electoral Participation Provisions (EPP) in the aftermath of civil wars have a discernible effect on the sustainability of the peace settlement (Matanock 2017, 2018). EPPs are meant to include the various combatants of a civil war into the post-conflict electoral process thereby transforming rebel groups, militias, and other armed forces into political parties. Such EPPs directly affect the likelihood of enduring peace through input legitimacy. At the same time, external monitoring of such post-war settlements not only provides a considerably less costly alternative to military interventions, the external intervention is also perceived as a lot more legitimate by local actors.

AFGHANISTAN AS AN EXAMPLE

The following examples from the Afghanistan intervention underscore the causal link between legitimacy and the success of external security governance. Following the terrorist attacks of September 11, 2001, a US-led international intervention force, which the UN Security Council backed under Chapter 7 (UNSC Resolution 1267), essentially took over the Afghan state, uprooted the Taliban government, and embarked on a comprehensive state-building attempt. At the end of 2014, most of the external military forces left the country, while the Taliban insurgency continued. A detailed analysis of security provision in Northeast Afghanistan reveals that the international intervention was highly successful in keeping the peace and building up Afghan national security forces (ANSF) – until about 2007, when the Taliban targeted the northeast again. It was only the so-called US surge in 2010 and 2011 that effectively controlled the insurgency – in conjunction with local militias (Koehler and Gosztonyi 2014).

Data from household surveys conducted in 80 villages of four provinces in Northeast Afghanistan from 2007 to 2015 (2,000 respondents per wave) have been used to evaluate the relationship between incidents of violence, subjective perceptions of security, and the evaluation of the legitimacy of various governors, including the International Security Assistance Force (ISAF; for the following see particularly Böhnke, Koehler, and Zürcher 2015, 2017; Koehler and Gosztonyi 2014). Incidents of violence in the provinces of Kunduz and Takhar increased from 2007 to 2010 and then decreased again (Koehler and Gosztonyi 2014, 244). These "objective" figures are only partially reflected in the subjective perceptions of security among the survey respondents, though. While large majorities continuously perceived the overall situation in Afghanistan as insecure, equally large majorities felt rather safe with regard to their own households. In contrast, when asked about "village security," the responses tend to reflect the ups and downs with regard to incidents of violence in the various provinces (Böhnke, Koehler, and Zürcher 2015, 27–29). In other words, perceptions of Afghan security and of the safety of one's own household appear to be driven by other factors than "objective" degrees of violence (see Chapter 3 on how to measure effectiveness).

Even more striking are the answers by Afghan people with regard to their evaluation of the security contributions of various governors, including the external intervention forces. To begin with, the Afghan armed forces and the national police received continuous high marks as contributing to public security. These numbers appear to suggest that local populations, even in a failed state, such as Afghanistan, still considered the state as responsible for providing security. We come back to that point in Chapter 8.

In contrast, criminals, warlords, and the Taliban are equally perceived as the greatest security threats throughout the time-period (Koehler and Gosztonyi 2014, 245). What varies strongly is the perception of ISAF and the external intervention forces as contributors to security. In 2007, almost 80 percent of the survey respondents perceived foreign forces as a positive contribution to security in their communities, the number dropped to 60 percent in 2009. In 2011 and 2013, only 5 percent and 14 percent of the respondents, respectively, saw foreign forces as positive security governors, while more and more people perceived them as a threat not only to security but also increasingly to their cultural values and identities (Böhnke, Koehler, and Zürcher 2015, 30–31).

The latter numbers appear to follow the augmented US counter-insurgency campaign in 2010 and 2011 mentioned above. While ISAF started with a high degree of legitimacy among the local population in the early 2000s, the anti-Taliban campaign of the 2010s appears to have had the opposite effect. Afghans in the northeast provinces increasingly saw the international intervention forces as part of the security problem, not the solution. Once the legitimacy was gone, it did not recover.

In contrast, international development actors enjoyed a much more positive image in Afghanistan. In 2007, 42 percent of the respondents saw them as positive contributors to local security, the numbers declined to 33 percent in 2009 and 26 percent in 2011, and went up again to 47 percent in 2013 (Böhnke, Koehler, and Zürcher 2015, 30). In other words, it is not external actors per se that are viewed in negative terms. Local populations see "soft interventions" through foreign aid and the provision of public services usually very positively, even as contributions to security (see below and Chapter 6 on the EU in the Western Balkans and the Southern Caucasus as well as Chapter 7 on multi-stakeholder partnerships for more details). At the same time, however, the data from Afghanistan also reveal that local populations clearly distinguish between types of foreign actors. For instance, the positive attitude toward foreign aid does not result in a better image of external armed forces (Böhnke, Koehler, and Zürcher 2015, 11).

A statistical analysis of the survey data from Northeast Afghanistan confirms the relationship between the perceptions of security, on the one hand, and the legitimacy of external actors, on the other, but with an important caveat. Stollenwerk finds that only those survey respondents who also attributed the increased security to ISAF considered the foreign forces legitimate (Stollenwerk 2018b). In other words, output legitimacy of external actors depends on two conditions: first, citizens must perceive the security situation as improved; second, they must attribute the improvement to the specific governors.

Overall, the evidence from Afghanistan corroborates the positive relationship between legitimacy and effective security governance. On the one hand, effective security governance increases the (output) legitimacy of the governors, including external armed forces, the more the effectiveness is attributed to them. On the other hand, the legitimacy of security governors is a pre-condition for their effectiveness, as the case of ISAF forcefully demonstrates. The more particularly US forces were engaged in counter-insurgency, the more they were perceived as security threats, and the less effective their military campaign became. This points to one of the "statebuilder's dilemmas" (Lake, D. 2016): the more external military forces become party to an ongoing conflict in order to restore the monopoly of the use of force, the more their counter-insurgency strategies contribute to the violence itself, as a result of which they lose their initial legitimacy, which in turn makes the counter-insurgency strategy less effective. The US learned this the hard way in Afghanistan. Moreover, the evidence from Afghanistan suggests that output legitimacy acquired through effective security governance can evaporate rather quickly when violent incidents increase again, which in turn tends to undermine its effectiveness.

In sum, we explain the variation in effective security governance primarily on grounds of the differences in legitimacy between consent-based missions, on the one hand, and military interventions without the agreement of national or local actors, on the other. Without a "license to govern," external interveners have to rely almost exclusively on coercive means of enforcement that are likely to meet resistance as a result of which the interveners will have to employ more force. International legitimacy – e.g. bestowed by a Chapter 7 resolution of the UNSC – only goes so far to legitimize interventions in ALS. Unless national and/or local actors "buy into" such legitimation, the domestic effects of international legitimacy in the affected country will be rather limited. This explains to a large extent why state-building interventions mostly fail. They lack input legitimacy and, thus, have to rely mostly on the expectations of the intervened that they will provide peace and security as well as other governance services, i.e., on output legitimacy.

Institutional Design: The Failure of Comprehensive State-Building and the Success of More Limited Efforts

Peace-keeping mandates have grown more complex over the past decades, encompassing the implementation of disarmament, demobilization, and re-integration tasks (DDR), the organization of elections or capacity-building of local civil society organizations (Hunt 2017; Karlsrud 2015; Shesterinina and Job 2016). Robust, multidimensional peace missions are more effective than more limited operations in preventing (relapse to) conflict (Doyle and Sambanis 2006; Fortna 2008; Gilligan and Sergenti 2008; Hegre, Hultman, and Nygård 2019). When it comes to broader governance outcomes, however, the opposite appears to be the case. The 1990s and 2000s saw several attempts at humanitarian interventions aiming at comprehensive state-building efforts – from Somalia in the early 1990s to Bosnia Herzegovina and Kosovo in the mid-to-late 1990s to Afghanistan in the 2000s, and Iraq following the 2003 US-led intervention. Most of these efforts failed, and our approach explains why. Above, we have already touched upon the problem of legitimacy: comprehensive state-building requires local legitimacy, which is rarely achieved, particularly since most external interveners lack input legitimacy. Here, we focus on institutional design, the second condition for successful governance, as discussed in Chapter 3.

A 2007 RAND study already hints at the problem (Dobbins, Jones, and DeGrasse 2007; quoted from Lake, D. 2016, 212–213). Accordingly, state-builders should concentrate on the following list: security, humanitarian relief, governance, economic stabilization, democratization, and development. In other words, they should build "Denmark" (see Chapter 1; for the history of the state-building paradigm see Woodward 2017, ch. 3, 4). Already the first item mentioned above – security – contains further specified tasks that are almost impossible to be achieved within a reasonable timeframe, namely peace-keeping, law enforcement, rule of law, and security sector reform (ibid.). Naturally, such a strategy leads to an attempt at wholesale transfers of – mostly Western – state institutions to areas of limited statehood, which has miserably failed over the past decades. It does not matter much in this context whether state-builders follow a Huntingtonian approach with a focus on state capacity (e.g. Fukuyama 2004) or try to focus simultaneously on security, capacity-building, democracy, and economic development as advocated by Acemoglu and Robinson (Acemoglu and Robinson 2012). The institutional design of what counts as stable state institutions almost always follows a Western script, which is ill-suited to the tasks at hand in many ALS and often results in decoupling, that is, a growing gap between institutional norms and behavioral practices. Complex mandates tend to overburden peace missions, which are "ill-structured" as organizations to affect the institutional changes necessary for sustainable peace- and state-building (Eckhard 2016; Karlsrud 2015; Lipson 2007; Schlöndorf 2011, 44–51).

However, it would be wrong to conclude from the failures of comprehensive state-building efforts that external contributions to security governance in ALS are impossible to achieve. As argued above, external interveners can stop the violence, protect civilians, and prevent genocide and massive human rights violations in accordance with the "responsibility to protect" (R2P; see Bellamy 2011). With an institutional design adequate for the tasks ahead, some comprehensive missions have been quite successful, even if they were carried out against the consent of the concerned state. Examples of such interventions include Bosnia Herzegovina and Kosovo, the latter without a UN mandate.

Secessionist movements, unsettled borders, ethnic tensions, deficient state capacity, and strong clientelistic networks have prevented Bosnia Herzegovina and Kosovo from developing into Western-type consolidated democratic states. Yet, the external interveners – from UN peace-keepers to the NATO-led Kosovo Force (KFOR) and the EU-led EU Forces (EUFOR) troops – have successfully supported development, albeit slow and with setbacks, of the two post-conflict Western Balkan societies toward stable peace, economic growth, and democracy (Biermann 2013; Börzel and Grimm 2018; Eckhard 2016; Krasniqi and Musaj 2015; Papadimitriou and Petrov 2013; Perry 2015). This achievement was only possible because the Western Balkans are in the "backyard" of the EU and, thus, NATO and the EU member states have been prepared to spend considerable resources and to stick around for more than 20 years, turning Bosnia Herzegovina and Kosovo into international protectorates. While Bosnia Herzegovina has become internationally sovereign, Kosovo still lacks both international and domestic sovereignty. In both countries, external actors continue to exercise significant authority. The EU is the largest donor and acts as an institution-builder and security-provider (Grimm and Mathis 2015). Between 2002 and 2011, the EU High Representative in Bosnia Herzegovina assumed the power and authority to oversee the implementation of the General Framework Agreement for Peace in Bosnia Herzegovina and the approximation of the territory to the EU. The EU has also taken over the responsibility for the economic reconstruction pillar under the United Nations Interim Administration Mission in Kosovo, as well as the subsequent European Union Rule of Law mission in Kosovo, that has overseen capacity-building in the rule-of-law sector since Kosovo's independence in 2008. Besides these direct state-building interventions, the EU's Stability Pact for South-Eastern Europe adopted in 2000 provided an integrated framework to promote post-conflict stabilization, state-building, and democratization (Friis and Murphy 2000). The Pact represents the beginning of the EU's open-ended commitment to the region, setting the stage for the Western Balkan countries' potential membership in the EU. With the *Stability and Association Process*, launched in 2000, the EU has linked post-conflict recovery in the Western Balkans with the process of EU integration. Bosnia Herzegovina and Kosovo do not meet yet the so-called Copenhagen Criteria, which requires them to develop into functioning democracies with market economies capable of applying the EU body of law as the condition for obtaining membership. However, they will continue to benefit from comprehensive financial and technical assistance through a variety of EU programs and pre-accession instruments for years to come (Börzel 2016). Moreover, membership conditionality provides a powerful incentive for incumbent elites to engage in costly governance reforms (Börzel and Schimmelfennig 2017; Richter 2012). Incentives include visa liberalization, technical assistance, and financial support for structural development and democratic institution-building, access to the European Single Market, and, ultimately, full EU membership.

The EU's comprehensive and open-ended commitment to state-building in the Western Balkans has remained the exception, though. Its limited successes result from devoting enormous financial and personal resources for state-building efforts, including an EU accession perspective for two tiny countries (Bosnia Herzegovina: 3.5 million inhabitants, 51,200 km^2; Kosovo: 1.8 million inhabitants, 10,900 km^2; in comparison Afghanistan: 35 million inhabitants, 653,000 km^2).

In contrast, most international operations aimed at providing security are much more limited in their scope, and, hence, more likely to be effective. The Australian-led intervention in Timor-Leste in 1999–2000 is a case in point (Blaxland 2015; Connery 2013; Martin and Mayer-Rieckh 2005; Robinson 2009). Following a UN-sponsored referendum for independence from Indonesia, which resulted in an overwhelming majority for the province's sovereignty, anti-independence militias instigated widespread violence, resulting in mass killings and the displacement of half a million people. Backed by a UNSC resolution and with the consent of the Indonesian government, a multinational peace-keeping force led by Australia (INTERFET, International Force East Timor) intervened to address the humanitarian and security crisis. It managed to restore the peace by driving out the militias. This particular mission not only had legitimacy; its mandate was also rather narrow. After violence had ended, INTERFET handed over to the United Nations Transitional Administration in East Timor.

Howard argues that UN peace-keeping missions are the more successful, the more they adjust to the local post-conflict environments and the more autonomous they are from the organizational prerogatives of UN headquarters (Howard 2007). In other words, institutional design matters, including a built-in capacity of peace-keeping missions for organizational learning. Campbell's study of peace-keeping in Burundi and elsewhere points in the same direction (Campbell 2018). Hegre et al. confirm this finding statistically based on a simulation of UN peace-keeping: "The more the UN is willing to spend on peace-keeping, and the stronger the mandates provided, the greater is the conflict-reducing effect" (Hegre, Hultman, and Nygård 2019, 3). They argue based on various simulations that, if the UN were to increase spending for peace-keeping and issue rather robust mandates, the initial costs would be high, but that this would drastically decrease particularly intra-state violence within a time-period of 10 years. Likewise, studies have found that peace missions with experienced, highly trained, and well-equipped staff are more effective in ending violence (Doyle and Sambanis 2006; Fortna 2008; Gilligan and Sergenti 2008; Seybolt 2007). Through an experimental design, Blair shows that the UN Mission in Liberia (UNMIL) had a demonstrable effect on improving the rule of law when citizens were exposed to the mission (Blair 2019; see also Chapter 6). Belgioioso, Salvatore, and Pickney (2020) show that UN peace-keeping missions have a strong effect on promoting non-violent protests in post-conflict societies, thereby turning violent conflict into peaceful democratic contestations. Matanock's study on external supervision of post-conflict elections including the conflict partners has already been mentioned (Matanock 2017).

Studies investigating the variation in effectiveness of SSR initiatives led by external actors yield similar results. As indicated above, the SSR template used by IOs and – mostly Western – state agencies changed over time to become more inclusive and more context-sensitive. The latter refers to institutional designs of police and military reforms that are better adapted to local conditions. Indeed, studies of changes in SSR approaches in Timor-Leste and Sierra Leone demonstrate that context-sensitive designs achieved better effects (on Timor-Leste see Dewhurst and Greising 2017; Dewhurst, Saraiva, and Winch 2016; on Sierra Leone see Bangura 2016, 2017). However, as Schröder et al. remind us, the resulting security governance arrangements rarely resemble Western-style policy and military institutions. The emerging security institutions are mostly mixtures of imported features and local-indigenous designs (Schröder, Chappuis, and Kocak 2014). At the same time, with their emphasis on local ownership, they are likely to enjoy at least some (input) legitimacy (see above).

The above analysis of various efforts by external actors to foster security governance yields two conclusions: First, success in comprehensive state-building by external actors through imposition and authoritative rule is extremely difficult and rather unlikely, as the examples of Afghanistan and Iraq demonstrate. Input legitimacy is only possible with the support of domestic actors for a trusteeship, even if they played no direct role in its creation (Kosovo and Bosnia Herzegovina). More common is the "state-builders' dilemma" between stability and legitimacy and between attempts to install regimes friendly to the interveners, on the one hand, and with the support of local populations, on the other (Lake, D. 2016, 2018). This dilemma often leads to state-building failures.

Second, this does not suggest that external efforts at fostering rule- and human rights-based security governance are bound to fail. Various GDAs, more focused peace-keeping missions, and SSR efforts can be successful under primarily two conditions:

1. The governors – external or otherwise – and their institutional solutions have to gain social acceptance by the governed, via input as well as output legitimacy.
2. More limited security tasks whose implementation can rely on institutional capacity and institutional designs with a built-in capacity for organizational learning appear to yield better results, even if the security governance institutions do not resemble "Western" templates.

Violent Non-State Actors (VNSA): Limited Effectiveness

We argued in Chapter 4 that not all VNSA (rebels, warlords, Islamist militants) are "predatory, abusive and disruptive for peace" (Podder 2013, 19). They do engage in (security) governance under certain conditions. We used the "stationary bandits" argument by Mancur Olson (Olson 1993) to suggest that they will be motivated to engage in security governance, if they need to keep a given territory and gain local as well as international legitimacy, for whatever reasons. Examples abound – from various warlords in Afghanistan, Islamist militants in the Middle East (Hamas, Hezbollah, even IS/Daesh) to rebel groups and transnational criminal networks in Latin America and elsewhere (overview in Berti 2018). The same holds true for tribal leaders and local authorities. But how successful are these groups with regard to effective security governance, i.e., keeping the peace? Under what conditions do these actors provide security as a more or less public good rather than a private or club good (Chojnacki and Branovic 2011), and how sustainable is security governance by VNSA or "traditional" leaders (see also Risse 2018b for the following).

Of course, one should not put the mark too high in this context: after all, the history of state formation in Europe suggests that it took centuries for VNSA to become "stationary bandits," to engage in taxation and rent extraction, and to gradually establish a monopoly of the use of force (see North, Wallis, and Weingast 2009; Tilly 1995). It took even more time before such a monopoly resulted in security as a public good for entire populations. This may be the reason why non-state actors are often found to be "more effective, accountable, efficient, legitimate, and accessible security providers" than state actors (Scheye 2009, 7–8; for a more critical perspective see Schröder 2018).

Warlords and Criminal Groups: Temporary Security Governance

Mukhopadhyay's study of Afghan warlords-turned-strongman-governors is rather instructive in this regard (Mukhopadhyay 2014; see Chapter 4). She argues that effective governance by warlords depended on two conditions: first, the warlords had to be powerful in terms of wealth and control over militias and other armed groups. Second, they had to face strong competition in the respective province. Under these conditions, they struck a bargain with the Afghan central government in Kabul, became "strongman governors" thereby exerting coercive control over their province. In a sense, these governors remained janus-faced, both formal state appointees and violent private actors, but it is precisely this combination that allowed them to govern their provinces – Balkh and Nangahar – hierarchically and to maintain an – albeit instable – peace (Mukhopadhyay 2014; see also Koehler and Gosztonyi 2014). Blair and Kalmanovitz tell a slightly different story about Ismail Khan, a prominent warlord in the Afghan province of Herat who refused to cut any deal with Kabul, but nevertheless managed to keep the peace:

He protected basic rights in Herat, providing security and ensuring public order more effectively than virtually any other authority in the country. ... by 2002, he had established nearly uncontested sovereignty in the province. He provided social services that might be interpreted as protecting welfare rights as well, including even the right to education. In the process, he won significant popular support. (Blair and Kalmanovitz 2016, 436)

In this particular case, the reinforcing relationship between governance effectiveness and legitimacy appears to have worked, at least temporarily (see Chapter 3), since Khan was ousted in 2004. As Marten maintains, warlords are unlikely to provide security in the long run. They are "specialists in violence who practice brute power politics and patronage, not outreach to a diverse constituency or accountability to stake-holders" (Marten 2013, 23). The ability of warlord-governors to rule hierarchically, including a monopoly of the use of force, is derived from their own "private" coercive means (militias; see Marten 2012, 2013). Strongman governors are unlikely to become state-builders, let alone democratic rulers (North, Wallis, and Weingast 2009; Wagner 2007). They mostly keep their military and economic resources to build their institutional power, which enable them to rule hierarchically and maintain a monopoly of the use of force. In the case of Afghanistan, their legitimacy was bestowed on them by the central government that, however, eventually became part of the larger patronage network itself (Felbab-Brown, Trinkunas, and Hamid 2017, 3; Marten 2013) – with the international peace-builders as bystanders unable to change the equation (see the argument about the "peacebuilders' contract," Barnett and Zürcher 2009). The usurpation of authority for personal enrichment and the brutal abuse of the local population by warlords affiliated with the central government have undermined both the legitimacy of the Afghan state and of the international community supporting it (Felbab-Brown, Trinkunas, and Hamid 2017, ch. 3). Thus, warlords might be motivated to provide security governance, but their short-term self-interests often prevents them from becoming governors in the long run.

Criminal groups are even more unreliable security providers than warlords. Smuggler rings, street gangs, or drug cartels may stop violence to the extent that they control a territory and its population, which they need as a base for their criminal activities (Davis 2009). Like rebel groups, they require some institutional capacity to enforce their rule, but also rely on social trust within its organization (Arlacchi and Ryle 1986), or the lack thereof in society (Gambetta 1988a). As Magaloni, Franco-Vivanco, and Melo (2020: 553) argue, when organized criminal groups "monopolize violence, they might establish forms of relatively orderly rule, delivering conflict resolution and a local police to sanction crimes, such as assault, rape, domestic violence, and robbery." However, the "pax mafiosa" (Felbab-Brown, Trinkunas, and Hamid 2017, 197) is profit-oriented and more often than not selective for those who are loyal to the network and pay. After all, (creating) insecurity through threatening or using violence is often part of the business model (racketeering, kidnapping, looting). Things are slightly different when organized crime is part of the funding for the governance provided by these groups (Davis 2009; Makarenko 2004). The Taliban and the FARC used profit from the illicit drug trade to provide law and order (Felbab-Brown, Trinkunas, and Hamid 2017, ch. 3, 5).

Rebel Groups and Other VNSA: Mixed Record

Rebel groups, (transnational) insurgents, and other VNSA share with warlords that they are often motivated to provide collective goods, the more they pursue political goals, such as overthrowing the central government or seceding from the state. But how effective is their security governance?

LEGITIMACY AND TRUST: LOCAL SUPPORT AND HONORING
COMMITMENTS

The empirical record appears to be mixed. Islamist militants, such as Hamas or Hezbollah, became security governors when they started controlling territory (for the following see Berti 2013, 2016, 2018; Berti and Gutiérrez 2016; Dingel 2016). After it won the elections in Gazah in 2007, Hamas gradually acquired the monopoly of the use of force. The same holds true for Hezbollah in southern Lebanon and parts of Beirut. At the same time, neither Hamas nor Hezbollah have become "normal" political players in the sense of refraining from violence against their opponents, both inside their territories and outside. They have remained VNSA that use force against anyone who opposes their authority. Hezbollah has become one of the most destabilizing violent actors in the Middle East. Hamas continues to regularly engage in violent acts against Israel, including its "collaborators" in Gazah. The Taliban and the IS/Daesh have fought each other as well as other competitors for power. They have also enforced their Islamist rule in the territories they control in Afghanistan, Iraq, and Syria, respectively, using brutal punishments, including stoning and beheadings (Felbab-Brown, Trinkunas, and Hamid 2017, ch. 3, 5), and in the case of IS/Daesh, even genocide.[10] In other words, the provision of security by Islamist militants oscillates between a public good, on the one hand, and a club good that is only

---

[10] www.ohchr.org/Documents/HRBodies/HRCouncil/CoISyria/A_HRC_32_CRP.2_en .pdf, last access August 27, 2018.

provided to supporters, as well as serious negative "bads" for those who are not, on the other. To the extent that they do provide security as a public good, the quest for local support and legitimacy appears to be key.

Fortna et al. corroborate this finding with regard to the funding sources of rebel groups and their subsequent use of terrorism in civil wars (Fortna, Lotito, and Rubin 2018). The more VNSA rely on civilian support for their funding, the less they engage in terrorist acts. Once again, the need to ensure legitimacy is key. At the same time, VNSA relying on lootable resources (such as drugs) do not need domestic support and, thus, resort to terrorist tactics.

Finally, the fate of the Colombia peace agreements appears to corroborate Matanock's argument discussed above about the relationship between (input) legitimacy, trust, and peace in post-conflict situations (Matanock 2017; cf. Cook, Jacobs, and Kim 2010; Widner 2004; Wong 2016). The peace agreement signed between Colombian president Santos and the FARC in 2016 became fragile (Felbab-Brown 2012, 95–98). Leftist rebels have been losing trust in the government's commitment to re-integrating former FARC fighters into society. The *Fuerza Alternativa Revolucionaria del Común*, the political successor of FARC, received less than one percent in the first parliamentary election in which they participated in March 2018. In the following presidential elections in May and June 2018, Iván Duque Márquez, a fierce critic of the peace agreement, won over Gustavo Petro, a former guerrilla head. Even before these elections, implementation of the peace agreement had stalled, particularly with regard to the demobilization of paramilitary groups and the land reform (Taula Calana Per La Pau I Els Drets Humans a Colòmbia and International Office of Human Rights – Action Colombia 2017). The Colombian government appears to be too weak to enforce its commitments. Nor does the Monitoring and Verification Mechanism, which the UNSC approved to ensure the security guarantees for the re-integration of rebel fighters, seem to work effectively. The power vacuum created by the demobilization of FARC has been filled by violent groups and criminal gangs competing for control over land, natural resources, and drugs. In other words, all three ingredients for the successful implementation of Electoral Participation Provisions (EPP) appear to be missing in this case: trust among the conflict partners to honor the agreements; input legitimacy generated through the inclusion of VNSA in the post-conflict political process; effective monitoring of the peace process by external governors. A study by Kreutz and Nussia corroborates the importance of trust relationships for post-conflict stability (Kreutz and Nussio 2019; for a similar finding with regard to Liberia see Karim 2020). The study relates to an earlier attempt of the

Colombian government to restore the monopoly of the use of force. Kreutz and Nussia argue that the peace agreement negotiated in 2002 with the paramilitaries was based on the trust of low-ranking ex-combatants in the commitment of the Colombian government to reciprocate demobilization with favorable legal treatment for acts of violence. More than 31,000 Colombian paramilitaries laid down their weapons between 2003 and 2006. The findings of the survey experiments show that inclusive institutions, such as re-integration programs, fostered increased trust among ex-combatants. This trust relationship, however, was eroded when the Colombian government decided to extradite former paramilitary leaders to the US in 2008 on drug-trafficking charges. This "betrayal" of the peace deal was followed by a re-mobilization into neo-paramilitary organizations and a resurgence of localized violence in 2008 and 2009. With the government of Iván Duque Márquez 10 years later, history repeats itself.

INSTITUTIONAL DESIGN: ENFORCEMENT CAPACITY

In addition to social trust and legitimacy, scholarship on VNSA also points to the significance of institutional capacities of rebel movements. A rebel army that cannot control its territory is also incapable of enforcing the peace and providing public security, as Kalyvas points out with regard to the Greek civil war during the 1940s (Kalyvas 2015). The same holds true for Museveni's National Resistance Army (NRA) in Uganda (Weinstein 2007, 175–180). Rebels in the Northern Ivory Coast gradually learned that they had to protect civilians and they increasingly interacted with the *dozo* (hunters), a network organization of "traditional" groups, in order to provide security governance (Förster 2015). In India, the Maoist Naxalites "graded the degree of protection they offered from the intermittent presence of rebel armed squads for basic protection up to an elaborate hierarchical system in liberated zones, with village defense squads at lower levels, a secondary force of local guerrilla squads, and the PLGA (People's Liberation Guerilla Army) at the apex" (Suykens 2015, 147). The story of Medellín, Colombia, is also instructive in this context: the leftist militias were able to maintain security due to superior organization and military discipline (Guitiérrez-Sanín 2015, 246). They became very popular and gained legitimacy, since they restored order and security in the areas they controlled. When their organizational capacity eroded, they were no longer able to keep order, and they also lost popular support. They then transformed into rent-seekers without any discipline (Guitiérrez-Sanín 2015). Finally, Reno reports how Charles Taylor's National Patriotic Front of Liberia

(NPFL) established a violent and patronage-based regime that provided security only as a club good in exchange for loot, if at all (Reno 2015a).

Jo's study of "compliant rebels" is also rather instructive in this context (see Jo 2015, ch. 5, for the following). One of her indicators is the degree to which rebel groups engage in violence against civilian non-combatants and, thus, respect their security. There is a lot of variation among rebel groups (ibid., 124). Examples of compliance include rebels in Iran, Myanmar, the Philippines, Guatemala, Chad, Sudan, the DRC, and elsewhere. Sometimes, there is variation within one and the same country, as Jo's case study of the DRC documents (ibid., 134–144). Relatedly, Herr compares the International Committee of the Red Cross (ICRC) efforts to commit rebel groups to International Humanitarian Law (IHL) more broadly defined with the so-called Geneva Call, an NGO which asks insurgents to sign up to three specific IHL norms, among them a commitment to refrain from sexual violence (Herr 2013). According to her study, Geneva Call has been more successful than ICRC in securing compliance by rebel groups, because its institutional design is more focused, covering only land mines, child soldiers, and sexual violence, and generates more throughput legitimacy through accountability mechanisms. While the ICRC relies on neutrality and confidentiality, Geneva Call recognizes rebels as legal parties to its agreements, satisfying their quest for international recognition. In return, however, they are held accountable for any violations for their international commitments being publicly named and shamed (ibid., 50–51).

In sum, institutional pre-conditions, the need to secure legitimacy, and – at least to some extent – trust relations, largely explain under what conditions rebel groups and other VNSA provide security as a public good: as to institutional design, the internal – hierarchical – organization and the subsequent ability of rebel leaders to keep the discipline within the group is crucial for the ability of VNSA to control territory and to keep the peace. In other words, rebel groups need to be organized like regular state armies. Moreover, the more – particularly politically motivated – VNSA require the support of local elites and populations to achieve their goals, the more these legitimacy needs not only motivate them to provide security as a public good (see Chapter 4), but they also increase the effectiveness of security governance.

Among the explanatory factors, legitimacy and social trust are clearly more important. The institutional capacity to enforce security through coercive means can also be used for terror, rape, and massive violence against civilian populations, as the example of Charles Taylor's NPFL in Liberia reminds us (Reno 2015a; see also Jo 2015, 71–72). In other words, whether or not the institutional capacity of VNSA is used for security governance rather than terror and violence against civilians depends on their need for local support and legitimacy, on the one hand, and the action capacity of local communities to demand security provision, on the other. The latter is based on social trust and cohesion. We come back to the last point below.

Chiefs, Tribal Leaders and Local Communities: Effective Peace-Builders

The contrast between VNSA, on the one hand, and local chiefs or tribal leaders as security governors, on the other, is striking. In many cases, these "traditional" authorities do not command substantial economic and military resources as a result of which their coercive power is rather limited. While they share "stationary banditry" with warlords, they require local legitimacy and the "license to govern" in order to be able to govern and to provide security as a public good. But, in contrast to warlords and many rebel groups, "traditional" leaders and clan elders usually exhibit long-term time horizons and are embedded through trust relations in local communities almost by definition, as a result of which their legitimacy enables them to provide effective (mediated) security. As argued in Chapter 4, local leaders are more likely to govern non-hierarchically through consensus-building in various councils and they have to rely on relationships of social trust in the community, in which they are embedded. As the following empirical examples suggest, their security governance is more sustainable than that of warlords and probably also of rebel groups and other VNSA.

Somalia is a least likely case of security governance. While particularly central Somalia has been a failed state since the early 1990s, the north-eastern province of Somaliland has done remarkable well despite an absent central state (Bradbury 2008; Glawion 2017, 151–170; Kaplan 2008; Lake 2016, 174–178; Menkhaus 2006/2007; Richards 2014). In particular, it has largely kept the peace (see Figure 5.3), and this effective security governance has been perceived as such by the population (Phillips 2019, 5). Previously, the province had been involved in a bloody war against the central state and its dictator, Siad Barre, which lasted until the mid-1990s. Violence subsided afterwards and Somaliland was able to build state-like structures. As Lake explains (Lake, D. 2016, 176), "potentially destabilizing conflicts were managed by the traditional councils of elders, representing the various clans and subclan factions" (for a more critical view see Balthasar 2013). Between 1991 and 1996 alone, 32 major mediation conferences took place in Somaliland, establishing a lasting peace until today. A USAID survey in Somaliland in 2016 found that more than 70 percent of the respondents perceived the security situation as very good. Even more people thought security had improved over the years, while less than five percent reported that it had experienced incidents of violence nearby (Robertson, Malla, and Oing 2017b, 25–26). These numbers compare favorably with the rest of Somalia, even though a majority of Somalis reported everywhere that the security situation had improved (less so in Mogadishu, see Robertson, Malla, and Oing 2017a, 26–27).

The factors outlined in Chapter 3 come together to explain the peace in Somaliland:

1. *Institutional design*: The clans and subclans are structured rather hierarchically. Wiseman or elders form councils to resolve conflicts and decide on compensation schemes for the victims of violence (Glawion 2017, 153). In cases of conflict between different clans, the sultan steps in. Thus, potentially violent conflicts are solved through mediation, leading to flexible outcomes. As Glawion explains, enforcement of decisions is key to successful mediation: "Decisions are enforced through the clan leaders' strong standing in society and the police using its limited means to punctually, but decisively, force deviators to adhere to the traditional elders' decisions" (ibid., 159).

2. *The "Shadow of Anarchy:"* In a very interesting article, Phillips claims that it was precisely the fear of war and chaos that helped Somaliland to keep the peace (Phillips 2019). Somalilanders constructed a powerful discourse according to which their quest for independence was justified on the grounds that Somaliland was able to keep the peace precisely because they did not need central state institutions. As Phillips explains, "(i)f Somalilanders return to war, they become just as susceptible to violence as other Somalis" (ibid., 3). She shows "that the very inability of a country's governance institutions to reliably contain violence can be discursively configured as a justification for maintaining peace" (ibid., 2). In other words, the "shadow of anarchy" created its own logic of appropriateness according to which Somaliland was supposed to keep the peace, *because* there were no central state institutions securing a monopoly of the use of force.

3. *Legitimacy and social trust*: Clan leaders enjoy a very high degree of legitimacy and social acceptance among the people, and this legitimacy is based on both personalized and group-based trust relations within the clans and subclans in Somaliland. The above-quoted USAID survey is instructive in this regard: first, trust in political institutions is generally much higher in Somaliland than in the rest of the country, with the neighboring province of Puntland running a

distant second, and the rest of Somalia exhibiting very low trust levels among the population (cf. Robertson, Malla, and Oing 2017b, 32; Robertson, Malla, and Oing 2017a, 36–37). Second, 85 percent of the respondents trust the Somaliland House of Elders a lot or somewhat, the number for Puntland is even higher, while only 59 percent trust their clan elders in Mogadishu (Robertson, Malla, and Oing 2017b, 32; Robertson, Malla, and Oing 2017a, 36–37). In other words, clan elders enjoy a very high degree of legitimacy based on what Weber calls "traditional authority" "resting in an established belief in the sanctity of immemorial traditions and the legitimacy of those exercising authority under them" (Weber 1978 (1922), 215; cf. Bagayoko, Hutchful, and Luckham 2016; Baker 2007; Cross 2016; Wisler and Onwudiwe 2009), and their positive impact on security governance through mediation reinforces this trend (through output legitimacy).

Legitimacy and Trust: Moral Authority and Local Collective Action

Other scholarship on "traditional" authorities corroborates the positive effect of legitimacy and trust on peace. A comparative study of "traditional" governance institutions in Uganda, Kenya, Tanzania, and Namibia finds relatively low levels of violent conflicts between the state and these institutions, between ethnic groups led by "traditional" leaders, or within these groups (Holzinger, Kern, and Kromrey 2017). In fact, the authors report only one violent conflict in their sample, namely between the kingdom of Buganda and the state of Uganda (ibid., 34). Interestingly enough, it matters little for the level of conflict whether or not indigenous governance institutions are recognized in the constitutional framework of the respective state (on this point see also Kötter 2015, 167–180). Similar to peace-building missions and military interventions, this seems to suggest that it is the empirical legitimacy bestowed on "traditional" leaders by their own people rather than the legitimacy derived from legal arrangements, be they domestic or international, that accounts for the peaceful relations. Beside their moral authority, "traditional" authorities can rely on social trust to solve collective action problems, making community members contribute to local security provision despite the costs involved.

Community-based policing in Africa and other parts of the world also demonstrates how local legitimacy and social trust matter for effective security governance in ALS. In Tanzania, the *sungusungu* village vigilante groups started to try and punish violent cattle raiders in the 1980s (Abrahams 1987). In 1989, the Tanzanian state officially recognized the *sungusungu* as local police forces and made participation mandatory for all male villagers. In the 1990s, the *ulinzi shirikishi* were introduced as neighborhood patrols that would be integrated with the state police and operate under state law, handing suspects over to the police rather than punishing them. But they have continued to be funded by community contributions, and their members are still recruited from each household, or, alternatively, formed by groups of young people, vetted by an elected security committee. These forms of participatory community policing have considerably improved neighborhood safety, which in turn has reinforced their legitimacy as traditional structures of security governance (Cross 2016).

In a similar vein, the *arbakai* in southeastern Afghanistan have helped to reduce violence within tribal communities. They are non-standing tribal police forces, to which each family is obliged to contribute one man when called upon (Schmeidl and Karokhail 2009). The embeddedness of traditional community-based policing in personalized trust relations allows these communities to overcome the collective action problem of risking one's life for the sake of community safety or paying others to do so, even though there is a tendency of commercialization, which tends to undermine the effectiveness of community-based policing (Cross 2016). While the *ulinzi shirikishi* and the *arbakai* are armed, "traditional" security actors are not always equipped with coercive power (anymore), particularly when they operate in parallel to state security forces. The Native Police Authorities in Sierra Leone, for instance, which played a key role during the civil war, have neither uniforms nor weapons. Rather than crime prevention and protection, their main task is to collect local taxes and market fees in the neighborhoods (Baker 2005). Even if they can deploy coercive force, compliance is often voluntary due to the adherence to shared tribal values and norms.

Moreover, a study of Xinjiang, China, shows the importance of local religious institutions for mitigating the effects of interethnic inequality and rivalry on violence (Cao et al. 2018). Cao et al. find that a high density of local mosques is associated with lesser degrees of ethnic violence even in areas with high interethnic inequalities. They argue that the mediating effect of religious institutions on ethnic conflict stems from two conditions, namely their abilities to provide public goods, on the one hand, and to serve as trusted sources of information between local communities and Chinese state authorities, on the other. In other words, these religious institutions are embedded in relationships of social trust within communities.

A key factor for effective security governance by "traditional authorities," religious organizations, but also VNSA (see above) (at least as perceived by the citizens) appears to be the ability of local communities to develop their own action capacity, which is in turn based on social cohesion and trust relations (see Chapter 3). Kaplan argues, e.g. that "(s)ocial cooperation and organization is therefore the key to help civilians overcome fear, manage their own communities, and deal with armed group pressure in an enduring manner" (Kaplan 2017, 4). His study shows through both quantitative and qualitative analyzes how community organizations based on social trust and cohesion overcame their collective action problems and adopted non-violent strategies to deal with civil war and VNSA and keep them in check. His main case is Colombia, but he extends his analysis to Afghanistan, Pakistan, Syria, and the Philippines. Krause's work on ethno-religious conflicts in eastern Indonesia and central Nigeria also points to community leaders building up collective action capacity in villages, which then managed to resist armed groups through non-violent strategies (Krause 2018). These results are corroborated by other work dealing with peace-building efforts through communal engagement and community-based NGOs (Anderson and Wallace 2013; Stephenson Jr. 2012).

Institutional Design: The Ambiguity of Enforcement Capacity

However, the positive effects of moral authority and local collective action on peace and security appears to be contingent on their institutional enforcement capacity, as Glawion shows through a comparison of Somaliland with South Sudan and the Central African Republic (CAR, see Glawion 2017, 151–170). In the two latter cases, not only clan leaders, but also religious organizations and NGOs, are active in peace-building and mediated security, with far less success. In South Sudan, clans are essentially "outgunned" by violent groups, both representing the central state and its opponent, who are engulfed in a civil war (and a war with Sudan). Here, state-armed forces are part of the problem, not the solution (see Chapter 8 for a discussion of the ambivalent role of the state in areas of limited statehood). The CAR is a case in between Somaliland and South Sudan with regard to the effectiveness of mediated security. The state and its police forces are absent, but various non-state actors including "traditional" leaders lack institutional capacity to enforce mediated security. In any event, these comparisons should prevent us from romanticizing "traditional" leaders (Förster and Koechlin 2018). Even if they are able to compensate for the lack of security provision by the state, "traditional" authorities may contribute to the competition between multiple local security providers, thereby inducing violent conflict (Goodfellow and Lindemann 2013; Krause and Milliken 2009; Schmeidl and Karokhail 2009). Nor do they necessarily have an interest in state-building, particularly if they have experienced central state actors as predatory and abusive (Menkhaus 2006/2007). Finally, "traditional" authorities can reproduce existing inequalities in power and resources and discriminate against women and minorities (Bagayoko, Hutchful, and Luckham 2016; Cross 2016; cf. Chapter 4).

To sum up: tribal chiefs and other "traditional" leaders, religious organizations, and community-based organizations appear to be comparatively better equipped to engage in effective security governance under adverse conditions than the above discussed warlords, rebel groups, and other VNSA. One important difference to these VNSA are the long time-horizons of community-based actors and groups. Other than that, our three explanatory factors (see Chapter 3) are all present in these instances and appear to reinforce each other: institutional capacity, particularly the ability to enforce peace agreements; social acceptance and legitimacy bestowed by the citizens in local communities; last but not least, strong relationships of social trust enhancing the action capacity of communities and community-based organizations.

At the same time, legitimacy and social trust may compensate for the weak or absent institutional capacity of "traditional" authorities to stop violence by the use of violence and to solicit participation in security governance arrangements, respectively.

Conclusions: Security Under Anarchy

Summary

This chapter has dealt with a "hard case" for "governance under anarchy" in ALS, the provision of peace and security as public goods. We have looked at external interveners, including international peace-keeping forces, and at VNSA, such as warlords, rebel groups, and other insurgents. We have also investigated the provision of mediated security by "traditional" authorities, such as tribal leaders and elders, as well as the role of local communities as peace-builders.

The good news is that effective security governance is possible, even under rather adverse conditions of civil war, at least temporarily. Each of the actors investigated in this chapter was able to provide security as a public good – under certain conditions. Interestingly enough, international peace-keepers as well as "traditional" leaders embedded in strong local communities emerge as the most effective security providers, even though the explanatory factors are different for the two groups of actors.

As to international peace-keeping in post-conflict environments, comprehensive state-building efforts have mostly been failures, but less complex tasks of security provision have not. The most important scope conditions for successful peace-keeping appear to be a strong military presence and sufficient resources (that is, institutional capacity) for the task at hand, on the one hand, and local legitimacy, on the other. Whether or not the external intervention is legitimized internationally (e.g. through a UN mandate), matters less for the effectiveness on the ground (it is probably more important for the social acceptance at home, particularly in liberal democracies).

In contrast, "traditional" authorities, such as clan elders, usually lack strong enforcement capacities, even if they have police forces at their disposal. Their success and effectiveness in mediated security governance and conflict resolution depend crucially on relationships of personalized and/or group-based trust within the local communities, including the latter's collective action capacities. The authority and legitimacy of chiefs and tribal leaders are derivative of such trust relations. The same holds true for religious leaders involved in peace-keeping. The effective security provision of these actors depends on their moral and/or charismatic legitimacy, which is grounded in personalized or group-based trust.

At the other end of the spectrum of effectiveness are warlords and criminal groups. The Afghan example shows that they may at times provide security as a public good, albeit under rather circumscribed conditions and of questionable quality. They are less dependent on social acceptance and legitimacy bestowed by local communities, because their rule and authority are mostly based on their coercive capabilities, on the one hand, and the patronage networks with state authorities and international organizations, on the other. This does not completely exclude security governance as a public good, but it is more likely that they provide security for their patronage and clientelistic networks, i.e., as a club good. Moreover, security provision is unlikely to be sustainable, since warlords are motivated by private gain that thrives on and creates insecurity in the first place. Finally, governance by profit-oriented and criminal VNSA comes at the price of "public bads," including human rights violations, human trafficking, and trade in illicit goods.

Rebel groups and other insurgents appear to occupy a middle position between the two in terms of their effectiveness as (public) security governors. We have argued in this chapter that they are able to keep the peace in the territory controlled by them, if three conditions are met: first, they must be motivated by concerns about their domestic and international legitimacy (see Chapter 4) and, second, they must have the institutional means and capacity to provide public security. Third, on the demand side, they have to deal with local communities with sufficient action capacity to pressure them into security governance. The latter ability is in turn based on social trust relations within and among communities.

Without the means, rebel groups lack the ability to govern. Without the legitimacy concerns, they lack the willingness to foster public security and to offer protection to the local population. Without trust relations, communities will be unable to demand security governance. Moreover, legitimacy may compensate for a lack of institutional capacity, particularly if rebels depend on local resources to pursue their political goals.

We have focused here on external state and VNSA as security providers in ALS. This is not to deny the role of other non-state actors. There is ample evidence that (I)NGOS, companies, and multistakeholder partnerships (MSPs) contribute to security governance, too (Deitelhoff and Wolf 2010a; Feil 2011; Jakobi and Wolf 2013; Hönke 2013b). However, their contributions tend to be more indirect through setting, helping implement, and complying with rules on the use of force rather than directly organizing and using force. The latter is particularly true for companies. Similar to VNSA, they often fuel conflict and violence by exploiting natural resources in conflict zones, by selling arms or military services to conflict parties, by trading goods (e.g. diamonds) conflict parties need to fight, or by financing their police and military forces directly (Avant 2005; Mandel 2002; Singer 2007). Private military and security companies profit by selling a collective good (security) to clients and take an interest in privatizing security rather than providing it as a truly public good (Krahmann 2010; Leander 2005). Even if their services are enlisted by states or international organizations, the effectiveness of private security companies (PSCs) is limited and their legitimacy for engaging in direct combat remains problematic, as the case of Blackwater in Iraq demonstrated (Deitelhoff 2010). For this reason, companies seeking to protect the safety of their operations and their workforce tend to refrain from directly taking security into their own hands. They hire private security or military companies or rely on public security forces supplying them with equipment or putting them on their payroll (Hönke 2013b; Zimmer 2010). Companies usually see the provision of peace and security as a core state responsibility and resist playing an active role in preventing, mitigating, and resolving violent conflict

(Bais and Huijser 2017; Börzel and Hönke 2012; Deitelhoff and Wolf 2010a). If they contribute, it is indirectly by addressing underlying causes of conflict, e.g. by cutting the trade with conflict-related goods (Jakobi 2013), promoting and protecting human rights and the rule of law (see Chapter 6), or contributing to welfare (see Chapter 7). This is also the case for (I)NGOs and MSPs, which cooperate with external state actors in promoting peace and stability rather than directly interfering with violent conflict (Jakobi and Wolf 2013).

The (Limited) Sustainability of Security Governance without a State

But how sustainable is (public) security governance by external as well as non-state actors, be they violent or not? Can it result in lasting peace, and under what conditions? Our overall assessment is skeptical, for the following reasons. First, we have already expressed our doubts that governance by warlords and criminal groups is able to provide public security in a sustainable way, since their interests and preferences to do so are likely to change according to varying circumstances, e.g. the needs to sustain patronage networks. Besides, there is no logic of appropriateness involved. Moreover, once warlords and criminal networks become security governors in a lasting sense, chances are that they are engaged in state-building as governments (see Tilly 1995).

Second, with regard to rebel groups and insurgents, the greatest spoilers of their attempts to provide public security are probably the state governments against which they rebel in the first place. National governments, however weak they might be with regard to areas of limited statehood, have little interest to support the quest for legitimacy by rebel groups, neither with regard to their domestic constituencies nor concerning the international community (on the latter see Krieger 2018). They are likely to deny rebel groups and insurgents their success in providing security governance, since they do not want to lose the civil war. To turn the argument around: security governance by rebel groups and insurgents can only be sustained if these groups are victorious in terms of either overthrowing the national government, seceding from the central state, or gaining domestic sovereignty as a quasi-state (as the examples of Timor-Leste and Somaliland show). In other words, sustainable security governance by rebels requires them to become state actors who enjoy a legitimate monopoly of the use of force.

Third, security governance by "traditional" or religious leaders appears to require rather exceptional circumstances, namely high trust relations among the governed (which is rare in ALS with rather culturally heterogeneous communities based on strongly ethnized identities).

Moreover, the presence of VNSA and predatory governments jeopardizes the peace-keeping role of "traditional" authorities. Somaliland represents the exception of the rule. It has all the ingredients of a quasi- or de-facto state (Bryden 2004; Jackson 1990; Pegg 1998) – except for international recognition. This explains why actors "promote peace and local policing systems quietly undermining efforts to revive the [central] state" (Menkhaus 2006/2007, 76).

Fourth, as to external actors and international peace-keeping forces, they usually lack the resources to engage in open-ended missions. However, these missions have to be open-ended so that potential spoilers on the ground cannot calculate their chances to overtake the country or the area, once the peace-keepers are gone (cf. the Afghan experience after 2014 where the Taliban could simply prepare for the time when ISAF would leave). Moreover, and equally important, open-ended missions are almost impossible to legitimize in the home countries of the peace-keepers, particularly in liberal democracies. Democratic parliaments usually require an "end date" for the mission that by definition jeopardizes its success. The cases of Bosnia Herzegovina and Kosovo are the exceptions to the rule, since EU peace-keepers have been engaged there for the past more than 20 years and their engagement is open-ended.

This is not to say that actors other than the state cannot provide public security and maintain the peace in ALS for limited time-periods. Warlords, rebel groups, traditional authorities, but also (multi-)national companies and (I)NGOS (Jakobi and Wolf 2013), have the institutional capacity and the motivation to engage in less complex security tasks, such as stopping the fight between conflicting parties, negotiating peace agreements, or restricting the trade in "conflict minerals" (Haufler 2015). This is better than nothing in war-torn countries, such as Afghanistan, which have experienced decades of violence. However, we are skeptical that long-term peace and security as a public good can be sustained in the absence of a state with at least some hierarchical governance capacity to coordinate the growing plurality of security providers (Beisheim et al. 2011b; cf. Chapter 8). The examples provided in this chapter also demonstrate that such a state needs to be legally restrained and politically accountable, since the means of violence in the hands of despots are by no means better than the rule of predatory VNSA who do not care about civilian populations. Last but not least, most cases of successful security governance by non-state (violent) actors resemble quasi-states in which these actors become public agents holding a legitimate monopoly of the use of force.

This chapter investigates the effectiveness of various efforts at promoting human rights, the rule of law, and democracy in areas of limited statehood. Conventional wisdom holds that the protection of liberal values requires a well-functioning state with full enforcement capacity (e.g. Acemoglu and Robinson 2012; Fukuyama 2012). Conventional wisdom also holds that violations of human rights and the rule of law mostly result from lack of (state) willingness rather than from lack of capacity. We take issue with both arguments (see also Börzel and Risse 2013; Risse 2017). First, human rights and the rule of law can be upheld even under rather adverse conditions of limited statehood. In many cases, we have to look for functional equivalents of "Western" democratic and rights-protecting institutions as well as courts (on functional equivalents in general see Draude 2007, 2012). Second, lack of (state) capacity can be as much a cause of non-compliance with human rights and the rule of law as lack of willingness. Moreover and more often than not, statehood is part of the problem and not of the solution in ALS, particularly in cases of rights-violating and predatory states (Ostrom 1999; Reno 2015b; Scott 1998). Simply strengthening statehood could, thus, worsen human rights conditions rather than improving the situation.

We suggest that the three conditions for effective governance – legitimacy, institutional design, and social trust – which we discussed in Chapter 3, explain effectiveness in human rights, rule of law, and democratic governance in ALS. As in Chapter 5, we look at the role of specific actors – external and domestic/local, state and non-state – in the effective promotion and protection of liberal values and institutions. Here, we focus in particular on regional organizations (ROs) as promoters of human rights, the rule of law, and of democracy, on (I)NGOs and Non-State Justice Institutions (NSJI), as well as on companies and non-state violent actors (NSVA).

Throughout the chapter, we adopt a broad understanding of what constitutes democratic governance (following Merkel 2010), which consists of participatory institutions, the rule of law (fair, transparent, and predictable justice institutions; independent courts; equal access to justice; etc.), and the protection of human rights. Rule of law and human rights are, hence, an integral part of democratic governance. Moreover, when we focus on "democracy," we refer particularly to participatory rights and institutions. With regard to the rule of law, we emphasize equal access to justice and independent justice institutions, as well as the fight against corruption. Last but not least, concerning human rights, the focus in this chapter is on political and civil rights (social and economic rights are covered in Chapter 7).

As in Chapter 5, we start our analysis with a general discussion of the governance puzzle with regard to liberal values and institutions, namely the (non-) correlation between democratic governance, on the one hand, and limited statehood, on the other. We then focus on the particular human rights and democracy problematique in ALS, followed by a discussion of the various actors mentioned.

The Puzzle: (In-) Effective Democratic, Rule of Law, and Human Rights Governance in Areas of Limited Statehood

Democracy, the rule of law, and human rights are no different from other issue-areas. We find no linear correlation between degrees of statehood and various aspects of democratic governance, as the following scatter plots demonstrate (see Figures 6.1–6.3).[1] Figure 6.1 shows an interesting pattern: first, consolidated statehood and liberal democracy are highly correlated, representing the "Western" liberal states of the OECD world. Second, however, countries with statehood scores between 0.5 and 0.8 cover the entire range from extreme autocracy to consolidated liberal democracies.[2] The fitted values line is misleading in this regard due to the extremely high standard deviation. For countries with substantial areas of limited statehood, there is no correlation between an (il)liberal polity and degrees of statehood. Take Sub-Saharan Africa, for example, probably the world's region with the highest concentration of ALS. In 2013, Polity IV coded South Africa, Namibia, Botswana, Kenya, Ghana, Niger, and Benin as democratic, while Angola, Tanzania, Uganda, Sudan, Ethiopia, Chad, and Cameroon were coded as "closed

---

[1] Unfortunately, we had to use different years in the 2010s, since data for the various measurements were not available in a given year. However, and overall, there is not much variation between 2010 and 2015.

[2] Note again that, given the measurements, statehood values below 0.5 represent countries with areas of extremely limited statehood. The countries below 0.4 statehood are essentially failed states.

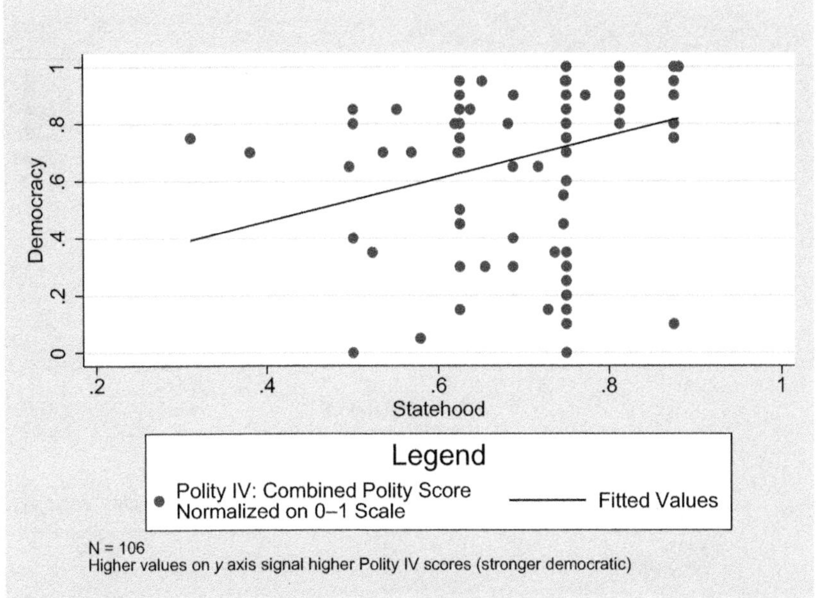

Figure 6.1 Democracy and statehood (2014)
Each dot represents the value for one country.
Source: Courtesy of Eric Stollenwerk, see Stollenwerk and Opper 2017. The democracy measurements use Polity IV data (http://www.systemicpeace.org/ polity/polity4.htm, last access March 29, 2018). For the statehood measurements see chapter 2.

anocracies," i.e., leaning toward autocratic systems.[3] In our dataset, these countries all encompass vast ALS.

An only slightly different picture emerges with regard to the rule of law and human rights (see Figure 6.2; see also Börzel and Risse 2013; Risse 2017 for the following). While the fitted values line appears to show that degrees of statehood and human rights are correlated, a more complex picture emerges upon a closer look at the data.

First, democratic countries with consolidated statehood are also rule of law and human rights-protecting states. This conforms to the literature (e.g. Simmons 2009, 2013). Second, at statehood levels between 0.9 and 0.6, where most countries with ALS are located, we find variation across the whole scale – from rights-protecting all the way down to the worst rights-violating states. Once again (not shown here, for evidence see

---

[3] See www.systemicpeace.org/polity/polity4x.htm, last access March 23, 2018.

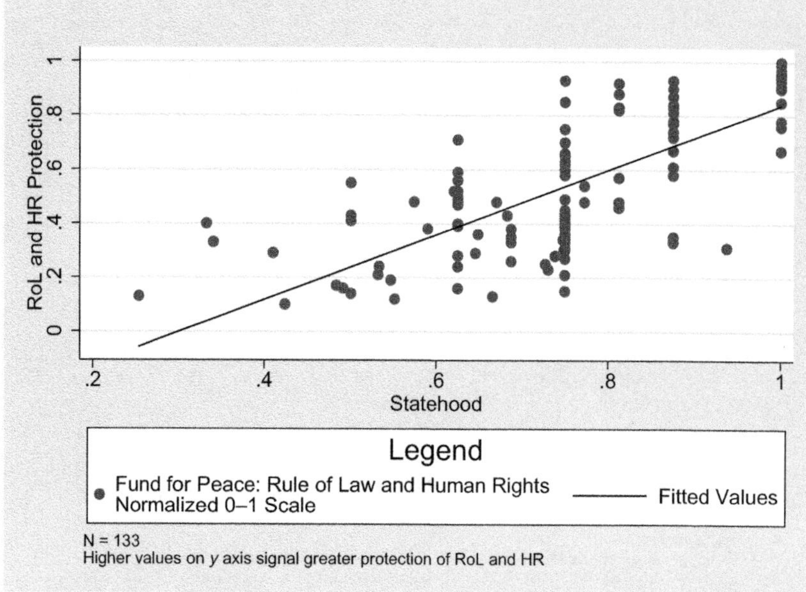

Figure 6.2 Rule of law (RoL), human rights (HR), and statehood (2015)
Low values indicate violations of human rights and the rule of law.
Source: Courtesy of Eric Stollenwerk. For statehood measurements see chapter 2 as well as Stollenwerk and Opper 2017. Rule of law and human rights data are taken from the Fund for Peace 2015: Human Rights and Rule of Law.[4]

Börzel and Risse 2013, 73–74), democracies fare better on average than autocratic states, of course. Yet, degrees of statehood as such are not correlated with the protection or violation of human rights and the rule of law at these medium levels of limited statehood. Take again sub-Sahara Africa: citizens of Benin, Botswana, Ghana, Lesotho, Namibia, and Senegal enjoy relatively high levels of political rights and civil liberties.

---

[4] The indicator looks at whether there is widespread abuse of legal, political and social rights, including those of individuals, groups, and institutions (e.g. harassment of the press, politicization of the judiciary, internal use of military for political ends, repression of political opponents). The indicator also considers outbreaks of politically inspired (as opposed to criminal) violence perpetrated against civilians. It comprises factors such as denial of due process consistent with international norms and practices for political prisoners or dissidents, and whether there is current or emerging authoritarian, dictatorial or military rule in which constitutional and democratic institutions and processes are suspended or manipulated (http://fundforpeace.org/fsi/indicators/p3/, last access July 29, 2018.

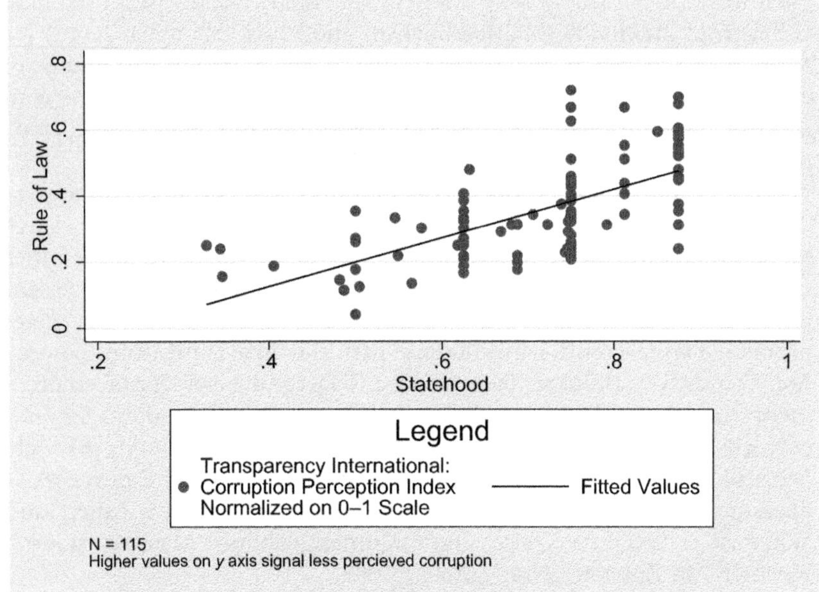

Figure 6.3 Corruption and statehood (2013)
Each dot represents the value for one country.
Source: Courtesy of Eric Stollenwerk. Statehood measurements in Stollenwerk
and Opper 2017; corruption data taken from Transparency International
Corruption Perception Index, which is a composite index combining several
surveys and polls on the perceptions of the degree of corruption by business, risk
analysts and the general public (https://www.transparency.org/news/feature/
corruption_perceptions_index_2017#table, last access March 29, 2018).

At the other end of the spectrum are Angola, Cameroon, Chad, Ethiopia,
South Sudan, and Zimbabwe, where political and civil rights are systematically violated. Many other African countries are located in between.[5]
Third, however and moving further to the left-hand side of Figure 6.2,
we find virtually no states at statehood levels below 0.6, i.e., in fragile and
failing states, which protect human rights and the rule of law. This
appears to suggest that the rule of law and human rights are unlikely to
be protected, once the state has lost the monopoly of the use of force and
civil war prevails. The data confirm that war zones are areas where
human rights are regularly and systematically violated.

---

[5] Data according to Freedom House, 2013 Report: www.freedomhouse.org/sites/default/
files/FIW%202013%20Charts%20and%20Graphs%20for%20Web_0.pdf, last access
March 28, 2018.

However, this latter finding has to be qualified. The datasets used here suffer from methodological nationalism and, thus, use mean scores for entire countries rather than regions or policy areas. There are "islands of excellence" even in failed states, as we discuss further in this chapter with regard to Somalia and the Democratic Republic of Congo (DRC), two quintessentially failed states.

Finally, a different measurement of the rule of law pertains to corruption (see Figure 6.3). Here, the picture slightly changes, since the country variation is closer to the fitted values line than in the other cases. In other words, corruption and degrees of limited statehood seem to correlate (see also Lee, Walter-Drop, and Wiesel 2014). There are probably two reasons for this finding: first, the dataset measures perception of mostly businesspeople who tend to factor the lack of rule enforcement (i.e., limited statehood) in their views of corruption. Second, corruption could indeed be the flip side of limited statehood, precisely because the use of public resources or income for private purposes is likely to result from limited state enforcement capacity (Shen and Wiliamson 2005; see also the argument about "shadow states," Koehler and Zürcher 2004; Zürcher 2007).

To sum up: the overall picture confirms what we have identified as the "governance puzzle" in ALS in Chapter 1. There is no linear correlation between democracy, the rule of law, and human rights, on the one hand, and degrees of statehood, on the other. This finding is not particularly surprising with regard to the consolidated end of the statehood spectrum: full-fledged autocratic states, such as North Korea, have both a monopoly of the use of force and the capacity to enforce decisions. Autocratic rule is particularly effective under conditions of fully consolidated statehood – and the same holds true for liberal democracies. The monopoly of the use of force and the enforcement capacity of consolidated states can be used to protect democracy and human rights or to preserve dictatorial rule.

At the other end of the statehood scale, we find fragile or failed states that have all but lost their enforcement capacities, including the monopoly of the use of force. We might still find some electoral democracies here (see Figure 6.1), but what does it mean if the elected officials are not in control of anything? Indeed, the data on the rule of law and human rights show that failed states are unlikely to be able to secure justice for all and equal rights if they cannot keep the peace (see Figures 6.2 and 6.3). In a way, it does not matter much whether a completely failed state is democratic or autocratic, since neither regime type can be enforced, although access to justice might be possible even under extremely adverse circumstances (see below). These examples notwithstanding, it follows that some minimum degree of statehood, particularly the control of the use of force, appears to be necessary for securing a liberal domestic order that encompasses democratic participation, the rule of law, and human rights.

The real puzzle concerns countries with a medium degree of limited statehood (or areas thereof), e.g. which might control the use of force, but lack the capacity to implement or enforce central decisions. We find most of the variation with regard to democratic participation, human rights, and the rule of law in this middle category of states. In these cases, state capacity does not seem to matter much. So, how can we explain this variation?

We start with further conceptualizing the problem, particularly with regard to human rights.

Human Rights and Democracy in Areas of Limited Statehood: A Matter of Institutional Capacity and Legitimacy

As argued above, it is empirically wrong to argue that democracy, rule of law, and human rights are impossible to protect under conditions of limited statehood, even though some minimum state capacity with regard to the monopoly of the use of force appears to be necessary. At the same time, we know that democracy, rule of law, and human rights go together in most cases (Simmons 2009). While the latter relationship is well established in the literature, previous scholarship has taken for granted that consolidated statehood is a pre-condition for the protection of human rights. Most studies – our own previous work included (see e.g. Risse, Ropp, and Sikkink 1999) – have conceptualized human rights violations as a matter of (state) willingness rather than capacity. The various theoretical approaches to explain human rights improvements – from the "boomerang effect" (Keck and Sikkink 1998) to the "spiral model" (Risse, Ropp, and Sikkink 1999) – have assumed that improving the human rights situation required changing state policies through a combination of sanctions, incentives, and persuasion. In areas of limited statehood, the problem, however, becomes more complex (see Börzel and Risse 2013; Risse 2017, for the following).

First, rights violations committed by state actors might be a question of both willingness and capacity. Table 6.1 conceptualizes human rights problems according to degrees of statehood and regime type (for the sake of the argument, both dimensions are treated as dichotomous, which is, of course, simplistic).

Human rights are mostly complied with in democratic consolidated states (top-right cell of Table 6.1) and violated by authoritarian regimes

Table 6.1 *Human rights by regime type and degree of statehood*

Statehood Level Regime Type	Limited Statehood	Consolidated Statehood
Democratic Regimes	Human rights violations due to lack of capacity	Mostly human rights compliance
Authoritarian Regimes	Human rights violations due to lack of willingness *and* capacity	Human rights violations due to lack of willingness

Source: Börzel and Risse 2013, 69

(bottom-right cell of Table 6.1). Since the latter are supposed to be able to enforce the law (consolidated statehood), compliance is a question of willingness. Yet, most countries in the real world – whether democracies or autocracies and, thus, irrespective of regime type – populate the left-hand cells of Table 6.1. The world is full of authoritarian as well as democratic regimes that try to govern areas of limited statehood. As Cole has shown, lack of state capacity matters a lot with regard to human rights violations (Cole 2015). He argues in particular that bureaucratic capacity improves human rights performance. The bottom-left cell of Table 6.1 is populated by authoritarian and semi-authoritarian regimes in countries with ALS where human rights are violated, because central governments lack both the willingness *and* the capacity to enforce compliance. The top-left cell of Table 6.1 contains democratic or democratizing regimes with ALS. For example, India, the world's largest democracy, belongs in this category. If we assume that democracies are willing to commit to and comply with human rights at least in principle, rights violations in countries populating the top-left cell of Table 6.1 occur mainly because a state is not in full control of parts of its territory, with regard to the police forces or the military. In other words, the compliance problem is a capacity issue in these cases. Human rights violations in ALS are committed because of two interconnected phenomena. First, weak central governments – even those committed to human rights – cannot protect them in ALS, e.g. because they do not control their own enforcement agencies, such as the police or the military. In such cases, human rights are violated by state agents outside the reach of central authorities. Second, lack of enforcement capacity enables non-state actors, such as warlords, private militias, (multinational) companies, or transnational criminal organizations, to become perpetrators of rights violations in ALS.

So, what explains the (non-)protection of human rights in ALS? Emphasizing human rights violations resulting from limited statehood directs our attention toward the "management school" in compliance research (particularly Chayes and Chayes 1993, 1995; see also Cole 2015). This group has argued that non-compliance with international regulations results from weak institutions, lack of resources, and resulting problems of involuntary defection rather than lack of willingness by governments. Interestingly enough, many IOs have long understood that support for building up sustainable institutions goes a long way in the promotion and protection of human rights, the rule of law, and democracy. Most of the resources spent on international democracy promotion by donors, such as the US and the EU, focus on capacity-building through financial and technical assistance (Magen, Risse, and McFaul 2009; see below). But there is a catch: helping to build state capacity from the outside is only likely to improve the human rights record of democratizing states (top-left cell in Table 6.1), while increasing administrative capacity of (semi-) authoritarian states will only make them more effective in repressing their citizens (bottom-left cell in Table 6.1). Nevertheless, the management school in compliance research emphasizes institutional capacity to secure human rights. In other words, this scholarship confirms our argument about institutional design and capacity-building as fostering effective governance in ALS (see Chapter 3).

Our argument about (empirical) legitimacy as another factor explaining effective governance also holds. It links up with the "legitimacy perspective" in compliance research (e.g. Hurd 1999). The more particular norms are considered appropriate and legitimate in a given collectivity, the more compliance with costly rules is likely. This could explain why democracy and civil rights protection might go together even in countries with areas of limited statehood. The more democratic values are considered legitimate by the citizens, the more political and civil rights might be secured even in the absence of functioning law enforcement institutions. Last but not least, if local communities cherish political and civil rights and consider them normatively appropriate, they can be protected under extremely adverse conditions (Berger 2017; Berger and Lake 2018; Lake, M. 2018). These findings point to the importance of vibrant civil society organizations to foster human rights change in ALS. In other words, state weakness can be compensated by civil society organizations and human rights NGOs, at least partially. We will demonstrate this point further below with regard to NSJI.

The legitimacy argument also implies that mechanisms to improve human rights conditions such as the "boomerang effect" (Keck and

Sikkink 1998) or the "spiral model" (Risse, Ropp, and Sikkink 1999, 2013) are likely to be effective in ALS, too. The "boomerang effect" describes alliances between local civil society organizations and NGOs, on the one hand, and transnational advocacy networks, on the other. The "spiral model" of human rights change consists of repeated "boomerang throws," which have been integrated in a dynamic model emphasizing various stages of human rights change.

With regard to the bottom-left cell of Table 6.1 (authoritarian regimes and ALS), the good news is that repressive governments have fewer means at their disposal to commit human rights violations under these circumstances, because many ALS are out of their reach. This opens up space for activists – local as well as transnational – as cultural brokers translating international human rights norms into local contexts and adapting them to these circumstances, as Lake argues with regard to remote areas of the DRC and Berger with regard to NGOs in rural Bangladesh (Berger 2017; Lake, M. 2018; on brokerage see Hönke and Müller 2018). In the context of authoritarian regimes, limited statehood might be a blessing for human rights promotion, since it allows other actors to circumvent the (repressive) state. This is particularly relevant for (I)NGOs, but also for IOs, ROs, and foreign governments (see below). The primary condition for effective human rights promotion by these actors is their legitimacy among the local communities.

With regard to liberal or liberalizing regimes (top-left cell of Table 6.1), central governments lack the capacity to enforce human rights standards in ALS. However, they can still use their limited capacity and their legitimacy as democratic rulers to foster human rights change as socializing agents and to assume a broker role in localization attempts. This is precisely what the "post-Arabellion" Tunisian government has been doing and what external actors, such as the EU, have been supporting (Dandashly 2015; van Hüllen 2013). Moreover, liberalizing regimes usually open political and social space for (I)NGOs and other civil society organizations to thrive, as was already argued in *The Power of Human Rights* (Risse, Ropp, and Sikkink 1999).

The bad news for areas of limited statehood – irrespective of regime type – is that human rights violations are likely to be committed by non-state actors, be it warlords, rebel groups, (multinational) companies, or even (I)NGOs. As a result, local conditions and the local balance of power in conjunction with transnational forces become even more relevant for human rights practices in ALS, as we argue below with regard to companies, on the one hand, and rebel groups, on the other.

In the following, we demonstrate empirically the validity of these considerations with regard to institutional capacity and legitimacy. As in Chapter 5, we concentrate on both external and internal governors. We begin with ROs.

Regional Organizations: Promoting and Protecting Human Rights, Democracy, and the Rule of Law

Since the end of the Cold War, IOs and states have systematically developed programs to promote democratic governance in ALS (inter alia Ottaway and Carothers 2000; Magen and Morlino 2008; Magen, Risse, and McFaul 2009; Whitehead 2001). Development cooperation, for instance, has become a primary tool for not only providing goods and services in target countries, but also for protecting and promoting human rights, the rule of law, or democracy. If states turned to the international level, they would go to the UN and its sub-organizations (Hafner-Burton 2012; Hafner-Burton, Mansfield, and Pevehouse 2015). Yet, ROs have gained an important role in such "governance transfer" (Börzel and van Hüllen 2015a) as an intermediate level between the nation-state and global institutions. Their broad mandate allows them to promote democratic governance in their member states and, in some cases, other countries. Today, almost any major RO prescribes and promotes some norms of democratic governance at the national level, irrespective of its original purpose. This even holds for strong proponents of the principles of national sovereignty and non-interference, such as the Association of Southeast Asian Nations (ASEAN) and the League of Arab States (LAS). Both have institutionalized the promotion of human rights in their member states in the 2000s: the Arab Human Rights Committee in 2008 and the ASEAN Inter-Governmental Commission on Human Rights in 2009.

ROs around the globe have not only institutionalized commitments to human rights, democracy, the rule of law, and the fight against corruption (for the following see Börzel and van Hüllen 2015a; Pevehouse 2016). They have also established similar instruments to ensure compliance, including the legal protection of human rights through either specific human rights courts or regional courts that also deal with human rights, suspension and/or military intervention clauses to sanction (massive) human rights violations and the interruption of the democratic (or constitutional) order, as well as election observation missions and election assistance (Kelley 2012). Overall, regional organizations use "harder" instruments, drawing on the use of force and sanctions to protect human rights and democracy, whereas the promotion of the rule of law and the fight against corruption is based on "softer" instruments of dialogue and capacity-building.

While ROs follow a global governance script, they differ in how far and to what extent they translate democratic governance principles into specific norms and rules. For instance, the North American Free Trade Agreement (NAFTA) and ASEAN focus more on the rule of law and the fight against corruption. ROs in Africa and South America are more concerned with democracy and human rights. When it comes to the specific content of human rights, some emphasize the importance of economic and social rights (especially ASEAN, but also Mercosur and the Southern African Development Community/SADC), whereas others pay more attention to civil and political rights (Organization of American States/OAS and African Union/AU). Similarly, ROs pick and choose among the instruments by which they actively promote and protect the adherence to democratic governance norms. ASEAN and LAS have been reluctant to commit their members to precise norms and to promote as well as protect them with hard instruments. African, European, and American ROs, in contrast, provide for the possibility of imposing sanctions, such as the suspension of membership. The AU, the Economic Community of West African States (ECOWAS), and SADC are the only ones that allow for the use of military force, even without the consent of the affected state. Finally, the gap between the prescription of norms, the instruments for their promotion and protection, and their actual enforcement is wider for some ROs than for others. Some ROs remain at the level of prescription (e.g. ASEAN, LAS), most have more (e.g. ECOWAS, SADC, AU) or less (e.g. Mercosur, Andean Community) elaborate instruments, but only a few implement measures on a regular basis. Mercosur took diplomatic sanctions against every threat to democracy that occurred in one of its member states. It politically intervened twice in Paraguay after attempted military coups in 1996 and 1999, respectively (Ribeiro Hoffmann 2007). It also suspended Venezuela's membership when President Maduro cracked down on the opposition in 2016. ECOWAS deployed military and police forces against unconstitutional power accessions in several member states (see below), but ignored the massive human rights violations by Boko Haram in Nigeria (Hartmann and Striebinger 2015). SADC forces intervened in Lesotho in 1978 to prevent a military coup. Yet, it continuously supported Zimbabwe's authoritarian president Mugabe despite human rights violations and electoral fraud (van der Vleuten and Hoffmann 2010). What is more, SADC dismantled its tribunal after it had issued a human rights ruling against Zimbabwe (Hulse and van der Vleuten 2015). While the Inter-American Court of Human Rights is as active as the European Court of Human Rights, its judgments are less likely to be upheld by its member states (Hawkins and Jacoby 2010). The EU postponed the accession of Romania and Bulgaria by three years for lack of sufficient compliance with the rule of law and the fight against corruption (Noutcheva and Bechev 2008). At the same time, Hungary and Poland have not faced any sanctions so far for undermining the independence of the judiciary and the media (Keleman 2017).

We lack systematic evaluations of the effectiveness of ROs as promoters and protectors of democratic governance in ALS. A review of the evidence on the practices of ROs, however, suggests that institutional design and legitimacy go a long way to explain variation:

1. ROs have to provide credible and sizeable incentives to pay off the costs of compliance for their member states. Since countries with ALS often score low on human rights, the rule of law, and democracy (see above), ROs have to strengthen the willingness as well as the capacity of state actors to implement and enforce democratic governance norms.
2. Since the enforcement capacity of both ROs and target states are limited, effective democratic governance ultimately depends on the domestic acceptance of the norms and the RO as the institution that promotes them.

Institutional Capacity: Locking in Domestic Reforms, Curbing Negative Externalities, and Signaling Commitment

A major reason for states joining ROs that engage in the promotion and protection of democratic governance is democratic lock-in. Governments of democratizing countries sign up to these ROs seeking to protect the democratic changes they introduced against authoritarian backlash (Moravcsik 2000; Pevehouse 2005). This also works for human rights and the rule of law. The Latin American member states of the OAS, for instance, endorsed the adoption of anti-corruption norms to lock in their domestic commitments to strengthen the rule of law and democracy (Lohaus 2015). But this does not explain why openly autocratic members of ECOWAS accepted a democracy clause that allows for the use of military force by majority decision (Hartmann and Striebinger 2015), or why the authoritarian membership of LAS adopted a human rights charter in 2004 (van Hüllen 2015). Why did human rights offenders like Brunei, Laos, Myanmar, and Vietnam not object to the establishment of a human rights commission in ASEAN (Jetschke 2015)?

First, promoting democratic governance at the regional level can help curb negative externalities by "bad" governance in the neighborhood. Massive human rights violations and coups d'état against governments, democratically elected or not, have the potential to destabilize the entire region by transnational refugee flows or roving rebel groups and militias. This is a particular problem when the concentration of ALS is high. It is no coincidence that AU, ECOWAS, and SADC have particularly strong democracy clauses.

Second, committing to democratic governance at the regional level helps satisfy the quest for international legitimacy. SADC, ECOWAS, and ASEAN have sought to attract foreign trade and aid by signaling commitment to generally accepted norms of democratic governance to international donors and investors (Hartmann and Striebinger 2015; Hulse and van der Vleuten 2015; Jetschke 2015). Such strategic signaling can also help deflect external pressure, e.g. from Western donors or international organizations (Davies 2013; Leininger 2015; Russo 2015).

The assumption is, of course, that ROs effectively promote and protect human rights, democracy, and the rule of law. Otherwise, they cannot lock in domestic reforms in democratizing countries. Nor would membership be a credible signal for non-democratic regimes. The institutional capacity of ROs to monitor and sanction compliance is therefore crucial. In their study on why newly democratic states are more likely to join more specialized economic than general purpose political organizations, Mansfield and Pevehouse argue that the former have the trade and financial leverage to make democratic backsliding costly (Mansfield and Pevehouse 2008). Their argument corroborates Hafner-Burton's findings that preferential trade agreements with hard human rights commitments reduce government repression (Hafner-Burton 2005).

Among the three ROs that have the authority to deploy military force to protect democratic governance, ECOWAS has been the most active (Hartmann and Striebinger 2015; Legler and Tieku 2010). Since enacting its democracy clause in 1999, ECOWAS has intervened several times, both politically and militarily, to protect democracy and human rights in one of its member states. In the humanitarian crisis that erupted after the 2010 elections in the Ivory Coast, ECOWAS threatened military intervention, backing Alassane Ouattara as the winner of the presidential elections. Ultimately, French and UN troops ended the conflict and saw Ouattara installed as president (Bellamy and Williams 2012; Speight 2014). Capacity problems prevented ECOWAS, as well as the AU, from getting involved on the ground (Abatan and Spies 2016). Nevertheless, the support of the two ROs legitimized the intervention by the former colonial power and the UN.

Capacity problems also plagued the intervention of ECOWAS in Mali, when President Amadou Toumani Touré was ousted by the military in 2012 over his handling of the Tuareg nationalist uprising in the northern part of the country (Lecocq et al. 2013). Political and economic sanctions by ECOWAS, reinforced by international pressure, made the rebels hand over power to a transition government, which, however, lasted less than a month. To end the armed conflict in the north and restore the constitutional order, ECOWAS obtained a UN mandate and established AFISMA (African-led International Support Mission), which received the logistical support of the EU (France and Germany). Due to lack of funding and personnel, however, ECOWAS handed over the mission to the UN after six months. In the end, French troops defeated Islamist forces (Boeke and Schuurman 2015). While the security situation is still fragile in the north, Mali returned to its constitutional order in May 2013 when Ibrahim Boubacar Keïta was elected president (Charbonneau and Sears 2014).

In 2016, ECOWAS effectively ended the attempted coup d'état in Gambia by longstanding president Yahya Jameh, who had been defeated at the polls by opposition leader Adama Barrow. Only when ECOWAS threatened military action, backed by the UN Security Council and the AU, did Jameh accept defeat and hand over power. Unlike in the case of Ivory Coast, ECOWAS this time had sufficient resources to make a credible threat, not least because it did not have to deal with an armed conflict or a humanitarian crisis (Hartmann 2017).

The political and military interventions of ECOWAS show that institutional capacity matters. The institutional design of ECOWAS facilitates collective action of its members. The Mediation and Security Council represents nine of the 15 member states. It can decide on political and military interventions by a two-thirds majority in cases of massive human rights violations as well as coup attempts. ECOWAS can also rely on the financial and military capabilities of its regional hegemon to avoid cumbersome decision-making processes. Nigeria pays for two-thirds of the ECOWAS budget and contributes the largest troop contingent (Hartmann and Striebinger 2015, 79). Moreover, the regional hegemon obtains procedural legitimacy for military interventions against threats emanating from its neighbors, which Nigeria used to initiate and lead within ECOWAS before 1999, but without proper legal base (Coleman 2007; Sabrow 2017).

Legitimacy: Domestic Acceptance of International Norms

The EU has actively promoted democratic governance in neighboring countries that either qualify for membership or seek closer relations with the EU (cf. van Hüllen and Börzel 2015). Its enlargement and neighborhood policies mostly rely on positive incentives. Unlike most ROs, the EU supports progress towards democratic governance rather than sanctioning violations (Schimmelfennig 2005). The prospects of obtaining a membership perspective, of becoming a formal candidate for accession, of opening accession negotiations, and ultimately of becoming a member, have proven a powerful incentive for governments to introduce democratic reforms and supported the transition of former communist countries in Central and Eastern Europe (Kelley 2004; Schimmelfennig and Sedelmeier 2004, 2005; Vachudova 2005). While membership is the most important factor of its effectiveness as a governor (Börzel and Schimmelfennig 2017), visa liberalization and deeper trade and security relations still give the EU substantial leverage, if consistently applied (Ademmer 2016; Börzel and Lebanidze 2017). Yet, as discussed above, in ALS, states do not (only) lack the willingness but the capacity to enforce human rights and the rule of law. External incentives for state actors to protect human rights and respect the rule of law do nothing to strengthen their enforcement capacity. The domestic legitimacy of international norms, in contrast, reduces the need for enforcement by mitigating the risk of domestic resistance and mobilizing local support for democratic governance.

The institutional capacity of the EU for promoting democratic governance is constant across its eastern neighbors that seek closer relations if not membership, but its effectiveness has varied considerably, e.g. concerning Georgia as compared to Armenia. A comparative study of Börzel and van Hüllen on the EU's efforts at state-building in the southern Caucasus shows that the variation can be explained by the legitimacy of anti-corruption norms (Börzel and van Hüllen 2014). Georgia responded to the EU's demands by reducing corruption, while the situation has not changed for the better in Armenia. In both countries, political elites used the fight against corruption selectively as an instrument against political opponents, employing enhanced state capacities to stabilize the incumbent regime. The social acceptance of anti-corruption norms, however, has been much higher in Georgia than in Armenia. In Georgia, corrupt practices have triggered moral outrage, which the political opposition could mobilize, resulting in public demands for effective political reforms. In Armenia, by contrast, corruption is widely accepted as the norm of particularism and a general culture of favoritism seems to prevail.

Van der Vleuten's research on SADC (non-)interventions corroborates the importance of legitimacy for the effectiveness of ROs as external promoters of democratic governance (van der Vleuten 2007; van der Vleuten and Hoffmann 2010). While SADC sent troops to defend democracy in Lesotho and to prevent an unconstitutional change of government in 1998, it refused to intervene in Zimbabwe, when Mugabe rigged his re-election in 2008. The threat of political instability to the region was equally high, so was international pressure. However, SADC's anti-apartheid and anti-colonialism identity delegitimized any criticism of Mugabe as "siding with the former colonial powers" (van der Vleuten and Hoffmann 2010, 752; cf. Hulse and van der Vleuten 2015).

To sum up, ROs promote and protect democratic governance, particularly if unconstitutional changes or massive human rights violations jeopardize the political stability of the entire region by transnational refugee flows or roving rebel groups and militias. The combination of institutional design and domestic legitimacy explains the varying success of ROs in promoting and protecting democratic governance. They require sufficient resources as well as institutional rules and procedures to facilitate collective action. Legitimacy is not only crucial for the willingness of states to act collectively in the first place. Domestic acceptance of external interventions also reduces the need for institutional capacity. ROs promoting and protecting their "own" norms of democratic governance tend to enjoy higher legitimacy than those that rely on global norms (Neuman 2008), even though the former usually build on the latter (Börzel and Stapel 2015).

At the same time, our findings with regard to the ability of ROs to promote democratic governance and the rule of law appear to be generalizable with regard to other external actors. With regard to Liberia, e.g. Blair shows that exposure of citizens to the UN Mission (UNMIL) improved the rule of law on the micro-level while also making people more aware of state corruption (Blair 2019). Our argument is also broadly consistent with Matanock's findings about the role of external actors in monitoring Electoral Participation Provisions (EPP), i.e., the inclusion of all parties to a conflict in the post-war electoral process leading to stable peace (see Chapter 5; Matanock 2018, 2017, ch. 7). The external election observers both enjoyed institutional capacity including an – albeit limited – "shadow of hierarchy" (the ability to enforce agreements and sanction non-compliance), but were also regarded as legitimate "intruders" into the post-conflict country's domestic sovereignty.

(I)NGOs and Non-State Justice Institutions (NSJI): Promoting Access to Justice and Fair Procedures

A major problem of ALS and the weak capacity of state institutions concerns the role of the judiciary. As mentioned above, corruption appears to be highly correlated with limited statehood and, in many cases, judicial independence and the wider rule of law suffers from corrupt state actors. Once the state judiciary is corrupted, a cornerstone of the rule of law no longer exists. The problem is exacerbated by the fact that most ALS exhibit normative and legal pluralism (overview in Swenson 2018). Afghanistan constitutes a prime example of a pluralism of different legal systems – state and international law, sharia law, and various tribal law systems – without a functioning collision regime that would specify the hierarchy and reach of the various legal norms and their sources (Röder 2009). While legal pluralism as such is almost ubiquitous, most legal systems in consolidated states exhibit meta-governance systems specifying the collision regimes that are missing in ALS (see Kötter and Schuppert 2009 for a detailed discussion). In other words, the problem for the rule of law is not the actual existence of legal and normative pluralism, but the absence of collision rules and regimes in ALS that specify which legal and normative standards apply in which situation and which take precedence.

Under these circumstances of corrupt state judiciaries and legal pluralism, many analysts put their hopes on various types of NSJI as functional equivalents of state courts, which could institute at least rudimentary features of the rule of law (overview in Kötter et al. 2015). We have discussed NSJI in Chapter 4, arguing that their informal and formal rules often resemble deliberative institutions. But how effective are such NSJI, and what accounts for effectiveness with regard to the rule of law? From a (positive) legal perspective, NSJI have to be incorporated into a state's law system in terms of common law, customary law, or self-government in order to strengthen the rule of law (Kötter 2015, 168). While many state constitutions – not just in the Global South, but also in Western consolidated states, such as the US and Germany – incorporate NSJI, they remain informal in many other states (overview in Kötter 2015). Moreover, since we are interested here in the rule of law as rule-based governance, we need to look beyond the legal status of NSJI and into their practices. The literature estimates that in ALS existing NSJI deal with 80 percent of all proceedings (Golub 2006, 106; Tamanaha 2011, 4; Wojkowska 2007, 12). But this number does not tell us much about the outcomes of these proceedings. In this context, we adopt the criteria for informal justice as established by the World Justice Project's Rule of Law Index referring to timeliness, impartiality, and protection of fundamental rights (World Justice Project 2018, 9). We add that NSJI need to provide equal access to justice in order to count as effective. We deliberately focus on the rule of law, but do not include the self-declared goal of many NSJI (see Chapters 4 and 5), namely to restore the peace in post-conflict communities. One measurement of effectiveness is significant in this context, though, namely the goal to re-integrate wrong-doers into the local communities rather than to punish them through exclusion.

Gauging the effectiveness of NSJI in such terms is extraordinarily difficult, since we lack data that can be assessed in a comparative way.[6] Moreover, most of the literature on NSJI does not evaluate the actual practices of these non-state courts and other dispute settlement systems, as a result of which we can only rely on a few detailed case studies. So, what do the available data tell us?

Berger's ethnographic micro-studies of NSJI in rural Bangladesh (Berger 2017, ch. 4) describe a *shalish* in a village mediating a conflict between two families that had turned violent, involving a third family from different villages. *Shalish* are the most prominent NSJI in Bangladesh, dating back to pre-colonial times, whereby local elders try to resolve disputes. In this case, the chairman of the local administration solved the conflict through extended negotiations involving the respect-ive families, as well as a group of respected elders from the communities. The resolution consisted of various compensatory payments between the three families as well as an elaborate reconciliation ceremony to restore the peace. The resolution did not involve punishment but was aimed at re-integrating the offenders into the community (for similar procedures among the Pastun *shuras* or *jirgas* in Afghanistan see Röder 2009, 289). While these reconciliation mechanisms might actually be better suited to prevent criminal acts and violence in the future than punishment through state criminal law, they have a clear downside (Berger 2017, 89): The language of "harmony" often serves to perpetuate unequal power rela-tions in local communities. Moreover, women are excluded from both *shalish* in Bangladesh and *shuras/jirgas* in Afghanistan (Schmeidl and Karokhail 2009).

Yet, Berger's studies also show how power relations can be mitigated and equal access to justice be ensured under certain conditions (Berger 2017, 9, ch. 6): With the help of the EU, so-called village courts were instituted in five Bangladeshi regions.[7] In four of the five regions, local NGOs and their fieldworkers implemented the village courts, while it was the project team of the United Nations Development Program (UNDP),

---

[6] While the World Justice Project now incorporates informal justice (as it calls it) into their Rule of Law Index, it does not use the data for the index, because of these methodological problems (World Justice Project 2018, 9).

[7] Interestingly enough, British colonial powers had instituted the original "village courts" in the nineteenth century. The EU sought to revive them.

which was in charge in the fifth region. The village courts quickly transformed into *shalish* NSJI ruling according to Islamic law. However, when NGO fieldworkers were present and active, the *shalish*/village courts did indeed provide access to justice for poor rural women thereby altering local power relations. In contrast, where the UNDP was directly involved, the village courts were not even activated.

Lake's book corroborates Berger's findings, but from a different angle (Lake, M. 2018): She seeks to explain the puzzle that courts in the eastern provinces of the DRC prosecuted sexual violence, particularly rape, much more thoroughly than courts in South Africa, a country with higher state capacity. What is more, the Congolese local courts became pioneers in the prosecution of war-related sexual violence, thereby applying the Rome statute of the International Criminal Court (ICC) directly as if it was national law. These local courts in the eastern DRC do not represent NSJI in the strict sense of the term, but "state" institutions. Lake, however, explains that "armed actors, NGOs, international organizations, religious groups, and/or civil society organizations have already assumed responsibility over many governance functions in certain parts of the country" (Lake, M. 2018, 131), including case management, justice sector administration, and legal training and oversight. Domestic and international NGOs were particularly involved in training prosecutors and judges in the complexities of international human rights law, including sexual violence. In other words, these courts were "state" judicial institutions only by name, while domestic and international NGOs enhanced their capacity and their functioning in accordance with the rule of law. In South Africa, in contrast, the much more effective central state institutions interfered with the judicial system in cases of sexual violence – while (I)NGOs deferred to these institutions rather than dealing directly with local courts. We discuss the ambivalent role of the state as inhibiting rather than promoting rule of law governance in Chapter 8.

Institutional Design: Enabling Deliberative Negotiations

Berger and Lake demonstrate that NSJI can indeed deliver successful and peaceful conflict resolution as well as equitable and fair dispute settlement (see also Kötter et al. 2015). However, the institutional design of the NSJI has to meet certain conditions, thereby enabling effective deliberative negotiations (see Chapter 4; Warren, Mansbridge, and Bächtiger et al. 2013; for the following see Risse 2018b, 324–325): 1) equal access to dispute settlement, particularly for underprivileged groups, which is mostly ensured by (I)NGOs; 2) power asymmetries receding in the background; 3) procedural fairness; 4) transparency; and 5) judges as honest brokers. A study of village assemblies in South India shows that deliberative institutions are not confined to NSJI in ALS (Parthasarathy, Rao, and Palaniswamy 2019).

Moreover, various case studies show that most NSJI do not strive to punish perpetrators of communal crimes and violence (although they do not exclude retributive measures). Rather, they seek to restore peace in local communities and to establish conciliatory measures (see above on Bangladesh; for Pakistan's FATA region see Röder and Shinwari 2015; for South Sudan see Diehl, Arol, and Malz 2015; for Ethiopia see Aneme 2015). In doing so, NSJI appear rather effective and rather similar – in ALS across continents. They seem to be superior to state-sponsored and formal court systems in ALS, which are mostly corrupted precisely because of the weak state institutions (on Northern Uganda see Latigo 2008; on the DRC Lake, M. 2018; on Afghanistan/Pakistan Barfield, Nojumi, and Thier 2006; Röder and Shinwari 2015; Shinwari 2011; on Bangladesh Berger 2017). In most cases, relations based on social trust within the community serves as a powerful functional equivalent for the law enforcement mechanisms otherwise provided by functioning state institutions.

Legitimacy: Moral Standing, Embeddedness, and Procedural Justice

Another reason for the effectiveness of NSJI is their *legitimacy* among local populations. A survey among Pakistanis in the FATA region revealed that traditional *jirgas* were considered far more legitimate than *jirgas* affiliated with the state (Röder and Shinwari 2015, 46; for similar data on Afghanistan see Böhnke, Koehler, and Zürcher 2017, 15–16). Two-thirds of the surveyed considered them protecting human rights (even when this was not the case under any "objective" measurement) and vast majorities supported that they should apply local customary law consistent with *sharia* law (Röder and Shinwari 2015, 46). Thus, legitimacy appears to be an important condition for the effectiveness of and compliance with deliberative NSJI. The higher the moral standing of the elders, chiefs, and senior leaders participating in or chairing these institutions in their local communities, the more they can act as "honest brokers" and deliver judgments that are considered fair and equitable by their constituents. The embeddedness of NSJI in and resonance with traditional norms and local understandings of justice appear to be another major source of their legitimacy. In contrast, it remains unclear whether the incorporation of NSJI in the state judicial systems or in the constitutional framework (as, for example, in South Africa, see

Rautenbach 2015; for a general overview see Holzinger et al. 2018; Kötter 2015) fosters the social acceptance of these dispute settlement systems in the eyes of the local populations.

At the same time, studies point to the following shortcomings of NSJI, which constrain their effectiveness. First, the informality of the institutional rules and structures implies that they can be manipulated and usurped by powerful political interests and factions. Therefore, it is crucial that NGOs and other civil society watchdogs are getting involved in the processes (Berger 2017; Latigo 2008). Second, it remains unclear whether NSJI can be effective in dealing with gross human rights violations and war crimes. The exclusion of women in most NSJI means that gender-related crimes are rarely dealt with at all or might be used to exculpate the perpetrators (see Merry 2006). Lake's analysis of local courts in the eastern DRC shows, however, that it is possible to tackle crimes related to sexual violence even under the most adverse circumstances (Lake, M. 2018) – if both local and international NGOs are involved. This confirms – once again – that (transnational) advocacy networks can be rather effective in ALS (see below; on advocacy networks in general see Keck and Sikkink 1998). Third, there seem to be limits with regard to scaling up NSJI beyond local communities and ethnic groups (Barfield, Nojumi, and Thier 2006; Wojkowska 2007). The example of *shalish* NSJI in Bangladesh (Berger 2017) suggests that disputes between villages and their communities can be tackled because they can rely on local legitimacy and social trust.

If these limits are taken into account, NSJI can deal rather effectively with even serious disputes within and between local communities – particularly in the absence of functioning law enforcement systems of the state, which is common for ALS. After all, one has to ask whether better alternatives are available to secure at least a minimum degree of rule of law, including the protection of human rights. As argued above, the state judicial system is thoroughly corrupt in many ALS, and/or political interference into the independence of court systems is widespread. In contrast, reciprocal and procedural fairness norms appear to be constitutive for most NSJI in ALS. The social acceptance and legitimacy of these institutions in local communities are based on precisely these norms, and almost all studies quoted above agree that local citizens trust their NSJI more than formal state legal institutions. At the same time, NSJI are vulnerable to power asymmetries, unless (I)NGOs and civil society activists level the playing field. In sum, and under certain conditions, NSJI can provide rather effective access to justice, particularly in rural ALS.

Violating or Protecting Human Rights? (Multinational) Companies and Rebel Groups

So far, we have discussed external state actors, such as ROs, as well as NSJI. We now turn to two types of actors who are primarily motivated by achieving private gains and, thus, are mostly seen as "problem causers" rather than "problem solvers" (Flohr et al. 2010, 7 with regard to companies), namely business and violent non-state actors (VNSA).[8] We argue that they may nevertheless serve as human rights protectors under specific circumstances.

Companies as Human Rights Protectors?

Reports on human rights violations by companies in ALS abound. Companies seeking to protect the security of their production sights pose significant human rights challenges (Le Billon 2006; Wettstein 2012). Their own security agents often abuse human rights or contribute to human rights abuses committed by state agencies, private security companies (PSC) or communal actors (Hönke 2013b). At the same time, thousands of corporations have joined transnational governance initiatives, such as the United Nationals Global Compact, the Business Principles for Countering Bribery, or the Voluntary Principles on Security and Human Rights, voluntarily committing themselves to respecting human rights, countering bribery and extortion, and improving their environmental and social performance. The corporate engagement in human rights governance has been largely driven by NGO and media campaigns, such as the one against Shell for its complicity in the death of Ogoni leader Ken Saro Wiwa in Nigeria in 1995 (Zimmer 2010), Coca-Cola for its involvement in the mistreatment and disappearance of labor union workers in Latin America (Gill 2007), or against companies trading natural resources originating in conflict zones (Bone 2004; Börzel and Hönke 2012). Rather than being merely norm takers, business in its quest for legitimacy is directly involved in the setting and developing of standards for appropriate behavior in ALS, often in cooperation with governments, IOs, and civil society groups (Deitelhoff and Wolf 2013; Flohr et al. 2010; Ruggie 2007a; cf. Tsutsui and Lim 2015). Not only are multinational corporations (MNCs) expected to honor their commitment; they shall also enforce them down the supply chain, on PSC they contract, and even on state actors, with whom they engage to protect the safety of their production sites and their workforce

---

[8] Please note that there is no normative judgment involved in this comparison. We neither regard companies as evil nor do we share any romanticism for VNSA.

(Börzel and Hönke 2012; Deitelhoff and Wolf 2013; Héritier, Müller-Debus, and Thauer 2009; Ruggie 2008). Human rights have become an integral part of the global script for corporate social responsibility (Meyer, Pope, and Isaacson 2015), which has been diffusing and has become part of world culture (Kinderman 2015). The spread of corporate codes of conduct and MSPs may indicate a "norm cascade within the business community" (Deitelhoff and Wolf 2013, 225), diffusing them through supply chain management and sectoral and regional initiatives (Black 2006). Yet, the way from commitment to compliance is already long, and respecting human rights by not violating them is not the same as actively protecting and promoting them. Effective governance is often impaired by the decoupling between formal behavioral prescriptions at the international, national, and corporate level, and actual corporate practices, on the ground.

THE VOLUNTARY PRINCIPLES ON SECURITY AND HUMAN RIGHTS: SOFT INSTITUTIONS AND WEAK LEGITIMACY

The Voluntary Principles on Security and Human Rights (VPSHR) are instructive in this regard.[9] Unlike the UN Guiding Principles on Business and Human Rights, the VPSHR do not only require business to "avoid infringements on the human rights of others" and "address averse human rights impacts in which they are involved."[10] They also broaden corporate social responsibility (CSR) from *respecting* toward *protecting* human rights for a business sector that has been prominently involved in human rights violations in ALS.

The extractive industry often operates in ALS where the allocation of resources and property rights are highly contested, and state security forces produce insecurity and violate human rights. Companies, in turn, seeking to protect their property or to extract private benefit from their mines and from the local population often cause violent conflict. The VPSHR are the only transnational human rights guidelines specifically directed to oil, gas, and mining companies. They were initiated by the US and UK governments in 2000 as a response to several incidents of human rights violations by security forces seeking to protect oil and mining installations of MNCs with headquarters in the UK and the US. To shield operations of key oil companies in Indonesia, Columbia, and Nigeria at the time, the two governments sat together with seven major Anglo-American extraction companies and jointly developed

---

[9] The following draws on Börzel and Hönke 2012.

[10] www.ohchr.org/documents/publications/GuidingprinciplesBusinesshr_eN.pdf, 11, last access August 19, 2019.

human rights guidelines that do not only ask companies to comply with human rights but to engage in protecting and promoting them in ALS.

While the VPSHR succeeded in committing companies to engage in human rights governance, their effectiveness has been hampered by their weak institutional design, on the one hand, and the lack of legitimacy of business as human rights governors, on the other.

As suggested by their very name, the VPSHR commit MNC on a voluntary basis. They lack centralized monitoring and sanctioning powers (Freeman and Hernandez Uriz 2003; Ruggie 2010).[11] Moreover, VPSHR membership is geographically concentrated and limited, further undermining its effectiveness.[12] While several major MNCs have joined, corporate membership remains confined to northern Europe and North America. Even though membership no longer requires that the home governments are participating, only a third of the major international metal mining companies have joined the initiative. Very few small and medium-sized companies have signed up. Government representativeness is similarly biased. Colombia is among the few host countries of MNCs with ALS that have joined so far. Important European countries, such as France and Germany, have declined to participate, as have all of the new major home countries for investors in oil and mining in Africa and elsewhere, including Brazil, Russia, India, China, and South Africa (the BRICS). Their institutional design in terms of their non-bindingness, weak monitoring and sanctioning capacity, and narrow membership severely reduces the effectiveness of the VPSHR (Hönke and Thauer 2014). Due to the limited data available and accessible, there remains a significant dearth in systematic evidence on corporate compliance with the VPSHR, too. The few studies that exist are often not fully independent of the company investigated (Jim Freedman Consulting 2006; Kapelus 2006). Or they are confined to an analysis of the incorporation of the VPSHR into corporate rules and management systems and the service agreements with contractors, on the one hand, and the extent to which corporate practices are consistent with the formal rules and procedures, on the other (e.g. Frynas 2000; Hofferberth 2010; Zalik 2004). There is hardly any work on the extent to which companies protect rather than merely respect human rights.

---

[11] The so-called participation criteria adopted in 2007 provide for the exclusion of participants if they fail to comply. However, this requires a unanimous decision by all members. Participants may also raise concerns that other participants have not met VPSHR standards or not made a sustained effort to effectively implement them (Hofferberth 2010).

[12] See   www.voluntaryprinciples.org/for-companies/;   www.voluntaryprinciples.org/for-companies/, last access August 12, 2018.

Börzel and Hönke (2012) consider effectiveness also in terms of whether the human rights situation actually improves on the ground (cf. Hönke 2013b). Their study shows that multinational mining companies operating in the DRC have incorporated the VPSHR into their corporate policies, management systems, and agreements with public and private security forces. They have also dedicated human, financial, and technical resources required for implementation projects and report on their progress and performance. Finally, companies have joined other international and regional initiatives, such as the Extractive Industries Transparency Initiative (EITI) or Pact Congo. Changes in the corporate practices are more difficult to detect. While their own security forces are increasingly trained and informed, companies are reluctant to do human rights trainings of PSCs or the local police and military. Nor do they engage in human rights dialogues with local communities and INGOs, which remain critical of corporate human rights policies and practices. In other words, mining companies still focus on respecting rather than protecting human rights.

Börzel and Hönke identify the weak legitimacy with state actors, local communities, and companies as a major cause for the limited effectiveness of the VPSHR on the ground. The problems mostly lie with the VPSHR's institutional design but go beyond the voluntary character, insufficient enforcement mechanisms, and vaguely defined performance criteria. Rather, they relate to the VPSHR's narrow understanding of security as protecting the companies' facilities and staff in the first place. The VPSHR require companies to reduce the negative effects of their corporate private security provision for others. Asking them to train public and private security agents in human rights may contribute to better security provision for the broader public. However, companies' willingness and ability to influence local police and military forces are limited (Deitelhoff and Wolf 2013). In order to secure the concession and political support for their operations, companies need to maintain good relations with agents at all levels of the state apparatus. They pay them for the enforcement of their contract and their property rights. As a result, and seeking to comply with the VPSHR, companies often come into conflict with competing norms at the local level, such as the "politics of the belly" (Bayart 1993), which require the payment of bribes and taxes. Moreover, while their statehood may be limited, states like the DRC still seek to protect their "Westphalian sovereignty," insisting that security provision is the prerogative of the state. Foreign companies are not allowed to get involved in any training of state security forces in the DRC (Hönke and Thauer 2014, 704–705). They have to work with the state and its security forces, which often results in the reproduction of autocratic and corrupt governance structures, facilitating extortion and human rights abuses rather than stopping them (Hönke 2012, 2013b; Reno 1998a, 2001). This is all the more the case, since many security problems of companies arise from the highly contested question of who has legitimate access to resources, of who shall have access to land, and who has to bear the costs of mining. To artisanal miners in the DRC, for example, the companies' claim to resources and land is illegitimate because it is based on a contract with a distant government in Kinshasa. Likewise, local communities expect the redistribution of company profits as they reclaim the right to make a living from "their resources" (Ogula 2012). Moreover, traditional norms and values that shape the understanding of local communities with regard to the responsibilities of social and economic institutions may raise further such expectations (Bruijn and Whiteman 2010; Whiteman 2009; Wiredu 1990). If they are not met, local conflicts over resources and property rights often turn violent and involve human rights violations, e.g. when artisanal miners are evicted by private security agents and state security forces or local communities are relocated by force (Garvin et al. 2009; O'Faircheallaigh 2012). Some companies have responded to the governance demands and expectations by providing development money, which is allocated within a community by an elected development committee. However, such participatory structures designed to foster local legitimacy often conflict with pre-existing local power structures and cause new competition over influence and resources (Geenen and Hönke 2014; Hönke 2012; Kraemer, Whiteman, and Banerjee 2013; Odoemene 2011; Ogula 2012).

In sum, the VPSHR are among the few governance instruments that not only commit companies to respect human rights when pursuing their own business, refraining from violations and addressing their averse human rights impact. They entail the more demanding task of transforming MNCs into human rights governors. However, our analysis shows limitations with regard to their effectiveness. The VPSHR's narrow conception of security undermines their social acceptance by local communities, who often contest the property rights of companies and expect them to contribute to the development of human security. Thus, the VPSHR are inherently weak as governance instruments. Training police and military forces in human rights and engaging with local communities in human rights dialogues does not only require substantial institutional capacity. It conflicts with local norms and conventions companies have to conform with to keep their operations running, which impairs the acceptance of and support by local managers. Likewise, state actors – particularly in ALS – reject the VPSHR's interference with their sovereign right to control and train their security forces.

So, what is the bottom-line with regard to companies and human rights governance? MNCs contribute to human rights governance because of legitimacy concerns mostly with regard to their customers and their home states in the Global North (see Chapter 4). Yet, motivation and effective governance are two different things in this case, even though the empirical evidence on the ground is still rather tenuous. Moreover, respecting and protecting human rights are two different things. Available studies tend to focus on compliance with human rights norms by companies in ALS. Where they look at protection, the evidence points to weak institutional design and capacities rendering transnational regulations, such as the VPSHR, rather ineffective. In addition, local legitimacy issues further inhibit companies from becoming human rights protectors in ALS. They might improve their compliance with human rights norms, but they still face significant obstacles when becoming human rights governors, also because companies do not rule the territory beyond their premises. This is different for rebel groups, at least in principle.

Taming Rebel Groups

There is a big difference between companies and VNSA. While companies (normally) do not control territory beyond their production sites, VNSA become "stationary bandits" under some conditions (see Chapter 4), and, thus, rule over areas of limited statehood. As a result, compliance with human rights norms and the rule of law mostly translates into human rights governance in the above defined way (see Chapter 2), since respecting human rights requires protecting the rights of citizens and non-combatants.

At first glance, however, it sounds almost preposterous to argue that VNSA not only comply with international human rights norms under certain conditions, but that they also promote human rights and the rule of law as governors in the territory that they control. *Boko Haram* in Nigeria has aimlessly killed thousands of civilians and abducted women and children. The Islamic State/*Daesh* has engaged in genocide and other crimes against humanity; the Revolutionary United Front in Sierra Leone massacred 6,000 people in January 1999; the Lord's Resistance Army in Uganda recruited children through abduction and used child soldiers as sex slaves (on the latter two examples see Jo 2015, 4). Stanton finds that around a third of 103 rebel groups fighting in civil wars between 1989 and 2010 "massacred civilians, burned civilian homes and crops and exploded bombs in populated places" (Stanton 2016, 4).

At the same time, the Sudan People's Liberation Movement – North (SPLM-N), the Popular Front for the Liberation of Saguia el Hamra and Rio de Oro (Polisario Front) in the Western Sahara, and the Moro Islamic Liberation Front / Bangsamoro Islamic Armed Forces (MILF/ BIAF) in the Philippines have signed the Geneva Call's "Deed of Commitment" banning the use of landmines. The Chin National Front/Army (CNF/CNA) in Myanmar as well as various rebel groups in India have even signed all three "Deeds of Commitment" pertaining to land mines, child protection, and gender issues. So did various Kurdish rebel groups and parties in Iran and Iraq, as well as several groups of the Free Syrian Army in Syria.[13] More than 40 percent of the rebel groups in Stanton's database did not engage in extreme atrocities, the destruction or burning of civilian homes or crops, the deliberate bombing or shelling of civilian targets, and forced expulsion (Stanton 2016, 4).

LEGITIMACY: THE QUEST FOR INTERNATIONAL AND DOMESTIC RECOGNITION

What explains the variation, and do the latter groups actually not only commit to human rights norms, but also comply with these norms? In her path-breaking analysis, Jo addressed these questions, focusing on civilian killings, child soldiering, and access to detention centers (Jo 2015; see also Jo and Bryant 2013). Her Rebel Groups and International Law (RGIL) database contains available data not only about the commitment of rebel groups to various humanitarian norms, but also about their compliance behavior, from 1989 to 2009. It shows, for example, that 51 percent of the rebel groups in the database are persistent compliers with regard to not killing civilians, while 22 percent kill civilians regularly (Jo 2015, 92; for similar findings see Stanton 2016). 165 rebel groups never used child soldiers, while 77 did (ibid., 90). With regard to granting the ICRC access to detention centers, compliance is much lower: only 47 out of 251 rebel groups granted full access during the time-period under consideration (ibid.).

Jo then conducts statistical analyses backed up by case studies to explain the variation. Her findings lend strong support to our arguments in this book: legitimacy-seeking rebel groups are far more likely to refrain from killing civilians and to allow ICRC officials into detention centers, while the statistical results for child soldiering are weaker (Jo 2015, 131–132, 162–165, 198–199). Jo measures legitimacy-seeking behavior through three proxies, namely whether the rebel group has a political

---

[13] See https://genevacall.org/how-we-work/armed-non-state-actors/, last access March 31, 2018.

wing and has formerly participated in a "normal" political process, whether it has secessionist aims, and whether it has foreign sponsors who care about human rights (ibid., 92–102). She argues that each of these factors requires the rebel group to seek social acceptance, with regard to domestic constituencies concerning the political process and secessionism, on the one hand, and with regard to international audiences concerning recognition and foreign sponsorship, on the other.

An instructive example concerns the above-mentioned MILF in the Philippines (Jo 2015, 166–180). In 2008, ca. 15 percent of its armed forces were child soldiers. At the time, MILF was already negotiating with UNICEF about child soldiers and subsequently signed a UN Action Plan to ban child soldiering, which it then implemented. This effort at gaining international recognition was part and parcel of MILF's attempt at reaching a peace agreement with the Philippine government, granting the region of Bangsamoro increased autonomy, which was finally signed in 2014. The implementation of the agreement stalled in 2018 as a result of Philippine domestic politics under the right-wing populist president Duterte. In July 2018, however, Duterte signed the constitution for the Bangsamoro Autonomous Region in Muslim Mindanao, which was then approved by a popular referendum in Bangsamoro in early 2019 (Kreuzer 2019).

These and other examples are corroborated by the study of Stanton on violence used by rebel groups in civil war. Similar to Jo, she combines quantitative analysis and case studies to show that rebel groups seeking recognition and acceptance at the domestic and international level are less likely to engage in violence against civilians. Indicative for the quest for domestic legitimacy are inclusive organizational structures that encourage accountability to civilian constituents. She also finds that rebel groups fighting autocratic governments are more inclined to turn to international actors for political support and assistance. This is why the Free Aceh Movement (GAM) lined up with rural Islamic teachers as well as with activists and civil society groups after the collapse of Suharto's autocratic rule in 1998 (Stanton 2016, 160–177; cf. Barter 2015). Acehnese organizations, such as the Islamic teachers (*ulama*), provided GAM with primarily local legitimacy given their embeddedness in and trust relations with local populations. The alliance with (transnational) advocacy groups and activists built before Indonesia's transition to democracy continued to provide GAM with international legitimacy. As a result, GAM gained the capacity to govern various rural communities through its own local government structure, tying it to the Acehnese population whose strong support made the use of violence superfluous.

The literature on rebel governance agrees on the importance of legitimacy-seeking as a major reason why rebels commit to and comply with human rights. Herr (2013) argues that a positive record on human rights does not only increase the chances of obtaining humanitarian aid, which rebel groups can distribute to core supporters, boosting their output legitimacy (cf. Kalyvas 2006; Metelits 2009). Rebels also gain recognition as legitimate actors in international and domestic politics (Herr 2013; Stanton 2016). States tend to delegitimize political insurgents as terrorists and criminals (Steinhoff 2009). They resist the possibility for rebel groups to become parties of international treaties. Since they contest the sovereignty of the state, international law denies them legal status even as combatants (Krieger 2018, 556). By signing up to non-governmental humanitarian rights initiatives, such as the Geneva Call, they appear like states (Bassiouni 2008). Participating in national elections fulfills a similar function by turning rebel groups into political parties. Electoral participation provisions in peace agreements make the recurrence of violence less likely in post-conflict societies (Matanock 2017; see ch. 5). Under these circumstances, the prospect of gaining (input-) legitimacy as future co-governors induces VNSA to engage in democracy-building in post-conflict societies. The greater these prospects, the more careful rebels are not to risk their credibility, reputation, and trust they have earned at the international and domestic level by respecting human rights (Herr 2013, 45; see also Jo 2015). Moreover, as Huang argues using quantitative as well as qualitative data, including an in-depth case study of Nepal, when VNSA – as "stationary bandits" (see Chapter 4) – depend on the resources of civilians to secure their rule, a likely side-effect is that the population mobilizes as a political force, creating political pressures for democratization in the post-war environment (Huang 2016). However, as we argued above (Chapter 3), this collective action capacity of civilians to pressure rebel groups depends crucially on their social cohesion, which is fostered by relationships of social trust.

INSTITUTIONAL DESIGN: INCLUSIVE HIERARCHY

These findings have implications for the effectiveness of international agreements regarding their institutional design. Herr shows that compliance with the deeds of commitment developed by Geneva Call is significantly higher than with the declarations given to and special agreements negotiated by the ICRC (cf. Bassiouni 2008; Steinhoff 2009). Both initiatives lack strong enforcement mechanisms. The ICRC is careful in protecting its role as a neutral intermediary between conflict parties and therefore reluctant to disclose information on norm violations.

The Geneva Call, in contrast, publicly reports on the performance of rebel groups, not only naming and shaming norm violators but also making sure that their initial commitment receives media attention. The Geneva Call also provides rebel groups with a seat at the international table where they can engage with states and civil society on humanitarian issues, which gives them recognition and fosters compliance through procedural legitimacy (Herr 2013). Finally, the scope of the Geneva Call is limited, focusing on compliance with three specific issues, land mines, child soldiers, and sexual violence. The ICRC tasks are more complex, seeking to increase compliance with humanitarian international law as such by non-state as well as state actors (Herr 2013).

Thus, it is not only the quest for legitimacy and social acceptance explaining rebel groups' compliance with basic human rights; institutional capacity matters, too. The organizational structure of a rebel group, particularly its ability to control the use of violence among its members, is also relevant for their adherence to human rights (Jo and Bryant 2013; cf. Humphreys and Weinstein 2006; Stanton 2016, 177–178; Weinstein 2007). Rebel groups need a hierarchical line of command to maintain internal discipline (Manekin 2013; Wood 2009). Alternatively, they can develop organizational structures that align combatants' preferences with those of commanders, e.g. through political education (Hoover Green 2016), or embed their members firmly in the communities within which they operate, fostering relations of mutual trust (Arjona 2016). The latter often involves the building of more inclusive governance institutions (Stanton 2016). Moreover, as Huang argues, if VNSA build inclusive governance institutions during wartime, chances are that these institutions survive the postwar settlement. In other words, how rebel groups govern civilians in times of war will affect how they will govern in the post-conflict era (Huang 2016).

But there is a caveat: VNSA's institutional capacity alone is ambivalent, since it can also be used for gross violations of human rights (Jo 2015, 71–72; Wood 2010). Only if and when rebel leaders strongly commit to human rights and international law, and to inclusive and participatory institutions, can the rebels' organizational structure be used to ensure compliant behavior (Jo and Bryant 2013; Stanton 2016). In this regard, the institutional capacity of rebel groups to control their members is no different from statehood: under authoritarian leadership, the control over the use of violence can undermine human rights governance. VNSA have to be strongly motivated (mostly through the quest for legitimacy) to commit to human rights, the rule of law, and to participatory governance so that their institutional capacity and internal organization matter for effective governance.

In sum, we find strong evidence that the quest for domestic and international legitimacy combined with institutional capacity goes a long way to explain why and when VNSA engage in effective governance with regard to human rights, the rule of law, and democracy.

Conclusions

Our discussion of (I)NGOs, ROs, NSJI, companies, and rebel groups demonstrates that the promotion and protection of human rights, the rule of law, and democracy can be effective even under rather adverse conditions of limited statehood where central authorities are unable or unwilling to enforce the law.

For each of these actors, legitimacy concerns offer the key explanation followed by particular institutional design conditions establishing the capacity to actually engage in democratic governance broadly defined. (I)NGOs can use the mechanisms of the "boomerang effect" and the "spiral model" (Keck and Sikkink 1998; Risse, Ropp, and Sikkink 1999) to improve human rights conditions and to exert pressures on other actors – state and non-state, domestic and international – to comply with human rights. In order to be successful, they need both the recognition as a human rights group and the institutional capacity to engage with IOs, foreign states, and transnational networks.

ROs tend to enjoy greater acceptance by target states and local populations than IOs or foreign states due to their greater proximity and more inclusive decision-making procedures. Their effectiveness as governors, however, depends on their institutional capacity to arrive at collective decisions and the necessary resources to implement them. The lack of financial and personnel resources has hampered African ROs in their attempts to stop coup d'états or mass killings.

NSJI need to be open, transparent, and inclusive to facilitate deliberative outcomes that substitute for non-existing state rule of law institutions. In the absence of centralized enforcement mechanisms, implementation relies more often than not on relations based on social trust within the community, as well as the legitimacy of NSJI among local populations.

Companies investing in ALS are increasingly expected not only to respect human rights but to also contribute to their enforcement against other actors. When their international reputation is at stake, multi-national firms have developed human rights policies and started to incorporate them in their local practices. Such policies are also increasingly handed down the supply chain and imposed on contracted private security companies. However, companies continue to pay state security forces for protecting their legal property rights and the security of their facilities and staff. Police and military usually refuse to be trained on human rights by foreign companies. As a result, the effectiveness of corporate human rights governance remains limited and often below the expectations of local communities.

Rebel groups, in contrast, engage in the governance of human rights, the rule of law, and even democracy in search of political support both at the local and at the international level. International recognition provides them with legitimacy as political actors rather than criminals or terrorists. They are also more likely to receive international funding, which they can use to secure the loyalty of their fighters as well as their core constituents. Domestic legitimacy provides VNSA with the crucial support of the people in the area of limited statehood where they rule. At the same time, the more local communities develop their own action capacity to mobilize for human rights and democracy, the more likely it is that rebel governance builds inclusive and participatory institutions. Inclusive organizational structures do not only provide additional input legitimacy at the local level. They also reduce the need for hierarchical control over the use of violence by rebel fighters. Last but not least, the more VNSA are included in the post-conflict settlement, including democratic processes, turning them into political parties, the more likely it is that the post-war peace actually lasts (see also Chapter 5).

Legitimacy then fulfills a double function for the effectiveness of human rights, the rule of law, and democracy in ALS. On the one hand, the quest for recognition and acceptance provides a powerful motive for actors to respect and protect human rights, the rule of law, and democracy. On the other hand, legitimacy reduces the need for the institutional capacity necessary to enforce the rule of law and democratic rules. Institutional design, in turn, influences both legitimacy, e.g. through inclusive and transparent decision-making procedures, and institutional capacity, e.g. by facilitating collective action or ensuring necessary resources. Last but not least, a virtuous circle is likely to develop between effective human rights, rule of law, and democratic governance, on the one hand, and input, throughput, as well as output legitimacy, on the other. At least, there is some evidence that the quest for human rights, the rule of law, and democracy can be satisfied even under rather dire circumstances in ALS.

7 Welfare

Chapter 5 investigated security governance by a variety of actors, while Chapter 6 looked at the rule of law, democracy, and human rights. This chapter completes the analysis by examining the degree to which collective goods and services in the area of welfare can be provided in areas of limited statehood. We focus on goods and services that will enhance the well-being of people rather than economic opportunities or economic growth. These include economic subsistence, public health, and environmental protection. Thus, this chapter also captures the fulfillment of social and economic rights, as covered by the International Covenant on Social, Economic, and Cultural Rights (ICSECR). The focus on these collective goods, which are also included in the UN Sustainable Development Goals (SDGs),[1] is exemplary in this chapter, there is no particular normative agenda involved suggesting that the collective goods under consideration are more important than others. As in the previous chapters, we observe an enormous variation of effective service delivery. We explain the variation by looking at the institutional design of the governance arrangements, at the social acceptance and empirical legitimacy of the governors, and the collective action capacity of the populations as enabled by relationships of social trust (for a similar attempt see Brixi, Lust, and Woolcock 2015).

As in the previous chapters, we concentrate on different types of actors rather than on particular collective services. The chapter begins with a general overview of the degree to which welfare governance is effectively provided in ALS. Data show a remarkable progress in the provision of basic goods and services to enhance social welfare. We then discuss the role of foreign aid, both bilateral as provided by various national governments and aid agencies, and multilateral through IOs, such as the World Bank and specialized UN agencies. This is followed by an analysis of two types of external governors, multinational corporations (MNCs) and

---

[1] https://sustainabledevelopment.un.org/?menu=1300, last access August 18, 2019.

multi-stakeholder partnerships (MSPs) with different motivations to provide governance (see Chapter 4). Finally, we examine the role of local actors, namely "traditional" chiefs and tribal leaders, as well as rebel groups and Islamist militants as violent non-state actors (VNSA).

Variation in the Provision of Welfare Governance

The general picture regarding the effective provision of welfare governance does not change much as compared to security (Chapter 5) and the rule of law, democracy, and human rights (Chapter 6). In the following, we provide an overview of the worldwide development with regard to some basic goods and services, such as nourishment, health, and the protection of the environment, followed by data on different degrees of limited statehood. The overall evolution in most areas has been quite positive, since service provision has improved on a global scale, particularly with regard to nourishment and health (for a general discussion see Sikkink 2017). With the number of ALS remaining stable over time, this is a first indication that limited statehood does not necessarily impair service provision.

Let us start with economic subsistence and food security as a basic collective good ensuring people's livelihood (Liese 2018). Overall, as Figure 7.1 indicates, food security has globally increased. Yet, undernourishment varies quite dramatically in ALS (Figure 7.2), even though the regression line shows a weak correlation between degrees of statehood and absence of hunger. Yet, the standard deviation for statehood values between 0.5 and 0.8, which include most countries with ALS, is quite substantial, mirroring the picture from Chapters 5 (security) and 6 (human rights, rule of law, democracy).

A similar picture emerges with regard to public health, measured here with regard to infant mortality (Figures 7.3 and 7.4; overview in Holzscheiter 2018). In general, and on a global scale, infant mortality rates have substantially dropped since 2000, but the differences between countries with ALS are, once again, striking. If we ignore areas of consolidated statehood (statehood values of 0.9) and fragile as well as failed states (statehood values of 0.4 and lower), some countries with ALS exhibit public health effectiveness as high as countries with consolidated statehood, while others still encounter substantial infant mortality rates. As in the case of undernourishment, the regression line is driven by the extreme statehood values at either end of the continuum.

The overall picture does not change much with regard to the protection of the environment (overview in Hamann, Hönke, and O'Riordan 2018). Figure 7.5 presents the values for the Environmental Performance

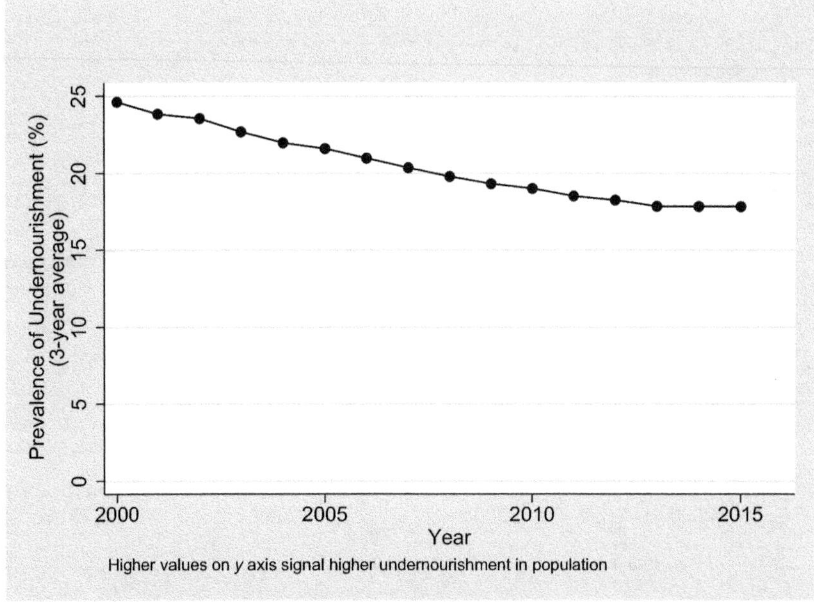

Figure 7.1 Undernourishment (2000–2015)
Courtesy of Eric Stollenwerk.
Source: Global Hunger Index; for details see Stollenwerk and Opper 2017, 6–7.

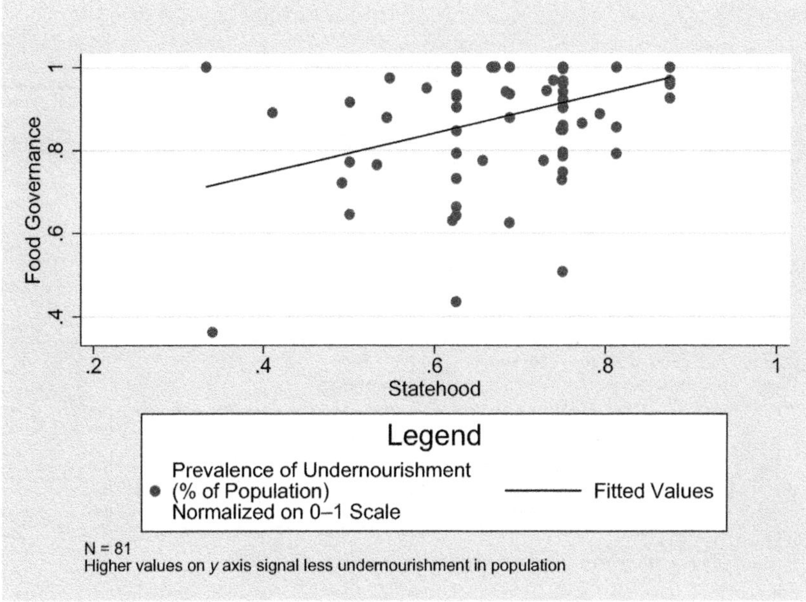

Figure 7.2 Undernourishment and statehood (2015)
Courtesy of Eric Stollenwerk. Each dot represents the value for one country.
Source: see figure 7.1. For the statehood indicators see chapter 2.

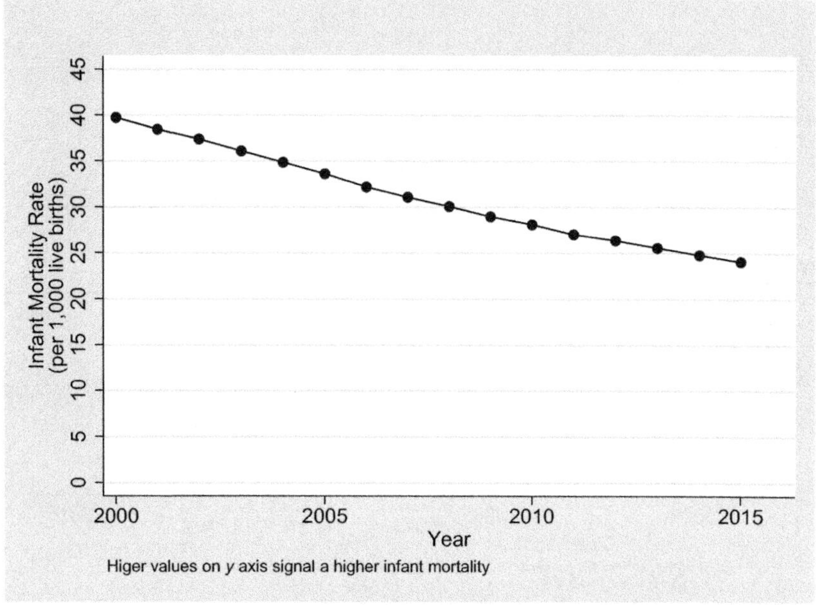

Figure 7.3 Evolution of infant mortality rates (2000–2015)
Courtesy of Eric Stollenwerk.
Source: World Bank data, for details see Stollenwerk and Opper 2017, 7.

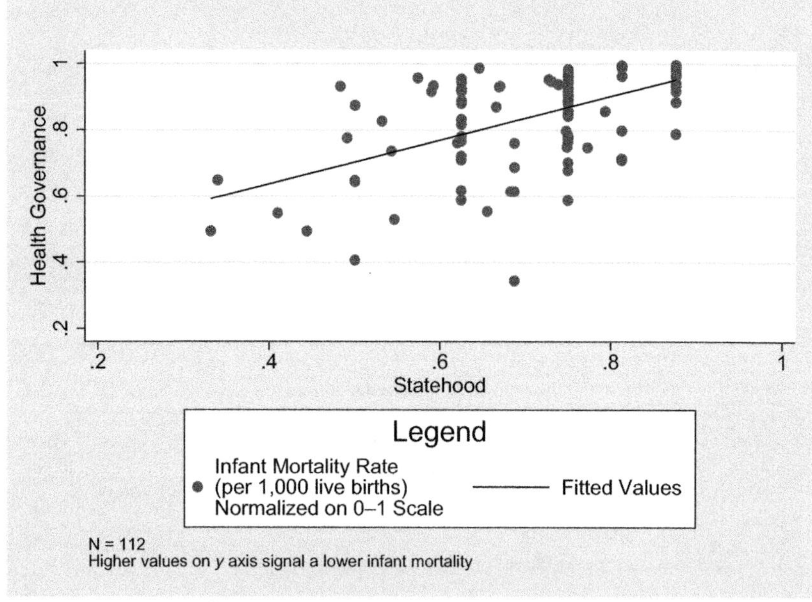

Figure 7.4 Infant morality and statehood (2015)
Courtesy of Eric Stollenwerk. Each dot represents the value for one country.
Source: See figure 7.3. For the statehood indicators see chapter 2.

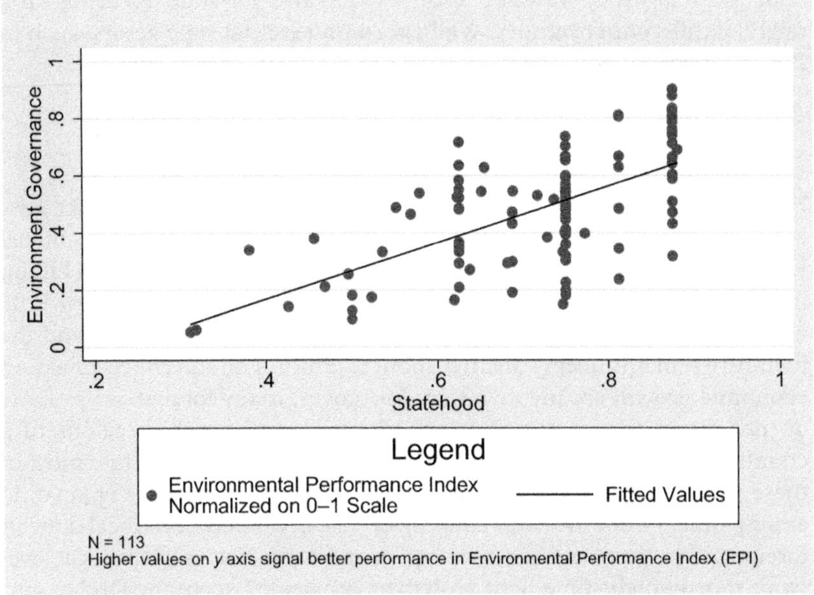

Figure 7.5 Environmental Performance Index (EPI) and statehood (2014)

Courtesy of Eric Stollenwerk. Each dot represents the value for one country. *Source*: Environmental Performance Index of Yale University, for details see Stollenwerk and Opper 2017, 5. See also Hamann, Hönke, and O'Riordan 2018, 503. For the statehood indicators see chapter 2.

Index, which contains several sub-indices of environmental standards, and degrees of statehood in 2014. Once again, the fitted values line is driven almost completely by countries with rather low statehood values, on the one hand, and consolidated states, on the other. In between and similarly to the picture above, the variation is significant and covers almost the entire spectrum from extremely low environmental protection to rather high standards.

It is rather striking that we do not see many differences between these three issue-areas of collective goods and services, at least as the overall picture is concerned. Some countries with ALS are doing quite well with regard to food security, health, and the environment, while others perform rather poorly. A more comprehensive statistical analysis of goods and services that includes education and basic infrastructure confirms the picture (Lee, Walter-Drop, and Wiesel 2014): There is no linear correlation between degrees of statehood, on the one hand, and the provision of collective goods and services, on the other.

In the following, we once again explain the variation focusing on a range of different governors. We begin with external state actors, such as IOs and foreign aid donors, and the provision of foreign aid.

IOs, Donor Agencies, and Aid Effectiveness

Foreign aid provides a powerful source of external actors to affect governance in ALS, particularly in low-income countries. Official Development Assistance (ODA) amounted to more than US$140 billion in 2016 (Dreher, Lang, and Ziaja 2018, 394). Yet, we still know little about the effectiveness of foreign aid (overview ibid., 395–399), and the literature remains deeply divided about it. Studies on the effects of aid on economic growth are inconclusive. Moreover, many foreign aid projects do not target the poorest, but are allocated in the richer regions of a country (Briggs 2016; see also Kotsadam et al. 2018, 66). While most of these works draw on country-level data, more recent studies emanating among others from the AidData project[2] use geo-referenced local data on foreign aid projects and also measure economic activities at the local level (with mostly night-time light growth as proxies). Except for Dreher and Lohmann (Dreher and Lohmann 2015), they demonstrate a rather consistent positive effect of foreign aid on economic growth (see e.g. Bitzer and Gören 2018 on World Bank projects; Khomba and Trew 2017 on Malawi; Civelli, Horowitz, and Teixeira 2017 on Uganda). Economic growth, of course, is not the same as welfare governance, even though it generates revenue to finance the provision of collective goods and services. There is research, however, that demonstrates a discernible effect of foreign aid on service provision. Kotsadam et al. show that foreign aid brings down infant mortality (Kotsadam et al. 2018). De and Becker have found similar results with regard to health, access to water, and education in Malawi (De and Becker 2015) as have Martorano et al. for Chinese ODA in Sub-Saharan Africa (Martorano, Metzger, and Sanfilippo 2018). Beath et al. demonstrate with regard to Afghanistan the positive effects of foreign aid on female empowerment (Beath, Christia, and Enikolopov 2013b). In sum, there is substantial evidence that external actors – states, IOs and donor agencies, but also non-state actors – can improve the effectiveness of welfare governance in ALS. Yet, these effects seem to be confined to the regional and local levels where aid is concentrated and do not necessarily have country-wide effects.

---

[2] See www.aiddata.org/, last access March 15, 2019.

As Dreher et al. point out, particularly areas of severely limited state-hood pose challenges to foreign aid (Dreher, Lang, and Ziaja 2018, 399–408). The "conditional effectiveness" literature has pointed out that aid effects depend on the quality of the institutions and the policies of recipient countries. Foreign aid is particularly effective in democratic systems, while it stabilizes autocracies and makes them more repressive. Moreover, DiLorenzo argues that aid that bypasses autocratic governments by being channeled through IOs and (I)NGOs might strengthen the former, since it reduces the willingness of citizens to resist their governments (DiLorenzo 2018).[3]

Three more problems are particularly severe in areas of very limited statehood and failed states: first, budget aid is often viewed as preferable to project aid, since it strengthens the autonomy of recipient governments. This might be less the case in areas where state institutions are too weak to prevent rent-seeking and corruption. Second, the absorption capacity of state administrations in ALS is weaker than elsewhere and these areas are poorer in most cases than other regions. As a result, aid levels often exceed 15 percent of the Gross Domestic Product (GDP) in those regions and are, therefore, likely to be less effective in generating growth (Dreher, Lang, and Ziaja 2018, 399, 406–407). Third, if ALS become war zones and are exposed to fighting, foreign aid could have adverse effects. Several studies have shown that foreign aid as an instrument of "winning hearts and minds" might induce VNSA, such as rebel groups, to increase fighting and even intentionally target civilians (Wood and Sullivan 2015 for Sub-Saharan Africa; Sexton 2016 for Afghanistan). In contrast, Gehring et al. suggest for geo-referenced World Bank and Chinese foreign aid projects in Sub-Sahara Africa that they actually reduce fighting (Gehring, Kaplan, and Wong 2019). Beber et al. point out that, on the one hand, UN peace-keeping operations substantially boost economic growth in areas in which they operate. On the other hand, they primarily create demand for low-skilled labor and their economic effects are short-lived, disappearing when the UN withdraws (Beber et al. 2019).

However, well-targeted and carefully designed projects are still likely to make a difference (Dreher, Lang, and Ziaja 2018, 408–409; see also the above-reported findings from the AidData project), even in fragile and failed states. Moreover, as Dietrich has shown, aid donors tend to bypass national governments in poorly governed countries and to use

---

[3] The normative consequences of this argument are unclear, though. Should donors refrain from helping citizens through "bypass aid" and leave them in poverty, because it might strengthen repressive governments?

(I)NGOs and other non-state actors instead (Dietrich 2013). These findings point to the significance of one of our three explanatory factors accounting for effective governance in ALS, namely institutional design.

Institutional design matters with regard to the effectiveness of foreign aid and the work of IOs. In this context, Lall has investigated the variation in IO effectiveness in terms of their goal achievement, their responsiveness to stakeholders, and their cost effectiveness (Lall 2017), using ratings from various development agencies. He shows that those development IOs, which enjoy policy autonomy from their principals, the member states, and have highly complex tasks to perform, are also more effective in achieving their objectives. In the food security sector, this explains the difference in performance between the World Food Programme (WFP), on the one hand, and the Food and Agriculture Organization (FAO), on the other (Lall 2017, 269–277). Honig adds to this the following observation: in a carefully designed quantitative and qualitative study, he shows that IOs and donor agencies, which grant their field agents sufficient leeway to adjust to local conditions, are also more effective. Those that are politically constrained by (particularly) parliamentary bodies do less well (Honig 2018). The effect is particularly pronounced in ALS, confirming our argument that flexible process management is a key to success (see also below). His study raises important questions with regard to the trade-off between input legitimacy (through parliamentary bodies) and the effectiveness of external actors in ALS.

Finally, the foreign aid literature adds to another issue of crucial significance in ALS, namely the effects of external actors' governance contributions to the legitimacy and capacity of state governments. This also includes the "virtuous circle" between legitimacy and effectiveness. One issue of concern in this context is whether foreign aid tends to delegitimize the weak state even further in ALS, as Bratton and others have suggested (e.g. Bratton 1989; Bräutigam 1992). In a series of experiments with regard to USAID projects supporting health governance in Bangladesh, Dietrich et al. show, however, that this is not the case (Dietrich, Mahmud, and Winters 2018; Winters, Dietrich, and Mahmud 2018). Information about donor financing not only improves the image of these donors (for similar findings with regard to China see Eichenhauer, Fuchs, and Brückner 2018). It also bolsters the legitimacy of local as well as state governments, and this effect is particularly strong among those citizens who perceive high levels of corruption in their country (Winters, Dietrich, and Mahmud 2018, 468; for similar findings with regard to Chinese and US aid in Sub-Saharan Africa see Blair and Roessler 2018). Unfortunately, the same holds true for "bypass" aid in autocratic regimes, which also tends to strengthen repressive governments (DiLorenzo 2018). In addition, D'Onofrio and Maggio show with regard to Uganda that foreign aid increases generalized trust among people. They find that "when a county received foreign aid, there is an increase in the likelihood that residents of that county feel more equal" (D'Onofrio and Maggio 2015, 7). In other words and in line with the general literature on social trust (Draude, Hölck, and Stolle 2018), foreign aid leads to the perception of lesser inequality, which then strengthens trust levels.

In sum, the literature on the overall effects of foreign aid on economic development in general remains inconclusive. However, the available data suggest that carefully designed aid that pays attention to local conditions is effective on the local and regional level in ALS. The findings not only support the "virtuous circle" hypothesis that governance effectiveness improves output-based legitimacy. They also challenge the claim that external governance contributions weaken the state in ALS. The opposite appears to be the case. Here, the generally positive image of foreign aid spills over to increasing state legitimacy, even in autocratic systems (if the government supports external governance, it cannot be altogether bad).

We now turn to non-state actors and begin with the governance contribution of MNCs.

Business as Governors: Beyond Voluntary Self-Regulation?

MNCs are unlikely welfare governors as their primary motivation is to make profit (see also Chapter 4). For decades, the literature on (economic) globalization has treated them as "footloose" agents moving from one country to the next depending on where the investment conditions are easiest and where social as well as environmental standards are lowest (Brühl et al. 2001; Chan and Ross 2003; Kaufmann and Segura-Ubiergo 2001; Lofdahl 2002; Rudra 2002; Xing and Kolstad 2002). In contrast, we argue in the following that MNCs and other business actors can indeed contribute to effective welfare governance in ALS thereby leading to a "race to the top" (Börzel et al. 2011; Börzel and Thauer 2013; Börzel and Hamann 2013). However, MNCs tend to be reluctant governors and their effectiveness in providing collective goods is strongly circumscribed by scope conditions.

Initiatives to make business contribute to governance in ALS draw on the functionalist rationale of bringing companies in to reach (greater) effectiveness (Cutler 2006, 200; Ruggie 2007b, 35). Systematic and comprehensive data on the effectiveness of business governance are still lacking. There is a literature on the social impact of firms on economic development and the environment. This scholarship finds both positive and negative effects on poverty, employment, health, education, basic utilities, or social conflict as a result of grievances (Aragón and Rud 2013; Chuhan-Pole, Dabalen, and Land 2017; Cust and Poelhekke 2015; Farooki 2012; Gamu, Le Billon, and Spiegel 2015; Jamali and Mirshak 2010; Kolk and Lenfant 2010; Lawrie, Tonts, and Plummer 2011; Steinberg 2019; Tordo 2011; Wegenast and Schneider 2017). In some cases, the positive externalities of commercial activities amount to governance contributions, e.g. when multinational mining or oil companies invest in basic infrastructure, such as roads, schools, hospitals, electricity, or sanitation, in exchange for access to natural resources (Ite 2005; Zafar 2007).

Evaluating the performance of MNCs in reducing their ecological and social footprints is more straightforward. Findings are equally mixed, though, pointing to a double commitment-compliance gap with regard to social and environmental regulation by business, on the one hand, and some demanding conditions to improve its commitment and compliance, on the other. We have seen a rapid growth of corporate regulatory initiatives, such as the United Nations Global Compact (UNGC), the Social Accountability 8000 (SA 8000), or the Global Reporting Initiative (GRI). Norms of corporate social responsibility (CSR) have diffused globally through transnational production networks and foreign direct investments (Dashwood 2012; Malesky and Mosley 2018; Thauer 2014b; Tsutsui and Lim 2015). While CSR has become part of world culture (Meyer, Pope, and Isaacson 2015), membership in global governance initiatives remains limited to large companies, typically with a brand name; it is also geographically concentrated in OECD countries (Utting 2015b). However, those companies that made voluntary commitments to minimize their negative externalities on the environment and local communities usually go beyond simply "green-" or "CSR-washing" their image (Dashwood 2012; Flohr et al. 2010; Pope and Wæraas 2016; Thauer 2014b). As Chapter 4 has shown, external regulation ("external shadow of hierarchy"), the absence of any service provision ("shadow of anarchy"), as well as global and local norms ("shadow of the community") motivate business to engage in governance in ALS, particularly with regard to environmental and social standards, but also by directly delivering services, such as health. The effectiveness of their governance contributions, however, is sometimes not only compromised by compliance problems but also by their limited scope.

Flohr et al. conducted a comprehensive study on the effectiveness of individual and collective self-regulatory arrangements, including MSPs such as UNGC, SA 8000, and GRI. They did not only consider company policies (output) and rule-consistent behavior (outcome). They also evaluated impact in terms of overall goal attainment, the evolution of new norms, as well as effects on third parties, other policy areas, and the role of the state (Flohr et al. 2010). Their findings show that companies move from commitment to compliance by incorporating regulatory standards into corporate rules and management systems. Their practices, however, often remain decoupled from these organizational changes. The headquarters of MNCs invest in communication campaigns seeking to socialize the management of their subsidiaries in ALS into social and environmental standards. Compliance management systems require country representatives to regularly report on their efforts to put company policies into practice and abide with transnational standards. While headquarters have a keen interest in enforcing corporate regulations to avoid reputational and financial damage (Frynas 2005; Thauer 2014b), local management often finds it difficult to comply with demanding rules, particularly if their local competitors are less committed to labor or environmental standards (Jastram and Schneider 2018).

Global value and supply chains are an important venue for the diffusion of transnational governance standards (Malesky and Mosley 2018). At the same time, compliance increases manufacturing costs thereby undermining the competitive advantage of investments in ALS. MNCs monitor compliance of their suppliers and subcontractors with agreed upon standards (Héritier, Müller-Debus, and Thauer 2009). They can terminate supply chain contracts or end joint ventures in case of violations. The example of the German chemical company BASF is instructive in this case: with regard to its South African operations, BASF threatened to end its relationship with the Lonmin company, which runs one of the world's largest platinum mines, if the British company continued to fail tackling community and environmental problems. The Lonmin-owned mine near Rustenburg had been the scene of the Marikana massacre, in which South African security forces killed 34 mineworkers during an illegal strike of thousands of workers for higher wages and better working conditions in mid-August 2012 (Alexander 2013). In response, Lomnin renewed its commitment to creating jobs, alleviating poverty, and providing housing for employees (Hamann 2019). Five years later, the Bapo Ba Mogale Traditional Authority of the community that had hosted the mine since the 1960s called for the suspension of Lonmin's operations because it failed to implement the promised social and labor plan. In the meantime,

BASF, which was the main customer of Lonmin, had conducted audits to support and ensure compliance with labor standards and the UN Global Compact principles.[4] Amid increasing public pressure, BASF declared in October 2017 that it reserved its right to terminate the cooperation if Lonmin did not improve its compliance with human rights and social as well as environmental standards.[5]

The research of Börzel and her collaborators on the contributions of MNCs in fighting HIV/AIDS and environmental pollution in Sub-Sahara Africa confirms the mixed record of governance by business. Effectiveness in terms of goal attainment is highest in the case of voluntary self-regulation at the company level (Börzel and Thauer 2013; Thauer 2014b). MNCs may go beyond international standards, such as the International Standardization Organization's (ISO) management systems, as well as the legal requirements of their host and their home countries. German-based car manufacturers require their South African subsidies to fully comply with all relevant European environmental process and product regulations and even go beyond European legislation. Auditing processes and systematic control provide for monitoring and enforcement mechanisms. At the same time, the scope of in-house regulation is often limited. Companies internalize negative externalities of their commercial activities, such as reducing environmental pollution or improving security at the workplace. They also engage in direct governance provision. Access to HIV/AIDS prevention and treatment programs, for instance, is often limited to their employees, contractors, their families, and the local communities in which they operate (Börzel and Thauer 2013; Thauer 2013a). Interestingly, this is why they are often considered more effective than public service provision, since state clinics "can be hard to get to, have long and public queues, and are prone to running out of the life-saving drugs people are queuing for" (Stephens 2019, 8). In other words, there appears to be a trade-off between the provision of healthcare as a public good and its effectiveness in ALS. The more healthcare is delivered as a club good, the more effective it is given the available resources.

The limited inclusiveness of business governance is not only due to the (long-term) costs of providing generally accessible public goods. On the one hand, companies and their shareholders increasingly accept the necessity to reduce, prevent, and rectify harmful effects of their economic activities, as the "moral minimum" of CSR (Simon, Powers, and

---

[4] www.zeit.de/2016/19/basf-metall-suedafrika-verantwortung, last access August 3, 2018.

[5] www.wiwo.de/unternehmen/auto/menschenrechte-basf-droht-vertrag-mit-platin-zulieferer-in-suedafrika-aufzuloesen/20510594.html, last access August 3, 2018.

Gunnemann 1972). On the other hand, they do not see it as their general responsibility to provide collective goods and services directly. Similar to many beneficiaries of business governance, companies consider the building and running of schools and hospitals or the electrification of local communities the task of the state (see also below).

Some studies have also pointed to the unintended consequences business governance can have for third parties, other policy areas, or power constellations at the local level. Effective governance by business may allow state actors to discharge their responsibility to protect the environment or provide public health and education (Hönke and Börzel 2014; Hönke and Thomas 2012). Local governments refer citizens asking for improved roads or housing to the company they are working for. The state's unwillingness or inability to support business contributions to governance often overburdens companies, which are then left alone to provide public services. As a result, their governance contributions are perceived as governance failures due to a "capacity-expectation gap."

The successful collaboration of the private and the public sector in improving regulatory standards and service delivery may not only create winners, either. The National Association of Automobile Manufacturers of South Africa (NAAMSA) successfully lobbied the South African government to issue stricter environmental regulation to keep low-regulating competitors from China, India, and South America and their cheaper cars out of the South African market. More precisely, the association – driven by mass-market producers with headquarters in Europe (particularly Germany) and Japan – feared an entrance of cheap Chinese and Indian cars on the South African car market and therefore pressed the government to issue stricter regulations with respect to emissions of new vehicles. In response to this lobbying attempt, the South African government raised the level of emission regulations as requested by NAAMSA, so that the cheap car competitors could not sell cars legally on the South Africa market. On the one hand, this has been a major contribution of MNCs to environmental governance following the logic of a "race to the top" rather than a race to the bottom (Börzel and Thauer 2013). On the other hand, it has compromised other governance objectives. Mobility is a prime social issue in South Africa, and immobility is a main barrier to employment for people who live in remote townships far away from the industrial centers. Keeping cheap cars out of the market, while being good for the environment, nevertheless hampers enhanced mobility and an inclusive labor market (Börzel, Hönke, and Thauer 2012, 12–15; cf. Thauer 2014b). Hence, this example demonstrates that raising standards may involve trade-offs – in this case between enhanced environmental protection, on the one hand, and enhanced mobility, on the other hand.

In sum, the overall contribution of business to governance in ALS is hard to assess given different measurement standards employed in the literature. We also lack large-n studies that isolate the effect of business on service provision. The growing number of case studies, however, demonstrate that – on balance – companies help close the governance gap and – under particular circumstances – are successfully "racing to the top." The question is rather what explains the variation with regard to the effectiveness of business contributions. In line with our theoretical framework (see Chapter 2), we account for the differences in governance effectiveness with regard to the institutional design of governance arrangements, residual statehood, and the legitimacy of business as governors.

Business contributions to governance appear to be most effective, the closer the governance task is to the day-to-day business operations. More complex tasks often overburden companies in terms of their financial and cognitive resources (Börzel and Hamann 2013; Börzel and Thauer 2013; Thauer 2014b). For instance, firms are rarely equipped to run schools or hospitals (Hönke and Börzel 2014). Moreover, the more regulatory and negotiation levels are involved, the more companies have to collaborate with other actors, which increases transaction costs and the risks of freeriding. To cope with complexity and tackle collective action problems, respectively, companies need to go beyond in-house regulation.

Institutional Conditions: The Case of South Africa and HIV/AIDS

While South Africa is not a failing or failed state, areas of limited statehood are widespread. The capacity of state actors to provide rules and services varies considerably across both territorial communities (provinces, local governments) and policy areas (cf. Börzel and Thauer 2013). HIV/AIDS is one of the most extreme cases of governance failure. South Africa belongs to the countries with the highest HIV/AIDS infection rates in the world. The South African state has lacked both capacity and, increasingly less though, the political will to comprehensively fight the disease. As shown in Chapter 4, firms are motivated to engage in governance if there is no other actor who provides the goods and services they require for the economic activities ("shadow of anarchy"). At the same time, tackling HIV/AIDS is an extremely complex governance task, which requires companies to engage beyond their premises. As such, HIV/AIDS in South Africa is instructive with regard to how the tension between the "shadow of anarchy" and task complexity affects the effectiveness of business contributions to welfare governance in ALS.

Companies that heavily rely on skilled labor and invest in the training of employees have a strong incentive to spend substantial resources for HIV/AIDS workplace programs and for comprehensive health care provision. Sick leaves, lower productivity, and social conflict associated with the disease can undermine the profitability of the investment in skills if the state fails to address the HIV/AIDS pandemic effectively. In South Africa, multinational automobile manufacturers, including BMW, Mercedes Benz, Volkswagen, General Motors, and Toyota, have also engaged in collective governance efforts. On the global level, many of these companies are members of the World Economic Forum Global Health Initiative or the Global Business Coalition on HIV/AIDS and other communicable diseases. Nationally, they work with the South African Business Coalition against HIV/AIDS, Business Unity South Africa and NAACAM, the National Association of Automotive Component Manufacturers, which organizes the suppliers of these big MNCs. On the local level, companies initiate many projects through local chambers of commerce to raise awareness of the disease in the population, to publicize preventive measures including condom use, and to improve health care services for those who have contracted the virus (for example, through the training of nurses and doctors in local clinics on the specifics of HIV/AIDS treatment). Associations help them push workplace programs onto their supply chains, which they usually share (Thauer 2013a; cf. Thauer 2014b).

Next to facilitating more complex governance tasks companies cannot tackle on their own, business associations or MSPs (see below) at the sectoral, regional or global level allow companies to level the playing field and prevent freeriding (Börzel, Thauer, and Hönke 2013; Dashwood 2012; Vandenbergh and Gilligan 2017). Collective governance initiatives often act as transmitters of peer pressure (Kollman and Prakash 2001), particularly on companies that are less visible and, hence, less likely to be targeted by shaming campaigns. In line with our argument in Chapter 4, large global companies in the South African mining sector, such as BHP Billiton and Anglo American, and some mid-sized companies that were targeted by a human rights campaign, such as Anglogold Ashanti, have taken the lead in the Social Responsibility Index of the Johannesburg Stock Exchange. At the same time, an increasing number of smaller mining enterprises have emerged in the course of the industry's restructuring process. They are mostly subcontracting firms, populate the more risk-friendly business segment of the mining industry, and hardly engage in governance. While smaller companies can freeride on the positive image produced by CSR-activities of major companies, the entire sector suffers reputational damage when a mining company gets under fire for violating environmental or human rights standards. Highly visible multinational companies concerned that one black sheep may ruin the reputation of their entire sector have therefore sought to set up sector-wide governance initiatives, such as the Mining/Metals and Sustainable Development process (Börzel, Hönke, and Thauer 2012, 18–19; cf. Hönke and Kranz 2013). They shall help prevent freeriding of both major competitors and smaller market players by setting and enforcing sector-wide standards.

Collective governance arrangements can increase the effectiveness of business governance by making companies contribute to governance in ALS that have not voluntarily committed themselves to reducing their negative externalities. Peer pressure to subscribe to and comply with voluntary standards, coupled with institutional monitoring and sanctioning mechanisms, may serve as functional equivalents for the state setting and enforcing collectively binding regulations. The more institutionalized these governance arrangements are, the higher their effectiveness (Hönke and Thauer 2014; Flohr et al. 2010).

Residual Statehood and the Provision of Public Goods

These governance arrangements, however, tend to reach their limits when it comes to delivering highly complex governance tasks as public goods beyond local communities. The more complex the service delivery, the more difficult it becomes to make the actors involved commit to precise and binding goals as well as to institute and put into practice monitoring and sanctioning mechanisms to ensure compliance. In-house HIV/AIDS workplace programs, for example, are highly institutionalized and their rolling out to employees is quite effective. However, combatting the pandemic requires a comprehensive health care system that reaches out to entire families and communities in order to prevent infection and provide care for infected people. To extend HIV/AIDS prevention and treatment programs beyond the locality in which they operate, companies require the cooperation of provincial and national state authorities. The state has to guarantee that public health institutions will take care of patients in case a firm decides to let staff go or if it moves away (cf. Börzel and Thauer 2013; Börzel, Hönke, and Thauer 2012; Hönke and Thauer 2014; Thauer 2014b). Likewise, compliance with voluntary environmental and social standards often requires a minimum of statehood. ISO 14001, for instance, is in essence a management system, which prescribes procedural rules. The level of substantive – that is, pollution limiting – standards in which this management system is embedded can vary. At a minimum, certification under ISO 14001 requires a company to implement the legal prescriptions prevailing in the country where its operations take place. In many areas, environmental regulation is a highly complex task to fulfill. National guidelines may exist, but they have to be applied at the local level and, for this, it takes an active state that is capable of setting these standards. How is a company supposed to undergo ISO 14001 certification without knowing the effluent, emission, and waste deposition limits it shall comply with (Thauer 2013b)? Statehood, finally, is often necessary to upscale club goods into truly public goods. Since business governance is most effective in the form of voluntary self-regulation, its geographical and social scope tends to be limited. To turn these governance services into public goods available to everybody, enforceable state regulations are often necessary. South African labor laws, for instance, have forced mining companies to guarantee the same pension and home-base care benefits to early-retired HIV-positive workers and dependents of deceased workers as to everybody else (Hönke 2013a).

Thus, residual statehood has a role to play for effective business governance in ALS (see also Chapter 8). Apart from state regulations, companies often depend on states with a minimum capacity to provide basic infrastructure (e.g. roads, ports, electricity grids) and public secur-ity in order to engage in governance effectively. However, residual state-hood is often janus-faced, it can also serve as a governance spoiler compromising and undermining service delivery. State actors may (ab) use their legal authority to impose some of their political and personal economic interests on firms. MNCs often rely on informal political networks to receive state contracts and licenses in many ALS. Companies then owe members of these networks personal favors (see also Chapter 5). State actors may also prevent companies from providing a particular common good and obstruct their CSR activities if these activities address issue-areas in a way not supported by government or opposition groups. In South Africa, the government has long opposed conventional theories about HIV/AIDS and therefore obstructed busi-ness engagement in combating the pandemic. Where they did not, medical treatment programs of firms still presuppose an agreement with local public health care institutions to take care of employees who leave the company. In exchange for this guarantee, MNCs frequently offer to extend their HIV/AIDS workplace program to parts of the local commu-nity. In East London, the government insisted on a highly exclusive deal: in exchange for the guarantee to take care of former employees of an MNC, the health department demanded to have its own employees enrolled in the company's workplace program (Börzel, Hönke, and Thauer 2012, 26–27). We will discuss these "dark sides of statehood" (Börzel, Thauer, and Hönke 2013, 242) in Chapter 8.

Norm Congruence and Domestic Legitimacy

Next to institutional design and residual statehood, legitimacy appears to be a crucial condition for effective business contributions to governance in ALS. Hönke and Thauer have shown that the congruence of norms on which business governance draws with domestic norms generates social acceptance and facilitates the cooperation of domestic actors with firms in the provision of welfare services. For instance, until the early 2000s, the South African government had rejected the transnational norm promoted by the WHO that the infection with HIV should be treated with antiretroviral drugs to delay the outbreak of AIDS. Only when international and domestic pressures forced the Mbeki government to abandon its resistance did business initiatives and MSPs with local authorities, chambers of commerce, and transnational NGOs for HIV/AIDS prevention and comprehensive treatment start to take effect (Hönke and Thauer 2014; cf. Börzel and Thauer 2013). As we already discussed in Chapter 6, the legitimation of business governance initiatives does not necessarily have to be provided by the state but can also come from traditional authorities. Some mining companies closely cooperate with traditional and faith healers (Stephens 2019, 11). Authorization by international or transnational institutions only yields legitimacy if their norms, rules, and procedures resonate with domestic standards for appropriate governance (see above; cf. Krasner and Risse 2014b). Finally, many beneficiaries of business governance still expect the state to take over, at least in the long run (Beisheim et al. 2011c). Local communities often resist the privatization of service delivery.

The literature has found only limited evidence for companies themselves seeking to increase their legitimacy as governors. They prefer to organize their governance contributions within institutional settings that are non-inclusive, non-transparent, and non-accountable (Börzel and Thauer 2013; Flohr et al. 2010, 234). Transnational norms often encourage the proactive engagement of companies with local communities. Participatory structures at the village level, such as elected development communities deciding on the allocation of company development funds, help mitigate conflict with local stakeholders and increase social acceptance of business as governors. Once again, the collective action capacity of local communities is crucial to induce companies to engage in effective governance, as Steinberg has shown with regard to mining companies in Africa (Steinberg 2019). At the same time, companies are often not willing nor able to meet local expectations for social investment (Banerjee 2011; Bruijn and Whiteman 2010; Ogula 2012). Business could certainly benefit from input- and throughput legitimacy to increase the effectiveness of its governance contributions. Yet, unlike other actors, most companies are not interested in becoming governors. They engage in governance to boost the legitimacy of their business operations vis-à-vis their stakeholders, which are often outside areas of limited statehood.

In sum, business contributions to effective welfare governance in ALS vary. They depend largely on their institutional design, in particular on their embeddedness in larger governance arrangements that also include their competitors. Moreover, residual statehood in terms of the provision of infrastructure as well as the ability of (local or national) governments to regulate business contributions (even in the absence of a viable "shadow of hierarchy," see Chapters 2 and 3) appears to be significant. At the same time, weak state actors often become governance spoilers. Last but not least and as argued before (see Chapters 3, 5, and 6), effective business governance relies on legitimacy and local support. The more the (transnational) norms promoted by business actors resonate with local understandings of what is appropriate, the more effective business governance becomes. Nevertheless, companies remain reluctant to actively foster their legitimacy as governors as their primary mission is to make profit. In short, business can indeed "race to the top" and provide public goods and services, but the scope conditions are rather demanding.

Multi-Stakeholder Partnerships (MSPs) and (I)NGOs: Institutional Design and Legitimacy

Companies prefer voluntary self-regulation for their governance contributions. At the same time, collective governance arrangements allow them to pool capacities, increase their impact, and solve collective action problems. Besides business associations and purely private governance initiatives, companies often form or join MSPs. By "making business and all actors of civil society part of the solution" (Michael Doyle, UN Asst. General Secretary, quoted in Beisheim, Liese, and Lorch 2014, 3; see Beisheim, Ellersiek, and Lorch 2018), MSPs held great promises for promoting sustainable development in ALS (Beisheim and Liese 2014b; Brinkerhoff 2002; Linder and Vaillancourt Rosenau 2000; Lund-Thomsen and Lindgreen 2014; Reinicke and Deng 2000; Witte, Reinicke, and Benner 2000). They are supposed to be more effective, flexible, and democratic than traditional forms of governance, resulting in higher standards, better methods of production, novel monitoring procedures, and new certification schemes. Not surprisingly, MSPs feature prominently as a major tool to accomplish the Sustainable

Development Goals (SDGs) of the UN.[6] There is plenty of evidence that MSPs have become key providers of collective goods and services in ALS, particularly in global health (Holzscheiter 2018; Schäferhoff 2014b).

The same holds true for (I)NGOs. In 2014, more than 17 percent of ODA was channeled through (I)NGOs and civil society organizations (Beisheim, Ellersiek, and Lorch 2018, 211; see also Dietrich 2013), while more than 60 percent of their budgets came from private donations (Büthe, Major, and Souza 2012, 572). US private donors and non-profit organizations exceed US ODA by 20–25 percent (Desai and Kharas 2018, 505).

Yet, despite involving a broad range of actors that pool their resources and participate in decision-making, the governance effectiveness of MSPs and INGOs appears to be disputed and inconclusive. Both actors have been criticized for privatizing standard setting (O'Rourke 2006) or for not reaching down to the most marginalized stakeholders, such as seasonal farmworkers and women workers (Gupta 2008; Ponte and Cheyns 2013; Khan and Lund-Thomsen 2011). One of the most comprehensive studies to date concludes that 80 percent of the 348 sustainable development MSPs covered were dysfunctional (Pattberg et al. 2012; cf. Bäckstrand 2006; Brinkerhoff 2002; Homkes 2011). The research of Beisheim et al. corroborates that many MSPs do not (fully) reach their goals (Beisheim and Liese 2014b; Beisheim et al. 2014). They analyzed 45 projects on health, social, and environmental policy in South Asia and East Africa. Effectiveness ranges from almost complete failures, e.g. the Alliance Against Hunger and Malnutrition, or the Children's Vaccine Initiative, to huge success stories, e.g. the Global Alliance for Vaccines and Immunization (GAVI) and the Global Fund to Fight AIDS, Tuberculosis and Malaria (GF), two giants among the MSPs in the public health sector and elsewhere (Beisheim et al. 2014; Schäferhoff 2014b; Kaan 2014; see also Chapter 4).

(I)NGOs display similar variation. One of the few comparative studies on the effectiveness of INGOs with regard to human security, which also includes some of the public goods discussed in this chapter, shows that INGOs can be hugely effective. At the same time, there is variation: "I find that the effect of these organizations is not monolithic; differences in organizational characteristics that reflect underlying motivations, issue focus, and state peculiarities condition when and where this vibrant and growing force of INGOs will be effective contributors to human security

---

[6] https://sustainabledevelopment.un.org/sdinaction, last access August 22, 2019.

outcomes" (Murdie 2014, 16; for a more skeptical view see Beisheim, Ellersiek, and Lorch 2018, 214–216).

One problem with the literature on MSPs and (I)NGOs is that they are often held to much higher performance standards than other actors, including VNSA, local chiefs and leaders, or states with weak capacities. Given that their main motivations are indeed to provide governance (other more self-interested goals notwithstanding, see Murdie 2014; Prakash and Gugerty 2010), they seem to be expected, therefore, to be effective, too. Many – particularly qualitative – studies hold them to Denmark-like standards in areas of limited statehood, at least implicitly, which raises measurement issues (see Chapter 2). We come back to this point in the concluding Chapter 8.

This is not to deny that the governance effectiveness of MSPs and (I)NGOs varies considerably, and this variation appears to be driven by factors related to institutional conditions, residual statehood, and legitimacy.

Institutional Design: Legalization, Flexible Process Management, and Residual Statehood

Beisheim et al. argue that the provision of services or standards associated with complex tasks, such as sustainable access to water and sanitation, fortified school meals, or auditable certification standards based on international workplace norms, can only be successful when transnational MSPs institutionalize the terms of obligation and monitoring. GAVI and the GF, for example, rely on precise rules to which all partners commit through contracts. Continued or additional funding is conditional upon compliance with these contracted rules and procedures, which is externally and centrally monitored (Beisheim and Campe 2012; Beisheim et al. 2014; Schäferhoff 2014b). In addition, GAVI and GF provide assistance for human resource development (e.g. training programs, improvement of working conditions), strengthen local leadership qualities, and build organizational and management capacities (e.g. strengthening communication structures and organizational culture). Their websites are exemplary in terms of transparency.[7]

Moreover, projects on the ground have to be managed in a flexible way as to be able to adjust to changing conditions. This also requires built-in learning capacities and a certain degree of autonomy of local agents (see also Lall 2017 for a similar argument on IOs in general). This flexibility is partly inconsistent with strong legalization requirements,

---

[7] See e.g. https://data.theglobalfund.org/home, last access August 22, 2019; www.gavi.org/results/, last access August 22, 2019.

since it requires a certain degree of local autonomy. Moreover, local project management needs to be organized "bottom up" so as to develop local ownership (also to gain legitimacy, see below; for details see Beisheim and Liese 2014b; Beisheim, Ellersiek, and Lorch 2018, 216–217; Beisheim et al. 2014).

Regarding residual statehood, the literature claims that MSPs are often absent in areas where the state does not control the use of force and lacks any capacity to set and enforce rules (Liese, Janetschek, and Sarre 2014). Naturally, MSPs prefer to operate in areas free of violent conflict, in which a somewhat functioning government administration provides a minimum of security and local infrastructure and they can cooperate with local partners to ensure successful project implementation through local ownership. At the same time, residual statehood can be as much of an impediment as in the case of business. Government authorities in India, for instance, acted as veto players or even spoilers blocking access of MSPs to local communities because they felt not sufficiently involved (Beisheim, Janetschek, and Sarre 2014).

Moreover, the most successful MSPs in the public health sector, such as GAVI and the GF, are indeed present in failed states, such as Afghanistan, South Sudan, Somalia, or the DRC.[8] Their reported results in terms of children immunized, the distribution of anti-malaria bednets, as well as tuberculosis and HIV/AIDS treatments are impressive. Unfortunately, the geographical coverage and distribution of MSP activities is not always clear, so we lack information about the degree to which these MSPs are actually able to enter war zones in these countries.

A study by Schäferhoff is highly instructive in this context (Schäferhoff 2014a, 2014b). He examined the effectiveness of health services in Somalia provided by the Global Fund. He showed that residual statehood and the absence of violence clearly mattered for effective governance. The GF was highly successful in distributing anti-malaria bednets throughout the country, including the warzone of central Somalia. Yet, GF projects combating HIV/AIDS succeeded only in comparatively peaceful regions, such as Somaliland, with stronger residual statehood. In other words, residual statehood and the absence of violence matter particularly for rather complex governance tasks that require multiple interventions and coordination among a diverse set of actors (see also Krasner and Risse 2014b).

Yet, degrees of statehood are not simply exogenous to external governance efforts. Various studies show that MSPs and INGOs can

---

[8] See the websites above.

strengthen state capacity in ALS. As argued above with regard to IOs, external MSP or INGO governance is unlikely to weaken limited statehood further (see also Chapter 8). Campbell et al. demonstrate, for example, that development INGOs strengthen state capacity in democracies (Campbell, DiGiuseppe, and Murdie 2019). Murdie and Hicks argue that health INGOs "help increase health spending [of the state] both by changing the policy-making climate and by aiding domestic efforts for increases in health spending" (Murdie and Hicks 2013, 543 [added by authors]; see also Murdie 2014).

Local Recognition and Legitimacy

Effectiveness also requires local stakeholders to recognize MSPs and INGOs as legitimate and their services as meeting local needs and being compatible with local customs (Beisheim, Janetschek, and Sarre 2014; see also Lund-Thomsen and Coe 2013; Khan and Lund-Thomsen 2011). This is often difficult as MSPs create their own rules and regulations to achieve their goals. These may replace or even compete with state or local regulation and customs. While state authorities may be involved in MSPs, they do not delegate or contract out the services the MSPs seek to provide. The effectiveness of GAVI suffered from the failure to communicate sufficiently a policy change to the governments of recipient countries, which caused substantial delays in the implementation of projects (Schäferhoff 2014b). Customizing their services to local needs, preferences, and habits, e.g. with regard to diets, requires institutional change management that allows MSPs to adapt project designs and project implementation (Beisheim, Janetschek, and Sarre 2014; Beisheim et al. 2014).

Another challenge for the legitimacy of MSPs is their perception as instruments of business interests that pursue their neoliberal agenda in privatizing collective goods and service provision (Brühl 2007; Bull and McNeill 2007; Miraftab 2004; Utting and Zammit 2009; Zammit 2003). Projects of the Water and Sanitation for the Urban Poor (WSUP) MSP, which aimed at improving access to water and sanitation, met with resistance in Indian slums due to concerns about the privatization of water supply (Beisheim and Liese 2014b; Beisheim et al. 2014, 661). GAVI experienced the power of community mobilization when local anti-vaccine activists challenged the necessity for new vaccines and nurtured fears of international companies driving up prices. The Global Alliance for Improved Nutrition (GAIN) faced fierce opposition by local activist networks that rejected food fortification as a mere supplement for adequate food supply (Beisheim et al. 2014, 660). It has also been criticized for targeting areas "according to the wealth of its potential clients" (Liese, Janetschek, and Sarre 2014, 141). As a result, GAIN often does not reach refugee camps, drought-prone, or remote rural areas.

Generating social acceptance for them and their projects, finally, often suffers from weak responsiveness and accountability of MSPs toward local stakeholders. (I)NGOs are concerned about their donors who expect quick and measurable results. So do executive boards and shareholders of companies. Local stakeholders, in turn, may lack the capacity to make use of participatory opportunities or are entangled in local power politics (Beisheim and Kaan 2010; Banks, Hulme, and Edwards 2015; Harrison 2002; Reich 2012). Flexible, inclusive, and transparent process management can help mitigate such power disparities. Thus, the secretariat of the Common Code for the Coffee Community (C4), setting minimum standards for economic, ecological, and social sustainability in the coffee sector, has documented meetings, facilitated exchange among the roasters and coffee-buying companies, the producer organizations, and civil society groups, and helped resolve conflicts among them. This generated ownership and relationships of personal trust among the different stakeholders. The secretariat also sought to strengthen the negotiation capacities of small coffee farmers (Beisheim and Kaan 2010; Kaan 2014). Involving local strongmen is another way to prevent them from sabotaging MSP projects as WSUP did in India when it consulted the local mafia that acts as illegal water providers. Since informal and illegal water cartels continue their illegal water connections, also in WSUP projects, these "mastans" compromise both the international and the domestic legitimacy of the MSP (Liese, Janetschek, and Sarre 2014). Conversely, effective MSPs have managed to build trust-based relationships with local stakeholders, often with the help of local brokers (Beisheim, Janetschek, and Sarre 2014; Beisheim and Kaan 2010). While companies are reluctant to share information about their business practices, NGOs and local communities tend to be suspicious of their stakes in providing governance. Process management, hence, helps fostering the input and throughput legitimacy of MSPs.

In sum, MSPs and (I)NGOs play crucial roles for welfare governance in ALS. They have helped to upscale efforts of setting and enforcing environmental and social standards and to provide key services in health, food, or education. The success of their governance contributions hinges upon important scope conditions, including particularly the institutional design of the governance arrangements and their legitimacy. The role of residual statehood is more ambivalent. On the one hand, a minimum of security and basic infrastructure provided by the state appears to be important for risk averse governors in their decision to engage. Moreover, more complex governance tasks are difficult to perform in warzones. On the other hand, residual statehood allows state authorities to block or hinder governance contributions by non-state actors if they feel their sovereignty undermined or their interest in rent-seeking not satisfied. Finally and importantly, external governance itself appears to strengthen rather than weaken residual state capacity. There is little evidence that MSPs and (I)NGOs substituting for limited statehood by providing much needed governance services weaken limited statehood even further. We come back to these points in Chapter 8.

Local Non-State Actors: VNSA and "Traditional" Authorities

We now turn to "local" non-state actors, namely VNSA and "traditional" authorities.

Rebel Groups and Religious VNSA: Public Services beyond Law and Order?

As we have seen in Chapters 4, 5, and 6, VNSA who hold control over territory are likely to turn into governors, if the state is absent, enlists them as "local strongmen" or if they are close to taking over the state. Warlords and criminal groups are profit-oriented. They engage in governance for instrumental reasons. Some order is necessary for them to collect their rents and conduct their illicit business. Exclusively relying on coercion is very costly. The use of excessive violence may increase domestic or international pressure on states to focus their limited capacities on prosecuting predatory warlords or brutal drug cartels. For example, when La Familia Michoacana, a major Mexican criminal organization, engaged in major atrocities, including the torture and murder of 12 Mexican federal policy officers, the Mexican government made it a top priority to bring La Familia down (Felbab-Brown, Trinkunas, and Hamid 2017, 114).

Moreover, delivering certain goods and services to local communities reduces the costs of territorial and social control by generating voluntary compliance through output legitimacy. Local strongmen, militias, drug cartels, or street gangs, therefore, do not only regulate violence and settle disputes. They also provide and protect job opportunities in the illegal economy (e.g. poppy or coca production) and distribute money for road pavement, schools, hospitals, churches, or sports facilities (Felbab-Brown, Trinkunas, and Hamid 2017, ch. 2, 6). However, because their primary goal is profit-making that relies on the use of violence, it remains questionable to what extent they transform from stationary bandits to governors. Their governance contributions tend to be selective, not sustainable, and come with severe "public bads" that are constitutive for rather than being negative consequences of their profit-seeking activities (see Chapter 5).

In contrast, identity-based groups have been found to be effective welfare governors among VNSAs (Arjona, Kasfir, and Mampilly 2015b; Bayat 2002; Berman 2009; Berti 2018; Ismail 2001; Kalyvas 2015; Walsh 2003). Ideology and religion provide not only an intrinsic motivation for rebel groups and religious militants to engage in governance; they are also an important source of input legitimacy. Seeking to establish a new or different order, the FARC in Colombia, the Maoist Naxalites in India, the Taliban in Afghanistan, or the IS/Daesh in Iraq and Syria distinguish themselves from other actors with whom they compete for control over territory. As they seek to step in for the state, take it over, or establish a new order, their governance contributions tend to center on providing law and order (see Chapters 5 and 6). Yet, particularly religious VNSA, such as Hamas in the Gaza Strip and Hezbollah in Lebanon, have set up and supported social institutions. This "Islamist social sector" (Roy 2011) plays a major role in welfare governance in ALS (cf. Grynkewich 2008).

The effectiveness of such welfare governance is often not too high, however. Moreover, VNSA governance contributions are often paid for by money raised through criminal activities involving kidnapping, drug trading, and human trafficking. Finally, when social service delivery becomes the terrain of political contestation and struggle over territorial control, violent non-state governors promote the fragmentation of welfare regimes, creating or exacerbating unequal access to public health, education, and other public goods (see below). Likewise, providing welfare along ideological or religious lines not only turns these services into club goods, it also undermines the building of generalized trust necessary to sustain the provision of truly public goods (see Chapter 3).

At the same time, in remote or marginalized areas, politically as well as religiously motivated VNSA may be the only governors willing and able to deliver social services in the first place. Moreover, their governance contributions are often still superior to "the chaotic efforts of a weak, feckless, and corrupt state" (Cammett 2014, 5, 13; Felbab-Brown, Trinkunas, and Hamid 2017, 9). FARC was the sole governance provider in areas where the state of Columbia had been largely absent. It used part of its income from drug trade for establishing clinics, vocational schools, and the organization of public works, e.g. road pavement.

It also blackmailed MNCs into investing in the delivery of basic social services. A survey of 1,500 people living in warzones found that around two-thirds used health services provided by FARC (Ratliff and Buscaglia 2001, 8–9). FARC also made coca farmers diversify their crops and grow food (Felbab-Brown 2012, 85).

The Islamic State/Daesh focused on setting and enforcing its version of Islamic Law. However, besides establishing an elaborate courts and police system, it created service offices in charge of distributing water, electricity, and food (Caris and Reynolds 2014). So have Hamas in Gaza and Hezbollah in Lebanon (Berti and Gutiérrez 2016; Cammett 2014; Roy 2011). The two Islamist organizations run or fund nurseries, kindergartens, primary and secondary schools, orphanages, youth and sports clubs, clinics, hospitals, and nursing homes. Besides "bricks-and-mortar" welfare institutions (Cammett 2014, 87), they provide food and financial assistance for medical services or school fees. In 2001, 25 percent of Palestinians in the West Bank and 87 percent in the Gaza Strip received food and cash assistance from Islamist social institutions. The majority has some association with Hamas, but not all of them are controlled by it. While Hamas spends the vast majority of its funds on welfare governance, Islamist charity and social organizations have multiple funding sources (Roy 2011, 138–141). Yet, particularly since Hamas seized control of Gaza in 2007, it has been able to reap the political benefits of Islamist welfare governance, not least because other Islamist social institutions no longer attempted to dissociate themselves politically from Hamas (Roy 2011, 6, 272). In Lebanon, religious organizations and charities – together with NGOs and for-profit institutions – account for 90 percent of the delivery of health care services and 60 percent of health care spending. While the state finances much of health and educational services, non-state actors are the main providers taking credit (Cammett 2014, 52–57).

EXTERNAL FUNDING AND FLEXIBLE INSTITUTIONS

Delivering social services beyond short-term food and financial assistance is a complex governance task that requires substantial institutional capacity. Islamist militants have received financial support from the Gulf region and Iran (Cammett 2014, 19; Roy 2011, 137–141). They also collect *zakat*, the charitable contributions Muslims are obliged to make, and other local and international donations. External financial support has become more restricted due to the efforts of the US, Europe, and Israel to counter the financing of terrorism by foreign charities and diaspora organizations contributing to Islamic social institutions (Gunning 2007). Despite external restrictions on their financing, however, Hamas and Hezbollah have maintained the capacity to deliver basic social services within the territories they control, particularly in comparison to other actors. In Lebanon, state institutions are weakened by the power-sharing arrangements among the different sectarian parties. In the Gaza Strip, the outbreak of the second intifada in 2000 turned the Islamic social sector into the second largest provider of food after the United Nations Relief and Works Agency for Palestine (UNRWA). Islamic medical institutions reached larger parts of the Palestinian population than the UNRWA, secular NGOs, and the Palestinian National Authority, which have suffered from funding shortages, have had only limited access to the population and were ridden by corruption, respectively (Roy 2011, 202–204).

Besides financial resources and territorial control, Roy attributes the quality of welfare provision by Islamic institutions in the Gaza Strip to their highly trained and professional staff, on the one hand, and their decentralized and localized institutions, which allow them to adapt to local conditions, on the other (Roy 2000; Roy 2011, 132–137, 140, 168). Likewise, Cammett emphasizes the "good management techniques" of Hezbollah (Cammett 2014, 19) and its targeted service delivery in Shi'a communities.

POPULAR ACCEPTANCE, LOCAL CULTURE, AND TRUST

Resource endowment and a flexible institutional infrastructure for service delivery are not sufficient for effective welfare provision. Identity-based VNSA have a tendency to restrict their services to their members. If membership is constitutive for access, non-members may be excluded. Moreover, Christians or Sunni Muslims may not want to attend a school or nursing home run by Hezbollah, particularly if welfare services are provided by their own group.

In her study on Hamas, Roy finds that "Islamic social service organizations typically had not (political) ideological criteria as condition for access (...), or for membership" (Roy 2011, 90). Hamas appears to open its kindergartens, schools, clinics, and hospitals to all Palestinians, regardless of political orientations. While enforcing Islamic rules, including the segregation of sexes and a conservative dress code for women, service delivery was "deeply embedded in local cultural norms that did not generally discriminate according to constituents' ideological vision or social class" (Roy 2011, 170). This local culture has also provided the basis for trust and solidarity beyond the in-group of Hamas supporters. Palestinians of all social classes, devout Muslims or not, have sent their children to kindergartens and schools associated with Hamas since they need their services or prefer "an Islamic curriculum and the moral teachings of Islam" (Roy 2011, 81). The impartiality of Islamist welfare institutions is also fostered by their working relationships with government authorities, particularly when their political parties pursue what Cammett refers to as a "state-centric" political strategy participating in government. For instance, Islamic schools adopt standard curricula approved by the Palestinian Ministry of Education. Hezbollah is less inclusive in its service delivery. While it does not deny access to Sunnis or Christians (Harb el-Kak 2000; Harik 2005), half of its institutions are located in communities with more than 90 percent Shi'a (Cammett 2014, 105). Families of Hezbollah fighters killed or injured receive most comprehensive access, followed by activists and core supporters. The Sunni Future Movement, in contrast, also serves more heterogeneous communities, including some heavily Christian areas (ibid., ch. 4 and 6).

Trust-based local institutions enhancing the collective action capacity of citizens also induce rebel groups to regulate the local economy. As Kubota argues, in such cases, "(t)he rebels may benefit from regulating an economy that returns both tax revenue and legitimacy" Kubota 2019, 7). In this case, VNSA behave similarly to (mining) companies faced with the resistance and demands of local communities (see above). Both actors provide governance in exchange for access to resources, on the one hand, and social acceptance, on the other.

Yet, the Achilles heel of Islamist groups and other VNSA in providing public services is that their legitimacy is almost entirely output-based. Except for their small in-group of supporters, they often lack other sources of legitimacy – let alone input-legitimacy – and, thus, have to provide effective governance in order to keep the virtuous circle between effectiveness and legitimacy running. If, for some reason, they are unable to deliver services, their support base is likely to dwindle, unless they invest in at least some degree of participatory governance (Arjona, Kasfir, and Mampilly 2015b). This is rather different with regard to "traditional" authorities such as tribal leaders.

"Traditional" Authorities as Development Brokers

Chiefs, elders, or "traditional" communities rarely have the resources to engage in comprehensive welfare governance. Yet, they often play an important role as development brokers in the implementation of social programs and development projects (on brokerage in general see Hönke and Müller 2018). In Sub-Sahara Africa, state-sponsored projects typically require some matching of resources by the recipient community since the state lacks the capacity to finance and administer welfare projects and programs at the local level. Local state actors are too weak to mobilize support on the ground, particularly in rural and remote areas (Migdal 1988). It is often up to "traditional" chiefs to organize labor, material, or additional funding within their communities for the construction of school buildings, clinics, or the pavement of roads (Baldwin 2016; Barkan, McNulty, and Ayeni 1991; Botchway 2001; Miguel and Gugerty 2005; Njoh 2017; Swidler 2013). Baldwin's quantitative study on 19 Sub-Saharan countries corroborates findings of various country studies that the effectiveness of welfare governance substantially improves when "traditional" chiefs are involved in the production of local public pubic goods (schools, sanitation, roads; Baldwin 2016). She argues that these leaders are particularly effective in public goods provision when they have long time-horizons (Baldwin 2019; for similar findings with regard to Oaxaca, Mexico, see Magaloni, Díaz-Cayeros, and Ruiz Euler 2019). Tsai finds similar forms of "co-production" (Baldwin 2016, 71) of welfare governance in China where local communities invoke tradition to mobilize citizen contributions to the construction of public roads or drainage channels (Tsai 2007). A study of Xinjiang, China, confirms these results with regard to the public service provision by (Islamic) religious institutions thereby reducing interethnic violence (Cao et al. 2018). So does Schäferhoff's study on public health provision in Somaliland (Schäferhoff 2014a, 2014b). Chiefs and elders served as development brokers for MSPs, such as the Global Fund, to provide effective governance with regard to malaria prevention and HIV/AIDS-related programs (see also Richards 2014).

Where local collective action fails, governance effectiveness is low. Acemoglu et al. find that powerful chiefs in Sierra Leone are associated with higher citizen participation in local development activities (Acemoglu, Reed, and Robinson 2014). They claim, however, that local collective action is ultimately used by "traditional" leaders for rent-seeking (see also Ntsebeza 2005). Baldwin contends that chiefs may benefit from local development projects they facilitate, as multinational companies do when they engage in governance. More often than not, however, constructing and improving local infrastructure (schools, roads, sanitation) still benefits community members. She supports her argument by showing that a gap in leadership, typically due to the death of the chief, diminishes the provision of key local public goods, such as the building of new schools and the filling of potholes in Zambia (Baldwin 2016, 107–120). Other studies on governance by indigenous communities yield more ambivalent results. The exercise of land rights, for instance, has been found to create and exacerbate conflict within indigenous communities (Connell and Howitt 1991; Kruse, Kleinfeld, and Travis 1982; Sawyer and Gomez 2008).

Finally, the collective action chiefs mobilize helps ensure the quality of local public goods provision. Organizing local protest against ineffective service delivery casts a "shadow of the community" that may not only induce state and other actors to engage in welfare governance (Hönke and Thauer 2014; cf. Chapter 4). It can also make them address problems of quality (Baldwin 2016, 106).

LIMITED STATEHOOD, SOCIAL TRUST, AND PERCEIVED EFFECTIVENESS

When and why do "traditional" authorities provide effective welfare governance in ALS? In the absence of the state, citizen engagement in welfare governance is voluntary. State actors are too weak to enforce governance contributions by citizens. They lack the capacity to raise necessary funding, e.g. by collecting mandatory taxes. Nor are they able to use available tax revenue and foreign aid to provide welfare services at the local level. The state leaves a "very limited bureaucratic footprint" (Baldwin 2016, 103), particularly in rural and remote areas.

"Traditional" authorities are local institutions in many ALS (see Chapters 4, 5, and 6). They have not much enforcement power, either. To overcome the ensuing collective action dilemma in the provision of local public goods, chiefs and clan elders rely on non-hierarchical modes of governance (see Chapter 4). They "operate as reservoirs of pooled collective obligations" (Swidler 2013, 326–327). Appealing to the moral obligation toward local "solidarity groups," based on common ethnicity, shared patrilineal descent, or worship of village guardian deities, "bestowing status and honor on those" who contribute, and invoking social sanctions for betraying social trust, play a key role (Baldwin 2016, 161; cf. Miguel and Gugerty 2005).

Chiefs and clan elders rely on their hereditary right to rule bestowed on them by a community that shares an identity rooted in ethnicity, family, or religion. "Traditional" leaders cultivate traditional norms and values organizing and presiding over ceremonies and rituals connecting the community to their ancestors (Williams 2010; Baldwin 2016, 105). This enables them to use social trust to overcome collective action dilemmas. Moreover, they enjoy high social acceptance as governors thereby also enhancing the empirical legitimacy of the service provision they help provide with other actors (central government, NGOs, IOs; see Baldwin 2019; Magaloni, Díaz-Cayeros, and Ruiz Euler 2019). Drawing on Africabarometer survey data, Baldwin finds that citizens in 19 Sub-Saharan countries perceive powerful chiefs and headmen to be crucial for the effective provision of local welfare projects and programs (Baldwin 2016; see also Williams 2010, ch. 6 on South Africa). A USAID sponsored survey shows similar results for Somaliland (Robertson, Malla, and Oing 2017b, 32).

Social embeddedness increases the legitimacy of "traditional" leaders in providing local services. The research of Diaz-Cayeros and colleagues on traditional governance in one of Mexico's prominent ALS, Oaxaca, shows that communities adopting *usos y construmbres* (see Chapter 4) yield higher levels of citizen participation and higher provision of electricity, education, and sewage than communities with elected municipal leaders (Díaz-Cayeros, Magaloni, and Ruiz Euler 2014; Magaloni, Díaz-Cayeros, and Ruiz Euler 2019). A similar study on 500 villages in Afghanistan finds that "traditional" leaders are more effective in distributing food aid than elected village councils if the latter are institutionally weak (Beath, Christia, and Enikolopov 2013a). Social embeddedness, finally, is not only a source of legitimacy. It also affects governance effectiveness by preventing "traditional" authorities from abusing their role for private gain. Local collective action, based on generalized trust, can also turn against "predatory rulers" and "local despots" (Mamdani 1996; Ntsebeza 2005; LiPuma and Koelble 2009), restraining their traditional authority in the absence of democratic accountability and effective rule of law (Börzel and Risse 2016; Hönke and Börzel 2014).

In sum, local non-state actors, such as rebel groups and Islamist militants, but also "traditional" authorities, are often major providers of collective goods and services in ALS. VNSA are janus-faced in this regard, since they are major causes for limited statehood in the first place through their efforts to overthrow the existing order by the use of force. At the same time, their quest for legitimacy often turns them into the main welfare governors in ALS. In contrast, "traditional" authorities, such as chiefs and elders, can mostly rely on other sources of – knowledge- as well as ethnicity-/kinship-based – legitimacy embedded in relationships of trust. Due to their limited capacity, they tend to be co-providers of governance mobilizing the collective action at the local level to implement social projects and programs in cooperation with other governors. At the same time, their governance contributions are likely to be more sustainable than those of VNSA, precisely because output legitimacy is not their only source of diffuse support.

These actors tend to have in common that access to their governance contributions is often identity-based, i.e., restricted to the members of the ideological, religious, or ethnic group they represent. As a result, the governance challenge is to move from the provision of club goods to inclusive public goods and services. This depends largely on local norms of impartiality and equality as well as the collective action capacity of the citizens in the respective areas of limited statehood.

Conclusions: The Role of Motivations for Sustainable Welfare Governance

This chapter has given an overview of welfare governance with regard to health, education, food security, environmental protection, and other public services in ALS. We showed that there is a general improvement on average across a wide range of governance services and including many countries of the Global South over the past decades. It is more than likely that governors other than the state have contributed to effective welfare governance in ALS. The chapter has covered a wide variety of such actors – from IOs and foreign donors to (multinational) companies, MSPs, (I)NGOs, VNSA, and "traditional" authorities. While we cannot present a quantitative scorecard, it is fair to conclude that effective welfare governance is possible in ALS even if the state is weak. However, this depends on two crucial conditions: the absence of large-scale violence and the provision of some minimum infrastructure (such as roads). In warzones, only most basic governance services (such as child immunization or the distribution of anti-malaria bednets, see Schäferhoff 2014a) can be effectively provided. In other words, most welfare governance does seem to require some residual statehood. We come back to this topic in the concluding Chapter 8.

If these two conditions – absence of large-scale violence and minimum infrastructure – are met, most governors covered in this chapter are able to provide effective services. This even includes business and VNSA that are primarily self-interested or profit-oriented. However, and in contrast to the other governors covered in this chapter, their governance contributions are hard to sustain effectively over long periods of time. Business as governor will step in as subsidiary service providers as long as nobody else is providing governance and its primary goals are not threatened. In other words, they might need social acceptance in order to govern, but they are not interested in legitimacy as the "right to rule" in the strict sense of the concept, since they only engage in governance if faced with powerful "shadows of hierarchy and of community" (see Chapter 3 and 4) or if nobody else does ("shadow of anarchy").[9] Besides, the institutional conditions for effective governance contributions of business are quite demanding. In general, it appears to be easier for companies to avoid negative externalities from their activities (e.g. environmental pollution) than to contribute positively to governance (e.g. in the area of HIV/AIDS prevention and care, see Börzel and Thauer 2013).

---

[9] We thank Eric Stollenwerk for pointing that out to us.

As to VNSA, we need to distinguish between politically or religiously motivated rebel groups, on the one hand, and criminal profit-seeking networks and organizations, on the other. The latter will only provide governance if it suits their (criminal) business interests (access to resources, support by local communities, etc.). The former have to have primarily legitimacy needs that lead them to provide effective welfare governance. However, the circle from effective governance to output legitimacy is likely to be disrupted by their opponents and rivals in governance, most prominently by state actors fighting them. It follows that rebel groups are only likely to sustain effective governance if they are close to victory, i.e., if they turn from governors to governments (Jo 2015).

With regard to the other governors covered in this chapter – IOs, foreign donors, MSPs, (I)NGOs, and "traditional" authorities – we can draw a somewhat more optimistic picture. While each of these actors also has self-interested goals, their primary motivation is to provide governance (see Chapter 4). Our analysis seems to indicate that their governance contributions are both effective and sustainable, under certain conditions. Recent studies that use geo-referencing and seek to overcome methodological nationalism demonstrate that foreign aid actually does improve local conditions – without weakening the state even further, but – on the contrary – contributing to increased state legitimacy. However, our survey of the literature shows that effective welfare governance by these actors depends on two crucial factors, namely:

- the institutional design of the governance arrangements that must be "fit for purpose" and adjusted to local conditions, including the necessary flexibility to change (even if this violates accountability rules, see Lall 2017);
- their "license to govern," i.e., empirical legitimacy bestowed by the citizens. In the case of "traditional" authorities, this license often results from relationships of (generalized) social trust.

If these two conditions are met, external as well as local non-state actors can indeed provide welfare governance services in areas of limited statehood in a sustainable fashion. This has important normative implications to which we come back in the concluding chapter.

8   Conclusions

This book provides ample evidence that areas of limited statehood are neither ungovernable nor ungoverned. This is, because governance, i.e., the setting of binding rules and the provision of collective goods and services, can be both effective and legitimate even if state institutions are too weak to implement and enforce decisions and/or to uphold a monopoly of the use of force.

The conclusions develop further some of the recurring themes of this book. The chapter consists of two parts. The first part provides a summary of our findings across the various actors, modes of governance, and issue-areas covered in this book. The second part is devoted to the implications of our arguments. We begin by discussing the ambivalent role of residual statehood in ALS as both enabler and spoiler of effective governance. Next, we analyze the complex relationship between the international system and ALS. On the one hand, as the "anarchy" metaphor indicates, there are important structural similarities between the international system and ALS. On the other hand, the international and the domestic/local in ALS are entangled in a complex system of multi-level governance. We conclude the book with discussing the policy implications of our findings. We advocate for Western democracies and IOs a paradigm shift from state-building to governance promotion.

Summary of the Findings

Our book set out to answer two interrelated research questions (see Chapter 1):

1. Why and when are actors – state and non-state, international, transnational, or domestic and local – motivated to provide governance in ALS, and how do they govern?
2. Under what conditions is "governance under anarchy" effective and legitimate?

Motivation and modes do not determine the success of governance in ALS. However, they do have an influence on conditions for effectiveness and legitimacy.

The Motivation to Govern

We find a multiplicity of governors in ALS (see particularly Chapter 4). These include international as well as regional (inter-governmental) organizations, foreign governments, aid and donor agencies, national, regional, and local governments, multi-stakeholder partnerships (MSPs), (I)NGOs and private foundations, (multinational) companies, warlords, religious and political rebel groups, as well as transnational criminal networks, "traditional" authorities including elders, tribal chiefs, religious leaders, and community-based organizations (CBOs). Many of these actors are not "natural" governors; some of them are part of the problem rather than part of the solution. Foreign governments often interfere in ALS to pursue their own economic and security interests, thereby rendering an already fragile situation even more dangerous (Lee 2018; see also Lake, D. 2018). UN peace-keepers have been found to violate human rights in the territory they control (Hirschmann 2017). (I)NGOs have been busy fighting among themselves for power and control in ALS rather than providing governance (Kristoff and Panarelli 2010). (Multinational) companies have violated basic human rights and destroyed the environment in many ALS (Hönke 2013b). Violent non-state actors (VNSA) – whether criminal or not – have turned ALS into warzones, rendering them ungovernable (Chojnacki and Branovic 2011). Many elders, tribal chiefs, and religious leaders have used ALS for rent-seeking and behaved in most repressive ways, particularly against women (Baldwin 2016).

At the same time, as we show in this book, even the most unlikely actors, such as Islamist VNSA, warlords, or mining companies, sometimes turn into governors. This raises the question what motivates actors to engage in the provision of rules and services, which requires substantial investment that cannot be directly passed on to the "consumers."

For a variety of state and non-state actors, governance is constitutive. This includes most donor agencies, IOs, (I)NGOs, MSPs, and private foundations. They may pursue their own egoistic self-interests rather than caring about the citizens in ALS and they often fail to govern effectively. Yet, they differ from other actors discussed in this book in that their very identity and purpose entail governance. Their official mandate obliges them to act in the public interest and makes them politically accountable and legally liable in case of failure (Scharpf 1991, 630).

Other actors discussed in this book are not institutionally motivated to govern and accept this role only reluctantly. (Multinational) companies want to make profit rather than provide collective goods. At best, their activities have positive externalities for citizens, such as jobs, income, and welfare benefits. Corporate social responsibility (CSR) seeks to change this by writing governance into the organizational purpose of companies. Rebel groups and other VNSA, if they are not just plunderers and racketeers, might seek to take over the state or parts of it in the future, which often includes governance. Elders, tribal chiefs, and religious leaders may exploit (natural) resources for their own benefits, but they also provide governance for their communities (Baldwin 2016). Likewise, local communities and CBOs might become complicit with VNSA in civil war (Kalyvas 2006). At the same time, they might develop some collective action capacity, engage in self-governance, or demand governance provision from other actors. (National as well as local) governments in ALS are also ambivalent governors: precisely because state institutions are either too weak to uphold and enforce the rule of law or the state is simply authoritarian, government actors often capture what remains of the state for rent-seeking purposes (Erdmann 2013; Erdmann and Engel 2007).

Our theoretical framework developed in Chapter 3 of this book explains why and when self-interested actors are motivated to govern. First, institutional conditions pertaining to statehood matter. Consolidated statehood in the Global North can cast an "external shadow of hierarchy" inducing otherwise self-interested actors, such as MNCs, to engage in governance. The US, the UK, and France have instituted laws obliging companies and their suppliers to comply with the social and environmental regulations of their home country when investing elsewhere, including in ALS. This also applies for state agencies as well as private donors and foundations, which are accountable to their home countries.

Interestingly enough, the opposite of the "shadow of hierarchy" induces primarily self-interested actors to engage in governance, too, namely the "shadow of anarchy." Foreign governments, (multinational) companies, but also rebel groups often cannot realize their own goals and self-interests when chaos and violence reign. Avoiding negative externalities spilling over from ALS (violent crimes, terrorism, but also refugee flows) often serves as a major motivation for foreign powers to intervene militarily, with or without a UN mandate. In some cases, weak states themselves invite external actors to take over crucial governance functions through Governance Delegation Agreements (Matanock 2014), including the acceptance of Chapter 6 UN peace-keeping operations.

Second, the quest for (international as well as domestic) legitimacy constitutes another major driver for actors to become governors. This applies to aid agencies, IOs, (I)NGOs, and MSPs, which have to legitimize their public mandates by demonstrating their engagement for the common good in their home countries, if only to generate public and private funding. But legitimacy concerns also serve as a major motivation for VNSA, such as rebel groups and religious fighters, to engage in governance (Cammett 2014; Jo 2015). VNSA as well as elders, tribal chiefs, and religious leaders are often faced with the "shadow of the (local) community" when citizens demand governance contributions from them, if the state is too weak or is to be overthrown (in the case of VNSA). This is particularly the case when local communities and CBOs develop collective action capacities. Similar dynamics are at work for MNCs when they are "sandwiched" between global norms as well as transnational mobilization through (I)NGO campaigns, on the one hand, and demands by local communities to provide collective goods, on the other hand. This dynamic conforms to the "spiral model" of human rights change, which has originally been proposed for repressive states (Risse, Ropp, and Sikkink 1999, 2013). Note, however, that companies rarely seek legitimacy as the "right to rule" in the strict sense. They are reluctant governors, seeking some degree of social acceptance at home and abroad, for their profit-making operations.

Third, social trust relations also foster motivations to govern. Personalized as well as group-based trust (see Chapter 3) generates the collective action capacity of local communities enabling them to both self-govern and to demand governance contributions from others. Moreover, social trust solves the enforcement problem by preventing cheating and free-riding in ALS.

In general, we find no direct correlation between motivations to govern and governance effectiveness. Of course, actors have to be willing to govern in order to be effective, but motivation does not equal success. Moreover, some governors are motivated to provide club goods rather than truly public goods and services, which mitigates their effectiveness and legitimacy as governors, as we will discuss below.

Modes of Governance

We find the entire spectrum of hierarchical as well as non-hierarchical modes of governance in areas of limited statehood (see Chapter 4). To begin with, hierarchical rule through command-and-control and the (threat of the) use of force is not confined to the (residual) state in ALS, which has all but lost its capacity to enforce decisions. External (military) interventions – whether invited (Chapter 6 UN Charter) or not (Chapter 7 UN Charter) – and international trusteeships or protectorates are one example (Lake, D. 2018).

Many non-state actors, such as VNSA and "traditional" authorities, also govern hierarchically. Once politically or religiously motivated rebel groups control some territory, they enjoy a monopoly of the use of force and have the capacity to enforce decisions, which they often use to govern (Berti 2018). Last but not least, elders, tribal chiefs, and religious leaders represent interesting cases of being able to rule hierarchically, not because they control means of violence, but because they enjoy such strong legitimacy backed up by social trust that they do not require strong enforcement capacities. Their rule is often enforced through social sanctioning systems, which can be as effective as physical punishment.

Other than that, non-hierarchical modes of governance prevail in most ALS. Various governors discuss and negotiate contractual relationships among themselves and with a multitude of stakeholders. GDA are only one example. IOs, donor agencies, MSPs, and (I)NGOs cooperate and coordinate activities among themselves as well as engaging with local communities. In most cases, they enter contracts with state actors, however weak they might be. We find few documented cases of deliberative governance in ALS. This might reflect a lack of research rather than the absence of modes of arguing and persuasion. In particular, CBOs, indigenous groups, and other "traditional" authorities appear to rely on deliberative negotiations (Baldwin and Holzinger 2019a; but see LiPuma and Koelble 2009). Moreover, a comparative study of non-state justice institutions (NSJI) around the world (see Chapter 4) shows that many of these institutions exhibit features conforming to the conditions that the literature has identified for deliberative negotiations (equal access; power asymmetries in the background; procedural fairness; transparency; orientation toward consensus-building, etc.). The more NSJI meet these criteria, the more effective they appear to be (see below).

The same holds true for participatory modes of governance, which are likely to generate input-legitimacy for the governors. Once the "ownership" principle of development cooperation is truly institutionalized rather than serving merely as a rhetorical device, both the effectiveness and legitimacy of governance increase. In this context, we find an interesting link between actor motivations and modes of governance: the more governors are motivated by a quest for legitimacy, the more they are likely to engage in non-hierarchical modes of coordination, including deliberative and participatory governance. As we will discuss below, this in turn has a positive impact on governance effectiveness in ALS.

Scope Conditions for Effective and Legitimate Governance

We now turn to the principal theme of the book, the exploration of the conditions of effective and legitimate governance in ALS. Our main message is that governance can be effective and legitimate even under the rather adverse conditions of limited statehood so that the "governance puzzle" identified in Chapter 1 can be solved. Most parts of the world will never be Denmark, but rules are set and complied with, and public goods as well as services can be delivered even if the state is weak or non-existing (see also Brixi, Lust, and Woolcock 2015). In every issue-area we investigated, we found examples of effective governance in ALS, in some cases even in failed states, such as Somalia. In other words, there is "evidence for hope," to quote Sikkink's book (Sikkink 2017).

At the same time, we do not indulge in Scott's "two cheers for anarchism" (Scott 2012). There are limitations for effective governance in ALS with regard to both issue-areas and types of actors:

- Security governance in terms of maintaining sustainable peace in ALS is unlikely to work without a monopoly of the use of force. The longer VNSA, such as rebel groups or warlords, are able to monopolize the use of force, the more they actually resemble a functioning state (Tilly 1995). Peace-keeping operations can substitute for a state monopoly of the use of force for a while, but they are only an interim solution. Some residual statehood appears to be necessary for security governance.
- Large-scale military interventions and comprehensive state-building operations are likely to fail, for two reasons (see also Lake, D. 2016). First, their intrusiveness into local governance requires substantial legitimacy bestowed by local elites and citizens, which is unlikely to be sustainable over a long period. Second, the financial and other resources necessary to sustain state-building exercises are enormous and open-ended. As a result, particularly democratic societies are unlikely to grant an unlimited "license to rule" for foreign lands. The EU's open-ended engagement in the Western Balkans only proves the point.
- With regard to particular governors, criminal organizations and warlords, who are not motivated politically or religiously, are unlikely to govern effectively and sustainably. Their primary purpose is rent- or

profit-seeking. They will only rule and provide collective goods to the extent that governance furthers these goals.

- The same holds true for (multinational) companies. They can indeed provide effective governance in some circumscribed area or with regard to particular services, but they are reluctant governors. Sooner or later, they are likely to refer to the state, particularly when governance goes beyond refraining from producing "public bads" or negative externalities.

These qualifications notwithstanding, "governance under anarchy" can be effective and sustainable, if the three scope conditions discussed in Chapter 3 are met: legitimacy of the governors and/or the governance arrangements; institutional design and residual statehood; and social trust. Each of these conditions has to be present to a minimum degree. Then, they can reinforce and also substitute for each other, at least partially.

LEGITIMACY

The number one condition for successful governance in areas of limited statehood is social acceptance by those being governed, bestowing a "right to rule" on the governors and governance institutions. As we have argued elsewhere, without legitimacy, there is no success (Krasner and Risse 2014b)! Our focus is on *empirical* legitimacy as the social acceptance of the governors and their governance arrangements by those being governed, that is, citizens and/or domestic and local elites (Chapter 3). Social acceptance is particularly relevant for security governance as well as the governance of human rights, the rule of law, and democracy (Chapters 5 and 6). As to the former, large-scale peace-keeping operations deeply intruding in the "Westphalian" sovereignty of states are particularly vulnerable to domestic legitimacy concerns. This explains why Chapter 6 operations, which require the consent of the host state, are usually more successful than Chapter 7 peace-keeping missions, which do not (Matanock 2014). While both have international legitimacy in terms of a UNSC mandate, the difference concerns their domestic legitimacy. Local empowerment and legitimacy is crucial for effective security governance by external peace-keepers (Campbell 2018). Domestic acceptance also explains why ROs are often more successful in the promotion of human rights, the rule of law, and democracy than IOs or foreign states, which are further away (Börzel and van Hüllen 2015a). The same holds true for MSPs and (I)NGOs with regard to welfare governance. As to VNSA, particularly politically or religiously motivated rebel groups – "stationary bandits" (Olson 1993) – do not only engage in governance because they seek international and domestic legitimacy. Their governance effectiveness with regard to all three issue-areas discussed here also increases, the more local communities bestow unto them the "right to govern." As a result, they are getting closer to achieving their goal of controlling the territory they hold or even the state. Last but not least, "traditional" authorities are particularly effective governors, precisely because they often enjoy legitimacy (Baldwin 2016, 2019). Elders, tribal chiefs, and religious leaders can also increase their effectiveness through participatory as well as deliberative modes of governance, which in turn generate input legitimacy (Chapter 6 on NSJI). In general, non-hierarchical modes of governance require less legitimacy than hierarchical modes as a result of which they are often also more effective.

In turn, lack of legitimacy explains governance failures to a large degree – from large-scale military and external state-building interventions to the very limited effectiveness of criminal networks (if they engage in governance rather than plunder). Lack of legitimacy also accounts for the difficulties that (multinational) companies have in providing effective governance. Local communities rarely bestow the "right to govern" on them, because they are considered as self-interested in profit-making. Moreover, local demands for corporate governance placed on them are often so high that companies are reluctant to engage in providing the required goods and services, which in turn decreases their legitimacy (on virtuous and vicious circles see below).

INSTITUTIONAL DESIGN AND RESIDUAL STATEHOOD

Our second scope condition for successful governance refers to institutional features of the governance arrangements. To begin with, they must be "fit for purpose" in terms of necessary resources, rules and decision-making procedures (design), as well as in-built learning capacity and flexibility to respond to changes in local conditions. As the institutionalist literature in International Relations (IR) has argued, institutions must be functionally adequate with regard to the cooperation problem at hand (see e.g. Koremenos, Lipson, and Snidal 2001; Martin 1992a; Zürn 1992). Global collaboration problems of the prisoners' dilemma variety (nuclear arms control, trade) require different solutions as compared to coordination problems (air traffic control). The same holds true for "governance under anarchy" in ALS (Beisheim and Liese 2014b). Moreover, institutions must be designed to deal with the task complexity at hand (Krasner and Risse 2014b). Child immunization or the distribution of anti-malaria bednets require a limited number of interventions and coordination among rather few actors. In contrast, combatting and preventing HIV/AIDS is a much more complex task, since it needs repeated interventions (and treatments) as well as the coordination among a multitude of different actors.

Since most governance problems require collaboration rather than coordination and deal with complex rather than simple tasks, the legalization literature can be used to deduce institutional requirements for effective governance in ALS (Abbott et al. 2000; Goldstein et al. 2000; for an application to ALS see Liese and Beisheim 2011). This literature suggests that governance structures are more likely to be more effective, the more the decision-making rules are precisely defined and the terms of obligation are well specified, and the more there are sufficient monitoring capacities and dispute settlement systems (preferably by independent authorities).

While this may sound rather trivial, it is remarkable how often we witness governance failures in ALS because adequate institutions are wanting. MSPs frequently fail, because the coordination among different types of actors proves extremely difficult (Beisheim and Liese 2014a). Lack of (financial) resources is another reason why comprehensive state-building interventions have been mostly unsuccessful. In contrast, more limited and circumscribed external interventions with regard to security, human rights, or the rule of law are often effective, because they command sufficient resources. Rebel governance often fails, because VNSA lack the institutional means and capacity to deliver public goods, such as security.

We also find that inclusive, participatory, deliberative, fair, and transparent institutions are likely to be rather effective in ALS, even if they prolong decision-making times. There might be a trade-off between efficiency and inclusiveness/deliberativeness, but we see little evidence that participatory and transparent institutions in ALS lack effectiveness. The reason is simple: since the enforcement capacities of the governors "under anarchy" are rather limited by definition, local "ownership" or "buy-in" is needed for effectiveness, both with regard to rule compliance and concerning service delivery. As theorized in Chapter 3, the causal mechanism runs from inclusive and fair institutional design via increased input and throughput legitimacy to effectiveness. A case in point in this regard are NSJI (see Chapter 6): the more NSJI design features resemble the criteria for deliberative institutions, the more effective they are in providing access to justice for underprivileged groups in ALS, e.g. women in rural areas (see e.g. Berger 2017; Lake, M. 2018). Less deliberative NSJI simply reproduce the local power structures, including clientelistic networks.

Last but not least, residual statehood matters in ALS. Yet, its effect is ambivalent. On the one hand, a state monopoly of the use of force in ALS serves as an enabling condition for effective governance by a variety of other actors in the realms of human rights, rule of law, education, health, basic subsistence, environmental protection, and the like. The same holds true for the provision of basic infrastructures, such as roads or electricity. On the other hand, weak state actors often use their (limited) capacities to spoil governance efforts by other actors, often citing "sovereignty" concerns, as the examples of the DRC, but also South Africa, illustrate (Börzel and Thauer 2013; Hönke and Börzel 2014; Lake, M. 2018). We come back to this point below.

SOCIAL TRUST

The third scope condition for effective governance in ALS is social trust. While there is ample evidence that personalized as well as particularistic or group-based trust relations promote effective and legitimate governance in ALS (see also Karim 2000), we find less indications for the presence of generalized trust in "imagined communities" (Anderson 1991) beyond personal knowledge or some group identifiers (see Chapter 3 for these distinctions, also Draude, Hölck, and Stolle 2018).

Social trust affects governance in ALS in various ways, both directly and more indirectly. First, as theorized by Ostrom and others (Ostrom 1990, 2000; Ostrom, Gardner, and Walker 1994), social trust enables effective self-governance directly by strengthening the action capacities of local communities. Personalized trust helps communities to overcome collective action problems in the absence of an enforcer and to solve problems such as the "tragedy of the commons" (Hardin 1968). Trust serves as a functional equivalent for the role of (consolidated) statehood in enforcing the law through some sanctioning capacity. The same holds true for group-based trust in comparatively homogenous ALS, Somaliland being a case in point. Trust enables self-governance directly (see e.g. Stephenson Jr. 2012; see also Krause 2018 for central Nigeria and eastern Indonesia; Kaplan 2017 for Colombia and elsewhere).

Second, social trust relations not only enable (local) communities and CBOs to engage in effective self-governance; the ensuing collective action capacity also allows them to mobilize and to demand effective governance from others, including rebel groups, companies, elders, tribal chiefs, and religious leaders. Here, social trust interacts with the other explanatory factors discussed in this book. For instance, social trust in communities bestows legitimacy to local leaders and "traditional" authorities, the more they are embedded in these communities. The collective action capacity of communities not only results in demands for effective governance, but also enhances legitimacy, e.g. through input legitimacy in inclusive and participatory institutions leading to a virtuous circle between inclusive, fair, and transparent institutional design, social trust, and (input- as well as throughput-legitimacy). We discuss these virtuous and vicious circles further below.

Motivations, Modes of Governance, and Effectiveness

As argued above, actor motivations to provide governance in ALS and their effectiveness have to be kept separate. IOs, (I)NGOs, MSPs, and foreign aid agencies might all be motivated to providing public goods and services, but they can fail miserably if they ignore institutional design and the need to coordinate activities or if they do not gain domestic acceptance and the "right to govern."

At the same time, we do find a nexus between motivations and effective governance in some cases, as indicated above. We refer here to actors who are primarily self-interested (or for whom we can assume that they are) – from external as well as domestic (national and local) state actors to (multinational) companies, VNSA, and tribal chiefs. Here, the primary distinction is whether actors' dominant goals are seeking power to control and govern a territory, a policy area, or a group of people or whether they are mainly interested in achieving other goals, such as profit-making or rent-seeking. The latter are usually "reluctant" governors who provide services or establish rules, because nobody else does it ("shadow of anarchy") or because they are forced to do so by somebody else ("shadows of external hierarchy and of [local] communities"). They are likely to refrain from governance, as soon as these external incentives and their cost-benefit calculations change. In other words, "reluctant governors" are unlikely to provide public goods and services or engage in rule-making and -implementation in a sustainable way. This explains, for example, why (multinational) companies are often rather ineffective governors and why they are more likely to be effective in the framework of strongly institutionalized MSPs (Chapter 7). It also explains why profit-seeking warlords and (transnational) criminal networks are rarely effective governors.

We do not mean to argue that other actors – state as well as non-state, domestic/local as well as international – are more effective by definition. They might still engage in power struggles over policies and institutions thereby enhancing political instability.[1] However, actors motivated by political power considerations are more likely to engage in sustainable and effective governance under the conditions specified in our

---

[1] Lake, following Riker 1980, refers to cycling in this context as a major governance problem in ALS, see Lake, D. 2018, 296–300.

framework. Since they want to rule, the right set of conditions can incentivize them to do so in a sustainable and effective manner.

Regarding the modes of governance and effectiveness, some are directly related to effectiveness, as our example of NSJI (see Chapter 6) demonstrates. In this particular case, the more the modes of governance of NSJI resemble the criteria specified for deliberative institutions, the more effective NSJI are in maintaining the rule of law, including fair trial and access to justice for under-privileged people in areas of severely limited statehood (Berger 2017; Lake, M. 2018).

In general, non-hierarchical modes of governance appear to be more effective than hierarchical ones in ALS, particularly because of the link between legitimacy and effectiveness. As external interveners have learned the hard way – from Bosnia-Herzegovina to Iraq and Afghanistan (Lake, D. 2016) – hierarchical and intrusive governance from the outside that includes establishing a monopoly of the use of force is hard to accomplish even if the interveners are primarily motivated to maintain peace and stability. The main reason for this, we argue, concerns the legitimacy requirements for effective hierarchical governance. Effectiveness can be enhanced through output legitimacy, as we have argued with regard to Afghanistan (Chapter 5; Stollenwerk 2018b). Yet, this condition is rather fragile and unlikely to be sustainable, also because the legitimacy requirements for external interveners at home and abroad are likely to clash: maintaining the peace under civil war conditions requires extensive military, political, and financial resources, which constituencies at home are rather reluctant to grant over extended periods of time.

In contrast, hierarchical rule by local leaders and "traditional" authorities appears to be more effective (Baldwin 2016, 2019), precisely because they are often bestowed with the "right to rule" by their communities. Here, legitimacy and social trust relations reinforce each other (see below). In this case, trust-based legitimacy enables elders, tribal chiefs, and religious leaders to govern hierarchically in an effective manner even though they do not usually command police and military forces to sanction wrong-doing. To put it differently: they can control the use of force through social means rather than military capabilities.

These might be exceptions to the rule, precisely because hierarchical governance by "traditional" authorities is often rather repressive, particularly against women. We submit, therefore, that non-hierarchical modes are generally more effective than hierarchical ones, because they are more likely to encourage self-governance, inclusion, fairness, and transparency. In other words, if their institutional design is adequate and

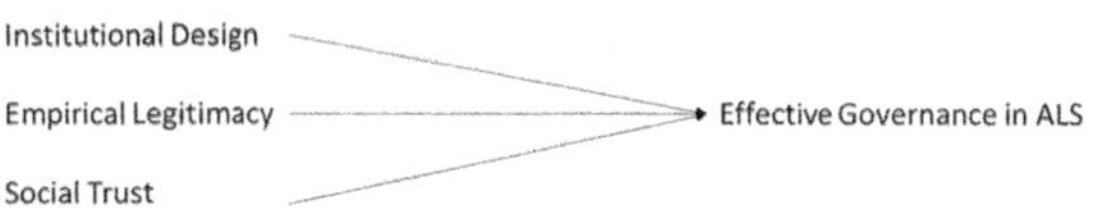

Figure 8.1 Complementary causal relations

functional to the tasks at hand, non-hierarchical modes of governance induce input as well as throughput legitimacy, which – as we argue throughout the book – is itself conducive to effectiveness (Beisheim and Liese 2014a). In other words, the institutional design of non-hierarchical modes of governance is key!

These considerations bring us to the issue of how our explanatory factors hang together, what explains legitimate governance, and which feedback loops our theoretical framework identifies.

Configurations of Effective Governance, Sources of Legitimacy, and Feedback Loops

CONFIGURATIONS OF EFFECTIVE GOVERNANCE

Throughout the book, we have used three sets of explanatory factors to account for the motivations of actors to become governors in ALS and for governance effectiveness: institutions, legitimacy, and social trust. While one could develop testable propositions to evaluate the causal power of these factors, we refrained from such an approach, for two reasons. First, propositions, such as "All else being equal, the more empirical legitimacy (social acceptance) the governors enjoy, the more effective they are" would have been rather trivial. Second, our approach is one of configurational causation, that is, we assume that various factors in combination produce the outcome of interest. It is very unlikely that any of our explanatory factors as such produces effective governance. For instance, in the case of external peace-keeping, (inclusive and well-funded) institutions combined with empirical legitimacy of the peace-keepers lead to effective governance, which is further enhanced if local communities are bound together by social trust relations fostering their collective action capacity (Chapter 5). The same holds true for successful MSPs in the realm of health governance (Chapter 7) or effective rebel governance with regard to human rights and the rule of law (Chapter 6). In these cases, the three causal factors complement each other in the sense that each contributes to the outcome of effective governance. If one of the factors is absent, efforts at governance are less likely to succeed (see Figure 8.1).

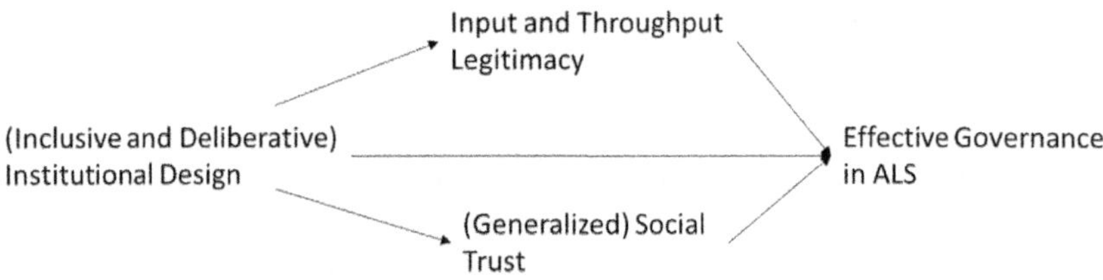

Figure 8.2 Effects of institutional design

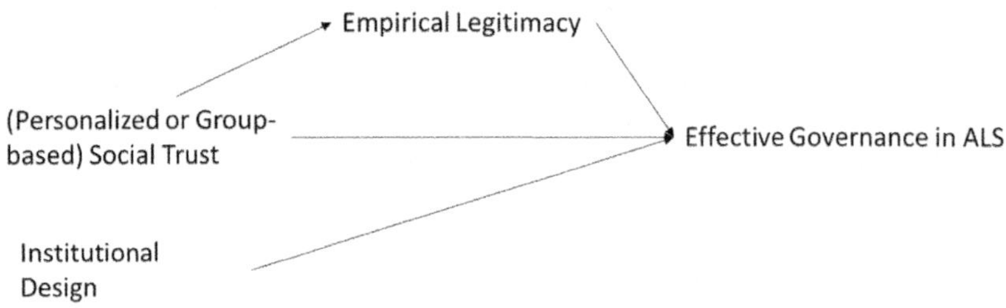

Figure 8.3 Social trust and its effects

The three factors also influence each other. In the case of NSJI (Chapter 6), the deliberative institutional design of the non-state courts not only affects rule of law governance directly, but is also likely to generate input and throughput legitimacy, which then leads to greater effectiveness (see Figure 8.2). Inclusive and fair institutions also are likely to lead to generalized social trust, which further enhances governance effectiveness (see also Figure 3.3, Chapter 3).

In the case of local communities, personalized or group-based social trust not only enhances their collective action capacity leading to effective self-governance. Trust also influences the legitimacy of local leaders and "traditional" authorities, which enables them to govern hierarchically and effectively (see Figure 8.3).

Last but not least, we also have configurations in which the demand for governance is affected by one set of factors, while other factors lead to the supply of (effective) governance (see Figures 8.4 and 8.5). In the case of MNCs, for example, an "external shadow of hierarchy" in combination with local mobilization and protest enabled by social trust among communities often leads to the demand for governance. Institutional design (e.g. risk-management structures and incorporation of supply chains) as well as social acceptance then bring about the supply of effective

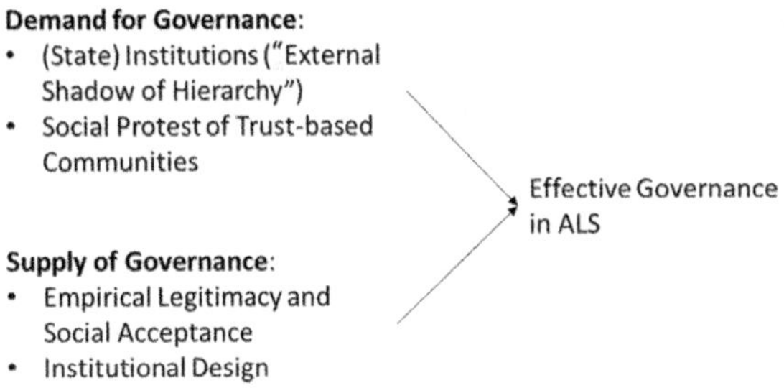

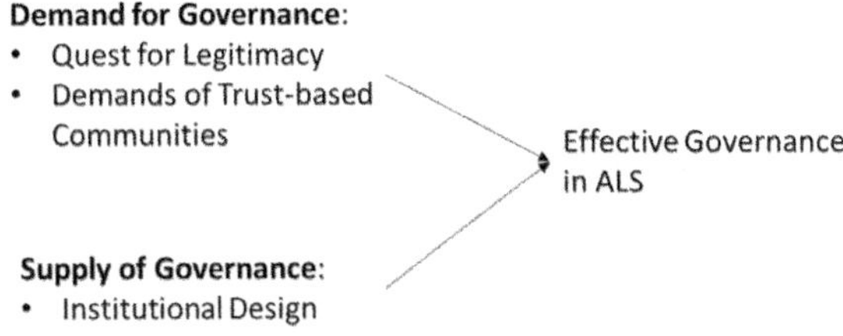

Figure 8.4 Demand and supply of governance: the case of MNCs

Figure 8.5 Demand and supply of governance: the case of rebel groups

governance. With regard to rebel governance, the quest for (international and domestic) legitimacy as well as the collective action capacity of local communities based on social trust influence the demand side, while institutional conditions (e.g. discipline, but also participatory institutions) are crucial on the supply side.

SOURCES OF LEGITIMACY AND THE VIRTUOUS CIRCLE BETWEEN LEGITIMACY AND EFFECTIVENESS

We argued throughout the book that empirical legitimacy, i.e., the social acceptance of the governors and the governance institutions by the governed bestowing upon them the "right to rule" is among the most crucial factors. As discussed in Chapter 3 and above, legitimate governance in areas of limited statehood has many sources (see Table 8.1). First, institutional design matters for social acceptance by generating input and throughput legitimacy (see Figure 8.2). Deliberative governance by NSJI, participatory governance by rebel groups, as well as the effective implementation of the "ownership" principle by external governors, such as IOs, MSPs, and INGOs, are cases in point. The failure to

Table 8.1 *Sources of legitimate governance in ALS*

Sources of Legitimacy	Examples for Indicators
Input: participatory governance	Satisfaction with election procedures
Throughput: procedural justice/ fairness/transparency	Perception of fair trials or transparent institutions
Output: effective governance	Satisfaction with service delivery
Social trust	Personal ties in local communities
"Traditional," religious, or knowledge-based authority	High esteem for elders, tribal chiefs, religious leaders, or leaders with particular claims to knowledge
Charismatic leadership	High esteem for leaders with particular charismatic characteristics
Ethnic belonging	Strong sense of ethnicized identity
Legal recognition	Recognition by international law

Source: Risse and Stollenwerk 2018a, 410

include local communities as well as CBOs in governance arrangements is likely to result in governance failures, even though this can be partially compensated by output legitimacy (see Campbell 2018 for peace-keeping; see below).

Second, as argued above (Figure 8.3), social trust also feeds into legitimate governance, particularly with regard to elders, tribal chiefs, and religious leaders as well as CBOs, who are deeply embedded in their communities. This can be both personalized trust through social integration in local communities, but also group-based trust through ethnic belongings and identities. Furthermore, the "right to rule" by local, religious, and "traditional" leaders often results from their claims to moral or knowledge-based authority as well as charisma. Here, Weber's sources of legitimacy (Weber 1978 [1922]) are visible in ALS.

Third, in contrast, we find that the international legal recognition of governors – such as IOs and their legal mandates, peace-keeping missions and their authorization by the UN Security Council – matters less in generating social acceptance in ALS (see particularly Chapter 5). External governors might be legitimated by international law to provide governance (Ladwig and Rudolf 2011; Rudolf 2007), but this international legitimacy matters less on the ground – unless it is in line or congruent with domestic or local standards of appropriateness (Börzel and van Hüllen 2014). This is the main reason why Chapter 6 peace-keeping missions as well as other GDA (Matanock 2014) are usually more successful than externally imposed trusteeships or protectorates (Lake and Farris 2014; Lake, D. 2016).

Even more important in the case of external governors, the legitimacy bestowed on them by their home countries through law and lines of political accountability (e.g. through parliaments) does not travel and affect their performance in ALS. Peace-keepers, IOs, MSPs, foreign aid agencies, and even MNCs might be ultimately accountable to and legitimated by the governments of their home or member states (in the case of IOs and MSPs). Yet, this does not matter much in ALS, where their effectiveness as governors depends crucially on local support (for peace-keepers see Campbell 2018). In fact, there are many cases where external governance in ALS is hampered by the need to seek the support of public opinion and legislators in the home countries, e.g. when it comes to the necessary material or financial resources, which are often wanting. International as well as home country legitimacy not only fails to contribute to local legitimacy in ALS; it might negatively affect the institutional design of the governance arrangement, thereby hampering effectiveness further.

Fourth, one particular source of legitimate governance in ALS is governance effectiveness itself, thereby generating output legitimacy (for the original argument see Scharpf 1999). Since legitimacy is also one of the most important sources of effective governance, this creates a virtuous (or, in case of negative feedback loops, a vicious) circle between legitimate and effective governance.

The virtuous circle argument has been originally developed with consolidated statehood in mind (Levi 1998; Levi and Sacks 2009; Levi 2018). Schmelzle and Stollenwerk have adapted the concept to the conditions of limited statehood (Schmelzle and Stollenwerk 2018b; see Figure 8.6), and several authors have put it to empirical tests (in Schmelzle and Stollenwerk 2018a). Since we have already discussed the loop from legitimacy to effectiveness (b → c → a in Figure 8.6), let us briefly explain the loop from effectiveness to legitimacy.

Most important for the virtuous circle to work is not so much the "objective" governance performance, but the (inter-) subjective beliefs by those being governed that they are indeed receiving the particular goods and services. As we have suggested in Chapter 3, "objective" and "subjective" indicators for governance performance can vastly diverge, particularly under conditions of limited statehood. For instance, it is remarkable how secure people often feel even in warzones with many instances of violence, particularly when they have experienced civil war for a long time (Stollenwerk 2018b, 2018c).

Schmelzle and Stollenwerk argue that four additional conditions are significant for the feedback loop from effectiveness to legitimacy to work

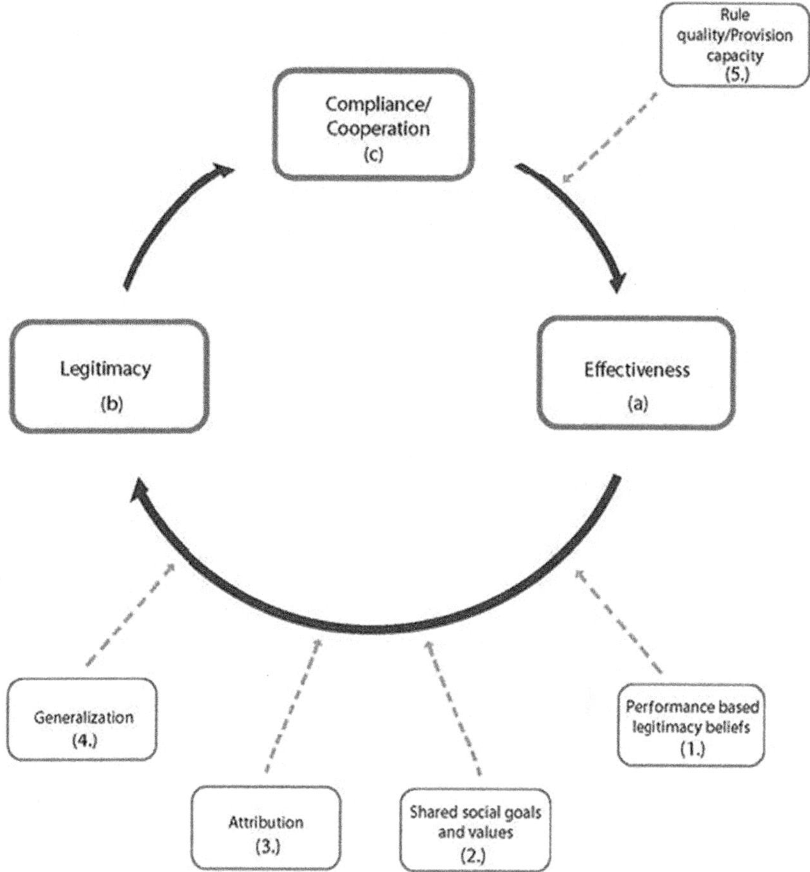

Figure 8.6 The virtuous circle between legitimacy and effectiveness
Source: Schmelzle and Stollenwerk 2018a, 459.

(Schmelzle and Stollenwerk 2018b, 459–460; see also McLoughlin 2015 on the non-linearity of the relationship):

- People have to incorporate successful governance in their legitimacy beliefs (condition 1 in Figure 8.6). For instance, if local communities only trust their leaders, other governors can be as effective as they want, their performance does not increase their legitimacy.
- Target populations must share values and goals with the governors (condition 2 in Figure 8.6). For example, effective education governance only leads to output legitimacy if the governed value education as important.

- The governed need to be able to attribute governance effectiveness to particular governors (condition 3 in Figure 8.6). This requirement has sparked a lively debate on whether successful governance by external and/or non-state actors might weaken an already weak state further. We come back to this debate below.

- Last but not least, the recognition by target populations and communities that governance has been successful must be translated from specific support for the governance task at hand to the diffuse support and legitimacy of the governors (condition 4 in Figure 8.6), as Easton suggested decades ago (Easton 1965; see also McLoughlin 2018 with regard to Sri Lanka).

While these conditions appear to be rather demanding, the evidence presented in this book suggests that the virtuous circle between legitimacy and effectiveness can indeed work even under rather adverse conditions of limited statehood. At the same time, the circle can quickly turn vicious (for external interveners in Afghanistan see Stollenwerk 2018b) if the governors do not perform as desired by the governed or if a lack of legitimacy leads to a lack of rule compliance or non-cooperation and resistance among the target populations (factor c in Figure 8.6). In other words, solely relying on output legitimacy in ALS is a risky proposition.

With these caveats in mind, however, we conclude our summary of the findings with a rather optimistic assessment. To reiterate: under the right conditions, effective and legitimate governance is possible "under anarchy," i.e., in areas of limited statehood. Countries do not need to reach the status of "Denmark" for their citizens to enjoy a decent living.

We now turn to the implications of our findings.

Implications

The Remains of the State in Areas of Limited Statehood

Our book has demonstrated that governance by non-state actors in ALS can be both effective and legitimate. At the same time, governance seems to require a minimum of residual statehood, which, however, needs to be restrained in order to avoid predatory statehood.

RESIDUAL STATEHOOD

Statehood gives state actors privileged resources for hierarchical coordination (Genschel and Zangl 2008a) in providing security and order, ensuring the (re-)allocation of values and safeguarding economic stability. The monopoly of the use of force and the capacity to set and enforce rules also matters for external and non-state governors by motivating them, on the one hand, and, facilitating effective and inclusive governance contributions, on the other (Börzel 2010b). In this context, we need to distinguish between statehood and state actors (governments). Statehood refers to the ability of central institutions to set and enforce rules as well as to uphold a monopoly of the use of force. Strictly speaking, the following considerations primarily refer to statehood as an institution rather than particular actors such as governments. In other words, external actors (foreign states or IOs) as well as internal ones (rebel groups, warlords, or "traditional" authorities) can all acquire statehood.

In this book, we have identified functional equivalents to statehood that motivate non-state actors, such as companies, rebel groups, or "traditional authorities", to engage in the effective provision of collective goods and services. Yet, at least some of these functional equivalents rely on residual statehood. Markets do not function without regulations, which are set and enforced by states. It is foreign states or IOs that commit companies to participate in effective governance. Community pressure is particularly effective when community members "invoke state authority" to induce non-state governance (Börzel, Hönke, and Thauer 2012) or when IOs and foreign states take up the claims of communities and exert pressure from above (Brysk 1993; Keck and Sikkink 1998).

Statehood not only incentivizes but also facilitates governance by external and non-state actors. Governance contributions by non-state actors presuppose the provision of some collective goods, such as political stability and security, but also basic infrastructure (cf. Beisheim et al. 2014). Companies are often unwilling to invest in conflict zones. Nongovernmental organizations require a minimum of security for their workers as well as (air)ports, roads, and railways to move around. In principle, such governance services do not have to come from state actors in ALS, which almost by definition lack the capacity to provide them. We have shown how warlords, rebel groups, and other VNSA may engage in peace-keeping and peace-making. They establish a monopoly of the use of force in the areas they control and set up basic administrations to coordinate external and domestic resources necessary for service delivery. In other words, they acquire statehood (see above). Moreover, weak states often rely on the – albeit equally limited – enforcement capacity of IOs and ROs to further governance. ROs then draw on statehood, too. For instance, many weak states try to lock in domestic reforms through ROs (Börzel and van Hüllen 2015a; Pevehouse 2005) or rely on regional courts to ensure the legal certainty that many companies expect before they do business in ALS (Alter 2014). Yet, to be credible, ROs have to include at least some member states with sufficient statehood to enforce regional norms and rules (e.g. Nigeria in ECOWAS, South Africa in SADC).

At least some residual capacity to set and enforce central rules is often important to ensure the effective and inclusive provision of collective goods and services by external and non-state actors. The successful implementation of many transnational governance initiatives still relies on the regulatory capacity of states in ALS. The Voluntary Principles of Security and Human Rights (Chapter 6), for instance, require host governments to cooperate in controlling the police and the military and improving their compliance with human rights standards (Börzel and Hönke 2012). The Kimberley process depends even more on a minimum of diamond-exporting states' capacity to implement the certification scheme. Participant countries are asked to put in place national legislation and institutions to monitor the scheme (Paes 2005). Monitoring and enforcement by state agencies not only contributes to the effectiveness of external and non-state governance. It also fosters inclusiveness. Labor regulations in South Africa, for example, have forced multinational mining companies to broaden the access to HIV/AIDS treatment (Hönke, 2013b) since they prohibit mandatory testing and automatic dismissal due to an HIV infection.

(Residual) statehood does not have to reside with state actors, as argued above. However, non-state actors that control a monopoly of the use of force as well as set and enforce collectively binding rules have to accept the public responsibility to use their statehood to serve the public interest rather than seek rents. The motivation to do so often comes from external statehood and from international law enforced by foreign states. External statehood, in turn, often suffers from its own problems of effectiveness and legitimacy (see above). At the same time, it would be wrong to assume that state actors in ALS are by definition bound by the common interest simply because they are in government (see below).

THE HORIZON OF LEGITIMACY

Non-state governance is not only effective in ALS. It is also socially accepted if it is efficient, inclusive, fair, and transparent. At the same time, many beneficiaries of governance services provided by non-state actors still seem to expect the state to take over, at least in the long run (Beisheim et al. 2011b). Local communities often resist the privatization of state functions and the overtaking of governance tasks by actors such as companies (Altvater and Mahnkopf 2002; Cutler 2003). The provision of *public* goods and services, particularly if they are complex and refer to basic human needs (e.g. security, clean water), is often considered a core task of the state (Leibfried and Zürn 2005; McLoughlin 2015). This coincides with the mind-set of many non-state actors, who are willing to help build the governance capacities of states but have little intention of substituting them (Deitelhoff and Wolf 2010b). Likewise, the international community engages in state-building in order to strengthen the capacity of state actors to set and enforce rules and provide collective goods and services (Brozus 2007). In other words, even in ALS, the state tends to define the expectations local citizens and external donors have not only with regard to which collective goods and services are provided but also by whom and to whom. The reference point for defining whether actors provide truly public or only club goods is often the nation-state, too (Jacob, Ladwig, and Schmelzle 2018).

In this context, one could argue that the provision of collective goods and services in ALS by actors other than the central or local governments is likely to weaken the state by undermining its legitimacy. The literature on aid dependency argues that governments heavily depending on foreign aid further delegitimize their state, whose legitimacy is already weak due to weak performance (e.g. Bräutigam and Knack 2004). Fortunately, there is little evidence that such a vicious circle may exist. Experimental studies show, for example, that foreign aid in fact increases the legitimacy of – particularly local – governments rather than decreasing it (Dietrich, Mahmud, and Winters 2018; Winters, Dietrich, and Mahmud 2018). As Dietrich et al. argue, a possible explanation of this spill-over effect would be that people ascribe foreign aid to their weak (local) government's efforts to bring in external actors and evaluate this positively. In other words, the "horizon of legitimacy" ensures that foreign governance contributions ultimately attributed to state efforts to improve citizens' lot. In a similar vein, a study of "traditional" authorities has shown that their legitimacy does not substitute the legitimacy of the state, but that the two are in fact complementary (van der Windt et al. 2019). This suggests that concerns about weakening the state further through the governance provision by other actors in ALS are exaggerated. Rather, there might be a "win-win" situation between state legitimacy, on the one hand, and the social acceptance of external and non-state governors, on the other. This has significant policy implications to which we come back towards the end of the chapter.

THE DARK SIDE OF (RESIDUAL) STATEHOOD

A certain degree of statehood may be necessary to make governance by non-state actors effective and legitimate. At the same time, such residual statehood can become part of the problem rather than the solution, when state actors use their limited capacity to set and enforce rules in order to seek private rents and consolidate their power rather than provide governance. Local authorities, for instance, have (ab)used their legal authority to impose their personal political and economic interest on firms. MNCs rely on informal political networks to receive state contracts and licenses in many ALS. Companies then owe members of these networks personal favors. Such "neopatrimonial collusion" (Hönke 2012; Pitcher, Moran, and Johnston 2009) reinforces the dark side of statehood when non-state actors provide governance in return for access to markets or the political system. Finally, state actors may invoke their residual statehood to spoil non-state efforts at rule-making and service delivery if non-state governance affects issue-areas that are sensitive to their claim to sovereignty not only with regard to the use of force (Hönke 2010b) but also welfare provision (cf. Beisheim, Janetschek, and Sarre 2014; Sehovic 2014). We find many instances in which residual statehood is used to spoil and to interfer with governance efforts by external and non-state actors rather than to support them. Lake's study of combating sexual violence is particularly instructive in this context. She shows that women's access to justice was better secured in ALS in the DRC beyond the reach of the state than in South Africa where the state was still strong enough to interfere with attempts to bring the perpetrators of sexual violence to justice (Lake, M. 2018).

Weak state capacity in ALS might not only spoil governance efforts by others, it can also turn governments into predators. Limited statehood by definition (Chapter 2) is unable to enforce the rules. As a result, state actors can usurp state capacity for private purposes, not only for rent-seeking, but also for outright preying on citizens (overview in Reno 2015b; see also Stollenwerk 2018c; Reno 2011; Robinson 1999). It is not surprising in this context that indicators for limited statehood highly correlate with various corruption indices (Lee, Walter-Drop, and Wiesel 2014). The state- (and euro-) centric view of the world too often turns a blind eye to state predation as a major cause of governance failure in ALS. It is precisely weak statehood that invites all kinds of "roving and stationary bandits" (Olson 1993) to exploit what remains of state institutions for predatory purposes.

What does this mean for residual statehood in ALS? On the one hand, we have argued above that some degree of statehood is necessary to ensure that governance provision by external as well as non-state actors is effective. On the other hand, residual statehood might be used by – national as well as local – governments not only to spoil governance, but to prey on the citizens.

Our findings indicate that the dark side of statehood is less likely to emerge if it is kept in check by institutional restraints (Börzel 2012). Unrestrained statehood is prone to despotism (Krasner 2018, 34–36). Institutional restraints, such as the rule of law and participatory institutions, can prevent statehood from becoming predatory or repressive (Fukuyama 2004; Olson 1993). The rule of law constrains the power of the executive by constitutional and legal norms, rules, and procedure that ensure the setting and enforcing of rules and the delivery of collective goods and services in a transparent, impartial, and predictable way. The norms, rules, and procedures are reviewed and enforced by an independent judiciary. Democratic procedures ensure elite and party competition. Citizens can vote their government out of power if they are dissatisfied with the governance provision. However, both restraints on statehood rely on formal institutions, which are weak in ALS. The literature on postcolonial politics, informal institutions, and resistance therefore focuses on societal mechanisms of accountability (see also Baldwin and Holzinger 2019a). Enbeddedness of state representatives in local commnunities that incorporate shared norms of public interest can hold them accountable and make them strive for inclusive governance outcomes (cf. Hönke and Börzel 2014). The findings of this book suggest that accountability through social embeddeness is particularly effective in communities that feature high levels of social trust. In sum, local mechanisms of accountability embedded in relationships of trust provide an alternative mechanism of ensuring that what remains of the state is restrained and not used for rent-seeking or predatory purposes.

THE TRANSFORMATION OF THE STATE

The above considerations lead to our final thoughts about limited statehood as compared to consolidated statehood. Interestingly enough, the role of statehood for governance in ALS is not so different from the role of statehood in contemporary consolidated states. It is a myth that democratic welfare states provide most public services hierarchically most of the time. As the literature on the "transformation of the state" demonstrates, the democratic and consolidated state in the Global North has transformed itself into a governance manager (Genschel and Zangl 2008; Kooiman 1993; Leibfried et al. 2015) or governance arena (Kohler-Koch 1996). Rather than hierarchically providing rules and collective services, state actors involve non-state actors to achieve more effective and legitimate governance (cf. Jessop 1998; Kooiman 1993; Mayntz 1993). Moreover, liberal democracies, while retaining their international sovereignty, have delegated parts of their "Westphalian" and domestic sovereignty to supranational ROs such as the EU. In a similar way, weak states with limited administrative capacity delegate governance tasks to other actors, e.g. foreign governments, IOs, and non-state actors. While delegation arrangements are usually heavily legalized (Matanock 2014), we can also observe cases in which the central state as well as local actors participate in more loosely coupled governance arrangements that resemble negotiation systems (for Afghanistan and Pakistan see Koehler and Wilke 2011). The state in these arrangements is "one player among many, which has decision-making as well as organizational competences, but cannot monopolize either" (Beisheim et al. 2011b, 257, our translation). Statehood in ALS can be as "negotiated" (Hagmann and Péclard 2010) or "mediated" (Menkhaus 2008; Raeymaekers, Menkhaus, and Vlassenroot 2008) as in consolidated states (see also below).

Of course, ALS differ from consolidated statehood in at least two ways. First, the "shadow of hierarchy" is missing; residual statehood is largely unable to threaten non-state and other actors with hierarchical governance, if they do not deliver (Chapter 2). Second, statehood is more often than not contested by, rather than shared or negotiated with other actors. The challenge for ALS is not that states are unable to monopolize the provision of governance. What is often missing is an institutionalized and uncontested "division of labor" between state and non-state governors. This often results in competing or at best "parallel" (Beisheim et al. 2011b, 261) or "complementary" (Idler and Forest 2015) governance, i.e., uncoordinated activities with some ad hoc arrangements among state and non-state actors. Since statehood is limited, state actors can neither hierarchically impose an order of divided and shared rule, nor can they settle conflicts and contestations (Beisheim et al. 2011a). To what extent non-state actors can provide such "meta governance" (Peters 2010) or rules about rule-making – without resorting to consolidated statehood – remains an open question. Bierschenk et al. (Bierschenk and De Sardan 2014) demonstrate what they call the "co-production of public services" by different combinations of state and non-state actors – domestic and international – in West Africa (Bierschenk 2014, 235–237; see also De Sardan 2014). The variation in effectiveness they observe is largely explained by institutional features similar to those identified in this book.

We need more research on whether the transformation of the state in ALS results in different varieties of (limited) statehood from the ones that have emerged in the world of consolidated statehood. What is missing are systematic comparisons of areas of limited statehood that overcome the problematic binaries of the "underdeveloped" Global South and the "developed" and "modern" Global North (Brandel and Randeria 2018;

Korf et al. 2018; Schlichte 2018) and investigate similarities and differences with regard to limited statehood rather than assuming them. How is the "retreat of the state" (Strange 1996) observed in industrialized democracies through privatization, marketization, and externalization different from the "discharging" (Hönke 2010b) and the "cunning state" (Randeria 2003) in Sub-Saharan Africa or India? Does the "globalized state" (Herren 2018) in Europe differ from the "internationalized state" (Schlichte 2018) in the Global South because supranational organizations, such as the EU, interfere with the "Westphalian sovereignty" of Western states rather than international donors? To what extent is multi-layered network governance in the twenty-first century different from colonial power-settings of nineteenth- and early twentieth-century imperialism (Herren 2018), or new modes of governance in the Middle Ages and early modern empires (Esders, Hölck, and Rinke 2018)?

Focusing on the transformation of the state and varieties of statehood appears to be more promising for future research than the debate on whether non-state governance ultimately strengthens or further weakens the state in ALS. As we argued above, there is little evidence that non-state governance in ALS weakens the state further. Development NGOs, for example, have been shown to strengthen state capacity, at least in democratic systems (Campbell, DiGiuseppe, and Murdie 2019). Or take Somalia, which is not only the quintessential failed state. It also provides an example of regionalized state-building by non-state governors (Menkhaus 2006/2007). Such "bottom-up state-building" (Podder 2014) may aim at preventing the revival of the central state, and the political goal of rebels or religious groups is to ultimately take over the state. However, rather than competition and opposition, the relationship between state and non-state governors in ALS more often than not entails cooperation and cooptation (Berti 2016; Staniland 2012). Our findings indicate that governance in ALS is neither an incipient form of state-formation nor does it necessarily prevent the consolidation of statehood. Whether the provision of rules and services by external and non-state actors is complementary to or competing with governance by the state depends on some form of meta-governance, whether provided by the (residual) state or by other actors, external as well as non-state.

In sum, sustainable governance in ALS requires some degree of statehood, particularly with regard to highly complex tasks. Moreover, the state remains the normative vantage point for governance in ALS; it "shows an amazing ability to survive both in the image of nation-statehood with its visible institutions, symbols and practices, and in the structure of relationships underlying contemporary modes of governance" (Raeymaekers, Menkhaus, and Vlassenroot 2008, 17). This may explain why the subjective assessment of citizens regarding the effectiveness of governance by the state is more positive than measurements by "objective" governance indicators (Stollenwerk 2018a). At the same time, governance by non-state and external/foreign actors does not weaken what remains of the state, but actually strengthens its legitimacy in the eyes of the citizens. Yet, residual statehood in ALS is often part of the problem rather than part of the solution, if not restrained by the rule of law and by participatory institutions. Predatory (residual) statehood is often worse than no statehood at all. Here, we agree with Scott's arguments, even though we do not share his "two cheers for anarchism" (Scott 2012, 2009).

Should countries with ALS then strive to become "Denmark"? Our book provides an empirical as well as a normative answer to the question. Let us start with the empirics. First, the "governance puzzle" in Chapter 1 (Figure 1.1) does indicate that many consolidated states rank very highly with regard to the provision of goods and services, while many ALS are less effectively governed. Second, however, becoming "Denmark" is not in the cards for most countries with ALS. Denmark as a governance model has always been the exception rather than the rule (Esders, Hölck, and Rinke 2018; Spruyt 1996). Third, as we have shown in this book, governance can be both effective and legitimate in ALS. Fourth, simply strengthening the state does not move a country toward "Denmark," since it can also increase the repressive or predatory capacity of a state, if statehood is not constrained by participatory institutions and the rule of law.

The normative issue is more difficult to tackle. On the one hand, the consolidated, democratic, and welfare state that is restrained by the rule of law, certainly marks civilizational progress – particularly when considering historical alternatives. Moreover, the standards against which non-state and external governors in ALS have to be held in order to render their provision of governance legitimate in a normative way are quite demanding. They are expected to provide public (governance) institutions that "make political participation and public accountability possible, and … imply strong role obligations to act inclusively, impartially, and reliably" (Jacob, Ladwig, and Schmelzle 2018, 577).

On the other hand, these standards also apply to state governance. Yet, many consolidated states have – throughout history – miserably failed in meeting these normative obligations; more statehood does not necessarily lead to better governance. Statehood is a means rather than an end for governance. The empirical reality, thus, obliges us to think outside the box and to overcome our state-centric view of the world. While "Denmark" represents public institutions that are normatively legitimate, it is neither the endpoint of history nor the (only) goal to strive for. Areas of limited statehood are the (empirical) norm not the deviation. Decentering the state requires us to think politics and political order beyond the state "all the way down," both in theoretical and in normative terms. We need to conceive of governance configurations, which approximate the normative ideal. "Denmark" is one possible configuration of "good governance," but not the only one. These considerations have important policy implications, which we will discuss below.

International Relations and Areas of Limited Statehood

COMPARING THE INTERNATIONAL SYSTEM WITH AREAS OF LIMITED STATEHOOD

The central message of this book is that effective and legitimate governance under anarchy is possible under certain specified conditions. This finding might still be news for researchers and practitioners dealing with fragile or failed states given the conventional wisdom (see Chapter 2). It is probably less surprising for International Relations scholars. For decades, IR scholars have struggled to explain under which conditions states as the main actors in the international system cooperate "under anarchy" (Oye 1986; see also Krasner 1983; Keohane 1989a; Müller 1993; Rittberger 1993, among others). The international system resembles areas of limited statehood insofar as there is no supreme authority with the capacity to uphold a monopoly of the use of force or to enforce rules and decisions. The "anarchy problematique" has always been the starting point for IR scholars rather than a deficiency that has to be overcome (for a rare exception see Wendt 2003). Similar to much of the literature of fragile and failed states, (neo)realists have concluded from this condition that the international system resembles the Hobbesian condition of a "state of nature" where war is frequent and can rarely be avoided (Morgenthau 1948; Waltz 1979; Mearsheimer 2001). They were challenged by neoliberal institutionalists who claimed that egoistic and self-interested states are likely to cooperate under certain conditions, if they cannot reach their goals otherwise (see Baldwin 1993). Later on, social constructivists entered the scene and claimed that we need to focus on the intersubjective quality of norms and on the role of ideas to understand international cooperation (Kratochwil 1989; Onuf 1989; Wendt 1999). Wendt in particular argued that "anarchy is what states make of it" (Wendt 1992), namely that it is up to the form and mode of state interaction whether the absence of a centralized enforcement authority results in enduring rivalries, stable cooperation, or even friendship. This debate culminated in the famous dictum that "governance without government" (Czempiel and Rosenau 1992) characterizes most of international relations. In other words, the international system – similar to ALS – does not consist of ungoverned spaces, only because a central authority that can enforce the rules does not exist.

Our argument on the conditions under which (self-interested) actors are likely to engage in governance in ALS owes a lot to this debate. Most recently, IR scholars have claimed that the international system exhibits elements of hierarchy, understood here as relationships of super- and subordination as well as of rule and authority (for comprehensive treatments see Lake, D. 2009; Zürn 2018). Our own understanding of hierarchy is more restrictive and refers back to Weber's concept of rule and authority ("Herrschaft"; see Chapter 2). However, the similarity to ALS is striking, since we do find hierarchical governance in ALS even in the absence of a functioning state.

Moreover, at least two of our three explanatory factors to account for governance motivations (Chapter 3) also feature prominently in the IR literature. First, as to institutional conditions, the "shadow of anarchy" resembles closely functional arguments in the neoliberal institutionalist literature. Self-interested states engage in international governance if they cannot realize their interests unilaterally (overview in Martin and Simmons 2013; see also Martin 1992b; Zürn 1992). The "shadow of the local community" shows similarities to transnational advocacy networks in IR that promote international norms, e.g. with regard to human rights and the environment (Finnemore and Sikkink 1998; Keck and Sikkink 1998). The "rational design" as well as the "legalization" literatures have inspired us concerning the functional design of governance arrangements (Goldstein et al. 2000; Koremenos, Lipson, and Snidal 2001; for an application to MSPs see Beisheim and Liese 2014a).

Second, the quest for legitimacy as a major motivation for actors, such as rebel groups (VNSA), to engage in governance in ALS also resonates with arguments in the IR literatures on the reasons why states engage in cooperation. From a more rationalist perspective, the literature on reputation has to be mentioned here (e.g. Crescenzi 2018; Mercer 1996). Sociological institutionalism emphasizes the "logic of appropriateness" to explain how actors (mostly states) come to cooperate and to sign up to as well as ratify international agreements (e.g. Finnemore and Sikkink 1998; March and Olsen 1998). We share with these literatures a focus on the desire of actors to be regarded as legitimate governors, be it in global affairs or ALS.

As to our third explanatory factor – social trust – IR scholars would not usually argue that international relations are trust-based, given what is at stake with regard to war and peace. However, more recent scholarship argues that social trust is crucial for multilateral cooperation and that without relationships of trust, diplomacy would not work (overview in Rathbun 2018; see also Mercer 2005; Rathbun 2011). Moreover, Wendt's social constructivist theory of IR uses social identification processes to account for the emergence of enduring relationships of friendship in international affairs (Wendt 1999). Last but not least, recent theories on international and regional organizations argue that collective identities and community-building beyond the nation-state (including social trust) are a necessary ingredient for states entering into open-end contract relations with others (Hooghe, Lenz, and Marks 2019; see also Risse 2010a). These arguments closely resemble our assertion that social trust relations enable local communities in ALS to overcome collective action problems (for a comparison of Ostrom's work and the IR literature on cooperation see Keohane and Ostrom 1994).

At the same time, the IR literature reminds us that the commitment to international cooperation and to international law does not equal compliance and problem-solving. In our language: the motivation to govern does not equal effective governance. In this context, there are similarities and differences between the governance problematique in international relations as compared to ALS. With regard to compliance with (costly) rules, ALS and the international system face similar problems, since the enforcement of collectively binding rules cannot rely on a centralized authority. However, unlike global governance, governance in ALS goes beyond rule-making and includes the direct provision of collective goods and services to citizens (Chapter 2).

Concerning rule compliance, however, our approach and the IR literature have a lot in common. The latter usually distinguishes between three approaches (overviews in Börzel et al. 2010; Hurd 1999; Raustiala and Slaughter 2002; for a comprehensive treatment see Börzel 2020). *Enforcement approaches* argue that rule compliance in IR is the more likely, the more norm violators are likely to face costs, which requires effective monitoring and sanctioning capacities of international regimes (Downs, Rocke, and Barsoom 1996). To the extent that governance in ALS involves hierarchical modes, rules can be enforced in such ways. Examples include (the threat of) using force by peace-keepers or rebel groups as well as the social sanctioning capacity of local communities and the rule by "traditional" authorities (Chapter 4).

Our argument about institutional design as accounting for effective governance in ALS closely resembles the *management school* in compliance research (Chayes and Chayes 1993, 1995). From this point of view, rule (non-) compliance is not so much a question of willingness, but of capacity (see Börzel and Risse 2013 for a discussion with regard to ALS). States might be fully committed to international norms and rules, but they lack the administrative capacities to implement them domestically, leading to what the literature calls "involuntary non-compliance." Our arguments about adequate institutional designs as a condition for effective governance are very similar in that governance arrangements must have sufficient material and ideational resources available and develop enough flexibility and intra-organizational learning capacities so as to be able to adjust to changing circumstances on the ground.

Last but not least, there is the *legitimacy approach* to (non-) compliance (Franck 1990; Hurd 1999; Schmelzle 2015). Accordingly, voluntary compliance with costly rules that are not in the short-term self-interest of actors is best ensured when governance actors and institutions enjoy legitimacy as the "right to govern." Legitimacy beliefs are grounded in the "logic of appropriateness" mentioned above. The more actors know what is appropriate in a given situation and/or the more they believe in the moral validity of the norm in question (see Checkel 2005 on this distinction), the more they are likely to follow the rules. This approach is almost identical with our argument that (empirical) legitimacy is probably the most important factor for effective governance in areas of limited statehood. Once again, the similarities between the international realm and ALS are striking.

Our approach also has something to offer to IR specialists. Two issues stand out. First, IR scholars have investigated the role and impact of transnational non-state actors for quite some time (Keohane and Nye 1971; overview in Risse 2013), particularly with regard to MNCs (Gilpin 1975 for an early contribution), transnational advocacy networks (Keck and Sikkink 1998), and epistemic communities (Haas 1992). However, the literature still concentrates on how transnational relations impact upon global and regional governance as conducted by states and IOs. Most scholarship remains rather state-centric and the literature on the (global and regional) governance contributions of non-state actors is still in its infancy (see e.g. Avant, Finnemore, and Sell 2010b; Cutler, Haufler, and Porter 1999; Haufler 1993, 1999). Research on ALS might help, since it sheds light on the multitude of non-state actors who actively engage in governance (Chapter 4). In fact, a focus on governance rather than state-led institutions and regimes enables scholars to study the contributions of non-state actors more systematically and to overcome state-centrism as well as "Western"-centrism (Draude 2012; on the latter point see Acharya and Buzan 2019).

Our second contribution to the larger IR literature is taken from the transformed role of the state in ALS (and elsewhere) discussed above.

A significant finding of our book that also resonates with the literature on the transformation of the state more generally (Leibfried et al. 2015) concerns state actors in ALS as governance managers and "meta-governors." The residual state (to the extent that it is not predatory) often coordinates the activities of other governors in ALS and sets the "rules of the game" according to which governance is provided. This transformed function of the state resonates with the emerging literature on authority in IR (e.g. Zürn 2018) and might actually advance the scholarship on hierarchy (e.g. Lake 2009; Zarakol 2017), which often conflates hierarchy as a particular mode of ruling with power relations in general. At least, a focus on meta-governance might shed new light on the role of state-led international institutions as well as IOs in the international system.

A third insight taken from our findings relates to the study of multi-level governance (MLG) systems in world politics.

GOVERNANCE IN ALS AS MULTI-LEVEL GOVERNANCE: LINKING THE
INTERNATIONAL AND THE DOMESTIC/LOCAL

So far, we have treated ALS and the international system as different levels of analysis, which is common in the field of political science, e.g. with its distinctions between the subfields of comparative politics and of IR. The reality, however, is more complex. Global governance and governance in ALS are linked and intertwined. The same actors that constitute the global governance system – states and their foreign policies, IOs, INGOs, MSPs, MNCs – are also among the most important governors in ALS, as we have argued throughout this book (particularly Chapter 4). As a result, governance in ALS can be treated as a "multi-level governance" (MLG) system.

Originally, the literature on MLG emerged in the framework of the EU with its different governance layers – from local/sub-national to national to supranational governance (Hooghe and Marks 2001; Kohler-Koch and Eising 1999; overview in Enderlein, Wälti, and Zürn 2010). This also allowed scholars to capture the role of non-state actors (business, interest groups, NGOs), which engage with local, national, and supranational authorities in setting and implementing EU policies forming multi-level formal and informal networks. By de-centering the state, multi-level governance is a useful approach to governance in ALS. First, multi-level governance is all about shared sovereignty, i.e., the pooling and delegating of political authority across the various local, national, and trans- as well as supranational levels. The same holds true for ALS. In many cases, external actors deeply interfere with the "Westphalian" as well as the domestic sovereignty of states with ALS.

Governance Delegation Agreements (GDA) are about sharing sovereignty between different levels (Matanock 2014) whereby national governments voluntary give up their right to rule in various issue-areas to external actors. Chapter 6 UN peace-keeping missions are typical examples (Chapter 5). In the case of trusteeships, protectorates, and Chapter 7 UN peace-keeping missions, external actors intrude in the "Westphalian" sovereignty of nation-states without their consent. So do the military interventions authorized by the AU or ECOWAS (Hartmann and Striebinger 2015).

Second, supranational authorities in MLG systems, such as the EU, rely on the capacities of the member states for the implementation and enforcement of their rules and decisions (Börzel 2020), which constitutes its own challenges for ensuring compliance. The same holds true for international law (IL) and ALS (Krieger 2018; see also Ladwig and Rudolf 2011). In general, IL is ill-equipped in dealing with weak states and ALS. On the one hand, IL has developed ever more demanding governance rules and standards that deeply intrude in the domestic sovereignty of states (Zürn 2018). This ranges from human rights and the rule of law to security governance, trade, education as well as public health, environmental protection (e.g. climate change), and biodiversity. The global governance system encompasses almost all issue-areas of governance. Moreover, the sanctioning and enforcement capacities of IOs and ROs have increased, including supranational courts and other dispute settlement systems (see Alter 2014; Alter and Hooghe 2016). On the other hand, IL assumes fully functioning and consolidated states that are willing and able to implement and enforce global governance norms. IL also presupposes the existence of a domestic collectivity for which decisions can be made and the existence of domestic political authority that is ultimately responsible. Of course, both conditions are missing in ALS.

As a result, the demands of IL and the realities of ALS often clash, leading to strong local resistance and contestation (Berger 2017; Zimmermann 2017; see also Zürn 2018). Moreover, as we have argued throughout this book, IL, including decisions by IOs as such, does not carry much weight in terms of generating legitimacy for governance in ALS. International law has to be aligned with local norms of appropriate behavior to generate legitimacy as a pre-condition for effective governance in ALS.

Finally, the MLG literature points to various legitimacy problems linked to the levels of governance (overview in Rittberger and Schroeder 2016; see also Risse 2006). In the EU, this relates to a "democratic deficit" pertaining to the (input) legitimacy of supranational institutions. With regard to MLG in ALS, these problems are exacerbated by the fact that the various (external) governors face very different accountability issues. Peace-keepers as well as foreign aid agencies are accountable to their sending states and their domestic mechanisms of bestowing legitimacy (national parliaments in liberal democracies). IOs and ROs are ultimately accountable to their member states. (Multinational) companies are accountable to their shareholders and – via market mechanisms – to their customers. INGOs have to compete for funding – usually in the Global North – and are ultimately accountable to these funders and their preferences, be they public or private. In ALS, contract relationships with – usually state governments – are the only way to hold these external actors accountable by those for whom they provide governance services. Even in these cases, the relationships of accountability and legitimacy with the home countries of external governors are stronger.

At the same time, as we have argued throughout this book, local legitimacy in ALS is key for effective governance. Without local acceptance, there is no success – irrespective of the lines of accountability to the various home countries! What if parliaments in home countries do not want to provide the necessary resources to ensure the effective institutional design of governance arrangements in ALS? What if home countries are eager to terminate long-term peace-keeping activities in cases in which a return to civil war is likely? These examples illustrate the inherent tensions and contradictions with regard to the legitimacy requirements for effective governments in ALS that are not easy to solve. To put it differently: institutionalizing "local ownership" principles to generate input legitimacy for governance by external actors almost inevitably clashes with the accountability issues these actors face. We come back to this question in the concluding section on the policy implications for external actors.

To sum up: the international system shares important features with areas of limited statehood. The "anarchy problematique" – the absence of an ultimate authority with the capacity to enforce decisions and to uphold a monopoly of the use of force – is common to both. At the same time, neither the international system nor ALS are ungoverned or ungovernable. It follows that many IR theories are highly relevant for explaining effective governance in ALS – and vice versa. Moreover, the global governance system and ALS are firmly intertwined in a multi-level governance system. This has numerous advantages insofar as the international community cannot simply ignore governance challenges in ALS – without creating severe repercussions for the international system, for global stability, and for peace, security, and the wealth of consolidated states. However, governance in ALS as multi-level governance creates its own problems since international law presupposes consolidated states and because of diverging legitimacy and accountability issues.

Policy Implications: From State Building to Governance Promotion

This book has significant implications for policies toward areas of limited statehood (see Brozus 2007, 2011; Brozus, Jetzlsperger, and Walter-Drop 2018; for the following). In the following and for pragmatic reasons, we particularly focus on policies by external state actors, such as Western liberal democracies and IOs as well as ROs (for the latter see Börzel and van Hüllen 2015a). In some cases, we also touch upon the role of companies and of (I)NGOs.

From the end of the Cold War through the 2000s, that is, for nearly two decades, the dominant Western and IO approach to ALS has been comprehensive liberal state-building understood mainly as transfers of Western liberal (state) institutions to ALS. The terrorist attacks of 9/11 added new urgency to the efforts, since fragile and failed states were quickly identified as one of the underlying factors enabling the rise of transnational terrorism. In fact, framing the problem of limited statehood as one of fragile, failing, or failed states almost automatically led to the conclusion that comprehensive state-building was the answer (Brozus, Jetzlsperger, and Walter-Drop 2018, 586–592; for comprehensive critiques see Lake, D. 2016; Woodward 2017). In addition, Western democracies, IOs and ROs, such as the EU, embarked upon democracy promotion efforts, which – again – implied the institutional transfer of Western-style institutions to liberalizing (weak) states (Babayan and Risse 2016; Lavenex and Schimmelfennig 2011; Magen, Risse, and McFaul 2009).

In the 2010s, Western governments and IOs gradually moved away from comprehensive state-building, particularly after the efforts in Iraq and Afghanistan had failed despite the enormous financial and other resources that had been spent. When Iraq and Afghanistan relapsed into conflict and civil war after the state-builders had left, the entire paradigm was challenged and a "new modesty" set in (Brozus, Jetzlsperger, and Walter-Drop 2018, 589). "Stabilization" became the new catchword with a focus on ceasefires and peace accords after civil wars coupled with empowering legitimate governance actors, mostly states. Some even advocated to leave fragile and failed states alone and to their own devices (for an earlier statement see Herbst 2004). Others argued in favor of "good enough governance" (Grindle 2004, 2011), understood as directing "attention to considerations of the *minimal* (emphasis in text) conditions of governance necessary to allow political and economic development to occur" (Grindle 2011, 200).

We find these approaches highly questionable. Comprehensive "state-building" has failed to accomplish its goals, as this book documents. "Stabilization" is too vague a concept as a result of which it can be filled with almost any content, including the stabilization of repressive, autocratic, and even predatory regimes. Leaving ALS alone is no viable solution either, for both normative-humanitarian and political reasons. Governance breakdowns and violent conflicts in ALS tend to produce immediate negative externalities, not only for neighboring countries, but also for Western democracies, as the most recent migration crises have amply documented. Last but not least, "good enough governance" has a rather paternalistic sound to it. While we should not orient foreign aid toward Western- or Euro-centric standards, who are we to decide about the aspirations of citizens in ALS? What are "minimal conditions of governance?" Freedom from torture and political imprisonment, but no religious freedoms, let alone gender rights? While this may sound polemical, it is difficult to discern from the outside which conditions for governance need to be fulfilled in order to enable a decent living for citizens.

We concur with the critics of comprehensive liberal state-building that a paradigm shift in Western and IO policies towards ALS is warranted. However, the lowering of standards and values with regard to human rights, democracy, the rule of law, economic well-being, education, public health, environmental protection, etc. is neither normatively nor politically desirable. Rather, we suggest a paradigmatic shift from top-down state-building to bottom-up "governance promotion" with a focus on "improving the delivery of basic governance services such as physical security, effective conflict regulation, and a minimum of participation in rule-making" (Brozus, Jetzlsperger, and Walter-Drop 2018, 595; see also Brozus 2011). Rather than institutional transfers, governance promotion starts from local conditions and contexts seeking to improve the situation from the ground up. It does not entail giving up on values such as human rights, democracy, the rule of law, market economy, social welfare, and the delivery of public services. Governance promotion furthers these goals through aligning with local actors and institutions that are conducive to effective and legitimate governance as conceptualized in this book.

A focus on governance promotion rather than state-building leads to the following policy recommendations:

1. Western governments, IOs, and ROs have to increasingly incorporate systematic risk analysis in order to identify potential crises and violent conflicts with the potential to produce negative externalities for their neighborhood and for regional as well as global orders. We suggest matching risk analysis with an evaluation of governance opportunities in the ALS concerned. Which actors – state and non-state – are likely to foster effective and legitimate governance to mitigate risks? Which governance institutions – whether state or non-state – are likely to engage in crisis prevention? In sum, risk assessments should be complemented by assessments of governance opportunities.

2. Focusing on governance promotion rather than state-building requires moving away from state-centric approaches. External actors need to engage (potential) local governors including "traditional" authorities, NGOs, as well as CBOs and NSJI. External actors should also include rebel groups and other VNSA as long as these actors commit to human rights and public goods provision. Nudging VNSA (and governments involved in civil war) toward negotiated settlements that involve post-conflict electoral participation has been shown to result in lasting peace (Matanock 2018).

3. Taking the "ownership" principle seriously requires inclusive and participatory engagement with these actors from the beginning and throughout the governance process. "Local ownership" is not only a pre-condition for effective governance, but also for strengthening legitimacy and social trust relations. At the same time, local governance is not per se legitimate, either in an empirical or in a normative sense. This also points to a careful analysis of local governance opportunities and risks.

4. Engaging non-state actors does not mean ignoring the (residual) state, whether on the national or local level. However, external state actors, agencies, and IOs (such as the IMF), which are legally obliged to work with governments, need to make tough choices. It makes no sense to engage predatory, repressive, and rent-seeking state actors, since strengthening their institutional capacities will only make them more repressive or predatory (see Risse 2021 for details). Rather, the emphasis should be on (local and national) governments in weak states that are embedded in rule-bound and participatory institutions. External actors should strengthen their capacity to become governance managers engaging in rule-setting for meta-governance, as outlined above.

5. Governance promotion requires focusing on results rather than institutions. Governance effectiveness should be measured in terms of

output, outcomes, and impact of service delivery rather than institutional buildup. How many girls have graduated from primary and secondary education, and what about their reading, writing, and mathematical skills? How many women in rural areas have access to justice institutions treating them in a fair and transparent way (irrespective of whether state courts or NSJI)? How many people in poor neighborhoods have access to clean water and sanitation? The UN Sustainable Development Goals (SDGs) and their indicators point in the right direction.

6. Institutional design matters, as we have argued throughout this book. Governance institutions have to be adequately resourced and equipped for the task at hand. They need to be flexible with in-built learning capacities to be able to adjust to changing local circumstances. Most important, external governance promoters should concentrate on inclusive, fair, and transparent governance institutions. Participatory and fair institutions are likely to increase input and throughput legitimacy of the governors. Experiencing such institutions will also strengthen generalized social trust among populations (Rothstein and Stolle 2008a). Thus, institutional design does not only lead to more effective governance, but also increases legitimacy.

7. External governors have to be acutely aware that the effectiveness of their contributions crucially depends on their social acceptance. Governance promotion from the outside requires paying as much attention to generating legitimacy as to providing public goods and services. Inclusive and transparent institution-building as well as working with local communities and CBOs is at least as important as rule-making and service provision. In this context, external actors have to be aware that their legitimacy at home or bestowed by international institutions, such as the UNSC, does not travel easily to ALS. Social acceptance and the "right to govern" have to be earned on the ground, thereby setting in motion the virtuous circle between legitimacy and effectiveness (see above; Schmelzle and Stollenwerk 2018b).

8. Last but not least, external actors have to be aware of the many trade-offs and goal conflicts that they are facing in ALS. This is one reason why heavy-handed comprehensive state-building interventions are to be avoided, even though the "responsibility to protect" (R2P) sometimes will require military interventions to prevent genocides and other gross violations of human rights. One trade-off that is particularly relevant for external actors is between securing public support in their home countries, on the one hand, and maintaining local social acceptance in ALS, on the other. The latter inevitably requires open-ended commitments, while publics at home mostly insist on exit

strategies. Moreover, governance effectiveness and inclusiveness might sometimes clash.

Ultimately, the central message in this book is one of hope. As we have demonstrated, effective and legitimate governance is possible in areas of limited statehood, even under adverse conditions of ethnically and religiously divided societies in post-conflict environments. Somaliland and parts of the DRC are cases in point. However, when ALS can be governed effectively and legitimately, this leads to a moral as well as political obligation and responsibility of liberal democracies and global institutions to contribute to effective and legitimate governance under anarchy.

References

Aas Rustad, Siri Camilla, Halvard Buhaug, Åshild Falch, and Scott Gates. 2011. All Conflict Is Local: Modeling Sub-National Variation in Civil Conflict Risk. *Conflict Management and Peace Science* 28 (1): 15–40.

Abatan, Ella, and Yolanda Spies. 2016. African Solutions to African Problems? The AU, R2P and Côte d'Ivoire. *South African Journal of International Affairs* 23 (1): 21–38.

Abbott, Kenneth W., Robert O. Keohane, Andrew Moravcsik, Anne-Marie Slaughter, and Duncan Snidal. 2000. The Concept of Legalization. *International Organization* 54 (3): 401–419.

Abrahams, Ray. 1987. Sungusungu: Village Vigilante Groups in Tanzania. *African Affairs* 86 (343): 179–196.

Abrams, Dominic, and Michael A. Hogg, eds. 1990. *Social Identity Theory.* London: Harvester Wheatsheaf.

Acemoglu, Daron, Tristan Reed, and James A. Robinson. 2014. Chiefs: Economic Development and Elite Control of Civil Society in Sierra Leone. *Journal of Political Economy* 122 (2): 319–368.

Acemoglu, Daron, and James E. Robinson. 2012. *Why Nations Fail. The Origins of Power, Prosperity, and Poverty.* New York: Crown Business.

Acharya, Amitav. 2014. *The End of American World Order.* Cambridge, UK: Polity Press.

Acharya, Amitav, and Barry Buzan. 2019. *The Making of Global International Relations: Origins and Evolution of IR at Its Centenary.* Cambridge, UK: Cambridge University Press.

Ademmer, Esther. 2016. *Russia's Impact on EU Policy Transfer to the Post-Soviet Space: The Contested Neighbourhood.* London: Routledge.

Alexander, Peter. 2013. Marikana, Turning Point in South African History. *Review of African Political Economy* 40 (138): 605–619.

Alter, Karen J. 2014. *The New Terrain of International Law: International Courts in International Politics.* Princeton, NJ: Princeton University Press.

Alter, Karen J., and Liesbet Hooghe. 2016. Regional Dispute Settlement. In *The Oxford Handbook of Comparative Regionalism*, edited by Tanja A. Börzel, and Thomas Risse. Oxford: Oxford University Press, 538–558.

Altvater, Elmar, and Birgit Mahnkopf. 2002. *Globalisierung der Unsicherheit. Arbeit im Schatten, schmutziges Geld und informelle Politik.* Münster: Westfälisches Dampfboot.

Amelina, Anna , Devrimsel D. Nergiz, Thomas Faist, and Nina Glick Schiller. 2012. *Beyond Methodological Nationalism. Research Methodologies for Cross-Border Studies.* London – New York: Routledge.

Amengual, Matthew. 2010. Complementary Labour Regulation: The Uncoordinated Combination of State and Private Regulators in the Dominican Republic. *World Development* 38 (3): 405–414.

An-Naim, Abdullahi Ahmed, and Francis M. Deng. 2010. *Human Rights in Africa: Cross-cultural Perspectives*. Washington, DC: Brookings Institution Press.

Anderson, Benedict. 1991. *Imagined Communities. Reflections on the Origin and Spread of Nationalism*. London: Verso.

Anderson, David M., and David Killingray. 1991. *Policing the Empire: Government, Authority, and Control, 1830–1940*. Manchester: Manchester University Press.

Anderson, David M., and Øystein H. Rolandsen. 2014. Violence as Politics in Eastern Africa, 1940–1990: Legacy, Agency, Contingency. *Journal of Eastern African Studies* 8 (4): 539–557.

Anderson, Mary B., and Marshall Wallace, eds. 2013. *Opting Out of War: Strategies to Prevent Violent Conflict*. Boulder, CO: Lynne Rienner.

Andonova, Liliana B., Edward D. Mansfield, and Helen V. Milner. 2007. International Trade and Environmental Policy in the Postcommunist World. *Comparative Political Studies* 40 (7): 782–807.

Aneme, Girmachew Alemu. 2015. Ethiopia: Legal and Judicial Plurality and the Incorporation of Traditional Dispute Resolution Mechanisms within the State Justice System. In *Non-State Justice Institutions and the Law. Decision-Making at the Interface of Tradition, Religion, and the State*, edited by Matthias Kötter, Tilmann J. Röder, Gunnar Folke Schuppert, and Rüdiger Wolfrum. Basingstoke: Palgrave Macmillan, 80–99.

Anheier, Helmut, Mary Kaldor, and Marlies Glasius. 2012. The Global Civil Society Yearbook. Lessons and Insights 2001–2011. In *Global Civil Society 2012. Ten Years of Critical Reflection*, edited by Sabine Selchow, Mary Kaldor, and Henrietta L. Moore. Basingstoke: Palgrave Macmillan, 2–26.

Aragón, Fernando M., and Juan Pablo Rud. 2013. Natural Resources and Local Communities: Evidence from a Peruvian Gold Mine. *American Economic Journal: Economic Policy* 5 (2): 1–25.

Arjona, Ana. 2015. Civilian Resistance to Rebel Governance. In *Rebel Governance in Civil War*, edited by Ana Arjona, Nelson Kasfir and Zachariah Mampilly. Cambridge, UK: Cambridge University Press, 180–202.

2016. *Rebelocracy. Social Order in the Colombian Civil War*. Cambridge, UK: Cambridge University Press.

Arjona, Ana, Nelson Kasfir, and Zachariah Mampilly. 2015a. Conclusion. In *Rebel Governance in Civil War*, edited by Ana Arjona, Nelson Kasfir and Zachariah Mampilly. Cambridge, UK: Cambridge University Press, 286–300.

Arjona, Ana, Nelson Kasfir, and Zachariah Mampilly, eds. 2015b. *Rebel Governance in Civil War*. Cambridge, UK: Cambridge University Press.

Arlacchi, Pino, and Martin Ryle. 1986. *Mafia Business: The Mafia Ethic and the Spirit of Capitalism*. London: Verso London.

Auld, Graeme, Steven Bernstein, and Benjamin Cashore. 2008. The New Corporate Social Responsibility. *Annual Review of Environment and Resources* 33: 413–435.

Autesserre, Séverine. 2014a. Going Micro: Emerging and Future Peacekeeping Research. *International Peacekeeping* 21 (4): 492–500.

2014b. *Peaceland. Conflict Resolution and the Everyday Politics of International Intervention.* Cambridge, UK: Cambridge University Press.

Avant, Deborah D. 2005. *The Market for Force: The Consequences of Privatizing Security.* Cambridge, UK: Cambridge University Press.

Avant, Deborah D., Martha Finnemore, and Susan K. Sell. 2010a. Who Governs the Globe? In *Who Governs the Globe?*, edited by Deborah Avant, Martha Finnemore and Susan K. Sell. Cambridge, UK: Cambridge University Press, 1–31.

2010b. *Who Governs the Globe?* Cambridge, UK: Cambridge University Press.

Axelrod, Robert A. 1984. *The Evolution of Cooperation.* New York: Basic Books.

Babayan, Nelli, and Thomas Risse, eds. 2016. *Democracy Promotion and the Challenges of Illiberal Regional Powers. Special Issue of 'Democratization'.* 22 (3).

Bäckstrand, Karin. 2006. Multi-stakeholder Partnerships for Sustainable Development: Rethinking Legitimacy, Accountability and Effectiveness. *European Environment* 16 (5): 290–306.

2008. Accountability of Networked Climate Governance: The Rise of Transnational Climate Partnerships. *Global Environmental Politics* 8 (3): 74–102.

Bagayoko, Niagale, Eboe Hutchful, and Robin Luckham. 2016. Hybrid Security Governance in Africa: Rethinking the Foundations of Security, Justice and Legitimate Public Authority. *Conflict, Security & Development* 16 (1): 1–32.

Bais, Karolien, and Mijnd Huijser. 2017. *The Profit of Peace: Corporate Responsibility in Conflict Regions.* London: Routledge.

Baker, Bruce. 2005. Who Do People Turn to For Policing in Sierra Leone? *Journal of contemporary African Studies* 23 (3): 371–390.

2007. Nonstate Providers of Everyday Security in Fragile African States. In *Fragile States and Insecure People? Violence, Security, and Statehood in the Twenty-First Century*, edited by Louise Andersen, Bjørn Møller and Finn Stepputat. Basingstoke: Palgrave Macmillan, 123–147.

Baldwin, David A., ed. 1993. *Neorealism and Neoliberalism: The Contemporary Debate.* New York: Columbia University Press.

Baldwin, David A. 1997. The Concept of Security. *Review of International Studies* 23 (1): 5–26.

Baldwin, Kate. 2016. *The Paradox of Traditional Chiefs in Democratic Africa, Cambridge Studies in Comparative Politics.* Cambridge, UK: Cambridge University Press.

2019. Elected MPs, Traditional Chiefs, and Local Public Goods: Evidence on the Role of Leaders in Co-Production From Rural Zambia. *Comparative Political Studies* 52 (12): 1925–1956.

Baldwin, Kate, and Katharina Holzinger. 2019a. Traditional Political Institutions and Democracy: Reassessing Their Compatibility and Accountability. *Comparative Political Studies* 52 (12): 1747–1774.

Baldwin, Kate, and Katharina Holzinger, eds. 2019b. *Traditional Political Institutions. Special Issue of "Comparative Political Studies"*, 52 (12).

Ball, Nicole. 2010. The Evolution of the Security Sector Reform Agenda. In *The Future of Security Sector Reform*, edited by Mark Sedra. Waterloo, ONT: Center of International Governance Innovation, 29–44.

Ballentine, Karen, and Heiko Nitzschke. 2004. Business and Armed Conflict: An Assessment of Issues and Options. *Die Friedens-Warte* 79: 35–56.

Balthasar, Dominik. 2013. Somaliland's Best Kept Secret: Shrewd Politics and War Projects as Means of State-Making. *Journal of Eastern African Studies* 7 (2): 218–238.

Banerjee, Abhijit. 2004. Who Is Getting the Public Goods in India? Some Evidence and Some Speculation. In *India's Emerging Economy*, edited by Kaushik Basu. Cambridge, MA: MIT Press, 183–213.

Banerjee, Subhabrata Bobby. 2008a. Corporate Social Responsibility: The Good, the Bad and the Ugly. *Critical Sociology* 34 (1): 51–79.

2008b. Necrocapitalism. *Organization Studies* 29 (12): 1541–1563.

2011. Voices of the Governed: Towards a Theory of the Translocal. *Organization* 18 (3): 323–344.

2018. Transnational Power and Translocal Governance: The Politics of Corporate Responsibility. *Human Relations* 71 (6): 796–821.

Bangura, Ibrahim. 2016. Assessing the Impact of Orthodox Security Sector Reform in Sierra Leone. CSG Papers: Kitchener, Ontario: Centre for Security Governance.

Bangura. 2017. The Gradual Emergence of Second Generation Security Sector Reform in Sierra Leone. CSG Papers: Kitchener, Ontario: Centre for Security Governance.

Banks, Nicola, David Hulme, and Michael Edwards. 2015. NGOs, States, and Donors Revisited: Still Too Close for Comfort? *World Development* 66: 707–718.

Baranyi, Stephen. 2012. Contested Statehood and State-Building in Haiti. *Revista de Ciencia Política* 32 (3): 723–738.

Barbato, Mariano, Sinja Hantscher, and Markus Lederer. 2016. Imagining Jihad. *Global Affairs* 2 (4): 419–429.

Barfield, Thomas, Neamat Nojumi, and J. Alexander Thier. 2006. *The Clash of Two Goods. State and Non-State Dispute Resolution in Afghanistan.* Washington, DC: United States Institute of Peace.

Barkan, Joel D., Michael L. McNulty, and M. A. O. Ayeni. 1991. 'Hometown' Voluntary Associations, Local Development, and the Emergence of Civil Society in Western Nigeria. *The Journal of Modern African Studies* 29 (3): 457–480.

Barnett, Michael N. 2017a. Conclusion: The World according to Paternalism. In *Paternalism beyond Borders*, edited by Michael N. Barnett. Cambridge, UK: Cambridge University Press, 316–344.

2017b. Introduction: International Paternalism: Framing the Debate. In *Paternalism beyond Borders*, edited by Michael N. Barnett. Cambridge, UK: Cambridge University Press, 1–43.

Barnett, Michael N., ed. 2017c. *Paternalism beyond Borders*. Cambridge, UK: Cambridge University Press.

Barnett, Michael N., and Christoph Zürcher. 2009. The Peacebuilder's Contract: How External State-building Reinforces Weak Statehood. In *Dilemmas of*

Statebuilding: Confronting the Contradictions of Post-War Peace Operations, edited by Roland Paris and Timothy Sisk. London: Routledge, 23–52.

Barrow, Clyde W. 1993. *Critical Theories of the State: Marxist, Neomarxist, Postmarxist*. Madison, WI: University of Wisconsin Press.

Barter, Shane Joshua. 2015. The Rebel State in Society: Governance and Accommodation in Aceh, Indonesia. In *Rebel Governance in Civil War*, edited by Ana Arjona, Nelson Kasfir and Zachariah Mampilly. Cambridge, UK: Cambridge University Press, 226–245.

Bassiouni, M. Cherif. 2008. The New Wars and the Crisis of Compliance with the Law of Armed Conflict by Non-state Actors. *The Journal of Criminal Law and Criminology* 98 (3): 711–810.

Bates, Robert H. 2008. *When Things Fall Apart. State Failure in Late-Century Africa*. Cambridge, UK: Cambridge University Press.

Bayart, Jean-François 1993. *The State in Africa: Politics of the Belly*. London and New York: Longman.

Bayat, Asef. 2002. Activism and Social Development in the Middle East. *International Journal of Middle East Studies* 34 (1): 1–28.

Bazirake, Joseph Besigye, and Paul Bukuluki. 2015. A critical reflection on the conceptual and practical limitations of the responsibility to protect. *The International Journal of Human Rights* 19 (8): 1017–1028.

Beath, Andrew, Fotini Christia, and Ruben Enikolopov. 2013a. Democratization, Division of Responsibilities and Governance Quality: Experimental Evidence on Local Institutions in Afghanistan. Available at http://econ-server.umd.edu/~davis/eventpapers/EnikolopovDemo.pdf; last access September 20, 2018. Cambridge, MA: MIT.

   2013b. Empowering Women through Development Aid: Evidence from a Field Experiment in Afghanistan. *American Political Science Review* 107 (03): 540–557.

Beber, Bernd, Michael J. Gilligan, Jenny Guardado, and Sabrina Karim. 2019. The Promise and Peril of Peacekeeping Economies. *International Studies Quarterly* 63 (2): 364–379.

Beisheim, Marianne, Tanja A. Börzel, Philipp Genschel, and Bernhard Zangl. 2011a. Einleitung: Der staatliche Beitrag zu Governance in Räumen konso-lidierter und begrenzter Staatlichkeit. In *Wozu Staat? Governance in Räumen begrenzter und konsolidierter Staatlichkeit*, edited by Marianne Beisheim, Tanja A. Börzel, Philipp Genschel and Bernhard Zangl. Baden-Baden: Nomos, 11–32.

   2011b. Governance jenseits des Staates. Das Zusammenspiel staatlicher und nicht-staatlicher Governance. In *Wozu Staat? Governance in Räumen begrenzter und konsolidierter Staatlichkeit*, edited by Marianne Beisheim, Tanja A. Börzel, Philipp Genschel and Bernhard Zangl. Baden-Baden: Nomos, 251–265.

Beisheim, Marianne, Tanja A. Börzel, Philipp Genschel, and Bernhard Zangl, eds. 2011c. *Wozu Staat? Governance in Räumen begrenzter und konsolidierter Staatlichkeit*. Baden-Baden: Nomos.

Beisheim, Marianne, and Sabine Campe. 2012. Transnational Public–private Partnerships' Performance in Water Governance: Institutional Design Matters. *Environment and Planning C: Government and Policy* 30 (4): 627–642.

Beisheim, Marianne, and Klaus Dingwerth. 2010. The Link between Standard-setting NGOs' Legitimacy and Effectiveness: An Exploration of Social Mechanisms. In *Evaluating Transnational NGOs. Legitimacy, Accountability, Representation*, edited by Jens Steffek and Kristina Hahn. Basingstoke: Palgrave Macmillan, 74–99.

Beisheim, Marianne, Annekathrin Ellersiek, and Jasmin Lorch. 2018. INGOs and Multi-Stakeholder Partnerships. In *The Oxford Handbook of Governance and Limited Statehood*, edited by Thomas Risse, Tanja A. Börzel and Anke Draude. Oxford: Oxford University Press, 210–230.

Beisheim, Marianne, Hannah Janetschek, and Joahanna Sarre. 2014. What's the 'Best Fit'? Partnership Project Design and Its Influence on Effectiveness. In *Transnational Partnerships. Effectively Providing for Sustainable Development*, edited by Marianne Beisheim and Andrea Liese. Basingstoke: Palgrave Macmillan, 161–189.

Beisheim, Marianne, and Christopher Kaan. 2010. Transnational Standard-Setting Partnerships in the Field of Social Rights: The Interplay of Legitimacy, Institutional Design, and Process Management. In *Democracy and Public-Private Partnerships in Global Governance*, edited by Magdalena Bexell and Ulrika Mörth. Basingstoke: Palgrave Macmillan, 122–144.

Beisheim, Marianne, and Andrea Liese. 2014a. Summing Up: Key Findings and Avenues for Future Research. In *Transnational Partnerships. Effectively Providing for Sustainable Development?*, edited by Marianne Beisheim and Andrea Liese. Basingstoke: Palgrave Macmillan, 193–216.

Beisheim, Marianne, and Andrea Liese, eds. 2014b. *Transnational Partnerships. Effectively Providing for Sustainable Development?* Basingstoke: Palgrave Macmillan.

Beisheim, Marianne, Andrea Liese, Hannah Janetschek, and Johanna Sarre. 2014. Transnational Partnerships: Conditions for Successful Service Provision in Areas of Limited Statehood. *Governance* 27 (4): 655–673.

Beisheim, Marianne, Andrea Liese, and Jasmin Lorch. 2014. Introduction: Transnational Partnerships for Sustainable Development. In *Transnational Partnerships. Effectively Providing for Sustainable Development?*, edited by Marianne Beisheim and Andrea Liese. Basingstoke: Palgrave Macmillan, 3–16.

Beisheim, Marianne, Andrea Liese, and Christian Vosseler. 2014. Who Governs Partnerships? On the Role of Boards, Donors, Partners, and Other Stakeholders. In *Transnational Partnerships. Effectively Providing for Sustainable Development?*, edited by Marianne Beisheim and Andrea Liese. Basingstoke: Palgrave Macmillan, 107–127.

Belgioioso, Margherita, Jessica Di Salvatore, and Jonathan Pinckney. 2020. Tangled up in Blue: The Effect of UN Peacekeeping on Nonviolent Protests in Post-Civil War Countries. *International Studies Quarterly* 0: 1-15. DOI: 10.1093/isq/sqaa015.

Bellamy, Alex J. 2011. *Global Politics and the Responsibility to Protect*. London: Routledge.

Bellamy, Alex J., and Paul D. Williams. 2012. Local Politics and International Partnerships: The UN Operation in Côte d'Ivoire (UNOCI). *Journal of International Peacekeeping* 16 (3–4): 252–281.

Bendel, Petra, Aurel Croissant, and Friedbert W. Rüb, eds. 2002. *Hybride Regime. Zur Konzeption und Empirie demokratischer Grauzonen*. Opladen: Leske & Budrich.

Benner, Thorsten, Charlotte Streck, and Jan Martin Witte. 2003. *Progress or Peril? Networks and Partnerships in Global Environmental Governance: The Post-Johannesburg Agenda*. Berlin: Global Public Policy Institute.

Benz, Arthur. 2001. *Der moderne Staat. Grundlagen der politologischen Analyse*. München-Wien: Oldenbourg.

    2004a. *Governance – Regieren in komplexen Regelsystemen*. Wiesbaden: VS Verlag für Sozialwissenschaften.

    2004b. Multilevel Governance – Governance in Mehrebenensystemen. In *Governance – Regieren in komplexen Regelsystemen*, edited by Arthur Benz. Wiesbaden: VS Verlag für Sozialwissenschaften, 125–146.

Benz, Arthur, and Iannis Papadopoulos, eds. 2006. *Governance and Democracy. Comparing National, European, and International Experiences*. London et al.: Routledge.

Berger, Tobias. 2017. *Global Norms and Local Courts. Translating 'the Rule of Law' in Bangladesh*. Oxford: Oxford University Press.

Berger, Tobias, and Milli Lake. 2018. Human Rights, Rule of Law, and Democracy. In *The Oxford Handbook of Governance and Limited Statehood*, edited by Thomas Risse, Tanja A. Börzel and Anke Draude. Oxford: Oxford University Press, 416–437.

Berman, Eli. 2009. *Radical, Religious, Violent: The New Economics of Terrorism*. Cambridge, MA: MIT Press.

Bernstein, Steven, and Benjamin Cashore. 2007. Can Non-State Global Governance be Legitimate? An Analytical Framework. *Regulation and Governance* 1 (4): 347–371.

Berti, Benedetta. 2013. *Armed Political Organizations. From Conflict to Integration*. Baltimore MD: Johns Hopkins University Press.

    2016. Rebel politics and the state: between conflict and post-conflict, resistance and co-existence. *Civil Wars* 18 (2): 118–136.

    2018. Violent and Criminal Non-State Actors. In *The Oxford Handbook of Governance and Limited Statehood*, edited by Thomas Risse, Tanja A. Börzel and Anke Draude. Oxford: Oxford University Press, 272–290.

Berti, Benedetta, and Beatriz Gutiérrez. 2016. Rebel-to-political and back? Hamas as a security provider in Gaza between rebellion, politics and governance. *Democratization* 23 (6): 1059–1076.

Besley, Timothy, and Torsten Persson. 2010. State Capacity, Conflict, and Development. *Econometrica* 78 (1): 1–34.

Bevir, Mark. 2008. *Key Concepts in Governance*. London: Sage.

Bevir, Mark, ed. 2011. *The SAGE Handbook of Governance*. London: Sage.

Biermann, Rafael. 2013. Secessionism, Irredentism and EU Enlargement to the Western Balkans: Squaring the Circle? In *European Integration and Transformation in the Western Balkans: Europeanization or Business as Usual?*, edited by Arolda Elbasani. London: Routledge, 157–169.

Bierschenk, Thomas. 2014. Sedimentation, Fragmentation, and Normative Double-Binds in (West) African Public Services. In *States at Work.*

Dynamics of African Bureaucracies, edited by Thomas Bierschenk and Jean-Pierre Olivier De Sardan. Leiden-Boston: Brill, 221–245.

Bierschenk, Thomas, and Jean-Pierre Olivier De Sardan, eds. 2014. *States at Work. Dynamics of African Bureaucracies*. Leiden-Boston: Brill.

Bitzer, Jürgen, and Erkan Gören. 2018. Foreign Aid and Subnational Development. A Grid Cell Analysis. AidData Working Papers. Williamsburg, VA: College of Williams and Mary, June.

Black, Nicky. 2006. Business Actions on Human Rights: Doing No Harm, Good Works, and Good Business in the Developing World. Cooperate Citizenship in Developing Countries. In *Corporate Citizenship in Developing Countries. New Partnership Perspectives*, edited by Mahad Huniche and Esben Rahbeck Pedersen. Copenhagen: Copenhagen Business School Press, 57–88.

Blair, Robert A. 2019. International Intervention and the Rule of Law after Civil War: Evidence from Liberia. *International Organization* 73 (2): 365–398.

Blair, Robert A., and Pablo Kalmanovitz. 2016. On the Rights of Warlords: Legitimate Authority and Basic Protection in War-Torn Societies. *American Political Science Review* 110 (3): 428–440.

Blair, Robert A., and Philip Roessler. 2018. The Effects of Chinese Aid on State Legitimacy in Africa: Cross-National and Sub-National Evidence from Surveys, Survey Experiments, and Behavioural Games. AidData Working Papers. Williamsburg VA: College of William and Mary, July.

Blaxland, John, ed. 2015. *East Timor Intervention: A Retrospective on INTERFET*. Melbourne: Melbourne University Publishing.

Böckenförde, Ernst Wilhelm. 1976. Die Bedeutung der Unterscheidung von Staat und Gesellschaft im demokratischen Sozialstaat der Gegenwart. In *Staat, Gesellschaft, Freiheit*, edited by Ernst Wilhelm Böckenförde. Frankfurt am Main, 395–431.

Boddewyn, Jean J., and Thomas L. Brewer. 1994. International-business Political Behavior: New Theoretical Directions. *Academy of Management Review* 19 (1): 119–143.

Boege, Volker. 2014. Vying for Legitimacy in Post-conflict Situations: The Bougainville Case. *Peacebuilding* 2 (3): 237–252.

Boeke, Sergei, and Bart Schuurman. 2015. Operation 'Serval': A Strategic Analysis of the French Intervention in Mali, 2013–2014. *Journal of Strategic Studies* 38 (6): 801–825.

Böhnke, Jan R., Jan Koehler, and Christoph Zürcher. 2015. Assessing the Impact of Development Cooperation in North East Afghanistan 2007–2013. Final Report. Bonn – Berlin: Federal Ministry for Economic Cooperation and Development.

Böhnke, Jan R. 2017. State Formation as It Happens: Insights from a Repeated Crosssectional Study of Afghanistan, 2007–2015. *Conflict, Security & Development*.

Boix, Carles. 2011. Democracy, Development, and the International System. *American Political Science Review* 105 (4): 809–828.

2015. *Political Order and Inequality. Their Foundations and Their Consequences for Human Welfare*. Cambridge, UK: Cambridge University Press.

Bone, Andrew. 2004. Conflict diamonds: The De Beers Group and the Kimberley Process. In *Business and Security*, edited by Alyson Bailes and Isabel Frommelt. Oxford: Oxford University Press, 129–147.

Booth, David. 2012. Aid Effectiveness: Bringing Country Ownership (and Politics) Back In. *Conflict, Security & Development* 12 (5): 537–558.

Börzel, Tanja A. 2007. European Governance – Verhandlungen im Schatten von Hierarchie und Wettbewerb. In *Die Europäische Union: Governance und Policy-Making, PVS – Politische Vierteljahresschrift, Sonderheft 2007/2*, edited by Ingeborg Tömmel. Wiesbaden: VS Verlag für Sozialwissenschaften, 61–91.

———. 2008. Der "Schatten der Hierarchie" – Ein Governance-Paradox? In *Governance in einer sich wandelnden Welt. PVS – Politische Vierteljahresschrift, Sonderheft 41*, edited by Gunnar Folke Schuppert and Michael Zürn. Wiesbaden: VS Verlag für Sozialwissenschaften, 118–131.

———. 2010a. European Governance – Negotiation and Competition in the Shadow of Hierarchy. *Journal of Common Market Studies* 48 (2): 191–219.

———. 2010b. Governance with or without the State? In *The Twilight of Constitutionalism?*, edited by Martin Loughlin and Petra Dobner. Oxford: Oxford University Press, 73–88.

———. 2010c. Governance with/out Government – False Promises or Flawed Premises? SFB Working Papers. Sonderforschungsbereich 700, Freie Universität Berlin (23).

———. 2012. How Much Statehood Does It Take – And What For? SFB Working Papers. Sonderforschungsbereich 700, Freie Universität Berlin (29).

———. 2013. Comparative Regionalism: European Integration and Beyond. In *Handbook of International Relations*, edited by Walter Carlsnaes, Thomas Risse and Beth A. Simmons. London: Sage, 503–530.

———. 2016. Building Member States. How the EU Promotes Political Change in Its New Members, Accession Candidates, and Eastern Neighbours. *Geopolitics, History, and International Relations* 8 (1): 76–112.

———. 2020. *Why Non-Compliance? The Politics of Law in the European Union*. Ithaca, NY: Cornell University Press.

Börzel, Tanja A., and Nicole Deitelhoff. 2018. Business. In *The Oxford Handbook of Governance and Limited Statehood*, edited by Thomas Risse, Tanja A. Börzel and Anke Draude. Oxford: Oxford University Press, 250–271.

Börzel, Tanja A., and Sonja Grimm. 2018. Building Good (Enough) Governance in Post-conflict Societies and Areas of Limited Statehood: The European Union and the Western Balkans. *Daedalus* 147 (1): 116–127.

Börzel, Tanja A., and Christine Hackenesch. 2013. Small Carrots, Few Sticks: EU Good Governance Promotion in Sub-Saharan Africa. *Cambridge Review of International Affairs* 26 (3): 536–555.

Börzel, Tanja A., and Ralph Hamann, eds. 2013. *Business and Climate Change Governance. South Africa in Comparative Perspective*. Basingstoke: Palgrave Macmillan.

Börzel, Tanja A., Adrienne Héritier, Nicole Kranz, and Christian Thauer. 2011. Racing to the Top? Regulatory Competition Among Firms in Areas of Limited Statehood. In *Governance Without a State? Policies and Politics in*

Areas of Limited Statehood, edited by Thomas Risse. New York: Columbia University Press, 144–170.

Börzel, Tanja A., Tobias Hofmann, Diana Panke, and Carina Sprungk. 2010. Obstinate and Inefficient. Why Member States Do Not Comply With European Law. *Comparative Political Studies* 43 (11): 1363–1390.

Börzel, Tanja A., and Jana Hönke. 2011. From Compliance to Practice. Mining Companies and the Voluntary Principles on Security and Human Rights in the Democratic Republic of Congo. SFB Working Papers. Sonderforschungsbereich 700, Freie Universität Berlin (25).

2012. *Security and Human Rights. Mining Companies between International Commitment and Corporate Practice*. Baden-Baden: Nomos.

Börzel, Tanja A., Jana Hönke, and Christian R. Thauer. 2012. Does It Really Take The State: Limited Statehood, Multinational Corporations, and Corporate Social Responsibility in South America. *Business and Politics* 14 (3): 1–32.

Börzel, Tanja A., and Bidzina Lebanidze. 2017. The Transformative Power of Europe" Beyond Enlargement: The EU's Performance in Promoting Democracy in Its Neighborhood. *East European Politics* 33 (1): 17–35.

Börzel, Tanja A., and Yasemin Pamuk. 2012. Pathologies of Europeanization. Fighting Corruption in the Southern Caucasus. *West European Politics* 35 (1).

Börzel, Tanja A., and Thomas Risse. 2005. Public-Private Partnerships. Effective and Legitimate Tools of Transnational Governance? In *Complex Sovereignty: On the Reconstitution of Political Authority in the 21st Century*, edited by Edgar Grande and Louis W. Pauly. Toronto: University of Toronto Press, 195–216.

2010. Governance Without a State – Can It Work? *Regulation and Governance* 4 (2): 113–134.

2013. Human Rights in Areas of Limited Statehood: The New Agenda. In *The Persistent Power of Human Rights. From Commitment to Compliance*, edited by Thomas Risse, Stephen S. Ropp, and Kathryn Sikkink. Cambridge, UK: Cambridge University Press, 63–84.

2016. Dysfunctional State Institutions, Trust, and Governance in Areas of Limited Statehood. *Regulation & Governance* 10 (2): 149–160.

Börzel, Tanja A., Thomas Risse, and Anke Draude. 2018. Governance in Areas of Limited Statehood: Conceptual Clarifications and Major Contributions of the Handbook. In *The Oxford Handbook of Governance and Limited Statehood*, edited by Thomas Risse, Tanja A. Börzel, and Anke Draude. Oxford: Oxford University Press, 3–25.

Börzel, Tanja A., and Frank Schimmelfennig. 2017. Coming Together or Driving Apart? The EU's Political Integration Capacity in Eastern Europe. *Journal of European Public Policy* 24 (2): 278–296.

Börzel, Tanja A., and Sören Stapel. 2015. Mapping Governance Transfer by 12 Regional Organizations. A Global Script in Regional Colors. In *Governance Transfer by Regional Organizations. Patching Together a Global Script*, edited by Tanja A. Börzel and Vera van Hüllen. Basingstoke: Palgrave Macmillan, 22–50.

Börzel, Tanja A., and Christian Thauer, eds. 2013. *Business and Governance in South Africa. Racing to the Top?* Basingstoke: Palgrave Macmillan.

Börzel, Tanja A., Christian R. Thauer, and Jana Hönke. 2013. Racing to the Top? In *Business and Governance in South Africa. Racing to the Top?*, edited by Tanja A. Börzel and Christian R. Thauer. Basingstoke: Palgrave Macmillan, 215–246.

Börzel, Tanja A., and Vera van Hüllen. 2014. State-Building and the European Union's Fight against Corruption in the Southern Caucasus: Why Legitimacy Matters. *Governance* 27 (4): 613–634.

Börzel, Tanja A., and Vera van Hüllen, eds. 2015a. *Governance Transfer by Regional Organizations. Patching Together a Global Script.* Basingstoke: Palgrave Macmillan.

2015b. Towards a Global Script? Governance Transfer by Regional Organizations. In *Governance Transfer by Regional Organizations. Patching Together a Global Script*, edited by Tanja A. Börzel and Vera van Hüllen. Basingstoke: Palgrave Macmillan, 3–21.

Botchway, Karl. 2001. Paradox of Empowerment: Reflections on a Case Study from Northern Ghana. *World Development* 29 (1): 135–153.

Bourdillon, Michael F. C. 1987. *The Shona Peoples: An Ethnography of the Contemporary Shona, with Special Reference to Their Religion.* Vol. 1. Harare: Mambo Press.

Bradbury, Mark. 2008. *Becoming Somaliland.* Bloomington, IN: Indiana University Press.

Braig, Marianne, and Ruth Stanley. 2007. Die Polizei – (k)ein Freund und Helfer? Die Governance der öffentlichen Sicherheit in Buenos Aires und Mexiko-Stadt. In *Regieren ohne Staat? Governance in Räumen begrenzter Staatlichkeit*, edited by Thomas Risse and Ursula Lehmkuhl. Baden-Baden: Nomos, 223–243.

Braithwaite, Valerie A., and Margaret Levi, eds. 1998. *Trust and Governance.* New York: Russell Sage Foundation.

Branch, Daniel. 2009. *Defeating Mau Mau, Creating Kenya: Counterinsurgency, Civil War, and Decolonization.* Cambridge, UK: Cambridge University Press.

Brandel, Andrew, and Shalini Randeria. 2018. Anthropological Perspectives on the Limits of the State. In *The Oxford Handbook of Governance and Limited Statehood*, edited by Thomas Risse, Tanja A. Börzel and Anke Draude. Oxford: Oxford University Press, 68–88.

Bratton, Michael. 1989. The Politics of Government-NGO Relations in Africa. *World Development* 17 (4): 569–587.

Bratton, Michael, and Nicolas van de Walle. 1994. Neopatrimonial Regimes and Political Transitions in Africa. *World Politics* 46 (4): 453–489.

1997. *Democratic Experiments in Africa.* Cambridge, UK: Cambridge University Press.

Bräutigam, Deborah A. 1992. Governance, Economy, and Foreign Aid. *Studies In Comparative International Development and Change* 27 (3): 3–25.

Bräutigam, Deborah A., and Stephen Knack. 2004. Foreign Aid, Institutions, and Governance in Sub-Saharan Africa. *Economic Development and Cultural Change* 52 (2): 255–285.

Brett, Edwin A. 1996. The Participatory Principle in Development Projects: The Costs and Benefits of Cooperation. *Public Administration and Development* 16 (1): 5–19.

Brewer, Marilynn B. 1981. Ethnocentrism and Its Role in Interpersonal Trust. In *Scientific Inquiry and the Social Sciences*, edited by Marilynn B. Brewer and Barry E. Collins. San Francisco: Jossey-Bass, 214–231.

2001. The Many Faces of Social Identity: Implications for Social Psychology. *Political Psychology* 22 (1): 115–125.

Briggs, Ryan C. 2016. Does Foreign Aid Target the Poorest? *International Organization* 71 (1): 187–206.

Brinkerhoff, Derick W., and Jennifer M. Brinkerhoff. 2002. Governance Reforms and Failed States: Challenges and Implications. *International Review of Administrative Services* 68 (4): 511–531.

Brinkerhoff, Jennifer M. 2002. *Partnership for International Development: Rhetoric or Results?* Boulder, CO: Lynne Rienner Publishers.

Brixi, Hana, Ellen Lust, and Michael Woolcock. 2015. Trust. Voice, and Incentives. Learning from Local Success Stories in Service Delivery in the Middle East and North Africa. Washington, DC: International Bank for Reconstruction and Development - The World Bank.

Brockmeier, Sarah, and Philipp Rotmann. 2018. Changing security governance. Lessons for External Support from Southeast Asia, Southern Africa, and Latin America. International Policy Analysis. Berlin: Friedrich Ebert Foundation.

Brosig, Malte, and Norman Sempijja. 2017. What Peacekeeping Leaves Behind: Evaluating the Effects of Multi-dimensional Peace Operations in Africa. *Conflict, Security & Development* 17 (1): 21–52.

Brown, L. David. 1998. Creating Social Capital: Nongovernmental Development Organizations and Intersectoral Problem Solving. In *Private Action and the Public Good*, edited by Walter W. Powell and Elisabeth S. Clemens. New Haven, CT: Yale University Press, 228–241.

Brown, L. David, and Mark H. Moore. 2001. Accountability, Strategy, and International Nongovernmental Organizations. *Nonprofit and Voluntary Sector Quarterly* 30 (3): 569–587.

Brozus, Lars. 2007. Governance in Räumen begrenzter Staatlichkeit als Problem der Politik. In *Regieren ohne Staat? Governance in Räumen begrenzter Staatlichkeit*, edited by Thomas Risse and Ursula Lehmkuhl. Baden-Baden: Nomos, 374–391.

2011. Applying the Governance Concept to Areas of Limited Statehood: Implications for International Foreign and Security Policy. In *Governance Without a State? Policies and Politics in Areas of Limited Statehood*, edited by Thomas Risse. New York: Columbia University Press, 262–280.

Brozus, Lars, Christian Jetzlsperger, and Gregor Walter-Drop. 2018. Policy. In *The Oxford Handbook of Governance and Limited Statehood*, edited by Thomas Risse, Tanja A. Börzel and Anke Draude. Oxford: Oxford University Press, 584–603.

Brühl, Tanja. 2007. Public–private Partnerships: Unlike Partners? Assessing New Forms of Regulation. In *Globalization. State of the Art and Perspectives*, edited by Stefan A. Schirm. London: Routledge, 143–161.

Brühl, Tanja, Tobias Debiel, Brigitte Hamm, Hartwig Hummel, and Jens Martens, eds. 2001. *Die Privatisierung der Weltpolitik. Entstaatlichung und Kommerzialisierung im Globalisierungsprozess.* Bonn: Dietz Verlag.

Bruijn, Eveline, and Gail Whiteman. 2010. That Which Doesn't Break Us: Identity Work by Local Indigenous 'Stakeholders'. *Journal of Business Ethics* 96 (3): 479–495.

Bryden, Matt. 2004. State-Within-a-Failed-State: Somaliland and the Challenge of International Recognition. In *States-Within-States: Incipient Political Entities in the Post-Cold War Era*, edited by Paul Kingston and Ian S. Spears. Basingstoke: Palgrave Macmillan, 167–188.

Brysk, Alison. 1993. From Above and From Below: Social Movements, the International System, and Human Rights in Argentina. *Comparative Political Studies* 26 (3): 259–285.

Buhaug, Halvard, and Päivi Lujala. 2005. Accounting for scale: Measuring geography in quantitative studies of civil war. *Political Geography* 24 (4): 399–418.

Bull, Benedicte, and Desmond McNeill. 2007. *Development Issues in Global Governance: Public-private Partnerships and Market Multilateralism.* London: Routledge.

Bull, Hedley. 1977. *The Anarchical Society. A Study of Order in World Politics.* New York: Columbia University Press.

Burges, Sean W. 2014. Brazil's International Development Co-operation: Old and New Motivations. *Development Policy Review* 32 (3): 355–374.

Bustillos, Lorena Ossio. 2015. Bolivia: Normative Equality between State and Customary Law. Utopia or the Future of Hybrid Normative Systems? In *Non-State Justice Institutions and the Law. Decision-Making at the Interface of Tradition, Religion, and the State*, edited by Matthias Kötter, Tilmann J. Röder, Gunnar Folke Schuppert and Rüdiger Wolfrum. Basingstoke: Palgrave Macmillan, 100–120.

Büthe, Tim, Solomon Major, and André de Mello e Souza. 2012. The Politics of Private Foreign Aid: Humanitarian Principles, Economic Development Objectives, and Organizational Interests in NGO Private Aid Allocation. *International Organization* 66 (4): 571–607.

Büthe, Tim, and Walter Mattli. 2011. *The New Global Rulers: The Privatization of Regulation in the World Economy.* Princeton, NJ: Princeton University Press.

Buur, Lars, and Helen Kyed. 2007. *State Recognition and Democratization in Sub-Saharan Africa: A New Dawn for Traditional Authorities?* New York: Springer.

Buzan, Barry, Ole Waever, and Jan de Wilde. 1998. *Security. A New Framework for Analysis.* Boulder CO: Lynne Rienner.

Buzasi, Katalin. 2014. Languages, communication potential and generalized trust in Sub-Saharan Africa: Evidence based on the Afrobarometer Survey. *Social Science Research* 49: 141–155.

Byrne, David. 2009. Complex Realist and Configurational Approaches to Cases: A Radical Synthesis. In *The Sage Handbook of Case-Based Methods*, edited by David Byrne and Charles C. Ragin. London: Sage, 101–112.

Call, Charles T. 2012. *Why Peace Fails: The Causes and Prevention of Civil War Recurrence.* Washington, DC: Georgetown University Press.

Cammett, Melani. 2014. *Compassionate Communalism: Welfare and Sectarianism in Lebanon.* Ithaca, NY: Cornell University Press.

Campbell, Susanna P. 2018. *Global Governance and Local Peace. Accountability and Performance in International Peacebuilding.* Cambridge, UK: Cambridge University Press.

Campbell, Susanna P., Matthew DiGiuseppe, and Amanda Murdie. 2019. International Development NGOs and Bureaucratic Capacity: Facilitator or Destroyer? *Political Research Quarterly* 72 (1): 3–18.

Cao, Xun, Haiyan Duan, Chuyu Liu, and Yingjie Wei. 2018. Local Religious Institutions and the Impact of Interethnic Inequality on Conflict. *International Studies Quarterly* 62 (4): 765–781.

Caris, Charles C., and Samuel Reynolds. 2014. ISIS Governance in Syria. Middle East Security Report 22. Washington, DC: Institute for the Study of War.

Carment, David. 2003. Assessing State Failure: Implications for Theory and Policy. *Third World Quarterly* 24 (3): 407–427.

Carment, David, Joe Landry, Yiagadeesen Samy, and Scott Shaw. 2015. Towards a Theory of Fragile State Transitions: Evidence from Yemen, Bangladesh and Laos. *Third World Quarterly* 36 (7): 1316–1332.

Chan, Anita, and Robert J. Ross. 2003. Racing to the Bottom. Industrial Trade without a Social Clause. *Third World Quarterly* 24 (6): 1011–1028.

Chandra, Kanchan. 2004. *Why Ethnic Parties Succeed. Patronage and Ethnic Head Counts in India.* Cambridge, UK: Cambridge University Press.

Charbonneau, Bruno, and Jonathan M Sears. 2014. Fighting for Liberal Peace in Mali? The Limits of International Military Intervention. *Journal of Intervention and Statebuilding* 8 (2–3): 192–213.

Chayes, Abram, and Antonia Handler Chayes. 1991. Compliance Without Enforcement: State Behaviour Under Regulatory Treaties. *Negotiation Journal* 7 (July): 311–330.

1993. On Compliance. *International Organization* 47 (2): 175–205.

1995. *The New Sovereignty. Compliance with International Regulatory Agreements.* Cambridge, MA: Harvard University Press.

Checkel, Jeffrey T. 1998. The Constructivist Turn in International Relations Theory. *World Politics* 50 (2): 324–348.

2005. International Institutions and Socialization in Europe: Introduction and Framework. *International Organization* 59 (4): 801–826.

Chojnacki, Sven, and Zeljko Branovic. 2011. New Modes of Security. The Violent Making and Unmaking of Governance in War-Torn Areas of Limited Statehood. In *Governance without a State? Policies and Politics in Areas of Limited Statehood*, edited by Thomas Risse. New York: Columbia University Press, 89–114.

Chowdhury, Arjun. 2018. *The Myth of International Order: Why Weak States Persist and Alternatives to the State Fade Away.* Oxford: Oxford University Press.

Chuhan-Pole, Punam, Andrew L. Dabalen, and Bryan Christopher Land. 2017. *Mining in Africa: Are Local Communities Better Off?* Washington, DC: World Bank Publications.

Cingolani, Luciana. 2013. The State of State Capacity: A Review of Concepts, Evidence and Measures. Working Paper Series on Institutions and Economic Growth. Maastricht: The United Nations University – Maastricht Economic and Social Research Institute on Innovation and Technology.

Civelli, Andrea, Andrew Horowitz, and Arilton Teixeira. 2017. Foreign Aid and Growth at the Sub-National Level. AidData Working Papers. Williamsburg VA: College of William and Mary, March.

Clapp, Jennifer. 2015. *Hunger in The Balance: The New Politics of International Food Aid*. Ithaca, NY: Cornell University Press.

Clark, Ian. 2005. *Legitimacy in International Society*. Oxford: Oxford University Press.

Clark, Phil. 2008. Ethnicity, Leadership and Conflict Mediation in Eastern Democratic Republic of Congo: The Case of the Barza Inter-Communautaire. *Journal of Eastern African Studies* 2 (1): 1–17.

Clunan, Anne L., and Harold A. Trinkunas, eds. 2010. *Ungoverned Spaces. Alternatives to State Authority in an Era of Softened Sovereignty*. Stanford, CA: Stanford University Press.

Coggins, Bridget L. 2015. Rebel Diplomacy: Theorizing Violent Non-State Actors' Strategic Use of Talk. In *Rebel Governance in Civil War*, edited by Ana Arjona, Nelson Kasfir and Zachariah Mampilly. Cambridge, UK: Cambridge University Press, 98–118.

Cole, Wade M. 2015. Mind the Gap: State Capacity and the Implementation of Human Rights Treaties. *International Organization* 69 (02): 405–441.

Coleman, Katharina P. 2007. *International Organisations and Peace Enforcement: The Politics of International Legitimacy*. Cambridge, UK: Cambridge University Press.

Collier, Paul. 2007. *The Bottom Billion: Why the Poorest Countries are Failing and What Can Be Done about It*. Oxford: Oxford University Press.

Collier, Paul, and Anke Hoeffler. 2004. Greed and Grievance in Civil War. *Oxford Economic Papers* 56 (4): 563–595.

Coni-Zimmer, Melanie. 2014. *Corporate Social Responsibility zwischen globaler Diffusion und Lokalisierung*. Baden-Baden: Nomos.

Connell, John, and Richard Howitt. 1991. Mining, Dispossession and Development. In *Mining and Indigenous People in Australasia*, edited by John Connell and Richard Howitt. Sydney: Sydney University Press, 1–17.

Connery, David. 2013. *Crisis Policymaking: Australia and the East Timor Crisis of 1999*. Canberra: ANU Press.

Conrad, Sebastian, and Shalini Randeria, eds. 2013. *Jenseits des Eurozentrismus. Postkoloniale Perspektiven in den Geschichts- und Kulturwissenschaften. 2nd rev. ed.* Frankfurt am Main: Campus.

Conrad, Sebastian, and Marion Stange. 2011. Governance and Colonial Rule. In *Governance without a State? Policies and Politics in Areas of Limited Statehood*, edited by Thomas Risse. New York: Columbia University Press, 39–64.

Conzelmann, Thomas, and Klaus Dieter Wolf. 2007. Doing Good While Doing Well? Potenziale und Grenzen grenzüberschreitender privatwirtschaftlicher Selbstregulierung. In *Macht und Ohnmacht internationaler Institutionen*, edited by Andreas Hasenclever, Klaus Dieter Wolf and Michael Zürn. Frankfurt am Main: Campus, 145–175.

Cook, Fay Lomax, Lawrence R. Jacobs, and Dukhong Kim. 2010. Trusting What You Know: Information, Knowledge, and Confidence in Social Security. *The Journal of Politics* 72 (2): 397–412.

Cortright, David, Conor Seyle, and Kristen Wall. 2017. *Governance for Peace: How Inclusive, Participatory and Accountable Institutions Promote Peace and Prosperity*. Cambridge, UK: Cambridge University Press.

Coser, Lewis A. 1956. *Functions of Social Conflict*. London: Routledge and Kegan Paul.

Crescenzi, Mark. 2018. *Of Friends and Foes: Reputation and Learning in International Politics*. Oxford: Oxford University Press.

Cross, Charlotte. 2016. Ulinzi Shirikishi: Popular Experiences of Hybrid Security Governance in Tanzania. *Development and Change* 47 (5): 1102–1124.

Curtis, Mark. 2016. *Gated Development. Is the Gates Foundation always a force for good?* London: Global Justice Now.

Cust, James, and Steven Poelhekke. 2015. The Local Economic Impacts of Natural Resource Extraction. *Annual Review of Resource Economics* 7 (1): 251–268.

Cutler, Claire A. 2003. *Private Power and Global Authority: Transnational Merchant Law and the Global Political Economy*. Cambridge, UK: Cambridge University Press.

2006. Transnational Business Civilization, Corporations, and the Privatization of Global Governance. In *Global Corporate Power*, edited by Christopher May. Boulder, CO: Lynne Rienner, 199–225.

Cutler, Claire A., Virginia Haufler, and Tony Porter, eds. 1999. *Private Authority and International Affairs*. Albany NY: State University of New York Press.

Czempiel, Ernst-Otto. 1981. *Internationale Politik: Ein Konfliktmodell*. Paderborn: Schöningh.

Czempiel, Ernst-Otto, and James Rosenau, eds. 1992. *Governance without Government: Order and Change in World Politics*. Cambridge, UK: Cambridge University Press.

D'Arcy, Michelle, and Marina Nistotskaya. 2016. State First, Then Democracy: Using Cadastral Records to Explain Governmental Performance in Public Goods Provision. *Governance* 30 (2): 193–209.

D'Onofrio, Alexandra, and Giuseppe Maggio. 2015. Does Foreign Aid Fuel Trust? AidData Working Paper. Williamsburg VA: College of William and Mary, December.

Dandashly, Assem. 2015. The EU Response to Regime Change in the Wake of the Arab Revolt: Differential Implementation. *Journal of European Integration* 37 (1): 37–56.

Dashwood, Hevina S. 2012. *The Rise of Global Corporate Social Responsibility: Mining and the Spread of Global Norms*. Cambridge, UK: Cambridge University Press.

Davies, Mathew. 2013. ASEAN and Human Rights Norms: Constructivism, Rational Choice, and the Action-Identity Gap. *International Relations of the Asia-Pacific* 13 (2): 207–231.

Davis, Diane E. 2009. Non-state Armed Actors, New Imagined Communities, and Shifting Patterns of Sovereignty and Insecurity in the Modern World. *Contemporary Security Policy* 30 (2): 221–245.

Davis, Diane E., and Anthony W. Pereira, eds. 2003. *Irregular Armed Forces and Their Role in Politics and State Formation.* Cambridge, UK: Cambridge University Press.

De, Rajlakshmi, and Charles Becker. 2015. The Foreign Aid Effectiveness Debate: Evidence from Malawi. AidData Working Papers. Williamsburg VA: College of William and Mary, March.

De la Rosa, Sybille, Ulrike Höppner, and Matthias Kötter, eds. 2008. *Transdisziplinäre Governanceforschung. Gemeinsam hinter den Staat blicken.* Baden-Baden: Nomos.

De Sardan, Jean-Pierre Olivier. 2014. The Delivery State in Africa. Interface Bureaucrats, Professional Cultures and the Bureaucratic Mode of Governance. In *States at Work. Dynamics of African Bureaucracies,* edited by Thomas Bierschenk and Jean-Pierre Olivier De Sardan. Leiden-Boston: Brill, 399–429.

Debiel, Tobias, Rainer Glassner, Conrad Schetter, and Ulf Terlinden. 2009. Local State-Building in Afghanistan and Somaliland. *Peace Review: A Journal of Social Justice* 21: 38–44.

Deitelhoff, Nicole. 2010. Private Security and Military Companies: The Other Side of Business and Conflict. In *Corporate Security Responsibility? Corporate Governance Contributions to Peace and Security in Zones of Conflict,* edited by Nicole Deitelhoff and Klaus Dieter Wolf. Basingstoke: Palgrave Macmillan, 177–201.

Deitelhoff, Nicole, Moira Feil, Susanne Fischer, Andreas Haidvogt, Klaus Dieter Wolf, and Melanie Zimmer. 2010. Business in Zones of Conflict and Global Security Governance: What Has Been Learnt and Where to from Here? In *Corporate Security Responsibility? Corporate Governance Contributions to Peace and Security in Conflict Zones,* edited by Nicole Deitelhoff and Klaus Dieter Wolf. Basingstoke: Palgrave Macmillan, 202–226.

Deitelhoff, Nicole, and Anna Geis. 2010. Entkernt sich der Leviathan? Die organisatorische und funktionelle Umrüstung der Militär- und Verteidigungspolitik westlicher Demokratien. *Leviathan* 3/2010: 389–410.

Deitelhoff, Nicole, and Klaus Dieter Wolf, eds. 2010a. *Corporate Security Responsibility? Corporate Governance Contributions to Peace and Security in Conflict Zones.* Basingstoke: Palgrave Macmillan.

Deitelhoff, Nicole, and Klaus Dieter Wolf. 2010b. Corporate Security Responsibility? Corporate Governance Contributions to Peace and Security in Zones of Conflict. In *Corporate Security Responsibility? Corporate Governance Contributions to Peace and Security in Zones of Conflict,* edited by Nicole Deitelhoff and Klaus Dieter Wolf. Basingstoke: Palgrave Macmillan, 1–25.

2013. Business and Human Rights. How Corporate Norm Violators Become Norm Entrepreneurs. In *The Persistent Power of Human Rights. From Commitment to Compliance,* edited by Thomas Risse, Stephen C. Ropp and Kathryn Sikkink. Cambridge, UK: Cambridge University Press, 222–238.

Dembinski, Matthias, and Thorsten Gromes. 2017. Ein Datensatz der humanitären militärischen Interventionen nach dem Zweiten Weltkrieg. Forschung DSF. Osnabrück: Deutsche Stiftung Friedensforschung.

DeRouen, Karl, Mark J. Ferguson, Samuel Norton, Young Hwan Park, Jenna Lea, and Ashley Streat-Bartlett. 2010. Civil war peace agreement implementation and state capacity. *Journal of Peace Research* 47 (3): 333–346.

DeRouen, Karl R., and David Sobek. 2004. The Dynamics of Civil War Duration and Outcome. *Journal of Peace Research* 41 (3): 303–320.

Desai, Raj M., and Homi Kharas. 2018. What Motivates Private Foreign Aid? Evidence from Internet-Based Microlending. *International Studies Quarterly* 62 (3): 505–519.

Dewhurst, Sarah, and Lindsey Greising. 2017. The Gradual Emergence of Second Generation Security Sector Reform in Timor-Leste. CSG Papers. Kitchener, Ontario: Centre for Security Governance.

Dewhurst, Sarah, Joana Saraiva, and Bronwyn Winch. 2016. Assessing the Impact of Orthodox Security Sector Reform in Timor-Leste. CSG Papers. Kitchener, Ontario: Centre for Security Governance.

Díaz-Cayeros, Alberto, Beatriz Magaloni, and Alexander Ruiz Euler. 2014. Traditional Governance, Citizen Engagement, and Local Public Goods: Evidence from Mexico. *World Development* 53: 80–93.

Die Bundesregierung. 2017. Krisen verhindern, Konflikte bewältigen, Frieden fördern. Leitlinien der Bundesregierung. Berlin.

Diehl, Katharina, Ruben Madol Arol, and Simone Malz. 2015. South Sudan: Linking the Chiefs' Judicial Authority and the Statutory Court System. In *Non-State Justice Institutions and the Law. Decision-Making at the Interface of Tradition, Religion, and the State*, edited by Matthias Kötter, Tilmann J. Röder, Gunnar Folke Schuppert and Rüdiger Wolfrum. Basingstoke: Palgrave Macmillan, 55–79.

Dietrich, Simone. 2013. Bypass or Engage? Explaining Donor Delivery Tactics in Foreign Aid Allocation. *International Studies Quarterly* 57 (4): 698–712.

Dietrich, Simone, Minhaj Mahmud, and Matthew S. Winters. 2018. Foreign Aid, Foreign Policy, and Domestic Government Legitimacy: Experimental Evidence from Bangladesh. *The Journal of Politics* 80 (1): 133–148.

DiLorenzo, Matthew. 2018. Bypass Aid and Unrest in Autocracies. *International Studies Quarterly* 62 (1): 208–219.

Dingel, Eva. 2016. *Power Struggles in the Middle East: The Islamist Politics of Hizbullah and the Muslim Brotherhood*. London: IB Tauris.

Dingwerth, Klaus. 2007. *The New Transnationalism: Transnational Governance and Democratic Legitimacy*. Basingstoke: Palgrave Macmillan.

Distelhorst, Greg, Jens Hainmueller, and Richard M. Locke. 2016. Does Lean Improve Labor Standards? Management and Social Performance in the Nike Supply Chain. *Management Science* 63 (3): 707–728.

Dobbins, James, Keith Crane Jones, and Beth Cole DeGrasse. 2007. *The Beginner's Guide to Nation-Building*. Santa Monica, CA: RAND Corporation.

Dominguez, Jorge I. 2001. Samuel Huntington and the Latin American State. In *The Other Mirror. Grand Theory through the Lens of Latin America*, edited by Miguel Angel Centeno and Fernando Lopez-Alves. Princeton, NJ: Princeton University Press, 219–239.

Donais, Timothy. 2009a. Empowerment or Imposition? Dilemmas of Local Ownership in Post-Conflict Peacebuilding Processes. *Peace & Change* 34 (1): 3–26.

2009b. Inclusion or Exclusion? Local Ownership and Security Sector Reform. *Studies in Social Justice* 3 (1): 117–131.

Dorff, Robert H. 2005. Failed States after 9/11: What Did We Know and What Have We Learned? *International Studies Perspectives* 6 (1): 20–34.

Downs, George W., David M. Rocke, and Peter N. Barsoom. 1996. Is the Good News about Compliance Good News about Cooperation? *International Organization* 50 (3): 379–406.

Doyle, Michael W., and Nicholas Sambanis. 2000. International Peacebuilding: A Theoretical and Quantitative Analysis. *The American Political Science Review* 94 (4): 779–801.

2006. *Making War and Building Peace: United Nations Peace Operations.* Princeton, NJ: Princeton University Press.

Draude, Anke. 2007. Wer regiert wie? Für eine äquivalenzfunktionalistische Beobachtung von Governance in Räumen begrenzter Staatlichkeit. SFB Working Papers. Sonderforschungsbereich 700, Freie Universität Berlin (2).

2008. Wer regiert wie? Eurozentrismus in der Governanceforschung und der Versuch einer methodischen Grenzüberschreitung. In *Transdisziplinäre Governanceforschung. Gemeinsam hinter den Staat blicken*, edited by Sybille De La Rosa and Matthias Kötter. Baden-Baden: Nomos, 100–118.

2012. *Die Vielfalt des Regierens. Eine Governance-Konzeption jenseits des Eurozentrismus.* Frankfurt am Main: Campus.

Draude, Anke, Lasse Hölck, and Dietlind Stolle. 2018. Social Trust. In *The Oxford Handbook of Governance and Limited Statehood*, edited by Thomas Risse, Tanja A. Börzel and Anke Draude. Oxford: Oxford University Press, 353–372.

Dreher, Axel, Valentin Lang, and Sebastian Ziaja. 2018. Foreign Aid. In *The Oxford Handbook of Governance and Limited Statehood*, edited by Thomas Risse, Tanja A. Börzel and Anke Draude. Oxford: Oxford University Press, 394–415.

Dreher, Axel, and Steffen Lohmann. 2015. Aid and growth at the regional level. *Oxford Review of Economic Policy* 31 (3–4): 420–446.

Dunning, Thad, and Lauren Harrison. 2010. Cross-cutting Cleavages and Ethnic Voting: An Experimental Study of Cousinage in Mali. *American Political Science Review* 104 (1): 21–39.

Easton, David. 1953. *The Political System.* New York: Alfred A. Knopf.

1965. *A Systems Analysis of Political Life.* New York: Wiley & Sons.

1975. A Re-assessment of the Concept of Political Support. *British Journal of Political Science* 5 (4): 435–457.

Eckert, Julia. 2009. Rechtsaneignung: Paradoxien von Pluralisierung und Entpluralisierung in rechtspluralen Situationen. In *Normative Pluralität ordnen. Rechtsbegriffe, Normenkollisionen und Rule of Law in Kontexten dies- und jenseits des Staates*, edited by Matthias Kötter and Gunnar Folke Schuppert. Baden-Baden: Nomos, 191–206.

Eckhard, Steffen. 2016. Political Guidance or Autonomy in Peacebuilding? EU Police Reform in Afghanistan and Kosovo. *International Peacekeeping* 23 (3): 363–388.

Eden, Lorraine, and Stefanie Lenway. 2001. Introduction to the Symposium "Multinationals: The Janus Face of Globalization." *Journal of International Business Studies* 32 (3): 383–400.

Eichenhauer, Vera Z., Andreas Fuchs, and Lutz Brückner. 2018. The Effects of Trade, Aid, and Investment on China's Image in Developing Countries. AidData Working Papers. Williamsburg VA: College of William and Mary, June.

Eisenstadt, Shmuel Noah. ed. 2002. *Multiple Modernities*. New Brunswick, NJ: Transaction Publishers.

2007. *Multiple Modernities – A Paradigm of Cultural and Social Evolution, ProtoSociology – A Journal of Interdisciplinary Research Vol. 24*. Frankfurt am Main.

Elbasani, Arolda, ed. 2013. *European Integration and Transformation in the Western Balkans: Europeanization or Business as Usual?* London: Routledge.

Ellersiek, Annekathrin. 2018. Education. In *The Oxford Handbook of Governance and Limited Statehood*, edited by Thomas Risse, Tanja A. Börzel and Anke Draude. Oxford: Oxford University Press, 479–497.

Enderlein, Henrik, Sonja Wälti, and Michael Zürn, eds. 2010. *Handbook on Multilevel Governance*. Aldershot: Edward Elgar.

Englebert, Pierre. 2002. Born-again Buganda or the Limits of Traditional Resurgence in Africa. *The Journal of Modern African Studies* 40 (3): 345–368.

Epstein, Marc J. 2008. *Making Sustainability Work. Best Practices in Managing and Measuring Corporate Social, Environmental and Economic Impacts*. Sheffield: Greenleaf Publishing.

Erdmann, Gero. 2013. Neopatrimonialism and Political Regimes. In *Routledge Handbook of African Politics*, edited by Nic Cheeseman and Dave Anderson. London – New York: Routledge, 59–69.

Erdmann, Gero and Ulf Engel. 2007. Neopatrimonialism Reconsidered: Critical Review and Elaboration of an Elusive Concept. *Commonwealth & Comparative Politics* 45 (1): 95–119.

Eriksen, Stein Sundstol. 2011. 'State Failure' in Theory and Practice: The Idea of the State and the Contradictions of State Formation. *Review of International Studies* 37 (1): 229–247.

Esders, Stefan, Lasse Hölck, and Stefan Rinke. 2018. Histories of Governance. In *The Oxford Handbook of Governance and Limited Statehood*, edited by Thomas Risse, Tanja A. Börzel and Anke Draude. Oxford: Oxford University Press, 131–147.

Esguerra, Alessandro. 2014. The Politics of Beginning. An Inquiry into Transnational Governance in Action. PhD. Dissertation, Berlin Graduate School for Transnational Studies (BTS), Freie Universität Berlin, Berlin.

2017. 'A Comment That Might Help Us to Move Along': Brokers in Negotiation Systems. In *Sustainability Politics and Limited Statehood*, edited by Alessandro Esguerra, Nicole Helmerich and Thomas Risse. London – New York: Palgrave Macmillan, 25–46.

Fanthorpe, Richard. 2005. On the Limits of Liberal Peace: Chiefs and Democratic Decentralization in Post-war Sierra Leone. *African Affairs* 105 (418): 27–49.

Farooki, Masuma. 2012. The Infrastructure and Commodities Interface in Africa: Time for Cautious Optimism? *Journal of International Development* 24 (2): 208–219.

Faude, Benjamin. 2014. Zur Dynamik interorganisationaler Beziehungen: Wie aus Konkurrenz Arbeitsteilung entsteht. *Politische Vierteljahresschrift* 49: 294–321.

Fearon, James D., and David D. Laitin. 1996. Explaining Interethnic Cooperation. *American Political Science Review* 90 (4): 715–735.

2003. Ethnicity, Insurgency, and Civil War. *American Political Science Review* 97 (1): 75–90.

2004. Neotrusteeship and the Problem of Weak States. *International Security* 28 (4): 5–43.

Feil, Moira. 2011. *Global Governance and Corporate Responsibility in Conflict Zones.* Basingstoke: Palgrave Macmillan.

Felbab-Brown, Vanda. 2012. *Aspiration and Ambivalence: Strategies and Realities of Counterinsurgency and State-building in Afghanistan.* Washington, DC: Brookings Institution Press.

Felbab-Brown, Vanda, Harold Trinkunas, and Shadi Hamid. 2017. *Militants, Criminals, and Warlords: The Challenge of Local Governance in an Age of Disorder.* Washington, DC: Brookings Institution Press.

Feldman, Shelley. 2003. Paradoxes of Institutionalisation: The Depoliticisation of Bangladeshi NGOs. *Development in Practice* 13 (1): 5–26.

Finnemore, Martha. 1993. International Organization as Teachers of Norms: The United Nations Educational, Scientific, and Cultural Organization and Science Policy. *International Organization* 47 (4): 565–597.

1996. Norms, Culture, and World Politics: Insights From Sociology's Institutionalism. *International Organization* 50 (2): 325–347.

2003. *The Purpose of Intervention: Changing Beliefs about the Use of Force.* Ithaca, NY: Cornell University Press.

Finnemore, Martha, and Kathryn Sikkink. 1998. International Norm Dynamics and Political Change. *International Organization* 52 (4): 887–917.

Fioretos, Orfeo, Tulia C. Falleti, and Adam Sheingate, eds. 2016. *The Oxford Handbook of Historical Institutionalism.* Oxford: Oxford University Press.

Fisher, Jonathan, and David M. Anderson. 2015. Authoritarianism and the Securitization of Development in Africa. *International Affairs* 91 (1): 131–151.

Fjelde, Hanne, and Indra De Soysa. 2009. Coercion, Co-optation, or Cooperation?: State Capacity and the Risk of Civil War, 1961–2004. *Conflict Management and Peace Science* 26 (1): 5–25.

Fjelde, Hanne, Lisa Hultman, and Desirée Nilsson. 2019. Protection Through Presence: UN Peacekeeping and the Costs of Targeting Civilians. *International Organization* 73 (1): 103–131.

Flanigan, Shawn Teresa. 2006. Charity as Resistance: Connections between Charity, Contentious Politics, and Terror. *Studies in Conflict & Terrorism* 29 (7): 641–655.

Flanigan, Shawn Teresa, and Mounah Abdel-Samad. 2009. Hezbollah's Social Jihad: Nonprofits as Resistance Organizations. *Middle East Policy* 16 (2): 122–137.

Flohr, Annegret, Lothar Rieth, Sandra Schwindenhammer, and Klaus Dieter Wolf. 2010. *The Role of Business in Global Governance. Corporations as Norm-Entrepreneurs*. Basingstoke: Palgrave Macmillan.

Förster, Till. 2015. *Dialogue Direct:* Rebel Governance and Civil Order in Northern Côte d'Ivoire. In *Rebel Governance in Civil War*, edited by Ana Arjona, Nelson Kasfir and Zachariah Mampilly. Cambridge, UK: Cambridge University Press, 203–225.

Förster, Till, and Lucy Koechlin. 2018. 'Traditional' Authorities. In *The Oxford Handbook of Governance and Limited Statehood*, edited by Thomas Risse, Tanja A. Börzel and Anke Draude. Oxford: Oxford University Press, 231–249.

Fortin, Jessica. 2010. A Tool to Evaluate State Capacity in Post-communist Countries, 1989–2006s. *European Journal of Political Research* 49 (5): 654–686.

Fortna, Virginia Page. 2004. Does Peacekeeping Keep Peace? International Intervention and the Duration of Peace after Civil War. *International Studies Quarterly* 48 (2): 269–292.

2008. *Does Peacekeeping Work? Shaping Belligerents' Choices after Civil War.* Princeton, NJ: Princeton University Press.

Fortna, Virginia Page, Nicholas J Lotito, and Michael A Rubin. 2018. Don't Bite the Hand that Feeds: Rebel Funding Sources and the Use of Terrorism in Civil Wars. *International Studies Quarterly* 62 (4): 782–794.

Franck, Thomas M. 1990. *The Power of Legitimacy Among Nations*. Oxford: Oxford University Press.

Fransen, Luc W., and Ans Kolk. 2007. Global Rule-setting for Business: A Critical Analysis of Multi-stakeholder Standards. *Organization* 14 (5): 667–684.

Freeman, Bennett, and Genoveva Hernandez Uriz. 2003. Managing Risk and Building Trust. The Challenge of Implementing the Voluntary Principles on Security and Human Rights. In *Business and Human Rights. Dilemmas and Solutions*, edited by Roni Sullivan. Sheffield: Greenleaf Publishing, 243–259.

Freitag, Markus, and Marc Bühlmann. 2009. Crafting Trust: The Role of Political Institutions in a Comparative Perspective. *Comparative Political Studies* 42 (12): 1537–1566.

Friedman, Milton. 1970. The Social Responsibility of Business Is to Increase Its Profits. *The New York Times Magazine* September 13: 121–125.

Friis, Lykke, and Anna Murphy. 2000. 'Turbo-Charged Negotiations': The EU and the Stability Pact for South Eastern Europe. *Journal of European Public Policy* 7 (5): 767–786.

Fromson, James, and Steven Simon. 2015. ISIS: The Dubious Paradise of Apocalypse Now. *Survival* 57 (3): 7–56.

Frynas, Jedrzej George. 2000. *Oil in Nigeria: Conflict and Litigation between Oil Companies and Village Communities*. Hamburg: Lit Verlag.

2005. The False Developmental Promise of Corporate Social Responsibility: Evidence from Multinational Oil Companies. *International Affairs* 81 (3): 581–598.

Fukuda-Parr, Sakiko, and Carlos Lopes. 2013. *Capacity for Development: New Solutions to Old Problems*. London: Routledge.

Fukuyama, Francis. 1992. *The End of History and the Last Man*. New York: Free Press.

2004. *State-building. Governance and World Order in the 21st Century*. Ithaca, NY: Cornell University Press.

2012. *The Origins of Political Order. From Prehuman Times to the French Revolution*. New York: Farar, Straus, and Giroux.

2014. *Political Order and Political Decay: From the Industrial Revolution to the Globalization of Democracy*. New York: Farrar, Straus and Giroux.

Fund for Peace. 2019. Fragile State Index. Annual Report 2019. Washington, DC: Fund for Peace.

Gambetta, Diego. 1988a. Mafia: The Price of Distrust. In *Trust: Making and Breaking Cooperative Relations*, edited by Diego Gambetta. Oxford: Blackwell, 158–175.

Gambetta, Diego, ed. 1988b. *Trust: Making and Breaking Cooperative Relations*. New York: Blackwell Publishers.

Gamu, Jonathan, Philippe Le Billon, and Samuel Spiegel. 2015. Extractive Industries and Poverty: A Review of Recent Findings and Linkage Mechanism. *The Extractive Industries and Society* 2 (1): 162–176.

Garcia-Johnson, Ronie. 2000. *Exporting Environmentalism: US Multinational Chemical Corporations in Brazil and Mexico*. Cambridge, MA: MIT Press.

Garvin, Theresa, Tara K. McGee, Karen E. Smoyer-Tomic, and Emmanuel Ato Aubynn. 2009. Community–Company Relations in Gold Mining in Ghana. *Journal of Environmental Management* 90 (1): 571–586.

Geenen, Sara, and Jana Hönke. 2014. 'Land Grabbing' by Mining Companies. Local Contentions and State Reconfiguration in South Kivu (DRC). In *Losing Your Land: Dispossession in the Great Lakes*, edited by An Ansoms and Thea Hilhorst. Rochester, NY: Boydell & Brewer, 58–81.

Gehman, Joel, Lianne M. Lefsrud, and Stewart Fast. 2017. Social License to Operate: Legitimacy by Another Name? *Canadian Public Administration* 60 (2): 293–317.

Gehring, Kai, Lennart Kaplan, and Melvin H. L. Wong. 2019. Aid and Conflict at the Sub-National Level: Evidence from World Bank and Chinese Development Projects in Africa. AidData Working Papers. Williamsburg VA: College of William and Mary, March.

Gehring, Thomas, and Benjamin Faude. 2014. A Theory of Emerging Order within Institutional Complexes: How Competition Among Regulatory International Institutions Leads to Institutional Adaptation and Division of Labor. *The Review of International Organizations* 9 (4): 471–498.

Genschel, Philipp, and Bernhard Zangl. 2008a. Metarmophosen des Staates – vom Herrschaftsmonopolisten zum Herrschaftsmanager. *Leviathan* 36 (3): 430–454.

2008b. Transformations of the State – From Monopolist to Manager of Political Authority. TranState Working Papers, 76, Bremen: Sfb 597 "Staatlichkeit im Wandel."

Ghani, Ashraf, and Clare Lockhart. 2009. *Fixing Failed states: A Framework for Rebuilding a Fractured World*. Oxford: Oxford University Press.

Gill, Lesley. 2007. 'Right There with You': Coca-Cola, Labor Restructuring and Political Violence in Colombia. *Critique of Anthropology* 27 (3): 235–260.

Gilligan, Michael J., and Ernest J. Sergenti. 2008. Do UN Interventions Cause Peace? Using Matching to Improve Causal Inference. *Quarterly Journal of Political Science* 3 (2): 89–122.

Gilligan, Michael J., and Stephen John Stedman. 2003. Where Do the Peacekeepers Go? *International Studies Review* 5 (4): 37–54.

Gilpin, Robert. 1975. *U.S. Power and the Multinational Corporation: The Political Economy of Foreign Direct Investment*. New York: Basic Books.

Glawion, Tim. 2017. Security Arena. Local Order Making in the Central African Republic, Somaliland, and South Sudan. PhD. Dissertation, Philosophische Fakultät der Universität Freiburg, Albert-Ludwigs-Universität, Freiburg.

2020. *The Security Arena in Africa: Local Order-Making in the Central African Republic, Somaliland, and South Sudan*. Cambridge, UK: Cambridge University Press.

Göhler, Gerhard, Ulrike Höppner, and Sybille De La Rosa, eds. 2009. *Weiche Steuerung. Studien zur Steuerung durch diskursive Praktiken, Argumente und Symbole*. Baden-Baden: Nomos.

Goldstein, Judith L., Miles Kahler, Robert O. Keohane, and Anne-Marie Slaughter, eds. 2000. *Legalization and World Politics. Special Issue of International Organization*. Cambridge, MA: MIT Press.

Golub, Stephen A. 2006. A House without a Foundation. In *Promoting the Rule of Law Abroad: In Search of Knowledge*, edited by Thomas Carothers. Washington, DC: Carnegie Endowment for International Peace, 105–136.

Goodfellow, Tom, and Stefan Lindemann. 2013. The Clash of Institutions: Traditional Authority, Conflict and the Failure of 'Hybridity' in Buganda. *Commonwealth & Comparative Politics* 51 (1): 3–26.

Grande, Edgar, and Louis W. Pauly, eds. 2005. *Complex Sovereignty. Reconstituting Political Authority in the Twenty-First Century*. Toronto: Toronto University Press.

Grant, Thomas D. 1998–1999. Defining Statehood: The Montevideo Convention and Its Discontents. *Columbia Journal of Transnational Law* 37: 403–414.

Gray, Kevin, and Barry K. Gills. 2016. South–South Cooperation and the Rise of the Global South. *Third World Quarterly* 37 (4): 557–574.

Greenhill, Brian, Layna Mosley, and Aseem Prakash. 2009. Trade-Based Diffusion of Labor Rights: A Panel Study, 1986–2002. *American Political Science Review* 103 (4): 669–690.

Griffin, Jennifer J., and Aseem Prakash. 2014. Corporate Responsibility: Initiatives and Mechanisms. *Business & Society* 53 (4): 465–482.

Grimm, Sonja, and Okka Lou Mathis. 2015. Stability First, Development Second, Democracy Third: The European Union's Policy towards the Post-Conflict Western Balkans, 1991–2010. *Europe-Asia Studies* 67 (6): 916–947.

Grindle, Merilee S. 2004. Good Enough Governance: Poverty Reduction and Reform in Developing Countries. *Governance* 17 (4): 525–548.

2011. Good Enough Governance Revisited. *Development Policy Review* 29 (s1): s199–s221.

Grøner Krogstad, Erlend. 2014. Local Ownership as Dependence Management: Inviting the Coloniser Back. *Journal of Intervention and Statebuilding* 8 (2–3): 105–125.

Grynkewich, Alexus G. 2008. Welfare as Warfare: How Violent Non-state Groups Use Social Services to Attack the State. *Studies in Conflict & Terrorism* 31 (4): 350–370.

Guitiérrez-Sanín, Francisco. 2015. Organization and Governance: The Evolution of Urban Militias in Medellín, Colombia. In *Rebel Governance in Civil War*, edited by Ana Arjona, Nelson Kasfir and Zachariah Mampilly. Cambridge, UK: Cambridge University Press, 246–264.

Gutiérrez-Sanín, Francisco, and Elisabeth Jean Wood. 2014. Ideology in Civil War: Instrumental Adoption and Beyond. *Journal of Peace Research* 51 (2): 213–226.

Gunning, Jeroen. 2007. Terrorism, Charities and Diasporas: Contrasting the Fundraising Practices of Hamas and al Qaeda Among Muslims in Europe. In *Countering the Financing of Terrorism*, edited by Thomas J. Biersteker and Sue E. Eckert. London: Routledge, 109–141.

Gupta, Aarti. 2008. Transparency under Scrutiny: Information Disclosure in Global Environmental Governance. *Global Environmental Politics* 8 (2): 1–7.

Gurr, Ted Robert. 1988. War, Revolution, and the Growth of the Coercive State. *Comparative Political Studies* 21 (1): 45–65.

Haas, Peter M., ed. 1992. *Knowledge, Power and International Policy Coordination, International Organization, Special Issue*. 46 (1).

Habermas, Jürgen. 1981. *Theorie des kommunikativen Handelns*. 2 Vols. Frankfurt am Main: Suhrkamp.

Hackenesch, Christine. 2015. Not as Bad as It Seems: EU and US Democracy Promotion Face China in Africa. *Democratization* 22 (3): 419–437.

2018. *The EU and China in African Authoritarian Regimes. Domestic Politics and Governance Reforms*. Basingstoke: Palgrave Macmillan.

Hafner-Burton, Emilie M. 2005. Trading Human Rights: How Preferential Trade Agreements Influence Government Repression. *International Organization* 59 (3): 593–629.

2012. International Regimes for Human Rights. *Annual Review of Political Science* 15: 265–286.

Hafner-Burton, Emilie M., Edward D. Mansfield, and Jon C. Pevehouse. 2015. Democratization and Human Rights Organizations. *British Journal of Political Science* 45 (1): 1–27.

Hagmann, Tobias, and Didier Péclard. 2010. Negotiating Statehood: Dynamics of Power and Domination in Africa. *Development and Change* 41 (4): 539–562.

Hale, Thomas, and David Held, eds. 2011. *Handbook of Transnational Governance*. Cambridge, UK: Polity Press.

Hall, Peter A., and Rosemary C. R. Taylor. 1996. Political Science and the Three New Institutionalisms. *Political Studies* 44 (5): 952–973.

Hall, Rodney Bruce, and Thomas J. Biersteker, eds. 2002. *The Emergence of Private Authority in Global Governance*. Cambridge, UK: Cambridge University Press.

Hamann, Ralph. 2004. CSR in Mining in South Africa. PhD Dissertation, University of East Anglia, Norwich.

2019. Dynamic De-responsibilization in Business–Government Interactions. *Organization Studies* 40 (8): 1193–1215.

Hamann, Ralph, and Nicola Acutt. 2003. How Should Civil Society (and the Government) Respond to 'Corporate Social Responsibility'? A Critique of Business Motivations and the Potential for Partnerships. *Development Southern Africa* 20 (2): 255–270.

Hamann, Ralph, Jana Hönke, and Tim O'Riordan. 2018. Environmental and Natural Resources. In *The Oxford Handbook of Governance and Limited Statehood*, edited by Thomas Risse, Tanja A. Börzel and Anke Draude. Oxford: Oxford University Press, 498–519.

Hammond, Ross A., and Robert A. Axelrod. 2006. The Evolution of Ethnocentrism. *Journal of Conflict Resolution* 50: 926–936.

Hampton, Jean. 1986. *Hobbes and the Social Contract Tradition*. Cambridge, UK: Cambridge University Press.

Harb el-Kak, Mona. 2000. Post-war Beirut: Resources, Negotiations, and Contestations in the Elyssar Project. *The Arab World Geographer* 3 (4): 272–288.

Hardin, Garrett. 1968. The Tragedy of the Commons. *Science* (162): 1243–1248.

Hardin, Russel. 2002. *Trust and Tustworthiness*. New York: Russell Sage Foundation.

Harik, Judith Palmer. 2005. *Hezbollah: The Changing Face of Terrorism*. London: IB Tauris.

Harrison, Elizabeth. 2002. 'The Problem with the Locals': Partnership and Participation in Ethiopia. *Development and Change* 33 (4): 587–610.

Hartmann, Christof. 2017. ECOWAS and the Restoration of Democracy in The Gambia. *Africa Spectrum* 52 (1): 85–99.

Hartmann, Christof, and Kai Striebinger. 2015. Writing the Script? ECOWAS's Military Intervention Mechanism. In *Governance Transfer by Regional Organizations. Patching Together a Global Script*, edited by Tanja A. Börzel and Vera van Hüllen. Basingstoke: Palgrave Macmillan, 68–73.

Hartmann, Martin. 2011. *Die Praxis des Vertrauens*. Berlin: Suhrkamp.

Hasenclever, Andreas, Peter Mayer, and Volker Rittberger. 1997. *Theories of International Regimes*. Cambridge, UK: Cambridge University Press.

Haufler, Virginia. 1993. Crossing the Boundary between Public and Private: International Regimes and Non-State Actors. In *Regime Theory and International Relations*, edited by Volker Rittberger. Oxford: Clarendon Press, 94–111.

1999. Self-Regulation and Business Norms. Political Risk, Political Activism. In *Private Authority and International Affairs*, edited by Claire A. Cutler, Virginia Haufler and Tony Porter. Albany NY: State University of New York Press, 199–222.

2001a. Is there a Role for Business in Conflict Management? In *Turbulent Peace: The Challenge of Managing International Conflict*, edited by Chester A. Crocker, Fen Hampson and Pamela Aall. Washington, DC: United States Institute of Peace, 659–675.

2001b. *A Public Role for the Private Sector – Industry Self-Regulation in a Global Economy.* Washington, DC: Carnegie Endowment for International Peace.

2015. Corporations, Conflict Minerals, and Corporate Social Responsibility. In *Corporate Social Responsibility in a Globalizing World*, edited by Kiyoteru Tsutsui and Alwyn Lim. Cambridge, UK: Cambridge University Press, 149–180.

Hawkins, Darren, and Wade Jacoby. 2010. Partial Compliance: A Comparison of the European and Inter-American Courts of Human Rights. *Journal of International Law and International Relations* 6 (1): 35–85.

Hay, Colin, Michael Lister, and David Marsh. 2006. *The State: Theories and Issues.* Basingstoke: Palgrave Macmillan.

Hayek, Friedrich A. von. 1948. *Individualism and Economic Order.* Chicago: University of Chicago Press.

Hegre, Havard, Lisa Hultman, and Håvard Mokleiv Nygård. 2019. Evaluating the Conflict-Reducing Effect of UN Peace-Keeping Operations. *The Journal of Politics* 81 (1): 215–232.

Hellmüller, Sara. 2013. The Power of Perceptions: Localizing International Peacebuilding Approaches. *International Peacekeeping* 20 (2): 219–232.

Helman, Gerald B., and Steven R. Ratner. 1992. Saving Failed States. *Foreign Policy* (89): 3–20.

Hendrix, Cullen S. 2010. Measuring State Capacity: Theoretical and Empirical Implications for the Study of Civil Conflict. *Journal of Peace Research* 47 (3): 273–285.

Hendry, Jamie. 2006. Taking Aim at Business. *Business and Society* 45 (1): 47–86.

Herbst, Jeffrey. 2004. Let Them Fail: State Failure in Theory and Practice. In *When States Fail. Causes and Consequences*, edited by Robert I. Rotberg. Princeton, NJ: Princeton University Press, 302–318.

Héritier, Adrienne, ed. 2002. *Common Goods. Reinventing European and International Governance.* Lanham MD: Rowman & Littlefield.

2003. New Modes of Governance in Europe: Increasing Political Capacity and Policy Effectiveness? In *The State of the European Union, Vol. 6: Law, Politics, and Society*, edited by Tanja A. Börzel and Rachel A. Cichowski. Oxford: Oxford University Press, 105–126.

Héritier, Adrienne, Anna Müller-Debus, and Christian Thauer. 2009. The Firm as an Inspector: Private Ordering and Political Rules. *Business and Politics* 11 (4): 1–32.

Héritier, Adrienne, and Martin Rhodes, eds. 2010. *New Modes of Governance in Europe. Governing in the Shadow of Hierarchy.* Basingstoke: Palgrave Macmillan.

Herr, Stefanie. 2013. Constraining the Conduct of Non-State Armed Groups. In *The Transnational Governance of Violence and Crime. Non-State Actors in Security*, edited by Anja P. Jakobi and Klaus Dieter Wolf. Basingstoke: Palgrave Macmillan, 40–60.

Herren, Madeleine. 2018. A Global History of Governance. In *The Oxford Handbook of Governance and Limited Statehood*, edited by Thomas Risse, Tanja A. Börzel and Anke Draude. Oxford: Oxford University Press, 148–166.

Herreros, Francisco. 2012. The State Counts: State Efficacy and the Development of Trust. *Rationality and Society* 24: 483–509.

Herrmann, Richard K., and Marilynn B. Brewer. 2004. Identities and Institutions: Becoming European in the EU. In *Transnational Identities: Becoming European in the EU*, edited by Richard K. Herrmann, Thomas Risse and Marilynn B. Brewer. Lanham, MD: Rowman & Littlefield, 1–22.

Heupel, Monika, Michael Zürn, and Gisela Hirschmann. 2017. *Protecting the Individual from International Authority: Human Rights in International Organizations*. Cambridge, UK: Cambridge University Press.

Hirschmann, Gisela. 2015. Guarding the Guards? Accountability in United Nations Peace Operations. PhD. Dissertation, Fachbereich Politik- und Sozialwissenschaft, Freie Universität Berlin, Berlin.

2017. UN Peacekeeping and the Protection of Bodily Integrity Rights: When Protectors Become Perpetrators. In *Protecting the Individual from International Authority: Human Rights in International Organizations*, edited by Michael Zürn, Monika Heupel and Gisela Hirschmann. Cambridge, UK: Cambridge University Press, 157–185.

Hobbes, Thomas. 1987 (1651). *Leviathan*. Frankfurt am Main: Suhrkamp.

Hobson, John M. 2000. *The State and International Relations*. Cambridge, UK: Cambridge University Press.

Hoeffler, Anke, and Verity Outram. 2011. Need, Merit, or Self-Interest. What Determines the Allocation of Aid? *Review of Development Economics* 15 (2): 237–250.

Hofferberth, Matthias. 2010. The Binding Dynamics of Non-Binding Governance Arrangements. The Emergence and Development of the Voluntary Principles on Security and Human Rights. https://ssrn.com/abstract=1643688, last access September 27, 2019.

Hölck, Lasse, and Stefan Rinke. 2016. Loyalität in Übersee: Legitimierung von Herrschaft in den Peripherien des spanischen Weltreiches, 16–19. Jahrhundert. *Geschichte und Gesellschaft* 42 (4): 574–591.

Hölck, Lasse, and Mónika Contreras Saiz. 2010. Educating Bárbaros: Educational Policies on the Latin American Frontiers between Colonies and Independent Republics (Araucania, Southern Chile/Sonora, Mexico). *Paedagogica Historica* 46 (4): 435–448.

Holland, Martin. 2003. Complementarity and Conditionality: Evaluating Good Governance. In *The European Union and the Third World*, edited by Martin Holland. Basingstoke: Palgrave Macmillan, 113–139.

Hollis, Duncan B. 2002. Private Actors in Public International Law: Amicus Curiae and the Case for the Retention of State Sovereignty. *Boston College International and Comparative Law Review* 25 (2): 235–255.

Holm, Petter. 1995. The Dynamics of Institutionalization: Transformation Processes in Norwegian Fisheries. *Administrative Science Quarterly* 40 (3): 398–422.

Holsti, Kalevi J. 2004. *Taming the Sovereigns. Institutional Change in International Politics*. Cambridge, UK: Cambridge University Press.

Holzinger, Katharina, Roos Haer, Axel Bayer, Daniela M. Behr, and Clara Neupert-Wentz. 2018. The Constitutionalization of Indigenous Group

Rights, Traditional Political Institutions, and Customary Law. *Comparative Political Studies* 52 (12): 1775–1809.

Holzinger, Katharina, Florian G. Kern, and Daniela Kromrey. 2016. The Dualism of Contemporary Traditional Governance and the State: Institutional Setups and Political Consequences. *Political Research Quarterly* 69 (3): 469–481.

2017. Traditional Institutions in Sub-Saharan Africa: Endangering or Promoting Stable Domestic Peace? Forschung DSF. Osnabrück: Deutsche Stiftung Friedensforschung.

Holzscheiter, Anna. 2018. Health. In *The Oxford Handbook of Governance and Limited Statehood*, edited by Thomas Risse, Tanja A. Börzel and Anke Draude. Oxford: Oxford University Press, 438–458.

Holzscheiter, Anna, Thurid Bahr, and Laura Pantzerhielm. 2016. Emerging Governance Architectures in Global Health: Do Metagovernance Norms Explain Inter-Organisational Convergence? *Politics and Governance* 4 (3): 5–19.

Homkes, Rebecca. 2011. Analysing the Role of Public-Private Partnerships in Global Governance. Institutional Dynamics, Variation and Effects. Dissertation at the London School of Economics and Political Science, London. Available at http://etheses.lse.ac.uk/269/1/Homkes%20Analysing%20the%20role%20of%20Public-private%20partnerships%20in%20global%20governance.pdf, last access August 5, 2018. London: London School of Economics and Political Science.

Honig, Dan. 2018. When Reporting Undermines Performance: The Costs of Politically Constrained Organizational Autonomy in Foreign Aid Implementation. *International Organization* 73 (1): 171–201.

Hönke, Jana. 2010a. Liberal Discourse and Hybrid Practise in Transnational Security Governance: Companies in Congo and South Africa in the 19th and 21st Centuries. PhD. Dissertation, Department of Political Science, Freie Universität Berlin, Berlin.

2010b. New Political Topographies. Mining Companies and Indirect Discharge in Southern Katanga (DRC). *Politique Africaine* 4 (120): 105–127.

2012. Multinationals and Security Governance in the Community. Participation, Discipline and Indirect Rule. *Journal of Intervention and Statebuilding* 6 (1): 89–105.

2013a. Between Cause and Cure. The Mining Industry and HIV/Aids Governance in South Africa. In *Business and Governance in South Africa. Racing to the Top?* edited by Tanja A. Börzel and Christian R. Thauer. Basingstoke: Palgrave Macmillan, 67–87.

2013b. *Transnational Companies and Security Governance. Hybrid Practices in a Postcolonial World.* London: Routledge.

Hönke, Jana, and Tanja A. Börzel. 2014. Restraint of Statehood and the Quality of Governance by Multinational Companies in Sub-Saharan Africa. SFB Working Papers. Sonderforschungsbereich 700, Freie Universität Berlin (65).

Hönke, Jana, and Nicole Kranz. 2013. Cleaning up Their Act, or More? Mining Companies and Environmental Protection in South Africa. In *Business and Governance in South Africa. Racing to the Top?* edited by Tanja A. Börzel and Christian R. Thauer. Basingstoke: Palgrave Macmillan, 152–179.

Hönke, Jana, and Markus Michael Müller. 2018. Brokerage, Intermediation, Translation. In *The Oxford Handbook of Governance and Limited Statehood*, edited by Thomas Risse, Tanja A. Börzel and Anke Draude. Oxford: Oxford University Press, 333–352.

Hönke, Jana, and Christian R. Thauer. 2014. Multinational Corporations and Service Provision in Sub-Saharan Africa: Legitimacy and Institutionalization Matter. *Governance* 27 (4): 697–716.

Hönke, Jana, and Esther Thomas. 2012. Governance for Whom? Capturing the Inclusiveness and Unintended Effects of Governance. SFB Working Papers. Sonderforschungsbereich 700, Freie Universität Berlin (31).

Hooghe, Liesbet, Tobias Lenz, and Gary Marks. 2019. *Community, Scale, and International Organization. A Postfunctionalist Theory of Governance.* Oxford: Oxford University Press.

Hooghe, Liesbet, and Gary Marks. 2001. *Multi-Level Governance and European Integration.* Lanham MD et al.: Rowman & Littlefield.

2003. Unraveling the Central State, but How? Types of Multi-level Governance. *American Political Science Review* 97 (2): 233–243.

Hoover Green, Amelia. 2016. The Commander's Dilemma: Creating and Controlling Armed Group Violence. *Journal of Peace Research* 53 (5): 619–632.

Howard, Lise Morjé. 2007. *UN Peacekeeping in Civil Wars.* Cambridge, UK: Cambridge University Press.

Huang, Reyko. 2016. *The Wartime Origins of Democratization: Civil War, Rebel Governance, and Political Regimes.* Cambridge, UK: Cambridge University Press.

Hulse, Merran, and Anna van der Vleuten. 2015. Agent Run Amuck: The SADC Tribunal and Governance Transfer Rollback. In *Governance Transfer by Regional Organizations. Patching Together a Global Script*, edited by Tanja A. Börzel and Vera van Hüllen. Basingstoke: Palgrave Macmillan, 84–104.

Hultman, Lisa, Jacob D. Kathman, and Megan Shannon. 2016. United Nations Peacekeeping Dynamics and the Duration of Post-Civil Conflict Peace. *Conflict Management and Peace Science* 33 (3): 231–249.

Humphreys, Macartan, and Jeremy M. Weinstein. 2006. Handling and Manhandling Civilians in Civil War. *American Political Science Review* 100 (3): 429–447.

Hunt, Charles T. 2017. All Necessary Means to What Ends? The Unintended Consequences of the 'Robust Turn' in UN Peace Operations. *International Peacekeeping* 24 (1): 108–131.

Huntington, Samuel P. 1968. *Political Order in Changing Societies.* New Haven: Yale University Press.

1993. The Clash of Civilizations? *Foreign Affairs* 72 (3): 22–49.

Hurd, Ian. 1999. Legitimacy and Authority in International Politics. *International Organization* 53 (2): 379–408.

Hurrelmann, Achim, Stephan Leibfried, Kerstin Martens, and Mayer Peter, eds. 2007. *Transforming the Golden-Age Nation State.* Basingstoke: Palgrave Macmillan.

Hutchison, Marc L., and Kristin Johnson. 2011. Capacity to Trust? Institutional Capacity, Conflict, and Political Trust in Africa, 2000–2005. *Journal of Peace Research* 48 (6): 737–752.

318   References

2017. Political Trust in Sub-Saharan Africa and the Arab Region. In *Handbook on Political Trust*, edited by Sonja Zmerli and Tom W. G. van der Meer. Cheltenham: Edward Elgar, 461–487.

Huyse, Luc. 2008. Introduction: Tradition-Based Approaches in Peacemaking, Transitional Justice, and Reconciliation Policies. In *Traditional Justice and Reconciliation after Violent Conflict. Learning from African Experiences*, edited by Luc Huyse and Marc Salter. Stockholm: International Institute for Democracy and Electoral Assistance, 1–24.

Huyse, Luc, and Marc Salter. eds. 2008. *Traditional Justice and Reconciliation after Violent Conflict. Learning from African Experiences*. Stockholm: International Institute for Democracy and Electoral Assistance.

Idler, Annette Iris, and James Forest. 2015. Behavioral Patterns Among (Violent) Non-state Actors: A Study of Complementary Governance. *Stability: International Journal of Security and Development* 4 (1): 1–19.

Ingelaere, Bert. 2008. The Gacaca Courts in Rwanda. In *Traditional Justice and Reconciliation after Violent Conflict. Learning from African Experiences*, edited by Luc Huyse and Marc Salter. Stockholm: International Institute for Democracy and Electoral Assistance, 25–60.

Inglehart, Ronald, and Christian Welzel. 2005. *Modernization, Cultural Change, and Democracy*. Cambridge, UK: Cambridge University Press.

Ismail, Salwa. 2001. The paradox of Islamist politics. *Middle East Report* (221): 34–39.

Ite, Uwem E. 2005. Poverty Reduction in Resource-Rich Developing Countries: What Have Multinational Corporations Got to Do with It? *Journal of International Development* 17 (7): 913–929.

Jackson, Paul. 2011. Security Sector Reform and State Building. *Third World Quarterly* 32 (10): 1803–1822.

Jackson, Paul, and Peter Albrecht. 2010. *Security Sector Transformation in Sierra Leone 1997–2007*. Basingstoke: Palgrave Macmillan.

Jackson, Robert H. 1990. *Quasi-States. Sovereignty, International Relations, and the Third World*. Cambridge, UK: Cambridge University Press.

Jackson, Robert H., and Carl Gustav Rosberg. 1982. *Personal Rule in Black Africa: Prince, Autocrat, Prophet, Tyrant*. Berkeley, CA: University of California Press.

Jacob, Daniel, Bernd Ladwig, and Cord Schmelzle. 2018. Normative Political Theory. In *The Oxford Handbook of Governance and Limited Statehood*, edited by Thomas Risse, Tanja A. Börzel and Anke Draude. Oxford: Oxford University Press, 564–583.

Jakobi, Anja P. 2013. Governing War Economies: Conflict Diamonds and the Kimberley Process. In *The Transnational Governance of Violence and Crime. Non-State Actors in Security*, edited by Anja P. Jakobi and Klaus Dieter Wolf. Basingstoke: Palgrave Macmillan, 84–105.

Jakobi, Anja P., and Klaus Dieter Wolf, eds. 2013. *The Transnational Governance of Violence and Crime. Non-State Actors in Security*. Basingstoke: Palgrave Macmillan.

Jamali, Dima, and Ramez Mirshak. 2010. Business-conflict Linkages: Revisiting MNCs, CSR, and Conflict. *Journal of Business Ethics* 93 (3): 443–464.

Jastram, Sarah, and Anna-Maria Schneider. 2018. *Sustainable Fashion – Governance and New Management Approaches*. New York et al.: Springer.

Jellinek, Georg. 1900 (1922). *Allgemeine Staatslehre*. Berlin: J. Springer.

Jessop, Bob. 1998. The Rise of Governance and the Risks of Failure: the Case of Economic Development. *International Social Sciences Journal* 50 (155): 29–45.

Jetschke, Anja. 2015. Why Create a Regional Human Rights Regime? The ASEAN Intergovernmental Commission for Human Rights. In *Governance Transfer by Regional Organizations. Patching Together a Regional Script*, edited by Tanja A. Börzel and Vera van Hüllen. Basingstoke: Palgrave Macmillan, 107–124.

Jim Freedman Consulting. 2006. OECD Audit of Anvil Mining Limited. Katanga Province, Democratic Republic of Congo. August 25, 2006.

Jo, Hyeran. 2015. *Compliant Rebels. Rebel Groups and International Law in World Politics*. Cambridge, UK: Cambridge University Press.

Jo, Hyeran, and Katherine Bryant. 2013. Taming of the Warlords: Commitment and Compliance by Armed Opposition Groups in Civil Wars. In *The Persistent Power of Human Rights: From Commitment to Compliance*, edited by Thomas Risse, Stephen C. Ropp and Kathryn Sikkink. Cambridge, UK: Cambridge University Press, 239–274.

Johson, Douglas H. 1991. From Military to Tribal Police: Protecting the Upper Nile of the Sudan. In *Policing the Empire: Governance, Authority, and Control 1830–1940*, edited by David M. Anderson and David Killingray. Manchester: Manchester University Press, 151–167.

Kaan, Christopher. 2014. Partnerships for Decent Work and Food – Special Focus: Standard Setting. In *Transnational Partnerships. Effectively Providing for Sustainable Development?*, edited by Marianne Beisheim and Andrea Liese. Basingstoke: Palgrave Macmillan, 63–86.

Kalyvas, Stathis N. 2006. *The Logic of Violence in Civil War*. Cambridge, UK: Cambridge University Press.

2015. Rebel Governance during the Greek Civil War. In *Rebel Governance in Civil War*, edited by Ana Arjona, Nelson Kasfir and Zachariah Mampilly. Cambridge, UK: Cambridge University Press, 119–137.

Kapelus, Paul. 2006. Anglo Gold Ashanti in the Democratic Republic of Congo: Management Challenges and Responses to Operating in a Weak Governance Area. New York: UN Global Compact.

Kaplan, Oliver. 2017. *Resisting War. How Communities Protect Themselves*. Cambridge, UK: Cambridge University Press.

Kaplan, Seth. 2008. The Remarkable Story of Somaliland. *Journal of Democracy* 19 (3): 143–157.

Karim, Sabrina. 2020. Relational State Building in Areas of Limited Statehood: Experimental Evidence on the Attitudes of the Police. *American Political Science Review* 114 (2): 536–551.

Karlsrud, John. 2015. *Norm Change in International Relations: Linked Ecologies in UN Peacekeeping Operations*. London: Routledge.

Kasara, Kimuli. 2007. Tax Me If You Can: Ethnic Geography, Democracy, and the Taxation of Agriculture in Africa. *American Political Science Review* 101 (1): 159–172.

Kasfir, Nelson. 2015. Rebel Governance – Constructing a Field of Inquiry: Definitions, Scope, Patterns, Order, Causes. In *Rebel Governance in Civil War*, edited by Ana Arjona, Nelson Kasfir and Zachariah Mampilly. Cambridge, UK: Cambridge University Press, 21–46.

Katzenstein, Peter J., ed. 1996. *The Culture of National Security. Norms and Identity in World Politics.* New York: Columbia University Press.

2012. *Anglo-America and Its Discontents: Civilizational Identities beyond West and East.* London: Routledge.

Katzenstein, Peter J., Robert O. Keohane, and Stephen D. Krasner. 1998. *International Organization at Fifty: Exploration and Contestation in the Study of World Politics. International Organization, Special Issue.* 52 (4).

Kaufmann, Robert R., and Alex Segura-Ubiergo. 2001. Globalization, Domestic Politics, and Social Spending in Latin America: A time-series Cross-section Analysis, 1973–97. *World Politics* 53 (4): 553–587.

Keane, John. 1988. Despotism and Democracy. The Origins of the Distinction between Civil Society and the State 1750–1850. In *Civil Society and the State*, edited by John Keane. London: Verso, 35–72.

Keck, Margaret E., and Kathryn Sikkink. 1998. *Activists beyond Borders. Advocacy Networks in International Politics.* Ithaca, NY: Cornell University Press.

Keleman, R. Daniel. 2017. Europe's Other Democratic Deficit: National Authoritarianism in Europe's Democratic Union. *Government and Opposition* 52 (2): 211–238.

Kell, Georg, and David Levin. 2003. The Global Compact Network: A Historic Experiment in Learning and Action. *Business and Society Review* 108 (2): 151–181.

Kelley, Judith G. 2004. *Ethnic Politics in Europe. The Power of Norms and Incentives.* Princeton, NJ: Princeton University Press.

2012. *Monitoring Democracy: When International Election Observation Works and Why It Often Fails.* Princeton, NJ: Princeton University Press.

Keohane, Robert O., ed. 1989a. *International Institutions and State Power.* Boulder, CO: Westview.

1989b. International Institutions: Two Approaches. In *International Institutions and State Power*, edited by Robert O. Keohane. Boulder, CO: Westview, 158–179.

1989c. Neoliberal Institutionalism. A Perspective on World Politics. In *International Institutions and State Power*, edited by Robert O. Keohane. Boulder, CO: Westview, 35–73.

2007. Governance and Legitimacy. Keynote Speech Held at the Opening Conference of the Research Center (SFB) 700. SFB-Governance Lecture Series Sonderforschungsbereich 700, Freie Universität Berlin (1).

Keohane, Robert O., and Joseph S. Nye jr., eds. 1971. *Transnational Relations and World Politics.* Cambridge, MA: Harvard University Press.

Keohane, Robert O., and Elinor Ostrom, eds. 1994. *Local Commons and Global Interdependence. Heterogeneity and Cooperation in Two Domains.* London: Sage.

Khagram, Sanjeev. 2004. *Dams and Development: Transnational Struggles for Water and Power.* Ithaca, NY: Cornell University Press.

Khan, Farzad Rafi, Kamal A. Munir, and Hugh Willmott. 2007. A Dark Side of Institutional Entrepreneurship: Soccer Balls, Child Labour and Postcolonial Impoverishment. *Organization Studies* 28 (7): 1055–1077.

Khan, Farzad Rafi, and Peter Lund-Thomsen. 2011. CSR as Imperialism: Towards a Phenomenological Approach to CSR in the Developing World. *Journal of Change Management* 11 (1): 73–90.

Khomba, Daniel Chris, and Alex Trew. 2017. Aid and Growth in Malawi. AidData Working Papers. Williamsburg VA: College of William and Mary, June.

Kinderman, Daniel. 2015. Explaining the Rise of National Corporate Social Responsibility: The Role of Global Framework, World Culture, and Corporate Interest. In *Corporate Social Responsibility in a Globalizing World*, edited by Kiyoteru Tsutsui and Alwyn Lim. Cambridge, UK: Cambridge University Press, 107–146.

Kingston, Paul, and Ian S. Spears, eds. 2004. *States-Within-States: Incipient Political Entities in the Post-Cold War Era*. Basingstoke: Palgrave Macmillan.

Klingebiel, Stephan. 2012. Accountability and the Effectiveness of Development Cooperation (March 1, 2012). Available at SSRN: https://ssrn.com/abstract=2181722 or http://dx.doi.org/10.2139/ssrn.2181722, last access September 27, 2019.

Knack, Stephen. 2003. Groups, Growth and Trust: Cross-country Evidence on the Olson and Putnam Hypotheses. *Public Choice* 117: 341–355.

Knight, Jack. 2001. Social Norms and the Rule of Law: Fostering Trust in a Socially Diverse Society. In *Trust in Society*, edited by Karen S. Cook. New York: Russel Sage Foundation, 354–373.

Koehler, Jan. 2008. Auf der Suche nach Sicherheit. Die internationale Intervention in Nordost-Afghanistan. SFB Working Papers; Sonderforschungsbereich 700, Freie Universität Berlin (17).

——— 2013. Institution-Centred Conflict Research. The Methodology and Its Application in Afghanistan, PhD. Dissertation, Department of Political and Social Sciences, Freie Universität Berlin, Berlin.

——— 2014. The Afghan Perspectives on ISAF – Changes and Trends in Northeast Afghanistan. In *From Venus to Mars? – Provincial Reconstruction Teams and the European Military Experience in Afghanistan, 2001–2014*, edited by Bernhard Chiari. Freiburg i. Br.: Rombach, 65–86.

Koehler, Jan, and Kristóf Gosztonyi. 2014. The International Intervention and Its Impact on Security Governance in North-East Afghanistan. *International Peacekeeping* 21 (2): 231–250.

Koehler, Jan, and Boris Wilke. 2011. Wie funktioniert Sicherheit ohne (viel) Staat? Befunde aus Nordostafghanistan and Pakistan. In *Wozu Staat? Governance in Räumen begrenzter und konsolidierter Staatlichkeit*, edited by Marianne Beisheim, Tanja A. Börzel, Philip Genschel and Bernhard Zangl. Baden-Baden: Nomos, 55–86.

Koehler, Jan, and Christoph Zürcher. 2004. Der Staat und sein Schatten. Zur Institutionalisierung hybrider Staatlichkeit im Südkaukasus. *WeltTrends* 12 (45): 84–96.

2007. Assessing the Contribution of International Actors in Afghanistan. Results from a Representative Survey. SFB Working Papers; Sonderforschungsbereich 700, Freie Universität Berlin (7).

Koelble, Thomas A., and Edward Li Puma. 2011. Traditional Leaders and the Culture of *Governance* in South Africa. *Governance* 24 (1): 5–29.

Kohler-Koch, Beate. 1996. Catching up with Change: The Transformation of Governance in the European Union. *Journal of European Public Policy* 3 (3): 359–380.

1998. Einleitung. Effizienz und Demokratie. Probleme des Regierens in entgrenzten Räumen. In *Regieren in entgrenzten Räumen. PVS – Politische Vierteljahresschrift, Sonderheft 29*, edited by Beate Kohler-Koch. Opladen: Westdeutscher Verlag, 11–25.

Kohler-Koch, Beate, and Rainer Eising, eds. 1999. *The Transformation of Governance in the European Union*. London: Routledge.

Kolk, Ans, and Francois Lenfant. 2010. MNC Reporting on CSR and Conflict in Central Africa. *Journal of Business Ethics* 93 (2): 241–255.

Kolk, Ans, Rob van Tulder, and Carlijn Welters. 2005. Setting New Global Rules? TNCs and Codes of Conduct. *Transnational Corporations* 14 (3): 1–28.

Kollman, Kelly, and Aseem Prakash. 2001. Green by Choice? Cross-National Variation in Firms' Responses to EMS-Based Environmental Regimes. *World Politics* 53: 399–430.

Kooiman, Jan, ed. 1993. *Modern Governance. New Government-Society Interactions*. London: Sage.

2003. *Governing as Governance*. London: Sage.

Koremenos, Barbara, Charles Lipson, and Duncan Snidal, eds. 2001. *Rational Design: Explaining the Form of International Institutions. Special Issue of International Organization.* 55 (4).

Koren, Ore, and Anoop K. Sarbahi. 2018. State Capacity, Insurgency, and Civil War: A Disaggregated Analysis. *International Studies Quarterly:* 62 (2): 274–288.

Korf, Benedikt, Timothy Raeymakers, Conrad Schetter, and Michael J. Watts. 2018. Geographies of Limited Statehood. In *The Oxford Handbook of Governance and Limited Statehood*, edited by Thomas Risse, Tanja A. Börzel and Anke Draude. Oxford: Oxford University Press, 167–187.

Kotsadam, Andreas, Gudrun Østby, Siri Aas Rustad, Andreas Forø Tollefsen, and Henrik Urdal. 2018. Development aid and infant mortality. Micro-level evidence from Nigeria. *World Development* 105 (May): 59–69.

Kötter, Matthias. 2015. Non-State Justice Institutions: A Matter of Fact and a Matter of Legislation. In *Non-State Justice Institutions and the Law. Decision-Making at the Interface of Tradition, Religion, and the State*, edited by Matthias Kötter, Tilmann J. Röder, Gunnar Folke Schuppert and Rüdiger Wolfrum. Basingstoke: Palgrave Macmillan, 145–187.

Kötter, Matthias, Tilmann Röder, Gunnar Folke Schuppert, and Rüdiger Wolfrum, eds. 2015. *Non-State Justice Institutions and the Law. Decision-Making at the Interface of Tradition, Religion and the State*. Basingstoke: Palgrave Macmillan.

Kötter, Matthias, and Gunnar Folke Schuppert, eds. 2009. *Normative Pluralität ordnen. Rechtsbegriffe, Normenkollisionen und Rule of Law in Kontexten dies- und jenseits des Staates*. Baden-Baden: Nomos.

Kraemer, Romy, Gail Whiteman, and Bobby Subhabrata Banerjee. 2013. Conflict and Astroturfing in Niyamgiri: The Importance of National Advocacy Networks in Anti-corporate Social Movements. *Organization Studies* 34 (5–6): 823–852.

Krahmann, Elke. 2010. *States, Citizens and the Privatisation of Security*. Cambridge, UK: Cambridge University Press.

Kranz, Nicole. 2013. Securing the Production Basis. Environmental Governance in the Food and Beverage Sector. In *Business and Governance in South Africa. Racing to the Top?*, edited by Tanja A. Börzel and Christian R. Thauer. Basingstoke: Palgrave Macmillan, 180–194.

Krasner, Stephen D., ed. 1983. *International Regimes*. Ithaca, NY: Cornell University Press.

1999. *Sovereignty. Organized Hypocrisy*. Princeton, NJ: Princeton University Press.

2004. Sharing Sovereignty. New Institutions for Collapsed and Failing States. *International Security* 29 (2): 85–120.

2018. Theories of Development and Areas of Limited Statehood. In *The Oxford Handbook of Governance and Limited Statehood*, edited by Thomas Risse, Tanja A. Börzel and Anke Draude. Oxford: Oxford University Press, 29–47.

Krasner, Stephen D., and Thomas Risse, eds. 2014a. *External Actors, State-Building, and Service Provision in Areas of Limited Statehood. Special Issue of "Governance,"* 27 (4).

Krasner, Stephen D., and Thomas Risse. 2014b. External Actors, State-Building, and Service Provision in Areas of Limited Statehood: Introduction. *Governance* 27 (4): 545–567.

Krasniqi, Gezim, and Mehmet Musaj. 2015. The EU's 'Limited Sovereignty-strong Control' Approach in the Process of Member State Building in Kosovo. In *The EU and Member State Building: European Foreign Policy in the Western Balkans*, edited by Soeren Keil and Zeynep Arkan, Abingdon: Routledge, 140–162.

Kratochwil, Friedrich V. 1989. *Rules, Norms, and Decisions. On the Conditions of Practical and Legal Reasoning in International Relations and Domestic Affairs*. Cambridge, UK: Cambridge University Press.

Krause, Jana. 2016. Non-violence and civilian agency in communal war: Evidence from Jos, Nigeria. *African Affairs* 116 (463): 261–283.

2018. *Resilient Communities: Non-Violence and Civilian Agency in Communal War*. Cambridge, UK: Cambridge University Press.

Krause, Keith, and Jennifer Milliken. 2009. Introduction: The Challenge of Non-state Armed Groups. *Contemporary Security Policy* 30 (2): 202–220.

Kreutz, Joakim, and Enzo Nussio. 2019. Destroying Trust in Government. Effects of a Broken Pact Among Colombian Ex-combatants. *International Studies Quarterly* 63 (4): 1175–1188.

Kreuzer, Peter. 2019. Ein Schritt näher am Frieden in Mindanao. Auf den Philippinen besteht Hoffnung auf das Ende eines jahrzehntelangen

Konflikts. PRIF Spotlight. Frankfurt am Main: Hessische Stiftung Friedens- und Konfliktforschung.

Krieger, Heike. 2018. International Legal Order. In *The Oxford Handbook of Governance and Limited Statehood*, edited by Thomas Risse, Tanja A. Börzel and Anke Draude. Oxford: Oxford University Press, 543–563.

Krieger, Heike, and Dieter Weingärtner, eds. 2012. *Streitkräfte und nicht-staatliche Akteure*. Baden-Baden: Nomos.

Kristoff, Madeline, and Liz Panarelli. 2010. *Haiti: A Republic of NGOs? Peace Brief*. Washington, DC: United States Institute of Peace, April 23.

Kruse, John A., Judith Kleinfeld, and Robert Travis. 1982. Energy Development on Alaska's North Slope: Effects on the Inupiat Population. *Human Organization* 41 (2): 97–106.

Kubota, Yuichi. 2019. The Rebel Economy in Civil War: Informality, Civil Networks, and Regulation Strategies. *International Studies Review*, 22 (3): 423–440.

Kumar, Krishan. 1997. *Public and Private in Thought and Practice: Perspectives on a Grand Dichotomy*. Chicago: University of Chicago Press.

Kwon, Huck-ju. 2005. *Transforming the Developmental Welfare State in East Asia*. Basingstoke: Palgrave Macmillan.

Kydd, Andrew H. 2005. *Trust and Mistrust in International Relations*. Princeton, NJ: Princeton University Press.

Ladwig, Bernd. 2007. Gebotene Fremdbestimmung? Normative Überlegungen zum Umgang mit zerfallen(d)er Staatlichkeit. In *Regieren ohne Staat? Governance in Räumen begrenzter Staatlichkeit*, edited by Thomas Risse and Ursula Lehmkuhl. Baden-Baden: Nomos, 354–373.

Ladwig, Bernd, and Beate Rudolf. 2011. International Legal and Moral Standards of Good Governance in Fragile States. In *Governance without a State? Policies and Politics in Areas of Limited Statehood*, edited by Thomas Risse. New York: Columbia University Press, 199–231.

Lake, David A. 2009. *Hierarchy in International Relations*. Ithaca, NY: Cornell University Press.

2016. *The Statebuilder's Dilemma. On the Limits of Foreign Intervention*. Ithaca, NY: Cornell University Press.

2018. Coercion and Trusteeship. In *The Oxford Handbook of Governance and Limited Statehood*, edited by Thomas Risse, Tanja A. Börzel and Anke Draude. Oxford: Oxford University Press, 293–311.

Lake, David A., and Christopher J. Farris. 2014. International Trusteeship: External Authority in Areas of Limited Statehood. *Governance* 27 (4): 569–587.

Lake, Milli. 2014. Organizing Hypocrisy: Providing Legal Accountability for Human Rights Violations in Areas of Limited Statehood. *International Studies Quarterly* 58 (3): 515–526.

2018. *Strong NGOs and Weak States. Human Rights Advocacy and Gender Justice in the Democratic Republic of Congo and South Africa*. Cambridge, UK: Cambridge University Press.

Lall, Ranjit. 2017. Beyond Institutional Design: Explaining the Performance of International Organizations. *International Organization* 71 (2): 245–280.

Lambach, Daniel, and Tim Dertwinkel. 2007. Breaking Down Breakdown: Localizing State Failure using GIS. In *Paper Presented at the International Studies Association, Annual Convention*. Chicago, February 28-March 3.

Lambach, Daniel, Eva Johais, and Markus Bayer. 2015. Conceptualising state collapse: an institutionalist approach. *Third World Quarterly* 36 (7): 1299–1315.

Laswell, Harold D. 1936. *Politics: Who Gets What, When, How?* New York: Whittlesey House.

Latigo, James Ojera. 2008. Northern Uganda: Tradition-Based Practices in the Acholi Region. In *Traditional Justice and Reconciliation after Violent Conflict. Learning from African Experiences*, edited by Luc Huyse and Mark Salter. Stockholm: International Institute for Democracy and Electoral Assistance, 85–120.

Lavenex, Sandra, and Frank Schimmelfennig, eds. 2011. *EU democracy promotion in the neighbourhood: from leverage to governance? Special Issue of 'Democratization'*. 18 (4).

Lawrie, Misty, Matthew Tonts, and Paul Plummer. 2011. Boomtowns, Resource Dependence and Socio-economic Well-Being. *Australian Geographer* 42 (2): 139–164.

Le Billon, Philippe. 2006. *Fuelling War: Natural Resources and Armed Conflicts*. London: Routledge.

2008. Corrupting Peace? Peacebuilding and Post-conflict Corruption. *International Peacekeeping* 15 (3): 344–361.

Leander, Anna. 2005. The Market for Force and Public Security: The Destabilizing Consequences of Private Military Companies. *Journal of Peace Research* 42 (5): 605–622.

Lecocq, Baz, Gregory Mann, Bruce Whitehouse, Dida Badi, Lotte Pelckmans, Nadia Belalimat, Bruce Hall, and Wolfram Lacher. 2013. One Hippopotamus and Eight Blind Analysts: A Multivocal Analysis of the 2012 Political Crisis in the Divided Republic of Mali. *Review of African Political Economy* 40 (137): 343–357.

Lederer, Markus. 2018. External State Actors. In *The Oxford Handbook of Governance and Limited Statehood*, edited by Thomas Risse, Tanja A. Börzel and Anke Draude. Oxford: Oxford University Press, 191–210.

Lee, Melissa M. 2018. The International Politics of Incomplete Sovereignty: How Hostile Neighbors Weaken the State. *International Organization* 72 (2): 283–315.

Lee, Melissa M., and Nan Zhang. 2017. Legibility and the Informational Foundations of State Capacity. *The Journal of Politics* 79 (1): 118–132.

Lee, Melissa M., Gregor Walter-Drop, and John Wiesel. 2014. Taking the State (Back) Out? A Macro-Quantitative Analysis of Statehood and the Delivery of Collective Goods and Services. *Governance* 27 (4): 635–654.

Lee, Sung Yong, and Alpaslan Özerdem, eds. 2015. *Local Ownership in International Peacebuilding: Key Theoretical and Practical issues*. London: Routledge.

Leeson, Peter T. 2007. Better Off Stateless: Somalia Before and After Government Collapse. *Journal of Comparative Economics* 35 (4): 689–710.

Legler, Thomas, and Thomas Kwasi Tieku. 2010. What Difference Can a Path Make? Regional Democracy Promotion Regimes in the Americas and Africa. *Democratization* 17 (3): 465–491.

Leibfried, Stephan, Evelyn Huber, Matthew Lange, Jonah D. Levy, Frank Nullmeier, and John D. Stevens, eds. 2015. *The Oxford Handbook of Transformations of the State*. Oxford: Oxford University Press.

Leibfried, Stephan, and Michael Zürn, eds. 2005. *Transformations of the State*. Cambridge, UK: Cambridge University Press.

Leininger, Julia. 2015. Against All Odds: Strong Democratic Norms in the African Union. In *Governance Transfer by Regional Organizations. Patching Together a Global Script*, edited by Tanja A. Börzel and Vera van Hüllen. Basingstoke: Palgrave Macmillan, 51–67.

Lenz, Tobias, Janine Bezuijen, Liesbet Hooghe, and Gary Marks. 2015. Patterns of International Organization: Task Specific vs. General Purpose. In *Internationale Organisationen. Politische Vierteljahresschrift, Sonderheft 49*, edited by Eugenia da Conceicao-Heldt, Martin Koch and Andrea Liese. Baden-Baden: Nomos, 131–155.

Lerner, Daniel. 1958. *The Passing of Traditional Society. Modernizing the Middle East*. New York: Free Press.

Levi-Faur, David. 2012. From "Big Government" to "Big Governance?". In *The Oxford Handbook of Governance*, edited by David Levi-Faur. Oxford: Oxford University Press, 3–18.

Levi, Margaret. 1988. *Of Rule and Revenue*. Berkeley, CA: University of California Press.

1998. A State of Trust. In *Trust and Governance*, edited by John Braithwaite and Margaret Levi. New York: Russell Sage Foundation, 77–101.

2018. The Who, What, and Why of Performance-based Legitimacy. *Journal of Intervention and Statebuilding* 12 (4): 603–610.

Levi, Margaret, and Audrey Sacks. 2009. Legitimating beliefs: Sources and indicators. *Regulation & Governance* 3 (4): 311–333.

Levi, Margaret, and Laura Stoker. 2000. Political Trust and Trustworthiness. *Annual Review of Political Science* 3 (1): 475–507.

Liese, Andrea. 2018. Food Security. In *The Oxford Handbook of Governance and Limited Statehood*, edited by Thomas Risse, Tanja A. Börzel and Anke Draude. Oxford: Oxford University Press, 459–478.

Liese, Andrea, and Marianne Beisheim. 2011. Transnational Public-Private Partnerships and the Provision of Collective Goods in Developing Countries. In *Governance without a State? Policies and Politics in Areas of Limited Statehood*, edited by Thomas Risse. New York: Columbia University Press, 115–143.

Liese, Andrea, Hannah Janetschek, and Johanna Sarre. 2014. Can PPPs Make It Anywhere? How Limited Statehood and Other Area Factors Influence PPP Effectiveness. In *Transnational Partnerships. Effectively Providing for Sustainable Development?*, edited by Marianne Beisheim and Andrea Liese. Basingstoke: Palgrave Macmillan, 131–160.

Linder, Stephen D., and Pauline Vaillancourt Rosenau. 2000. Mapping the Terrain of the Public-Private Policy Partnership In *Public-Private Policy*

Partnerships, edited by Pauline Vaillancourt Rosenau. Cambridge, MA: MIT Press, 1–18.

Lindvall, Johannes, and Jan Teorell. 2016. State Capacity as Power: A Conceptual Framework. STANCE Working Paper Series 2016(1). Lund: Lund University.

Linke-Behrens, Luisa, and Lisa van Hoof-Maurer. 2016. External Authoriy. Compensating for Limited Statehood in the Provision of Collective Goods? SFB Working Papers; Sonderforschungsbereich 700, Freie Universität Berlin (70).

Lipset, Seymour Martin. 1959. Some Social Requisites of Democracy. Economic Development and Political Legitimacy. *American Political Science Review* 53 (1): 69–105.

Lipson, Michael. 2007. Peacekeeping: Organized Hypocrisy? *European Journal of International Relations* 13 (1): 5–34.

LiPuma, Edward, and Thomas A. Koelble. 2009. Deliberative Democracy and the Politics of Traditional Leadership in South Africa: A Case of Despotic Domination or Democratic Deliberation? *Journal of Contemporary African Studies* 27 (2): 201–223.

Liss, Carolin. 2013. Private Military and Security Companies in Maritime Security Governance. In *The Transnational Governance of Violence and Crime. Non-State Actors in Security*, edited by Anja P. Jakobi and Klaus Dieter Wolf. Basingstoke: Palgrave Macmillan, 193–213.

Lockart, Clare. 2018. Sovereignty Strategies: Enhancing Core Governance Functions as a Postconflict & Conflict-Prevention Measure. *Daedalus* 147 (1): 90–103.

Lofdahl, Corey L. 2002. *Environmental Impact of Globalization and Trade. A Systems Study*. Cambridge, MA: MIT Press.

Lohaus, Mathis. 2015. Ahead of the Curve: The OAS as a Pioneer of International Anti-Corruption Efforts. In *Governance Transfer by Regional Organizations. Patching Together a Global Script*, edited by Tanja A. Börzel and Vera Van Hüllen. Basingstoke: Palgrave Macmillan, 159–176.

Lopes, Carlos, and Thomas Theisohn. 2003. *Ownership, Leadership and Transformation. Can We Do Better for Capacity Development?* New York: Earthscan.

Lowndes, Vivien, and Chris Skelcher. 1998. The Dynamics of Multi-organizational Partnerships. An Analysis of Changing Modes of Governance. *Public Administration* 76 (2): 313–333.

Luhmann, Niklas. 1989. *Vertrauen. Ein Mechanismus zur Reduktion sozialer Komplexität*. Stuttgart: Enke.

Lumsdaine, David. 1993. *Moral Vision in International Politics: The Foreign Aid Regime, 1949–1989*. Princeton, NJ: Princeton University Press.

Lund-Thomsen, Peter, and Neil M. Coe. 2013. Corporate Social Responsibility and Labour Agency: The Case of Nike in Pakistan. *Journal of Economic Geography* 15 (2): 275–296.

Lund-Thomsen, Peter, and Adam Lindgreen. 2014. Corporate Social Responsibility in Global Value Chains: Where Are We Now and Where Are We Going? *Journal of Business Ethics* 123 (1): 11–22.

Ly, Pierre. 2012. The Effect of Ownership in NGO's Commercial Ventures. *Annals of Public and Cooperative Economics* 83 (2): 59–179.

Mac Ginty, Roger, and Oliver Richmond. 2016. The Fallacy of Constructing Hybrid Political Orders: A Reappraisal of the Hybrid Turn in Peacebuilding. *International Peacekeeping* 23 (2): 219–239.

Madsen, Peter M. 2009. Does Corporate Investment Drive a "Race to the Bottom" in Environmental Protection? A Reexamination of the Effect of Environmental Regulation on Investment. *Academy of Management Journal* 52 (6): 1297–1318.

Magaloni, Beatriz, Alberto Díaz-Cayeros, and Alexander Ruiz Euler. 2019. Public Good Provision and Traditional Governance in Indigenous Communities in Oaxaca, Mexico. *Comparative Political Studies* 52 (12): 1841–1880.

Magaloni, Beatriz, Edgar Franco-Vivanco, and Vanessa Melo. 2020. Killing in the Slums: Social Order, Criminal Governance, and Policy Violence in Rio de Janeiro. *American Political Science Review* 114 (2): 552–572.

Magen, Amichai, and Leonardo Morlino, eds. 2008. *Anchoring Democracy: External Influence on Domestic Rule of Law Development*. London: Routledge.

Magen, Amichai, Thomas Risse, and Michael McFaul, eds. 2009. *Promoting Democracy and the Rule of Law. American and European Strategies*. Basingstoke: Palgrave Macmillan.

Maihold, Günther. 2016. Intervention by Invitation? Shared Sovereignty in the Fight against Impunity. *European Review of Latin America and Carribean Studies* (101): 5–31.

Makarenko, Tamara. 2004. The Crime-terror Continuum: Tracing the Interplay between Transnational Organised Crime and Terrorism. *Global crime* 6 (1): 129–145.

Malesky, Edmund J., and Layna Mosley. 2018. Chains of Love? Global Production and the Firm-Level Diffusion of Labor Standards. *American Journal of Political Science* 62 (3): 712–728.

Mamdani, Mahmood. 1996. *Citizen and Subject: Contemporary Africa and the Legacy of Late Colonialism*. Princeton, NJ: Princeton University Press.

2018. *Citizen and Subject: Contemporary Africa and the Legacy of Late Colonialism*, 2nd. ed. Princeton, NJ: Princeton University Press.

Mampilly, Zachariah Cherian. 2012. *Rebel Rulers: Insurgent Governance and Civilian Life During War*. Ithaca, NY: Cornell University Press.

Man, Joyce Yanyun, ed. 2013. *China's Environmental Policy and Urban Development*. Cambridge, MA: Lincoln Institute of Land Policy.

Mandel, Robert. 2002. *Armies without States: The Privatization of Security*. Boulder, CO: Lynne Rienner.

Manekin, Devorah. 2013. Violence against Civilians in the Second Intifada: The Moderating Effect of Armed Group Structure on Opportunistic Violence. *Comparative Political Studies* 46 (10): 1273–1300.

Mann, Michael. 1984. The Autonomous Power of the State: Its Origins, Mechanisms and Results. *European Journal of Sociology* 25 (2): 185–213.

Mansfield, Edward D., and Jon C. Pevehouse. 2008. Democratization and the Varieties of International Organizations. *Journal of Conflict Resolution* 52 (2): 269–294.

March, James G., and Johan P. Olsen. 1989. *Rediscovering Institutions. The Organizational Basics of Politics*. New York; London: The Free Press.

1998. The Institutional Dynamics of International Political Orders. *International Organization* 52 (4): 943–969.

Marijan, Branka. 2017. The Gradual Emergence of Second Generation Security Sector Reform in Bosnia-Herzegovina. CSG Papers. Kitchener, Ontario: Centre for Security Governance.

Marten, Kimberley. 2012. *Warlords: Strong-Arm Brokers in Weak States*. Ithaca, NY: Cornell University Press.

2013. Warlords and Governance. In *The Transnational Governance of Violence and Crime. Non-State Actors in Security*, edited by Anja P. Jakobi and Klaus Dieter Wolf. Basingstoke: Palgrave Macmillan, 23–39.

Martin, Ian, and Alexander Mayer-Rieckh. 2005. The United Nations and East Timor: From self-determination to state-building. *International Peacekeeping* 12 (1): 125–145.

Martin, Lisa L. 1992a. *Coercive Cooperation: Explaining Multilateral Economic Sanctions*. Princeton, NJ: Princeton University Press.

1992b. Interests, Power, and Multilateralism. *International Organization* 44 (4): 765–792.

Martin, Lisa L., and Beth A. Simmons. 2013. International Organizations and Institutions. In *Handbook of International Relations. Second Edition*, edited by Walter Carlsnaes, Thomas Risse and Beth Simmons. London: Sage, 326–351.

Martorano, Bruno, Laura Metzger, and Marco Sanfilippo. 2018. Chinese Development Assistance and Household Welfare in Sub-Saharan Africa. AidData Working Papers. Williamsburg VA: College of William and Mary, May.

Matanock, Aila M. 2014. Governance Delegation Agreements: Shared Sovereignty as a Substitute for Limited Statehood. *Governance* 27 (4): 589–612.

2017. *Electing Peace. From Civil Conflict to Political Participation*. Cambridge, UK: Cambridge University Press.

2018. External Engagement: Explaining the Spread of Electoral Participation Provisions in Civil Conflict Settlements. *International Studies Quarterly* 62 (3): 656–670.

Mayntz, Renate. 1993. Modernization and the Logic of Interorganizational Networks. In *Societal Change between Market and Organization*, edited by John Child, Michel Crozier and Renate Mayntz. Aldershot: Avebury, 3–18.

2004. Governance im modernen Staat. In *Governance – Regieren in komplexen Regelsystemen*, edited by Arthur Benz. Wiesbaden: VS Verlag für Sozialwissenschaften, 65–76.

2009. *Über Governance. Institutionen und Prozesse politischer Regelung*. Frankfurt am Main: Campus.

Mayntz, Renate, and Fritz W. Scharpf., eds. 1995a. *Gesellschaftliche Selbstregulierung und politische Steuerung*. Frankfurt am Main.: Campus.

1995b. Steuerung und Selbstorganisation in staatsnahen Sektoren. In *Gesellschaftliche Selbstregulierung und politische Steuerung*, edited by Renate Mayntz and Fritz W. Scharpf. Frankfurt am Main: Campus, 9–38.

McEwan, Cheryl, and Emma Mawdsley. 2012. Trilateral Development Cooperation: Power and Politics in Emerging Aid Relationships. *Development and Change* 43 (6): 1185–1209.

McLoughlin, Claire. 2015. When Does Service Delivery Improve the Legitimacy of a Fragile or Conflict-Affected State? *Governance* 28 (3): 341–356.

2018. When the Virtuous Circle Unravels: Unfair Service Provision and State De-legitimation in Divided Societies. *Journal of Intervention and Statebuilding* 12 (4): 527–544.

Mearsheimer, John J. 2001. *The Tragedy of Great Power Politics*. New York – London: W. W. Norton.

Menaldo, Victor. 2012. The Middle East and North Africa's Resilient Monarchs. *The Journal of Politics* 74 (3): 707–722.

Menkhaus, Ken. 2006/2007. Governance without Government in Somalia. Spoilers, State Building, and the Politics of Coping. *International Security* 31 (3): 74–106.

2008. The rise of a Mediated State in Northern Kenya: The Wajir Story and Its Implications for State-building. *Afrika Focus* 21 (2): 23–38.

Mercer, Jonathan. 1996. *Reputation and International Politics*. Ithaca, NY: Cornell University Press.

2005. Rationality and Psychology in International Politics. *International Organization* 59 (1): 77–106.

Merkel, Wolfgang. 2010. *Systemtransformation. Eine Einführung in die Theorie und Empirie der Transformationsforschung, 2nd ed.* Wiesbaden: VS Verlag für Sozialwissenschaften.

Merry, Sally E. 2006. *Human Rights and Gender Violence. Translating International Law into Local Justice.* Chicago: University of Chicago Press.

Merz, Sibille. 2012. 'Missionaries of the New Era': Neoliberalism and NGOs in Palestine. *Race & Class* 54 (1): 50–66.

Messner, J. J., Nate Haken, Patricia Taft, Hannah Blyth, Kendall Lawrence, Sebastian Pavlou, and Felipe Umaña. 2015. Fragile States Index: The Book. Washington, DC: The Fund for Peace.

Messner, J. J., Nate Haken, Patricia Taft, Hannah Blyth, Kendall Lawrence, Charlotte Bellm, Sagal Hashi, Nicole Patierno, and Leo Rosenberg. 2016. *Fragile States Index 2016*. Washington, DC: Fund for Peace.

Metelits, Claire. 2009. *Inside insurgency: Violence, Civilians, and Revolutionary Group Behavior*. New York: New York University Press.

Meyer, John M. 1987. The World Polity and the Authority of the Nation State. In *Institutional Structure: Constituting State, Society and the Individual,* edited by George M. Thomas, John W. Meyer, Francisco O. Ramirez and John Boli. London: Sage, 41–70.

Meyer, John W, Shawn Pope, and Andrew Isaacson. 2015. Legitimating the Transnational Corporation in a Stateless World Society. In *Corporate Social Responsibility in a Globalizing World,* edited by Kiyoteru Tsutsui and Alwyn Lim. Cambridge, UK: Cambridge University Press, 27–72.

Michalopoulos, Stelios, and Elias Papaioannou. 2016. The Long-Run Effects of the Scramble for Africa. *American Economic Review* 106 (7): 1802–1848.

Migdal, Joel S. 1988. *Strong Societies and Weak Sates. State-Society Relations and State Capabilities in the Third World*. Princeton, NJ: Princeton University Press.

2001. *State in Society: Studying How States and Societies Transform and Constitute One Another*. Cambridge, UK: Cambridge University Press.

Miguel, Edward, and Mary Kay Gugerty. 2005. Ethnic Diversity, Social sanctions, and Public Goods in Kenya. *Journal of Public Economics* 89 (11–12): 2325–2368.

Miller, Michael R. Castle. 2015. The Ciudades Modelo Project: Testing the Legality of Paul Romer's Charter Cities Concept by Analyzing the Constitutionality of the Honduran Zones for Employment and Economic Development. *Willamette Journal of International Law and Dispute Resolution* 22 (2): 271–312.

Miraftab, Faranak. 2004. Public-private Partnerships: The Trojan Horse of Neoliberal Development? *Journal of Planning Education and Research* 24 (1): 89–101.

Mitchell, Timothy. 1991. The Limits of the State: Beyond Statist Approaches and Their Critics. *American Political Science Review* 85 (1): 77–96.

Miura, Satoshi, and Kaoru Kurusu. 2015. Why Do Companies Join the United Nations Global Compact? The Case of Japanese Signatories. In *Corporate Social Responsibility in a Globalizing World*, edited by Kiyoteru Tsutsui and Alwyn Lim. Cambridge, UK: Cambridge University Press, 286–320.

Mobekk, Eirin. 2010. Security Sector Reform and the Challenges of Ownership. In *The Future of Security Sector Reform*, edited by Mark Sedra. Waterloo, ONT: Centre for International Governance Innovation, 230–243.

Mol, Arthur P. J. 2001. *Globalization and Environmental Reforms: The Ecological Modernization of the Global Economy*. Cambridge, MA: MIT Press.

Moravcsik, Andrew. 2000. The Origins of Human Rights Regimes: Democratic Delegation in Postwar Europe. *International Organization* 54 (2): 217–252.

Morgenthau, Hans J. 1948. *Politics among Nations*. Vol. Brief edition, 1993. New York: McGraw Hill.

Morton, Bill. 2013. An Overview of International NGOs in Development Cooperation. In *Working with Civil Society in Foreign Aid*, edited by UNDP. New York: UNDP, 325–352.

Mosse, David. 2011. *Adventures in Aidland: The Anthropology of Professionals in International Development*. New York: Berghahn Books.

Muchlinski, Peter T. 2001. Human Rights and Multinationals: Is There a Problem? *International Affairs* 77 (1): 31–47.

Mukhopadhyay, Dipali. 2014. *Warlords, Strongman Governors, and the State in Afghanistan*. Cambridge, UK: Cambridge University Press.

Müller, Harald. 1993. *Die Chance der Kooperation*. Darmstadt: Wissenschaftliche Buchgesellschaft.

2004. Arguing, Bargaining, and All That: Communicative Action, Rationalist Theory and the Logic of Appropriateness in International Relations. *European Journal of International Relations* 10 (3): 395–435.

Müller, Markus-Michael. 2012. *Public Security in the Negotiated State: Policing in Latin America and Beyond*. Basingstoke: Palgrave Macmillan.

Mungiu-Pippidi, Alina. 2015. *The Quest for Good Governance: How Societies Develop Control of Corruption*. Cambridge, UK: Cambridge University Press.

Murdie, Amanda. 2014. *Help or Harm: The Human Security Effects of International NGOs*. Stanford, CA: Stanford University Press.

Murdie, Amanda, and Alexander Hicks. 2013. Can International Nongovernmental Organizations Boost Government Services? The Case of Health. *International Organization* 67 (3): 541–573.

Murphy, Dale. 2000. *The Structure of Regulatory Competition: Corporations and Public Policies in a Global Economy*. Oxford: Oxford University Press.

Mwangi, Wagaki, Lothar Rieth, and Hans Peter Schmitz. 2013. Encouraging Greater Compliance: Local Networks and the United Nations Global Compact. In *The Persistent Power of Human Rights: From Commitment to Compliance*, edited by Thomas Risse, Stephen C. Ropp and Kathryn Sikkink. Cambridge, UK: Cambridge University Press, 203–221.

Naurin, Daniel, and Christine Reh. 2018. Deliberative Negotiation. In *The Oxford Handbook of Deliberative Democracy*, edited by André Bächtiger, John Dryzek, Jane Mansbridge and Marc E. Warren. Oxford: Oxford University Press, 728–741.

Neuman, Gerald L. 2008. Import, Export, and Regional Consent in the Inter-American Court of Human Rights. *European Journal of International Law* 19 (1): 101–123.

Nishtar, Sania. 2004. Public–private 'Partnerships' in Health – A Global Call to Action. *Health Research Policy and Systems* 2 (1): 2–5.

Njoh, Ambe J. 2017. *Planning in Contemporary Africa: The State, Town Planning and Society in Cameroon*. London: Routledge.

Norris, Pippa. 2012. *Making Democratic Governance Work: How Regimes Shape Prosperity, Welfare, and Peace*. Cambridge, UK: Cambridge University Press.

North, Douglass C. 1986. The New Institutional Economics. *Journal of Institutional and Theoretical Economics* (142): 230–237.

  1990. *Institutions, Institutional Change, and Economic Performance*. Cambridge, UK: Cambridge University Press.

North, Douglass C., John Joseph Wallis, and Barry R. Weingast. 2009. *Violence and Social Orders. A Conceptual Framework for Interpreting Recorded Human History*. Cambridge, UK: Cambridge University Press.

Noutcheva, Gergana, and Dimitar Bechev. 2008. The Successful Laggards: Bulgaria and Romania's Accession to the EU. *East European Politics and Society* 22 (1): 114–144.

Ntsebeza, Lungisile. 2005. *Democracy Compromised: Chiefs and the Politics of the Land in South Africa*. Leiden: Brill.

Nyberg, Tove. 2015. International Commission against Impunity in Guatemala: A Non-Traditional Transitional Justice Effort. *Revue Quebecoise de Droit International* 28 (1): 157–184.

O'Brien, Robert, Anne Marie Goetz, Jan Aart Scholte, and Marc Williams. 2000. *Contesting Global Governance. Multilateral Economic Institutions and Global Social Movements*. Cambridge, UK: Cambridge University Press.

O'Faircheallaigh, Ciaran. 2012. International Recognition of Indigenous Rights, Indigenous Control of Development and Domestic Political Mobilisation. *Australian Journal of Political Science* 47 (4): 531–545.

O'Rourke, Dara. 2006. Multi-stakeholder Regulation: Privatizing or Socializing Global Labor Standards? *World Development* 34 (5): 899–918.

Ochoa, Jerjes Aguirre, and Zoe Infante Jiménez. 2012. Police Force Crisis and State Legitimacy in México. *Asian Social Science* 8 (15): 86–92.

Odoemene, Akachi. 2011. Social Consequences of Environmental Change in the Niger Delta of Nigeria. *Journal of Sustainable Development in Africa* 11 (2): 123–135.

Oetzel, Jennifer, and Kathleen Getz. 2012. Why and How Might Firms Respond Strategically to Violent Conflict? *Journal of International Business Studies* 43 (2): 166–186.

Offe, Claus. 2009. Governance. An 'Empty Signifier'? *Constellations* 16 (4): 550–562.

Ogula, David Clyde Neintare. 2012. Corporate Social Responsibility: Case Study of Community Expectations and the Administrative Systems, Niger Delta *The Quality Report* 17 (73): 1–27.

Olivier, NJJ. 1969. *The Governmental Institutions of the Bantu Peoples of Southern Africa. Recueils de la Societies Jean Bodin XII.* Brussels: Fondation Universitaire de Belgique.

Olson, Mancur. 1993. Dictatorship, Democracy, and Development. *American Political Science Review* 87 (3): 567–576.

Onuf, Nicholas Greenwood. 1989. *World of Our Making: Rules and Rule in Social Theory and International Relations.* Columbia, SC: University of South Carolina Press.

Oosterveld, Willem, and Renaud Galand. 2012. Justice Reform, Security Sector Reform and Local Ownership. *Hague Journal on the Rule of Law* 4 (1): 194–209.

Osiander, Andreas. 2001. Sovereignty, International Relations, and the Westphalian Myth. *International Organization* 55 (2): 251–287.

Ostrom, Elinor. 1990. *Governing the Commons. The Evolution of Institutions for Collective Action.* Cambridge, UK: Cambridge University Press.

 2000. Collective Action and the Evolution of Social Norms. *The Journal of Economic Perspectives* 14 (3): 137–158.

 2002. Toward a Behavioral Theory Linking Trust, Reciprocity, and Reputation. In *Trust and Reciprocity. Interdisciplinary Lessons for Experimental Research*, edited by Elinor Ostrom and James Walker. New York: Russell Sage Foundation, 19–79.

Ostrom, Elinor, Roy Gardner, and James Walker. 1994. *Rules, Games, and Common-Pool Resources.* Ann Arbor, MI: University of Michigan Press.

Ostrom, Vincent. 1999. Cryptoimperialism, Predatory States, and Self-governance. In *Polycentric Governance and Development: Readings from the Workshop in Political Theory and Policy Analysis*, edited by Michael D. McGinnis. Ann Arbor, MI: University of Michigan Press, 166–185.

Ottaway, Marina, and Thomas Carothers. 2000. *Funding Virtue: Civil Society Aid and Democracy Promotion.* Washington, DC: Carnegie Endowment for International Peace.

Oye, Kenneth A., ed. 1986. *Cooperation under Anarchy.* Princeton, NJ: Princeton University Press.

Paes, Wolf-Christian. 2005. 'Conflict' Diamonds to 'Clean' Diamonds: The development of the Kimberley Process Certification Scheme. In *Resource Politics in Sub-Saharan Africa*, edited by Andreas Mehler and Andreas Basedau. Hamburg: Institute for African Studies, 305–324.

Paller, Jeffrey. 2014. Shame and Honor: The Everyday Practice of Accountability in African Democracies. *Paper presented at the American Political Science Association Meeting*, Washington DC, August 27–31.

Papadimitriou, Dimitris, and Petar Petrov. 2013. State-building without Recognition: A Critical Retrospective of the European Union's Strategy in Kosovo (1999–2010). In *European Integration and Transformation in the Western Balkans: Europeanization or Business as Usual?*, edited by Arolda Elbasani. London: Routledge, 121–137.

Paris, Roland. 2011. Ordering the World: Academic Research and Policymaking on Fragile States. *International Studies Review* 13 (1): 58–71.

Paris, Roland, and Timothy D. Sisk. 2009. *The Dilemmas of Statebuilding: Confronting the Contradictions of Postwar Peace Operations*. London: Routledge.

Parthasarathy, Ramya, Vijayendra Rao, and Nethra Palaniswamy. 2019. Deliberative Democracy in an Unequal World: A Text-As-Data Study of South India's Village Assemblies. *American Political Science Review* 113 (3): 623–640.

Pattberg, Philipp H., Frank Biermann, Sander Chan, and Aysem Mert. 2012. *Public-Private Partnerships for Sustainable Development: Emergence, Influence and Legitimacy*. Cheltenham: Edward Elgar.

Pegg, Scott. 1998. *International Society and the De facto State*. Aldershot: Ashgate.

Perkins, Richard, and Eric Neumayer. 2012. Does the 'California Effect' Operate Across Borders? Trading-and Investing-up in Automobile Emission Standards. *Journal of European Public Policy* 19 (2): 217–237.

Perry, Valery. 2015. Not-so-great Expectations: The EU and the Constitutional Politics of Bosnia and Herzegovina. In *The EU and Member State Building in the Balkans: European Foreign Policy in the Western Balkans*, edited by Soeren Keil and Zeynep Arkan. London: Routledge, 163–187.

Peters, B. Guy. 2010. Governing in the Shadows. SFB Lecture Series; Sonderforschungsbereich 700, Freie Universität Berlin (3).

Pevehouse, Jon C. 2005. *Democracy from Above: Regional Organizations and Democratization*. Cambridge, UK: Cambridge University Press.

2016. Regional Human Rights and Democracy Governance. In *Oxford Handbook of Comparative Regionalism*, edited by A. Tanja Börzel and Thomas Risse. Oxford: Oxford University Press, 486–512.

Phillips, Sarah G. 2019. Proximities of Violence: Civil Order beyond Governance Institutions. *International Studies Quarterly* 63 (3): 680–691.

Piattoni, Simona. 2001. *Clientelism, Interests, and Democratic Representation. The European Experience in Historical and Comparative Perspective*. Cambridge, UK: Cambridge University Press.

Pierre, Jon, and B. Guy Peters. 2000. *Governance, Politics and the State*. Basingstoke: Palgrave Macmillan.

Pingeot, Lou, and Wolfgang Obenland. 2014. In Whose Name? A critical view on the Responsibility to Protect. Bonn – New York: Global Policy Forum, Rosa Luxemburg Stiftung – New York Office.

Pitcher, Anne, Mary H. Moran, and Michael Johnston. 2009. Rethinking Patrimonialism and Neopatrimonialism in Africa. *African Studies Review* 52 (1): 125–156.

Plant, Raymond. 2010. *The Neo-liberal State*. Oxford: Oxford University Press.

Podder, Sukanya. 2013. Non-state Armed Groups and Stability: Reconsidering Legitimacy and Inclusion. *Contemporary Security Policy* 34 (1): 16–39.

2014. Mainstreaming the Non-state in Bottom-up State-building: Linkages between Rebel Governance and Post-conflict Legitimacy. *Conflict, Security & Development* 14 (2): 213–243.

Ponte, Stefano, and Emmanuelle Cheyns. 2013. Voluntary Standards, Expert knowledge and the Governance of Sustainability Networks. *Global Networks* 13 (4): 459–477.

Pope, Shawn M. 2015. Why Firms Participate in the Global Corporate Social Responsibility Initiative, 2000–2010. In *Corporate Social Responsibility in a Globalizing World*, edited by Kiyoteru Tsutsui and Alwyn Lim. Cambridge, UK: Cambridge University Press, 251–285.

Pope, Shawn M., and Arild Wæraas. 2016. CSR-Washing is Rare: A Conceptual Framework, Literature Review, and Critique. *Journal of Business Ethics* 137 (1): 173–193.

Portes, Alejandro. 1998. Social Capital: Its Origins and Applications in Modern Sociology. *Annual Review of Sociology* 24: 1–24.

Potoski, Matthew, and Aseem Prakash. 2006. Racing to the Bottom? Trade, Environmental Governance, and ISO 14001. *American Journal of Political Science* 50 (2): 350–364.

Prakash, Aseem. 2000. *Greening the Firm. The Politics of Corporate Environmentalism*. Cambridge, UK: Cambridge University Press.

Prakash, Aseem, and Jennifer J. Griffin. 2012. Corporate Responsibility, Multinational Corporations, and Nation States: An Introduction. *Business and Politics* 14 (3): 1–10.

Prakash, Aseem, and Mary Kay Gugerty, eds. 2010. *Advocacy Organizations and Collective Action*. Cambridge, UK: Cambridge University Press.

Prakash, Aseem, and Matthew Potoski. 2007. Investing Up: FDI and the Cross-Country Diffusion of ISO 14001 Management Systems. *International Studies Quarterly* 51 (3): 723–744.

Pratten, David, and Atreyee Sen. 2008. *Global Vigilantes: Perspectives on Justice and Violence*. London: Hurst.

Prigge, Judit. 2011. Friedenswächter. Institutionen der Streitbeilegung bei den Amhara in Äthiopien. SFB Working Papers; Sonderforschungsbereich 700, Freie Universität Berlin (28).

Przeworski, Adam. 1991. *Democracy and the Market. Political and Economic Reforms in Eastern Europe and Latin America*. Cambridge, UK: Cambridge University Press.

Przeworski, Adam, and Fernando Limongi. 1997. Modernization: Theories and Facts. *World Politics* 49 (2): 155–183.

Pugh, Michael. 2005. The Political Economy of Peacebuilding: A Critical Theory Perspective. *International Journal of Peace Studies* 10 (2): 23–42.

Putnam, Robert D. 1993. *Making Democracy Work. Civic Traditions in Modern Italy*. Princeton, NJ: Princeton University Press.

1995. Turning in, Turning out: The Strange Disappearance of Social Capital in America. *PS: Political Science and Politics* 28 (4): 664–683.

2000. *Bowling Alone: The Collapse and Revival of American Community*. New York: Simon and Schuster.

Raeymaekers, Timothy, Ken Menkhaus, and Koen Vlassenroot. 2008. State and Non-state Regulation in African Protracted Crises: Governance without Government? *Afrika Focus* 21 (2): 7–21.

Raleigh, Clionadh, Andrew Linke, Havard Hegre, and Joakim Karlsen. 2010. Introducing ACLED: An Armed Conflict Location and Event Dataset. *Journal of Peace Research* 47 (5): 651–660.

Randeria, Shalini. 2003. Cunning States and Unaccountable International Institutions: Legal Plurality, Social Movements and Rights of Local Communities to Common Property Resources. *European Journal of Sociology / Archives Européennes de Sociologie* 44 (01): 27–60.

Rathbun, Brian C. 2011. Before Hegemony: Generalized Trust and the Creation and Design of International Security Organizations. *International Organization* 65 (2): 243–273.

2018. Trust in International Relations. In *The Oxford Handbook of Social and Political Trust*, edited by Eric M. Uslaner. Oxford: Oxford University Press, 687–706.

Ratliff, William E., and Edgardo Buscaglia. 2001. *War and Lack of Governance in Colombia: Narcos, Guerrillas, and U.S. Policy*. Stanford, CA: Hoover Institution on War, Revolution, and Peace.

Rauch, James, and Peter B. Evans. 2000. Bureaucratic Structure and Bureaucratic Performance in less Developed Countries. *Journal of Public Economics* 75 (1): 49–71.

Raustiala, Kal, and Anne-Marie Slaughter. 2002. International Law, International Relations, and Compliance. In *Handbook of International Relations*, edited by Walter Carlsnaes, Beth Simmons and Thomas Risse. London et al.: Sage, 538–558.

Rautenbach, Christa. 2015. South Africa: Legal Recognition of Traditional Courts – Legal Pluralism in Action. In *Non-State Justice Institutions and the Law. Decision-Making at the Interface of Tradition, Religion, and the State*, edited by Matthias Kötter, Tilmann J. Röder, Gunnar Folke Schuppert and Rüdiger Wolfrum. Basingstoke: Palgrave Macmillan, 121–151.

Rautenbach, Christa, Jan C. Bekker, and Nazeem M. I. Goolam. 2010. *Introduction to Legal Pluralism in South Africa, 3rd ed.* Durban, South Africa: Butterworths.

Raynolds, Laura T. 2014. Fairtrade, Certification, and Labor: Global and Local Tensions in Improving Conditions for Agricultural Workers. *Agriculture and Human Values* 31 (3): 499–511.

Rayroux, Antoine, and Nina Wilén. 2014. Resisting Ownership: The Paralysis of EU Peacebuilding in the Congo. *African Security* 7 (1): 24–44.

Reich, Hannah. 2012. "Local Ownership" in Conflict Transformation Projects. Partnerships, Participation or Patronage. Occasional Paper No. 22. Berlin: Berghof Research Center for Constructive Conflict Management.

Reinhard, Wolfgang. 2007. *Geschichte des modernen Staates*. München: C. H. Beck.

Reinicke, Wolfgang H., and Francis Deng. 2000. *Critical Choices. The United Nations, Networks, and the Future of Global Governance*. Ottawa et al.: International Development Research Center.

Renders, Marleen, and Ulf Terlinden. 2010. Negotiating Statehood in a Hybrid Political Order: The Case of Somaliland. *Development and Change* 41 (4): 723–746.

Reno, William S. 1998a. Mines, Money, and the Problem of State-Building in Congo. *African Issue* 26 (1): 14–17.

1998b. *Warlord Politics and African States*. Boulder CO: Lynne Rienner.

2001. How Sovereignty Matters: International Markets and the Political Economy of Local Politics in Weak States. In *Intervention & Transnationalism in Africa: Global-Local Networks of Power*, edited by Thomas M. Callaghy, Ronald Kassimir and Robert Latham. Cambridge, UK: Cambridge University Press, 197–215.

2009. Explaining Patterns of Violence in Collapsed States. *Contemporary Security Policy* 30 (2): 356–374.

2010. Persistent Insurgencies and Warlords: Who Is Nasty, Who Is Nice, and Why. In *Ungoverned Spaces: Alternatives to State Authority in an Era of Softened Sovereignty*, edited by Anne Clunan and Harold Trinkunas. Stanford: Stanford University Press, 57–76.

2011. *Warfare in Independent Africa*. Cambridge, UK: Cambridge University Press.

2015a. Predatory Rebellions and Governance: The National Patriotic Front of Liberia, 1989–1992. In *Rebel Governance in Civil War*, edited by Ana Arjona, Nelson Kasfir and Zachariah Mampilly. Cambridge, UK: Cambridge University Press, 265–285.

2015b. Predatory States and State Transformation. In *The Oxford Handbook of Transformations of the State*, edited by Stephan Leibfried, Evelyne Huber, Matthew Lange, Jonah D. Levy and John D. Stephens. Oxford: Oxford University Press, 730–744.

2017. Fictional States & Atomized Public Spheres: A Non-Western Approach to Fragility. *Daedalus* 146 (4): 139–151.

Ribeiro Hoffmann, Andrea. 2007. Political Conditionality and Democratic Clauses in the EU and Mercosur. In *Closing or Widening the Gap? Legitimacy and Democracy in Regional Integration Organizations*, edited by Andrea Ribeiro Hoffmann and Anna van der Vleuten. Aldershot: Ashgate, 173–189.

Rice, Susan E., and Stewart Patrick. 2008. *Index of State Weakness in the Developing World*. Brookings Global Economy and Development: Washington, DC: The Brookings Institution.

Richani, Nazih. 2005. Multinational Corporations, Rentier Capitalism, and the War System in Colombia. *Latin American Politics and Society* 47 (3): 113–144.

Richards, Rebecca. 2014. *Understanding Statebuilding: Traditional Governance and the Modern State in Somaliland*. Aldershot: Ashgate.

Richter, Solveig. 2012. Two at One Blow? The EU and Its quest for Security and Democracy by Political Conditionality in the Western Balkans. *Democratization* 19 (3): 507–534.

Rihoux, Benoît, and Charles C. Ragin. 2008. *Configurational Comparative Methods. Qualitative Comparative Analysis (QCA) and Related Techniques*. London: Sage.

Riisgaard, Lone. 2009. Global Value Chains, Labor Organization and Private Social Standards: Lessons from East African Cut Flower Industries. *World Development* 37 (2): 326–340.

Riker, William H. 1980. Implications from the Disequilibrium of Majority Rule for the Study of Institutions. *The American Political Science Review* 74 (2): 432–446.

Rinke, Stefan, Mónika Contreraz Saiz, and Lasse Hölck. 2011. *Regieren an der Peripherie. Amerika zwischen Kolonien und unabhängigen Republiken.* Stuttgart: Heinz.

Risse, Thomas. 2000. 'Let's Argue!' Communicative Action in World Politics. *International Organization* 54 (1): 1–39.

2006. Transnational Governance and Legitimacy. In *Governance and Democracy. Comparing National, European and International Experiences*, edited by Arthur Benz and Ioannis Papadopoulos. London: Routledge, 179–199.

2010a. *A Community of Europeans? Transnational Identities and Public Spheres.* Ithaca, NY: Cornell University Press.

2010b. Rethinking Advocacy Organizations? A Critical Comment. In *Advocacy Organizations and Collective Action*, edited by Aseem Prakash and Mary Kay Gugerty. Cambridge, UK: Cambridge University Press, 283–294.

ed. 2011a. *Governance without a State? Policies and Politics in Areas of Limited Statehood.* New York: Columbia University Press.

2011b. Governance in Areas of Limited Statehood: Introduction and Overview. In *Governance without a State? Policies and Politics in Areas of Limited Statehood*, edited by Thomas Risse. New York: Columbia University Press, 1–35.

2013. Transnational Actors and World Politics. In *Handbook of International Relations, 2nd Edition*, edited by Walter Carlsnaes, Thomas Risse and Beth Simmons. London: Sage, 426–452.

2017. Human Rights Change in Areas of Limited Statehood: Of Spiral Models, Localization, and Translation. In *Human Rights Futures*, edited by Stephen Hopgood, Jack Snyder and Leslie Vinjamuri. Cambridge, UK: Cambridge University Press, 135–158.

2018a. Arguing and Deliberation in International Relations. In *The Oxford Handbook of Deliberative Democracy*, edited by André Bächtiger, John Dryzek, Jane Mansbridge and Marc E. Warren. Oxford: Oxford University Press, 518–534.

2018b. Hierarchical and Non-Hierarchical Coordination. In *The Oxford Handbook of Governance and Limited Statehood*, edited by Thomas Risse, Tanja A. Börzel and Anke Draude. Oxford: Oxford University Press, 312–332.

2021. Building Governance Capacity in Areas of Limited Statehood. In *Macroeconomic Policy in Fragile States*, edited by Ralph Chami, Raphael Espinoza and Peter Montiel. Oxford: Oxford University Press.

Risse, Thomas, Tanja A. Börzel, and Anke Draude. eds. 2018. *The Oxford Handbook of Governance and Limited Statehood.* Oxford: Oxford University Press.

Risse, Thomas, and Ursula Lehmkuhl. eds. 2007. *Regieren ohne Staat? Governance in Räumen begrenzter Staatlichkeit*. Baden-Baden: Nomos.

Risse, Thomas, Stephen C. Ropp, and Kathryn Sikkink. eds. 1999. *The Power of Human Rights: International Norms and Domestic Change*. Cambridge, UK: Cambridge University Press.

eds. 2013. *The Persistent Power of Human Rights. From Commitment to Compliance*. Cambridge, UK: Cambridge University Press.

Risse, Thomas, and Eric Stollenwerk. 2018a. Legitimacy in Areas of Limited Statehood. *Annual Review of Political Science* 21 (1): 403–418.

2018b. Limited Statehood Does Not Equal Civil War. In *Civil Wars, Violence, and International Responses. Special Issue of Daedalus* 147 (1): 104–115.

Rittberger, Berthold, and Philipp Schroeder. 2016. The Legitimacy of Regional Institutions. In *The Oxford Handbook of Comparative Regionalism*, edited by Tanja A. Börzel and Thomas Risse. Oxford: Oxford University Press, 579–599.

Rittberger, Volker, ed. 1993. *Regime Theory and International Relations*. Oxford: Clarendon Press.

2004. Transnationale Unternehmen in Gewaltkonflikten. *Die Friedenswarte* 79 (1–2): 15–34.

Robertson, Lawrence, Lucas Malla, and Lauren Oing. 2017a. Somalia Program Support Services. Somali Perceptions Survey, Part 1 – The Emerging Federal States, Mogadishu, and Puntland. Washington, DC: USAID.

Robertson. 2017b. *Somalia Program Support Services. Somali Perceptions Survey, Part 2: Somaliland*. Washington, DC: USAID.

Robinson, Geoffrey. 2009. *"If You Leave Us Here, We Will Die": How Genocide Was Stopped in East Timor*. Princeton, NJ: Princeton University Press.

Robinson, James E. 1999. When Is a State Predatory? CESifo Working Paper: 178 Munich: Center for Economic Studies and Ifo Institute.

Röder, Tilmann J. 2009. Kollisionen zwischen shari'a, Gesetz und Stammestradition in Afghanistan. In *Normative Pluralität ordnen. Rechtsbegriffe, Normenkollisionen und Rule of Law in Kontexten dies- und jenseits des Staates*, edited by Matthias Kötter and Gunnar Folke Schuppert. Baden-Baden: Nomos, 257–301.

Röder, Tilmann J., and Naveed A. Shinwari. 2015. Pakistan: Jirgas Dispensing Justice without State Control. In *Non-State Justice Institutions and the Law. Decision-Making at the Interface of Tradition, Religion, and the State*, edited by Matthias Kötter, Tilmann J. Röder, Gunnar Folke Schuppert and Rüdiger Wolfrum. Basingstoke: Palgrave Macmillan, 25–54.

Romer, Paul. 2010. Technologies, rules, and progress: The Case for Charter Cities. Working Papers id:2471, eSocialSciences. Available at https://ideas.repec.org/p/ess/wpaper/id2471.html, last access September 20, 2019.

Rotberg, Robert I., ed. 2003. *State Failure and State Weakness in a Time of Terror*. Washington, DC: Brookings Institution Press.

2004a. The Failure and Collapse of Nation-States: Breakdown, Prevention, and Repair. In *When States Fail. Causes and Consequences*, edited by Robert I. Rotberg. Princeton, NJ: Princeton University Press, 1–50.

ed. 2004b. *When States Fail. Causes and Consequences*. Princeton, NJ: Princeton University Press.

2014. Good Governance Means Performance and Results. *Governance* 27 (3): 511–518.

Rothstein, Bo. 2011. *The Quality of Government: Corruption, Social Trust, and Inequality in International Perspective*. Chicago: University of Chicago Press.

Rothstein, Bo, and Dietlind Stolle. 2003. Social Capital, Impartiality and the Welfare State: An Institutional Approach. In *Generating Social Capital: Civil Society and Institutions in Comparative Perspective*, edited by Marc Hooghe and Dietlind Stolle. New York: Palgrave, 191–210.

2008a. Political Institutions and Generalized Trust. In *The Handbook of Social Capital*, edited by Dario Castiglione, Jan W. Van Deth and Guglielmo Wolleb. Oxford: Oxford University Press, 273–302.

2008b. The State and Social Capital: An Institutional Theory of Generalized Trust. *Comparative Politics* 40 (4): 441–459.

Rouveroy van Nieuwaal, Emile Adriaan Benvenuto, and Rijk van Dijk, eds. 1999. *African Chieftaincy in a New Socio-Political Landscape*. Hamburg: Lit-Verlag.

Roy, Sara. 2000. The Transformation of Islamist NGOs in Palestine. *Middle East Report* 30 (214): 24–27.

2011. *Hamas and Civil Society in Gaza: Engaging the Islamist Social Sector*. Princeton, NJ: Princeton University Press.

Rudolf, Beate. 2007. Zwischen Kooperation und Intervention: Die Durchsetzung völkerrechtlicher Standards guten Regierens in Räumen begrenzter Staatlichkeit. In *Regieren ohne Staat? Governance in Räumen begrenzter Staatlichkeit*, edited by Thomas Risse and Ursula Lehmkuhl. Baden-Baden: Nomos, 331–373.

Rudra, Nita. 2002. Globalization and the Decline of the Welfare State in Less-developed Countries. *International Organization* 56 (2): 411–445.

Rueschemeyer, Dietrich, and Peter B. Evans. 1983. The State & Economic Transformation: Towards an Analysis of the Conditions Underlying Effective Intervention. In *Bringing the State Back In*, edited by Peter B. Evans, Dietrich Rueschemeyer and Theda Skocpol. Cambridge, UK: Cambridge University Press, 44–77.

Ruggeri, Andrea, Han Dorussen, and Theodora-Ismene Gizelis. 2017. Winning the Peace Locally: UN Peacekeeping and Local Conflict. *International Organization* 71 (1): 163–185.

Ruggie, John G. 2004a. How to Marry Civic Politics and Private Governance. In *The Impact of Global Corporations on Global Governance*, edited by Carnegie Council on Ethics and International Affairs. New York: Carnegie Council on Ethics and International Affairs, 10–15.

2004b. Reconstituting the Global Public Domain: Issues, Actors and Practices. *European Journal of International Relations* 10 (4): 499–532.

2007a. Business and Human Rights: Mapping International Standards of Responsibility and Accountability for Corporate Acts. Report of the Special Representative of the Secretary-General on the Issue of Human Rights and Transnational Corporations and Other Business Enterprises. New York: UN.

2007b. Global Markets and Global Governance: The Prospects for Convergence. In *Global Liberalism and Political Order: Toward a New Grand Compromise*, edited by Steven F. Bernstein and Louis W. Pauly. Albany, NY: State of New York University Press, 23–50.

2008. Protect, Respect and Remedy: A Framework for Business and Human Rights. Report of the Special Representative of the Secretary-General on the Issue of Human Rights and Transnational Corporations and Other Business Enterprises. New York: UN.

2010. Remarks at Mid-Year Special Session Voluntary Principles on Security and Human Rights. US Department of State, Washington, DC.

2018. Multinationals as Global Institution: Power, Authority and Relative Autonomy. *Regulation & Governance* 12 (3), 317–333.

Russo, Alessandra. 2015. A 'Potemkin Village'? Governance Transfer by the CIS. In *Governance Transfer by Regional Organizations. Patching Together a Global Script*, edited by Tanja A. Börzel and Vera Van Hüllen. Basingstoke: Palgrave Macmillan, 141–158.

Rustow, Dankwart A. 1968. Modernization and Comparative Politics. *Comparative Politics* 1 (1): 37–51.

Sabel, Charles F., and Jonathan Zeitlin, eds. 2010. *Experimentalist Governance in the European Union. Towards a New Architecture*. Oxford: Oxford University Press.

Sabrow, Sophia. 2017. Local Perceptions of the Legitimacy of Peace Operations by the UN, Regional Organizations and Individual States – A Case Study of the Mali Conflict. *International Peacekeeping* 24 (1): 159–186.

Sageman, Marc. 2011. *Leaderless Jihad: Terror Networks in the Twenty-first Century*. Philadelphia: University of Pennsylvania Press.

Said, Edward W. 1979. *Orientalism*. New York: Random House.

Salehyan, Idean, David Siroky, and Reed M. Wood. 2014. External Rebel Sponsorship and Civilian Abuse: A Principal-Agent Analysis of Wartime Atrocities. *International Organization* 68 (3): 633–661.

Sampson, Robert J. 2012. *Great American City: Chicago and the Enduring Neighborhood Effect*. Chicago: University of Chicago Press.

Sampson, Robert. J., Stephen W. Raudenbush, and Felton Earls. 1997. Neighborhoods and Violent Crime: A Multilevel Study of Collective Efficacy. *Science* 277 (5328): 918–924.

Santiso, Carlos. 2001. International Co-operation for Democracy and Good Governance: Moving toward a Second Generation? *European Journal of Development Research* 13 (1): 154–180.

Sarkees, Meredith Reid, and Frank Wayman. 2010. *Resort to War: 1816–2007*. Washington, DC: CQ Press.

Sawyer, Suzana, and Terence Gomez. 2008. Transnational Governmentality and Resource Extraction: Indigenous peoples, Multinational Corporations, Multinational Institutions and the State. Geneva: UNRISD.

Schäferhoff, Marco. 2011. Die Bereitstellung von Gesundheitsleistungen in Räumen begrenzter Staatlichkeit – Wie viel Staat ist zur effektiven Erbringung von Governance-Leistungen notwendig? In *Wie viel Staat wofür? Governance in Räumen konsolidierter und begrenzter Staatlichkeit*, edited by Marianne Beisheim, Tanja A. Börzel, Philipp Genschel and Bernhard Zangl. Baden-Baden: Nomos, 117–142.

2014a. External Actors and the Provision of Public Health Services in Somalia. *Governance* 27 (4): 675–695.

2014b. Partnerships for Health – Special Focus: Service Provision. In *Transnational Partnerships: Effectively Providing for Sustainable Development?*, edited by Marianne Beisheim and Andrea Liese. Basingstoke: Palgrave Macmillan, 45–62.

Schäferhoff, Marco, Sabine Campe, and Christopher Kaan. 2009. Transnational Public-Private Partnerships in International Relations. Making Sense of Concepts, Research Frameworks, and Results. *International Studies Review* 11 (3): 451–474.

Scharpf, Fritz W. 1991. Die Handlungsfähigkeit des Staates am Ende des zwanzigsten Jahrhunderts. *Politische Vierteljahresschrift* 32 (4): 621–634.

1997. *Games Real Actors Play. Actor-Centered Institutionalism in Policy Research.* Boulder, CO: Westview.

1999. *Governing in Europe. Effective and Democratic?* Oxford: Oxford University Press.

Scheye, Eric. 2009. *State-Provided Service, Contracting Out, and Non-State Networks. Justice and Security as Public and Private Goods and Services.* Paris: INCAF.

Schimmelfennig, Frank. 2005. Strategic Calculations and International Socialization: Membership Incentives, Party Constellations and Sustained Compliance in Central and Eastern Europe. *International Organization* 59 (4): 827–860.

Schimmelfennig, Frank, and Ulrich Sedelmeier. 2004. Governance by Conditionality: EU Rule Transfer to the Candidate Countries of Central and Eastern Europe. *Journal of European Public Policy* 11 (59 (4)): 661–679.

2005. *The Europeanization of Central and Eastern Europe.* Ithaca, NY: Cornell University Press.

Schlichte, Klaus. 2018. A Historical-Sociological Perspective on Statehood. In *The Oxford Handbook of Governance and Limited Statehood*, edited by Thomas Risse, Tanja A. Börzel and Anke Draude. Oxford: Oxford University Press, 48–67.

Schlöndorf, Elisabeth. 2011. Against the Odds. Successful UN Peace Operations – A Theoretical Argument and Two Cases. Baden-Baden: Nomos.

Schmeidl, Susanne, and Masood Karokhail. 2009. The Role of Non-state Actors in 'Community-based Policing' – An Exploration of the Arbakai (Tribal Police) in South-Eastern Afghanistan. *Contemporary Security Policy* 30 (2): 318–342.

Schmelzle, Cord. 2011. Evaluating Governance: Effectiveness and Legitimacy in Areas of Limited Statehood. SFB Working Papers. Sonderforschungsbereich 700, Freie Universität Berlin (26).

Schmelzle. 2015. *Politische Legitimität und zerfallene Staatlichkeit.* Frankfurt am Main: Campus.

Schmelzle, Cord, and Eric Stollenwerk. 2018a. *Virtuous or Vicious Circle? Governance Effectiveness and Legitimacy in Areas of Limited Statehood, Special Issue of the Journal of Intervention and Statebuilding*, 12 (4).

2018b. Virtuous or Vicious Circle? Governance Effectiveness and Legitimacy in Areas of Limited Statehood. *Journal of Intervention and Statebuilding* 12 (4): 449–467.

Schmidt, Vivien A. 2013. Democracy and Legitimacy in the European Union Revisited: Input, Output and 'Throughput'. *Political Studies* 61 (1): 2–22.

Schmidt, Volker H. 2006. Multiple Modernities or Varieties of Modernity? *Current Sociology* 54 (1): 77–97.

Schneckener, Ulrich, ed. 2004. *States at Risk. Fragile Staaten als Sicherheits- und Entwicklungsproblem*. Berlin: Stiftung Wissenschaft und Politik.

2009. Spoilers or Governance Actors? Engaging Armed Non-State Groups in Areas of Limited Statehood. SFB Working Papers; Sonderforschungsbereich 700, Freie Universität Berlin (17).

Schröder, Ursula. 2018. Security. In *The Oxford Handbook of Governance and Limited Statehood*, edited by Thomas Risse, Tanja A. Börzel and Anke Draude. Oxford: Oxford University Press, 375–393.

Schröder, Ursula, Fairlie Chappuis, and Deniz Kocak. 2013. Security Sector Reform from a Policy Transfer Perspective: A Comparative Study of International Interventions in the Palestinian Territories, Liberia and Timor-Leste. *Journal of Intervention and Statebuilding* 7 (3): 381–401.

2014. Security Sector Reform and the Emergence of Hybrid Security Governance. *International Peacekeeping* 21 (2): 214–230.

Schuppert, Gunnar Folke, ed. 2005. *Governance-Forschung. Vergewisserung über Stand und Entwicklungslinien*. Baden-Baden: Nomos.

Schuppert, Gunnar Folke. 2007. Was ist und wozu Governance? *Die Verwaltung* 40 (4): 465–514.

2009. *Staat als Prozess. Eine staatstheoretische Skizze in sieben Aufzügen*. Frankfurt am Main: Campus.

Schuppert, Gunnar Folke, and Michael Zürn, eds. 2008. *Governance in einer sich wandelnden Welt. PVS – Politische Vierteljahresschrift, Sonderheft 41.*

Scott, James C. 1998. *Seeing Like a State: How Certain Schemes to Improve the Human Condition Have Failed*. New Haven, CT: Yale University Press.

2009. *The Art of Not Being Governed. An Anarchist History of Upland Southeast Asia*. New Haven, CT: Yale University Press.

2012. *Two Cheers for Anarchism: Six Easy Pieces on Autonomy, Dignity, and Meaningful Work and Play*. Princeton, NJ: Princeton University Press.

Sehovic, Annamarie Bindenagel. 2014. *HIV/AIDS and the South African State: Sovereignty and the Responsibility to Respond*. Aldershot: Ashgate.

Selsky, John W., and Barbara Parker. 2005. Cross-Sector Partnerships to Address Social Issues. Challenges to Theory and Practice. *Journal of Management* 31 (6): 849–873.

Sexton, Renard. 2016. Aid as a Tool against Insurgency: Evidence from Contested and Controlled Territory in Afghanistan. *American Political Science Review* 110 (4): 731–749.

Seybolt, Taylor B. 2007. *Humanitarian Military Intervention: The Conditions for Success and Failure*. Oxford: Oxford University Press.

Shen, Ce, and John B. Wiliamson. 2005. Corruption, Democracy, Economic Freedom, and State Strength: A Cross-national Analysis. *International Journal of Comparative Sociology* 46 (4): 327–345.

Sherman, Jake. 2001. Private Sector Actors in Zones of Conflict. In Research Challengers and Policy Responses, IPA workshop report. New York: International Peace Academy.

Shesterinina, Anastasia, and Brian L. Job. 2016. Particularized Protection: UNSC Mandates and the Protection of Civilians in Armed Conflict. *International Peacekeeping* 23 (2): 240–273.

Shinwari, Naveed A. 2011. Understanding Jirga: Legality and Legitimacy in Pakistan's Federally Administered Tribal Areas. Islamabad, Pakistan: Community Appraisal & Motivation Programme (CAMP) Head Office.

Sikkink, Kathryn. 2011. *The Justice Cascade: Human Rights Prosecutions and World Politics*. New York: W. W. Norton.

2017. *Evidence for Hope. Making Human Rights Work in the 21st Century*. Princeton, NJ: Princeton University Press.

Simmons, Beth A. 2009. *Mobilizing for Human Rights. International Law in Domestic Politics*. Cambridge, UK: Cambridge University Press.

2013. From Ratification to Compliance: Quantitative Evidence on the Spiral Model. In *The Persistent Power of Human Rights. From Commitment to Compliance*, edited by Thomas Risse, Stephen C. Ropp and Kathryn Sikkink. Cambridge, UK: Cambridge University Press, 43–59.

2019. Border Rules. *International Studies Review* 21 (2): 256–283.

Simmons, Beth A., and Lisa L. Martin. 2002. International Organizations and Institutions. In *Handbook of International Relations*, edited by Walter Carlsnaes, Thomas Risse and Beth A. Simmons. London et al.: Sage, 192–211.

Simon, John G., Charles W. Powers, and Jon P. Gunnemann. 1972. The Responsibilities of Corporations and Their Owners. In *Ethical Theory and Business*, edited by Tom L. Beauchamp, Norman E. Bowie and Denis Gordon Arnold. Englewood Cliffs: Prenctice-Hall, 60–75.

Singer, Peter Warren. 2007. *Corporate Warriors: The Rise of the Privatized Military Industry*. Ithaca, NY: Cornell University Press.

Singh, Ajit, and Ann Zammit. 2004. Labour Standards and the 'Race to the Bottom': Rethinking Globalization and Workers' Rights from Developmental and Solidaristic Perspectives. *Oxford Review of Economic Policy* 20 (1): 85–104.

Sjöstedt, Martin. 2013. Aid Effectiveness and the Paris Declaration: A Mismatch between Ownership and Results-Based Management? *Public Administration and Development* 33 (2): 143–155.

Skocpol, Theda. 1985. Bringing the State Back In: Strategies of Analysis in Current Research. In *Bringing the State Back In*, edited by Peter B. Evans, Dieter Rueschenmeyer and Theda Skocpol. Cambridge, UK: Cambridge University Press, 3–37.

Slaughter, Anne-Marie. 2004. *A New World Order*. Princeton, NJ: Princeton University Press.

Smith, C. N. 2008. Consumers as Drivers of Corporate Social Responsibility. In *The Oxford Handbook of Corporate Social Responsibility*, edited by Andrew Crane, Abagail McWilliams, Dirk Matten, Jeremy Moon and Donald S. Siegel. Oxford: Oxford University Press, 303–323.

Sobek, David. 2010. Masters of their domains: The role of state capacity in civil wars. *Journal of Peace Research* 47 (3): 267–271.

Soifer, Hillel. 2008. State Infrastructural Power: Approaches to Conceptualization and Measurement. *Studies in Comparative International Development* 43 (3–4): 231–251.

Spann, Michael. 2014. Charter Cities and Development: Examining a Paradox. In *The Politics of Development: A Survey*, edited by Heloise Weber. London: Routledge, 167–192.

Spar, Deborah L., and Lane T. LaMure. 2003. The Power of Activism: Assessing the Impact of NGOs on Global Business. *California Management Review* 45: 78–101.

Speight, Jeremy. 2014. Warlord Undone? Strongman Politics and Post-conflict State-building in Northeastern Côte d'Ivoire (2002–2013). *Canadian Journal of African Studies/La Revue canadienne des études africaines* 48 (2): 223–241.

Spinellis, Dionysios. 1996. The Phenomenon of Corruption and the Challenge of Good Government. In *OECD Symposium on Corruption and Good Governance*. OECD Working Papers 78. Paris.

Spruyt, Hendrik. 1996. *The Sovereign State and Its Competitors: An Analysis of Systems Change*. Princeton, NJ: Princeton University Press.

Staniland, Paul. 2012. States, Insurgents, and Wartime Political Orders. *Perspectives on Politics* 10 (2): 243–264.

Stanton, Jessica A. 2016. *Violence and Restraint in Civil War: Civilian Targeting in the Shadow of International Law*. Cambridge, UK: Cambridge University Press.

Stedman, Stephen John. 1997. Spoiler Problems in Peace Processes. *International Security* 22 (2): 5–53.

Stein, Arthur A. 1990. *Why Nations Cooperate: Circumstances and Choice in International Relations*. Ithaca, NY: Cornell University Press.

Steinberg, Jessica. 2019. *Mines, Communities, and States. The Local Politics of Natural Resource Extraction in Africa*. Cambridge, UK: Cambridge University Press.

Steinhoff, Dawn. 2009. Talking to the Enemy: State Legitimacy Concerns with Engaging Non-State Armed Groups. *Texas International Law Journal* 45: 297–322.

Stephens, Sian. 2019. HIV in South African Industry: The Experience of Healthcare in an Area of Limited Statehood. Middlesex University, unpublished manuscript

Stephenson Jr., Max, ed. 2012. *Peacebuilding through Community-Based NGOs: Paradoxes and Possibilities*. Sterling, VA: Kumarian Press.

Stewart, Megan A, and Yu-Ming Liou. 2017. Do Good Borders Make Good Rebels? Territorial Control and Civilian Casualties. *The Journal of Politics* 79 (1): 284–301.

Stokke, Olav. 2013. *Aid and Political Conditionality*. London: Routledge.

Stolle, Dietlind. 2002. Trusting Strangers. The Concept of Generalized Trust in Perspective. *Österreichische Zeitschrift für Politikwissenschaft* 31 (4): 397–412.

Stolle, Dietlinde, and Thomas R. Rochon. 1998. Are all Associations Alike? Member Diversity, Associational Type, and the Creation of Social Capital. *American Behavioral Scientist* 42 (1): 47–65.

Stollenwerk, Eric. 2017. Measuring Statehood on the Sub-National Level in Nigeria. In *Measuring Statehood on a Sub-National Level: A Dialogue among Methods*, SFB Working Papers; Sonderforschungsbereich 700, Freie Universität Berlin (71), edited by Angela Heuchler, Luisa Linke-Behrens and Leon Schettler, 9–16.

2018a. Measuring Governance and Limited Statehood. In *The Oxford Handbook of Governance and Limited Statehood*, edited by Thomas Risse, Tanja A. Börzel and Anke Draude. Oxford: Oxford University Press, 106–127.

2018b. Securing Legitimacy? Perceptions of Security and ISAF's Legitimacy in Northeast Afghanistan. *Journal of Intervention and Statebuilding* 12 (4): 506–526.

2018c. A Virtuous Circle of Governance? The Interplay between Effectiveness and Legitimacy in Areas of Limited Statehood. PhD. Dissertation, Department of Political and Social Sciences, Freie Universität Berlin, Berlin.

Stollenwerk, Eric, and Jan Opper. 2017. Codebook. The Governance and Limited Statehood Dataset. SFB 700 "Governance in Areas of Limited Statehood": Freie Universität Berlin.

Strange, Susan. 1996. *The Retreat of the State. The Diffusion of Power in the World Economy*. Cambridge, UK: Cambridge University Press.

Sullivan, John P., and Robert J. Bunker. 2002. Drug Cartels, Street Gangs, and Warlords. *Small Wars and Insurgencies* 13 (2): 40–53.

Sutherland, Alex, Ian Brunton-Smith, and Jonathan Jackson. 2013. Collective Efficacy, Deprivation and Violence in London. *British Journal of Criminology* 53 (6): 1050–1074.

Suykens, Bert. 2015. Comparing Rebel Rule Through Revolution and Naturalization: Ideologies of Governance in Naxalite and Naga India. In *Rebel Governance in Civil War*, edited by Ana Arjona, Nelson Kasfir and Zachariah Mampilly. Cambridge, UK: Cambridge University Press, 138–157.

Swenson, Geoffrey. 2018. Legal Pluralism in Theory and Practice. *International Studies Review* 20 (2): 438–462.

Swidler, Ann. 2013. Cultural Sources of Institutional Resilience: Lessons from Chieftaincy in Rural Malawi. In *Social Resilience in the Neoliberal Era*, edited by Peter A. Hall and Michele Lamont, Cambridge, UK: Cambridge University Press, 319–345.

Szablowski, David. 2007. *Transnational Law and Local Struggles: Mining Communities and the World Bank*. Oxford: Oxford University Press.

Szekely, Ora. 2015. Doing Well by Doing Good: Understanding Hamas's Social Services as Political Advertising. *Studies in Conflict & Terrorism* 38 (4): 275–292.

Tajfel, Henri. 1974. Social Identity and Intergroup Behavior. *Social Science Information* 13 (2): 65–93.

Talentino, Andrea Kathryn. 2007. Perceptions of Peacebuilding: The Dynamic of Imposer and Imposed Upon. *International Studies Perspectives* 8 (2): 152–171.

Tamanaha, Brian Z. 2011. The Rule of Law and Legal Pluralism in Development. *Hague Journal on the Rule of Law* 3 (1): 1–17.

2015. Introduction: A Bifurcated Theory of Law in Hybrid Societies. In *Non-State Justice Institutions and the Law. Decision-Making at the Interface of Tradition, Religion, and the State*, edited by Matthias Kötter, Tilmann J. Röder, Gunnar Folke Schuppert and Rüdiger Wolfrum. Basingstoke: Palgrave Macmillan, 1–21.

Tanis, Martin, and Tom Postmes. 2005. A Social Identity approach to Trust: Interpersonal Perception, Group Membership and Trusting Behaviour. *European Journal of Social Psychology* 35: 413–424.

Taula Calana Per La Pau I Els Drets Humans a Colòmbia, and International Office of Human Rights – Action Colombia. 2017. One Year Since the Start of the Implementation of the Peace Agreement in Colombia. Report of the Taula Calana Per La Pau I Els Drets Humans a Colòmbia and the International Office of Human Rights – Action Colombia (OIDHACO) Brussels: Taula Calana Per La Pau I Els Drets Humans a Colòmbia and International Office of Human Rights – Action Colombia.

Taylor, Peter Leigh. 2005. In the Market but not of it: Fair Trade Coffee and Forest Stewardship Council Certification as Market-based Social Change. *World Development* 33 (1): 129–147.

Thauer, Christian R. 2013a. Coping with Uncertainty. The Automotive Industry and the Governance of HIV/AIDS in South Africa. In *Business and Governance in South Africa. Racing to the Top?* edited by Tanja A. Börzel and Christian R. Thauer. Basingstoke: Palgrave Macmillan, 45–66.

2013b. Upgrading the Periphery? The Contribution of Car Companies to Environmental Governance in South Africa. In *Business and Governance in South Africa. Racing to the Top?*, edited by Tanja A. Börzel and Christian R. Thauer. New York: Palgrave Macmillan, 128–151.

2014a. Goodness Comes From Within. Intra-organizational Dynamics of Corporate Social Responsibility. *Business and Society* 53 (4): 483–516.

2014b. *The Managerial Sources of Corporate Social Responsibility. The Spread of Global Standards*. Cambridge, UK: Cambridge University Press.

The Development Assistance Committee. 2015. States of Fragility. Meeting Post-2015 Ambitions. Paris: Organization for Economic Cooperation and Development.

Theisohn, Thomas, and Carlos Lopes. 2013. *Ownership Leadership and Transformation: Can We Do Better for Capacity Development*. London: Routledge.

Thomas, Esther. 2014. Sustainable Conflict Management by Multinational Mining Companies in Areas of Limited Statehood. PhD. dissertation, Otto-Suhr-Institute of Political Science, Freie Universität Berlin, Berlin.

Thomas, M. A. 2015. *Govern Like Us. U.S. Expectations of Poor Countries*. New York: Columbia University Press.

Thomson, Janice E. 1994. *Mercenaries, Pirates, and Sovereigns. State-Building and Extraterritorial Violence in Early Modern Europe*. Princeton, NJ: Princeton University Press.

1995. State Sovereignty in International Relations: Bridging the Gap between Theory and Empirical Research. *International Studies Quarterly* 39 (2): 213–233.

Tilly, Charles. 1975. *The Formation of the National State in Western Europe*. Princeton, NJ: Princeton University Press.

1985. War Making and State Making as Organized Crime. In *Bringing the State Back In*, edited by Peter B. Evans, Dietrich Rueschemeyer and Theda Skocpol. Cambridge, UK: Cambridge University Press, 169–191.

1995. *Coercion, Capital, and European States, AD 900–1992*. Vol. 2. Oxford: Blackwell.

Tordo, Silvana. 2011. *National Oil Companies and Value Creation*. Washington, DC: World Bank Publications.

Tripathi, Salil. 2005. International Regulation of Multinational Corporations. *Oxford Development Studies* 33 (1): 117–131.

Tsai, Lily L. 2007. *Accountability without Democracy. Solidarity Groups and Public Goods Provision in Rural China*. Cambridge, UK: Cambridge University Press.

Tsutsui, Kiyoteru, and Alwyn Lim, eds. 2015. *Corporate Social Responsibility in a Globalizing World*. Cambridge, UK: Cambridge University Press.

Turner, John C. 1987. *Rediscovering the Social Group. A Self-Categorization Theory*. Oxford: Oxford University Press.

Tyler, Tom R. 1997a. Citizen Discontent with Legal Procedures: A Social Science Perspective on Civil Procedure Reform. *The American Journal of Comparative Law* 45 (4): 871–904.

1997b. Procedural Fairness and Compliance with the Law. *Schweizerische Zeitschrift für Volkswirtschaft und Statistik* 133 (2/2): 219–240.

Ubhenin, Oscar Edoror. 2017. Domain without Subjects. Traditional Rulers in Post-Colonial Africa. *Taiwan Journal of Democracy* 13 (2): 31–54.

Ubink, Janine. 2016. *Traditional Authorities in Africa. Resurgence in an Era of Democratisation*. Leiden: Leiden University Press.

Utting, Peter. 2015a. Corporate Accountability, Fair Trade and Multi-stakeholder Regulation. In *Handbook of Research on Fair Trade*, edited by Raynolds, Laura T. and Elizabeth A. Bennett. Cheltenham: Edward Elgar, 61–79.

2015b. Corporate Social Responsibility and the Evolving Standards Regime: Regulatory and Political Dynamics. In *Corporate Social Responsibility in a Globalizing World*, edited by Kiyoteru Tsutsui and Alwyn Lim. Cambridge, UK: Cambridge University Press, 73–106.

Utting, Peter, and Ann Zammit. 2009. United Nations-business Partnerships: Good Intentions and Contradictory Agendas. *Journal of Business Ethics* 90 (1): 39–56.

Vachudova, Milada Anna. 2005. *Europe Undivided: Democracy, Leverage and Integration After Communism*. Oxford: Oxford University Press.

van der Vleuten, Anna. 2007. Contrasting Cases: Explaining Interventions by SADC and ASEAN. In *Closing or Widening the Gap? Legitimacy and Democracy in Regional Integration Organizations*, edited by Andrea Ribeiro Hoffmann and Anna Van der Vleuten. Aldershot: Ashgate, 155–172.

van der Vleuten, Anna, and Andrea Ribeiro Hoffmann. 2010. Explaining the Enforcement of Democracy by Regional Organizations: Comparing EU, Mercosur and SADC. *JCMS: Journal of Common Market Studies* 48 (3): 737–758.

van der Windt, Peter, Macartan Humphreys, Lily Medina, Jeffrey F. Timmons, and Maarten Voors. 2019. Citizen Attitudes toward Traditional and State Authorities: Substitutes or Complements? *Comparative Political Studies* 52 (12): 1810–1840.

van Hüllen, Vera. 2013. The 'Arab Spring' and the Spiral Model: Tunisia and Morocco. In *The Persistent Power of Human Rights: From Commitment to*

Compliance, edited by Thomas Risse, Stephen C. Ropp and Kathryn Sikkink. Cambridge, UK: Cambridge University Press, 182–199.

2015. Just Leave Us Alone: The Arab League and Human Rights. In *Governance Transfer by Regional Organizations. Patching Together a Global Script*, edited by Tanja A. Börzel and Vera van Hüllen. Basingstoke: Palgrave Macmillan, 125–140.

van Hüllen, Vera, and Tanja A. Börzel. 2015. Why Being Democratic Is Just Not Enough: The EU's Governance Transfer. In *Governance Transfer by Regional Organizations. Patching Together a Global Script*, edited by Tanja A. Börzel and Vera van Hüllen. Basingstoke: Palgrave Macmillan, 227–244.

Vandenbergh, Michael P., and Jonathan M. Gilligan. 2017. *Beyond Politics: The Private Governance Response to Climate Change*. Cambridge, UK: Cambridge University Press.

Vogel, David. 1995. *Trading Up: Consumer and Environmental Regulation in a Global Economy*. Cambridge, MA: Harvard University Press.

2007. *The Market for Virtue: The Potential and Limits of Corporate Social Responsibility*. Washington, DC: Brookings Institution Press.

Vogel, David, and Robert Kagan, eds. 2004. *Dynamics of Regulatory Change: How Globalization Affects National Regulatory Policies*. Berkeley – Los Angeles: University of California Press.

vom Hau, Matthias. 2015. State Theory: Four Analytical Traditions. In *The Oxford Handbook of Transformations of the State*, edited by Stephan Leibfried, Evelyne Huber, Matthew Lange, Jonah D. Levy and John D. Stephens. Oxford: Oxford University Press, 131–151.

von Billerbeck, Sarah B. K. 2015. Local Ownership and UN Peacebuilding: Discourse versus Operationalization. *Global Governance* 21 (2): 299–315.

Wagner, R. Harrison. 2007. *War and the State: The Theory of International Politics*. Ann Arbor, MI: University of Michigan Press.

Walsh, John. 2003. Egypt's Muslim Brotherhood. *Harvard International Review* 24 (4): 32–36.

Waltz, Kenneth N. 1979. *Theory of International Politics*. Reading, MA: Addison-Wesley.

Wardak, Ali. 2004. Jirga – A Traditional Mechanism of Conflict Resolution in Afghanistan. Glamorgan, UK: University of Glamorgan.

Warren, Marc E., Jane Mansbridge, and André Bächtiger et al. 2013. Deliberative Negotiations. In *Negotiating Agreement in Politics*, edited by Jane Mansbridge and Cathie Jo Martin. Washington, DC: American Political Science Association, 86–120.

Waygood, Steve. 2006. *Capital Market Campaigning. The Impact of NGOs on Companies, Shareholder Value and Reputational Risk*. London: Risk Books.

Weber, Max. 1978 (1922). *Economy and Society*. Berkely – Los Angeles: University of California Press.

Wegenast, Tim, and Gerald Schneider. 2017. Ownership Matters: Natural Resources Property Rights and Social Conflict in Sub-Saharan Africa. *Political Geography* 61: 110–122.

Wegenast, Tim, Georg Strüver, Juliane Giesen, and Mario Krauser. 2017. At Africa's Expense? Disaggregating the Social Impact of Chinese Mining

Operations. GIGA Working Paper 308. Hamburg: German Institute for Global and Area Studies.

Weinstein, Jeremy M. 2007. *Inside Rebellion. The Politics of Insurgent Violence.* Cambridge, UK: Cambridge University Press.

Wendt, Alexander. 1992. Anarchy Is What States Make of It: The Social Construction of Power Politics. *International Organization* 88 (2): 384–396.

  1999. *Social Theory of International Politics.* Cambridge, UK: Cambridge University Press.

  2003. Why a World State Is Inevitable. *European Journal of International Relations* 9 (4): 491–542.

Wenger, Andreas, and Daniel Möckli. 2003. *Conflict Prevention: The Untapped Potential of the Business Sector.* Boulder, CO: Lynne Rienner.

Westerwinter, Oliver. 2013. Formal and Informal Governance in the UN Peacebuilding Commission. In *The Transnational Governance of Violence and Crime. Non-State Actors in Security,* edited by Anja P. Jakobi and Klaus Dieter Wolf. Basingstoke: Palgrave Macmillan, 61–83.

Wettstein, Florian. 2012. CSR and the Debate on Business and Human Rights: Bridging the Great Divide. *Business Ethics Quarterly* 22 (4): 739–770.

Wheeler, David. 2001. Racing to the Bottom? Foreign Investment and Air Pollution in Developing Countries. *Journal of Environment and Development* 10 (3): 225–245.

Whelan, Glen, and Judy Muthuri. 2017. Chinese State-owned Enterprises and Human Rights: The Importance of National and Intra-organizational Pressures. *Business & Society* 56 (5): 738–781.

Whitehead, Laurence, ed. 2001. *The International Dimensions of Democratization: Europe and the Americas.* Oxford: Oxford University Press.

Whiteman, Gail. 2009. All My Relations: Understanding Perceptions of Justice and Conflict between Companies and Indigenous Peoples. *Organization Studies* 30 (1): 101–120.

Wickham-Crowley, Timothy. 2015. Del Gobierno de Abajo al Gobierno de Arriba... and Back: Transitions to and from Rebel Governance in Latin America, 1956–1990. In *Rebel Governance and Civil War,* edited by Ana Arjona, Nelson Kasfir and Zachariah Mampilly. Cambridge, UK: Cambridge University Press, 47–73.

Widner, Jennifer A. 2004. Building Effective Trust in the Aftermath of Severe Conflict. In *When States Fail: Causes and Consequences,* edited by Robert I. Rotberg. Princeton, NJ: Princeton University Press, 222–236.

Williams, J. Michael. 2010. *Chieftaincy, the State, and Democracy: Political Legitimacy in Post-apartheid South Africa.* Bloomington, IN: Indiana University Press.

Williams, Patrick, and Laura Chrisman, eds. 1994. *Colonial Discourse and Postcolonial Theory. A Reader.* New York: Columbia University Press.

Williamson, Oliver E. 1996. *The Mechanisms of Governance.* Oxford: Oxford University Press.

Winters, Matthew S., Simone Dietrich, and Minhaj Mahmud. 2018. Aiding the Virtuous Circle? International Development Assistance and Citizen Confidence in Government in Bangladesh. *Journal of Intervention and Statebuilding* 12 (4): 468–483.

Wiredu, Kwasi. 1990. An Akan Perspective on Human Rights. In *Human Rights in Africa: Cross-Cultural Perspectives*, edited by Abdullahi Ahmed An-Naim and Francis M. Deng. Washington, DC: Brookings Institution, 243–260.

Wisler, Dominique, and Ihekwoaba W. Onwudiwe. 2009. Rethinking Police and Society. In *Community Policing: International Patterns and Comparative Perspective* edited by Dominique Wisler and Ihekwoaba W. Onwudiwe. Boca Raton, FL: CRC Press, 1–18.

Witte, Jan Martin, and Wolfgang H. Reinicke. 2005. *Business Unusual: Facilitating United Nations Reforms through Partnerships*. New York: United Nations Global Compact Office.

Witte, Jan Martin, Wolfgang H. Reinicke, and Thorsten Benner. 2000. Beyond Multilateralism: Global Public Policy Networks. *Internationale Politik und Gesellschaft* 2 (2): 176–188.

Wojkowska, Ewa. 2007. Doing Justice: How Informal Justice Systems Can Contribute. Oslo: United Nations Development Programme/Oslo Governance Centre.

Wolff, Stefan. 2011. The regional dimensions of state failure. *Review of International Studies* 37 (3): 951–972.

Wong, Pui-Hang. 2016. How Can Political Trust be Built After Civil Wars? Evidence from Post-conflict Sierra Leone. *Journal of Peace Research* 53 (6): 772–785.

Woo-Cumings, Meredith, ed. 1999. *The Developmental State*. Ithaca, NY: Cornall University Press.

Wood, Elisabeth Jean. 2009. Armed Groups and Sexual Violence: When Is Wartime Rape Rare? *Politics & Society* 37 (1): 131–161.

Wood, Geoff. 1997. States without Citizens: The Problem of the Franchise State. In *NGOs, States and Donors: Too Close for Comfort*, edited by David Hulme and Michael Edwards. Basingstoke: Palgrave Macmillan, 79–92.

Wood, Reed M. 2010. Rebel Capability and Strategic Violence against Civilians. *Journal of Peace Research* 47 (5): 601–614.

Wood, Reed M., Jacob D. Kathman, and Stephen E. Gent. 2012. Armed Intervention and Civilian Victimization in Intrastate Conflicts. *Journal of Peace Research* 49 (5): 647–660.

Wood, Reed M., and Christopher Sullivan. 2015. Doing Harm by Doing Good? The Negative Externalities of Humanitarian Aid Provision during Civil Conflict. *The Journal of Politics* 77 (3): 736–748.

Woodward, Susan L. 2017. *The Ideology of Failed States. Why Intervention Fails*. Cambridge, UK: Cambridge University Press.

World Justice Project. 2018. Rule of Law Index 2017–2018. Washington, DC: The World Justice Project.

Xing, Yuquinq, and Charles Kolstad. 2002. Do Lax Environmental Regulations Attract Foreign Investment? *Environmental and Resource Economics* 21 (1): 1–22.

Yom, Sean L., and F. Gregory Gause III. 2012. Resilient Royals: How Arab Monarchies Hang On. *Journal of Democracy* 23 (4): 74–88.

Young, Robert. 2001. *Postcolonialism. A Historical Introduction.* Oxford: Blackwell.

Zadek, Simon, Xiaohong Chen, Li Zhaoxi, Jia Tao, Zhou Yan, Kelly Yu, Maya Forstater, and Guy Morgan. 2009. Responsible Business in Africa. Chinese Business Leaders' Perspectives on Performance and Enhancement Opportunities. Corporate Social Responsibility Initiative Working Paper No 54. AccountAbility and the Enterprise Research Institute, Development Research Centre of the State Council of P.R. China (DRC-ERI), November 2009. Available at www.accountability21.net, last access September 27, 2019.

Zafar, Ali. 2007. The Growing Relationship between China and Sub-Saharan Africa: Macro-Economic, Trade, Investment, and Aid Links. *The World Bank Research Observer* 22 (1): 103–130.

Zalik, Anna. 2004. The Niger Delta: 'Petro Violence' and 'Partnership Development'. *Review of African Political Economy* (101): 401–424.

Zammit, Ann. 2003. *Development at Risk: Rethinking UN-Business Partnerships.* Geneva: The South Center and UNRISD.

Zarakol, Ayşe. ed. 2017. *Hierarchies in World Politics,* Cambridge, UK: Cambridge University Press.

Zaum, Dominik. 2013. International organizations, legitimacy, and legitimation. In *Legitimating International Organizations,* edited by Dominik Zaum. Oxford: Oxford University Press, 3–25.

Zimmer, Melanie. 2010. Oil Companies in Nigeria: Emerging Good Practice or Still Fuelling Conflict. In *Corporate Security Responsibility? Corporate Governance Contributions to Peace and Security in Zones of Conflict,* edited by Nicole Deitelhoff and Klaus-Dieter Wolf. Basingstoke: Palgrave Macmillan, 58–84.

Zimmermann, Lisbeth. 2017. *Global Norms with a Local Face. Rule-of-Law Promotion and Norm-Translation.* Cambridge, UK: Cambridge University Press.

Zürcher, Christoph. 2007. When Governance Meets Troubled States. In *Staatszerfall und Governance,* edited by Marianne Beisheim and Gunnar Folke Schuppert. Baden-Baden: Nomos, 11–28.

Zürn, Michael. 1992. *Interessen und Institutionen in der internationalen Politik. Grundlegung und Anwendung des situationsstrukturellen Ansatzes.* Opladen: Leske & Budrich.

1998. *Regieren jenseits des Nationalstaates. Globalisierung und Denationalisierung als Chance.* Frankfurt am Main: Suhrkamp.

2000. Democratic Governance beyond the Nation-State: The EU and Other International Institutions. *European Journal of International Relations* 6 (2): 183–221.

2002. Politik in der postnationalen Konstellation. Über das Elend des methodologischen Nationalismus. In *Politik in einer entgrenzten Welt. 21. wissenschaftlicher Kongress der Deutschen Vereinigung für Politische Wissenschaft,* edited by Christine Landfried. Köln: Verlag Wissenschaft und Politik, 181–203.

2013. Globalization and Global Governance. In *Handbook of International Relations. Second Edition*, edited by Walter Carlsnaes, Thomas Risse and Beth Simmons. London: Sage, 401–425.

2018. *A Theory of Global Governance. Authority, Legitimacy, and Contestation.* Oxford: Oxford University Press.

Index